IN THE TRENCHES
Volume 4

IN THE TRENCHES

Selected Speeches and Writings
of an American Jewish Activist
Volume 4: 2004–2005

DAVID A. HARRIS

Executive Director,
American Jewish Committee

KTAV Publishing House, Inc.

Copyright © 2006
David A. Harris

Library of Congress Cataloging-in-Publication Data

Harris, David A.
  In the trenches : selected speeches and writing of an American
Jewish activist / David A. Harris.
  v. cm.
  Contents: v. 1. 1979-1999
  ISBN 0-88125-693-5 (v. 1)
  ISBN 0-88125-779-6 (v. 2) 2000-2001
  ISBN 0-88125-842-3 (v. 3) 2002-2003
  ISBN 0-88125-927-6 (v. 4) 2004-2005
  1. Jews--Politics and government--1948- 2. Jews--Soviet
Union--Emigration and immigration. 3. Arab-Israeli conflict.
4. Jews--Europe--Social conditions--20th century. 5. Antisemitism.
6. American Jewish Committee--Officials and employees--Biography.
7. Holocaust, Jewish (1939-1945)--Influence. I. Title.
DS140.H36 2001
305.892'4'009045--dc21   00-058958

Distributed by
KTAV Publishing House, Inc.
930 Newark Avenue
Jersey City, NJ 07306
www.ktav.com

*To the American Jewish Committee,
my safe harbor of civility, decency,
and integrity in a stormy world.*

CONTENTS

2. SPEECHES AND TESTIMONY

3. ISRAEL ADVOCACY GUIDE

4. RADIO COMMENTARY

5. PRINT MEDIA

6. AJC INSTITUTIONAL

FOREWORD

"Vision," said Jonathan Swift, "is the art of seeing things invisible." An effective leader must be a visionary who looks to the future, discerns broad trends, absorbs and acts upon their unseen implications. I have been privileged to work over the last two years with such a farsighted leader, David Harris.

Within the first years of this new millennium, there has been no more significant trend than globalization—of the economy, as workers participate in a global marketplace; of ideas, as the Internet and its search engines connect distant communities and expose alternate ideologies; of people, as populations move in search of opportunity; and of politics, as the fate of nations becomes increasingly bound together through international and regional entities. David Harris, for whom the expression globetrotter is perhaps an understatement—and whose family history, education, and even maybe a "gene" for diplomacy have all prepared him for international statesmanship—grasps profoundly the globalizing trends of our time and has incorporated them into the agenda of the American Jewish Committee.

In countless ways, under David's leadership, AJC, over the past two years, has steadily expanded its horizons—opening a Transatlantic Institute in Brussels, enabling the completion of a significant Holocaust memorial and museum at Belzec, defending Israel's right to be accorded the same respect as other nations at the UN and in the International Red Cross, launching the Latino and Latin American Affairs Institute, and most recently, establishing the Africa Institute.

A glance at this book's table of contents will tell you some of David's recent destinations: Istanbul, Thessaloniki, Rome, Caracas, Lima, Buenos Aires, and Prague. Far more than an itinerary, this book illuminates his ever-expanding worldview, as well as hinting at how the world has come to see him. Within the past two years, he has been the recipient of the French Legion of Honor, the Polish Commander's Cross of Merit with Stars, the most prestigious medal Poland bestows on foreigners, and the Golden Cross, the German military's highest civilian honor. But it is not only foreign countries that have come to recognize his distinction. Through his writings, radio broadcasts, timely responses to the media, and presentations around the country, his has become a highly regarded voice of passion, erudition, and reason on a range of issues affecting America, American Jewry, human rights, and the defense of democratic values.

I am sure that you will enjoy reading David's insightful commentary as much as I have enjoyed being his partner and colleague in working for a better future for the Jewish people and all humanity.

E. Robert Goodkind
President
American Jewish Committee

IN THE TRENCHES

TRENCHES

Volume 4

INTRODUCTION

When I was an undergraduate in the late 1960s, like many of my contemporaries, I believed that anything was possible. America was changing before our eyes. A controversial war in Vietnam was under growing challenge. President Lyndon Johnson was forced to announce that he would not run for a second full term of office. Universities were opening up and students were getting a voice in the conduct of affairs on campus. And American minorities—and women—were demanding, and finally getting, the rights that had largely been denied to them in years past.

It translated into the "triumphant conviction of strength," in the words of Joseph Conrad describing his own youth. There was an intoxicating sense of power and impact, of an unstoppable force—a belief that on our watch we could create something new and better.

Lord Byron, the English poet identified with Rome and the quest for Italian nationhood, once wrote: "I shall soon be twenty-six. Is there anything in the future that can possibly console us for not always being twenty-five!" It so happens that I entered the Jewish communal world, in Rome in 1975, at the age of twenty-five.

In my case, what "consoled" me was an unerring belief, rooted in my previous experience, that my generation could have the same decisive impact on Jewish issues as we had had on American political and social matters. Surely that would translate into helping the world understand the legitimacy of Israel's case, contributing to peacemaking, strengthening Jewish identity, marginalizing anti-Semitism, etching the Holocaust indelibly onto the world's conscience, ensuring the well-being of Jewish communities around the world, and fostering a climate of interfaith and interethnic respect and cooperation.

Much progress on these fronts has been achieved in the past three decades, more than might have been previously imagined. But even as I stubbornly cling to my idealism during the bumpy journey through

3

middle age, the arrogance of my youth, which declared no challenge to be beyond the capacity of our generation to solve, has yielded to a grudging recognition that some issues just don't lend themselves to easy solutions or—gasp!—might actually outlive us. Or, put another way, I suppose I've crossed the threshold and now understand Aristotle's definition of youth: "[Those who] have exalted notions because they have not yet been humbled by life or learned its necessary limitations."

And so there is Book 4 of *In the Trenches* and, yes, it grapples during the years 2004 and 2005 with many of the same issues as did the three previous volumes. And I suspect that if I'm fortunate enough to be able to prepare Book 5, the subject matter won't be all that different, either, given the way the world looks at the start of 2006. Just in case anyone was wondering, the lion and the lamb don't appear ready yet to lie down together in eternal peace and friendship.

But I'm not complaining, far from it. I have what I consider to be the world's best job. And that's why I chose to dedicate this book to the American Jewish Committee, my professional home since 1979.

The AJC's dogged determination to make the world a better place for all, its impressive record of achievement, its abiding belief in the power of reason, and its openness to discourse and debate all attract me. In a world sometimes gone mad, the innate courage, principle, and decency of the American Jewish Committee make the organization stand tall. And at a time when Jews the world over have good reason for concern, the steady hand of this organization reassures me.

Hokey as it may sound, I am grateful each and every day for the privilege of working at AJC. I am surrounded by lay and staff colleagues who share a passion for the defense of democracy, pluralism, and human rights and a commitment to a robust Jewish future. And I am particularly indebted to those who helped make this book possible. While I am solely responsible for the contents, I most assuredly could not have undertaken this task alone.

Bob Goodkind, AJC's national president and a prominent New York attorney, has offered support and encouragement from the first day he took office in 2004. He exemplifies the consistent quality of our lay leadership.

Roselyn Bell, our director of publications and in-house editor par excellence, pored over every word and punctuation mark in this manuscript with infinite patience and dedication. She saved me from more than one embarrassment.

Larry Grossman, the editor of AJC's *American Jewish Year Book*, has always made himself available to read my drafts and offer helpful comments, both big and small.

The same is true of Rebecca Neuwirth, director of special projects, who has sat by my side for nearly seven years and has been a valuable—or, I should say, invaluable—sounding board for just about every article, essay, or speech I've written.

Linda Krieg, our art director, was tasked with conceptualizing an original cover for this volume, having already designed the first three in the series, and once again she came through with flying colors.

Cyma Horowitz and Michele Anish, the indefatigable librarians of AJC's superb Blaustein Library, have always risen to the challenge of locating and substantiating every request for information, no matter how seemingly obscure.

Many of the pieces in this volume were published separately in the media. Ken Bandler, our public relations and communications director, was the middleman in just about every case, for which I am thankful.

Maxine Kaye, a recent Barnard College graduate now working as my senior assistant, helped organize this publishing project, which was anything but easy. She did so in what has become her signature style—unassuming, efficient, and congenial. The Jewish future looks bright indeed with individuals like Maxine coming up through the ranks.

Helen Allen, my administrative assistant, took care of the nuts and bolts—the typing and retyping, filing, and retrieving—without which I never would have made it even to first base. Helen was always there for me, even long after the building emptied out.

As always, Bernie Scharfstein and the team at KTAV Publishing House have been a joy to work with.

And last but by no means least, my family has been my pillar of strength.

By example far more than by words, my mother, Nelly Harris, inspired me to try to make a difference in the world.

I was blessed growing up to be surrounded within a few blocks by two sets of grandparents, one set of great-grandparents, an aunt and uncle, and cousins galore, each of whom touched me with the connective tissue in time and space that is the Jewish people. That's all the more reason why I'm so heartbroken to see the atomizing of the American family, precisely because I know what it means to have an extended family within easy reach.

And my beloved wife, Jou Jou, and our three wonderful sons, now happily joined by our first daughter-in-law, are a constant reminder of the blessings I've had.

I. LETTERS

Letter from Juan
January 12, 2004

My name is Juan.* Actually, that's not my real name, but it will have to do. I'm an illegal alien living in the United States. I've been here just over three years. It's been tough, very tough, but I'm proud of what I've accomplished.

I came here with absolutely nothing except a will to work hard and earn some money. I left behind my country, Paraguay, my parents and siblings, my two children, and everything that was familiar and dear to me. I had no choice. I love my country, but it couldn't offer me anything. Even though I had a few college courses under my belt, I could find work only at all kinds of odd jobs—from door-to-door salesman to long-distance truck driver. There was no job security and certainly no prospect for the future—hence my decision to emigrate.

Paraguay is a vast landlocked country, roughly the size of California, but with just under six million inhabitants. It became independent in 1811, after 275 years of Spanish rule. There are two official languages—Spanish and Guarani. The population is largely mestizo, a mixture of Spanish and indigenous Guarani Indian. The Catholic Church predominates. There is a small but highly successful community of Mennonites who came in waves from Europe and Canada, and settled in the Chaco region, near the Bolivian border. The Jewish community, centered in the capital of Asuncion, is tiny but, like the Mennonites, seemingly well-to-do. There are some Chinese immigrants. And, as I'll discuss shortly, there are a fair number of Arabs, mostly from Lebanon.

Like many Latin American nations, Paraguay came to democracy only recently, after decades of stultifying authoritarian rule and economic stagnation under "President-for-life" Alfredo Stroessner.

* Juan is a fictitious person. He is a composite of several Latin American migrants living in the New York area whom I have met in recent years.

7

Just over one-third of the population lives below the poverty line. The unemployment rate today is close to 20 percent. Corruption is widespread and systemic. Money talks. With money, just about anything becomes possible; without money, everything is out of reach.

Nowhere is all this more evident than in my hometown of Ciudad del Este, in eastern Paraguay, the country's second largest city. Perhaps you've heard of it. If not, it's a name you should remember, all the more so in this era of global terrorism.

My city is in a region called the tri-border area, where Argentina, Brazil, and Paraguay meet. On our side of the border is the Itaipu Dam, which created one of the largest hydroelectric projects in the world. On the Argentine side is the city of Puerto Iguazu. And on the Brazilian side, which is connected by the Puente de la Amistad ("Friendship Bridge"), are the famous Iguazu Falls, a major tourist site. I don't know the exact number, but I'd say that thousands of people cross the bridge every day, mostly Brazilians on shopping expeditions. Border controls are lax to nonexistent.

Ciudad del Este, I'm sorry to say, is best known not for shopping or sightseeing, but for its black market, smuggling, money laundering, drugs and arms trafficking, and Islamic extremism.

The city was founded less than fifty years ago. The construction of the Itaipu Dam in the 1970s and 1980s caused a rapid growth in the population as many moved to my city for work in the booming service and commerce industries. Arabs became the principal merchants and to this day dominate the business sector. Most of the Arabs are Shiite Muslims from Lebanon. Across the Parana River, in Foz do Iguazu, Brazil, there is another Arab Muslim community with its mosques.

It wasn't until ten years ago that people began talking about Ciudad del Este and the tri-border region. Until then, no one seemed to pay much attention to what went on in the area. The law-abiding people, of whom there were many, kept their heads down and went about their business quietly, knowing that the last thing to do in a largely lawless place like this was to draw attention to themselves.

But with the two terrorist bombings in Buenos Aires—the first against the Israeli Embassy in 1992, the second against the Jewish

Community Center in 1994—our area was suddenly in the news. There were reports that the attackers had a connection to the Arab community, numbering about 20,000, in Ciudad del Este. Rumors began swirling that the terrorists had been given logistical support or financial assistance or safe haven in our city or the surrounding area. Leaders of the Arab community denied the allegations.

Then things seemed to quiet down, at least until September 11. Since then, there have been investigations, accusations, raids, and arrests, all focused on some members of the Arab community and involving suspected links to Hezbollah, Hamas, and Al-Qaeda. A few people were detained, some of whom were subsequently released. Others, including the Hezbollah point man in the region, managed to flee across the border to Brazil. And incriminating material, including Hezbollah recruitment propaganda and evidence of financial remittances to the terrorist organization, has been found.

I left just over three years ago, but stay in close touch with my family. I have to say that we were all surprised by the reports. We knew the Arabs as local businessmen and neighbors, and we saw them gather to pray on Fridays in the Prophet Mohammed Mosque. We understood that as a community they were quite successful, which came from a combination of skilled entrepreneurship and, we presumed, cross-border smuggling, the pirating of compact discs and the like, which, as I've said, is not uncommon in our region. The alleged links with international terrorism, whether in Buenos Aires or the Middle East, though, came as a big surprise.

I'm certainly no expert on international terrorism, but I can tell you that, despite some recent well-publicized steps, law enforcement still has a long way to go if it wants to monitor effectively what's going on in Ciudad del Este and its neighboring cities. I know from my friends just how porous the borders are, even if Argentina has noticeably tightened its frontier, and how free-wheeling and unchecked the economy is in my city. There are any number of unpatrolled airstrips and waterways, which create endless opportunities for people to move in and out of the region with ease. People can also make lots of (unreported) money, which can be moved around—in the country or out of the country—without too much difficulty.

Back to my own journey. After lots of agonizing, I decided to take the plunge and go to the United States. Everyone said that was the place for me. I was lucky. I didn't have to turn to a "coyote," the name given to professional smugglers, for help, nor did I have one of those gruesome overland trips depicted in the film *El Norte*. By a quirk of fate, I had been born on the Argentine side of the border and therefore had two passports—Argentine and Paraguayan.

At the time I planned my departure, Argentine citizens, unlike Paraguayans, didn't need an American visa to enter the country. That made life a lot easier for me. As a Paraguayan, getting a U.S. visa can be tricky. For instance, if you're from the town of Caraguatay, located between Asuncion and Ciudad del Este, you're likely to be turned down flat. It's widely known that just about every young person from that town tries to get to America, and many have done so, mostly illegally.

In my case, the Argentine passport was sufficient. I flew to New York, showed my passport, was given a tourist visa and, like many others, simply overstayed.

I was in my early thirties, healthy, strong as a bear, and eager to go to work. My goal was to make enough to live on and to send back as much money as I could for my two children, who were living with my ex-wife. Long-term, my hope was to find a way to bring my children to America.

I could write a book about my first three years. I spoke just a little English, which I had learned in school in Paraguay, but was far from fluent. I had a few Paraguayan contacts, but they had arrived not much before me. I knew nothing about the American economy or its social system.

I found my first job on a farm on Long Island. That was backbreaking work, and I lasted about three months. Then a friend told me I'd be better off elsewhere, so I moved upstate and became a pizza delivery man. Incidentally, that first winter introduced me to snow, something I'd never seen before, much less driven in.

Once I got the hang of driving here, which essentially involves obeying rules that are largely ignored in my country, and a sense of the geography, I got a job as a cab driver. It wasn't long, however, before

I realized that the owners, fellow South Americans, were treating me unfairly. They kept for themselves all the lucrative rides to airports and into Manhattan, while I was left with local calls that yielded very little. And so I worked even harder, twelve to fourteen hours per day, six, even seven, days a week, to put some money aside toward my dream of one day opening my own competing company. I'm proud to say that, together with a few compatriots, I have now started that company, and it's doing well.

Any American reading this is bound to ask questions, most of which are variations on the same theme: How can an illegal immigrant start a business? The short answer is that it's surprisingly easy. And we've managed to do everything by the books. We are licensed and insured, we accept credit cards, and we deal directly with local authorities. I could write a book—or, more precisely, a manual—on this subject as well.

But what I want to convey is that, believe me, I take no pride in being illegal. Given the choice, it's not the way I would opt to live. Please understand that the last thing I wanted was to leave my country, my family, especially my children, and my friends, without the possibility of returning to them.

Do you have any idea how painful it is to know that my children are growing up without me, while the best I can do is make regular phone calls and send holiday gifts and money? I can't see them. There's no way I can go back for a visit and be sure that I can return here, as border controls have tightened since September 11. And there's no way for me now to bring the children here, even though my ex-wife has agreed in principle that they'd be far better off in America than in Paraguay. I've explored all kinds of schemes, but the chances of success aren't very high. I suppose my best hope is for an amnesty that will legalize my status, all the more so after President Bush's potentially encouraging comment on undocumented aliens of January 7. Then I would hope to file for my children's legal immigration.

I know there's some resentment in America about this influx of illegals from Latin America. At times, I feel it personally. The local police, for instance, seem to go out of their way to harass us. I can't tell you the number of times I've been stopped for no apparent reason while driving. They always seem to be looking for some excuse to give me a ticket. But we're here in America for the very same reason that others have come—in search of opportunity denied us elsewhere and a better life for ourselves and our families. And we're prepared to do the work that others don't seem to want. Who are the maids, housekeepers, gardeners, dishwashers, parking attendants, nighttime office cleaners, day laborers, and agricultural workers of today? (But we're also entrepreneurs and who knows what else.)

There are moments, though, when I feel that, as a group, we're practically invisible. Yes, society wants us to do the tough jobs, but then some people look at us as if we are lesser human beings, or nonexistent. Or they lump us all together and see us monolithically as "those Latinos."

I've now been here long enough to meet a lot of Latinos from various countries—Ecuador, Guatemala, Mexico, and Peru. Many came here legally; others, like myself, didn't. Some are with families; others are not. Some plan to return to their countries; others see their future in America. Some are well-educated; others are practically illiterate. Some have learned English; others are still struggling. In other words, while most of us speak Spanish (either as a first or, if we were raised to speak an Indian dialect, second language) and are Catholic (though a growing number have been drawn to Evangelical churches), we are a far more varied community than outsiders might think. Moreover, Peru is not Paraguay, and Ecuador is not El Salvador. Each country is different.

There are many things about America I like, even if I can't entirely adjust to a country whose national sport isn't soccer. After living in a country rife with corruption and with only limited economic opportunity, I find it a breath of fresh air to live here. America's infrastructure is also very impressive, as is the care given the environment. And I'm struck by the diversity of people here.

For example, I had never actually met a Jew before coming here, but now several of my regular customers are Jews. I have to confess that I didn't know much about Jews while living in Paraguay, other than that they were concentrated in Asuncion. I heard they were rich and that some Catholics believed they were responsible for killing Jesus, but I myself wasn't familiar with any Jews. In fact, I remember asking one of my customers if Jews celebrated Christmas. I couldn't imagine that anyone didn't. Now I know better.

Speaking of Jews, I read in one of the Paraguayan newspapers that Israel had decided to close its embassy in Asuncion. That's a shame. Israel is not well enough understood in my country, and the Arab community is very active. But there's a natural connection to Israel because it's seen as the Holy Land, the birthplace of Christianity. I hope Israel will reconsider its decision.

All in all, I've discovered that life isn't always fair. That's why I'm here alone and not in my country with my family. But I think I was born with an optimistic disposition. I try not to dwell too long on my difficulties. I have faith. I believe in God. I trust that things will work out for the best in the end. One way or another, I'll get my kids here, legalize my status, maybe remarry, and perfect my English.

My taxi company is doing well and I'm making more money than I ever imagined possible when I was working on the Long Island farm, even if it doesn't give me much time off. Earlier this fall, I even agreed to drive to a suburb of Denver to pick up a teenager and bring him to New York, at the request of a customer. I guess I had no idea how big this country really is and therefore charged too little. In all, I drove about 75 hours back and forth with just a couple of hours of sleep in the car. It turned out the teenager was the son of a "coyote" who couldn't let his son fly because he had no valid identification! Live and learn.

Why do I share my life story with you?

First, I suppose it's because of what I said a moment ago: I want to humanize us, the invisible people. Each of us Latinos has a story to tell, and no two stories are identical.

Second, maybe by recounting stories like mine, I can help in a small way to narrow the gap between the tens of millions of Latinos in the U.S. and other Americans.

And third, having been in the New York area on September 11, I came to understand the evil of terrorism. By coincidence, I come from a city that is on the global terrorist map. Perhaps by telling my story, I can shine the spotlight a bit on a city I love but one that contains within it dangerous elements that, if left unchecked, could contribute to a major terrorist incident somewhere in the world.

Letter from Chappaqua
February 29, 2004

Once upon a time, Chappaqua was an unknown northern Westchester town, often confused in people's minds with either Chautauqua or Chappaquiddick. No longer. Ever since an ex-president and his wife, now the senator from New York, unexpectedly moved here, the place has become plenty well known. What hasn't changed, though, is the beauty and tranquillity of the area.

That makes it all the more jarring, on a quiet weekend day, to contemplate the world in which we live. From my desk, looking out at tree tops framed by snow-covered hills, it's hard to imagine the complex and often ugly realities which we face daily.

This past week was another sobering reminder.

Yet again a Palestinian suicide bomber took Israeli lives—eight dead, sixty injured—on a bus in the center of Jerusalem, as the toll from such terrorist attacks nears one thousand, the proportional equivalent of 50,000 American fatalities. And the Israeli number would be far higher were it not for the extraordinary efforts of security forces to prevent, through intelligence and interception, more than 90 percent of all planned attacks.

The International Court of Justice in The Hague held a politically motivated hearing on Israel's security barrier that is expected, given the court's composition, to offer an advisory opinion in favor of the Palestinians and refer the matter back to the United Nations, fertile ground for Israel-bashing.

The current issue of the *New York Times Sunday Magazine* has yet another article on the difficulties faced by many "frightened, angry, and dispirited" Jews in France, including a description of an incident that occurred while an American Jewish Committee delegation was visiting last month. A prominent Jewish singer named Shirel was performing in the eastern town of Macon in the presence of Bernadette Chirac, the First Lady, when a group of French Arab youths began chanting "Death to the Jews." Sadly, the chant itself is nothing new these days, but the fact that the presence of Madame Chirac did not deter the youngsters reveals the depth of the problem, both for France's large Jewish community and for French society as a whole.

And Mel Gibson's deeply troubling new film, a direct challenge to the liberalizing spirit of the Second Vatican Council, opened in thousands of cinemas across the country and appears headed, for reasons worthy of examination at another time, for box-office success. That's bad enough. Even worse, as the film makes its way overseas, there could be more problems. In countries where the Jewish communities are small and the web of Christian-Jewish cooperation not nearly as well developed as here, the level of Jewish anxiety is likely to be even higher. And it's very possible that Arab countries will use the film to show Jews in the worst possible light. Remember how, in May 2001, the Syrian president, in the presence of Pope John Paul II, reawakened the deicide charge.

In thirty years of communal service, I can't recall a more unsettling, unnerving, and unpredictable period, and it's not as if the past three decades were all milk and honey. In my frequent meetings with Jewish audiences, whether in synagogues, homes, schools and colleges, or organizational settings, it's clear that people are worried, more so than they have been in a very long time.

Everything seems to be happening at once, they note, and it's almost too much to process—Gibson's film, dangers to Jews in Europe, security threats, suicide bombings, vilification of Israel, fiery anti-Semitic rhetoric in the Islamic world, and, increasingly, anecdotal stories of anti-Jewish comments or incidents in their own communities.

Just in the last few weeks, one New Jersey grandmother told me that her five-year-old grandson had come to visit her after school, but without the kippah he normally wears. When she asked why, he told her that he had learned that "some people don't like us" and therefore it was better to take off the skullcap outside of school.

At a high school sports event in Westchester, a Jewish player for one team, the son of friends, was taunted with the "k" word by players on the other team. Meanwhile, a Long Island resident who works on Wall Street told me the other evening that he has become much more low-key about his Jewish identity and support for Israel at work because he "senses hostility." And parents of college-bound kids wonder aloud what their children might face on campus as Jews and whether they'll know how to deal with potentially troublesome situations.

Given this state of affairs, it may seem a bit of a stretch to introduce some counterbalancing news. Surely there will be those who wonder if I've taken leave of my senses or become hopelessly woolly-headed. Neither is the case, to the best of my knowledge at least, but it's important precisely at this moment in time, when there may be a temptation to yield to despair, to remind ourselves that the current picture is not unremittingly bleak. And perhaps this will provide a measure of hope that we are far from being alone or defenseless.

First, it was in 1654, exactly 350 years ago, that Jews arrived here, in what was then called New Amsterdam. They came from Recife, Brazil, fleeing the extension of the Portuguese Inquisition to that part of the world. The story of the ensuing three-and-a-half centuries simply has no precedent in Jewish history. We have evolved to become the freest, most successful, most integrated, most prosperous, and most influential Diaspora Jewish community ever.

To say the least, we have received a great deal from this country—unparalleled freedom, opportunity, acceptance, and equality. In turn, we have contributed mightily to America's growth and development in virtually every sphere imaginable. We should not pass up the upcoming opportunity to celebrate this landmark anniversary with unreserved joy and gratitude.

Second, there are signs everywhere of American Jewish energy and vitality. Jews who care about being Jewish, more mindful than ever of the dangers to the Jewish future posed by assimilation and eventual disappearance, are intensifying their involvement and commitment. The evidence is everywhere—in day schools, camps, synagogues, universities, community centers, new groupings, publications, the Internet, you name it. The result in the years ahead may be a community slightly smaller than today, but still more vibrant, literate, and engaged.

Third, we live in the single most powerful and dynamic nation in the world. This counts for something.

America continues to stand tall and proud as a beacon of hope and freedom. America is uniquely positioned to assist Israel in its quest for security and peace. America maintains a special relationship with Israel unlike any other country's ties with the Jewish state. America is prepared to use its power of veto in the UN Security Council, even when it may be a minority of one, to block anti-Israel resolutions. America is prepared to speak out on the dangers of global anti-Semitism while some other countries would rather look the other way or bury their heads in the sand. America is prepared to walk out of a UN-sponsored conference on racism in Durban when it turns into a hate fest. And America is prepared to use its diplomatic might to protect endangered Jewish communities in far-flung places.

Fourth, despite an unprecedented campaign of terror and violence directed against it, Israel's will both to defend itself and to carry on with daily life remains unshakable. It is, in fact, a powerfully inspiring story.

When one thinks about what Israelis are shouldering—the defense burden, the narrow margin for error, the elusive search for peace, the danger of suicide bombings anywhere and everywhere, the microscopic and often unsympathetic scrutiny of the international media, automatic majorities arrayed against them in international organizations, a tourism meltdown, economic travails, and domestic fault lines—the miracle of this country and its successes to date boggle the mind. A recent visit to Israel was another welcome reminder of a democratic country unbowed, unbent, and determined to live life to its fullest, even as it grapples with a never-ending stream of challenges.

Fifth, there have been some rather noteworthy changes in this tumultuous region.

For the foreseeable future, at least, Iraq as a regional threat is out of the picture. That's no small feat. After all, this was a country openly calling for Israel's elimination, which provided hefty financial payments to the families of Palestinian suicide bombers and launched thirty-nine Scud missiles at Israel in the 1991 Gulf War.

So, too, at least in large measure, is Afghanistan, which under Taliban rule was a haven for terrorist groups, including, of course, Al-

Qaeda. The Taliban have been removed from government and wide swaths of the country, if not entirely from the Afghan-Pakistani border region.

Libya appears to have undergone a change of heart, sobered, no doubt, by the fate of Saddam Hussein, and the interception of equipment headed for Tripoli's fledgling nuclear weapons program.

Syria continues to talk tough, but finds itself in an unenviable strategic position. Turkey, to its north, is close to the United States and Israel, and will not soon forget Syria's harboring of anti-Turkish Kurdish terrorist groups not that long ago. Iraq, to its east and southeast, is now occupied by 100,000 American soldiers. Jordan, to the south, is pro-American. Israel, to the southwest, sits atop the Golan Heights with a clear view of Damascus. And Syria's longtime and indefensible occupation of Lebanon is finally getting some scrutiny from the international community.

Iran poses the greatest threat in the region, but two recent developments bear noting. There can be no doubt about Iran's intention to develop nuclear weapons. Much in this regard has been unearthed in recent months with the help of the International Atomic Energy Agency (IAEA). While the United States and Europe may not entirely see eye-to-eye on the proper policy response, there is no longer any significant disagreement on the intelligence assessment, which itself is a major step forward. Further, the Iranian elections held earlier this month have revealed the true nature of the regime, shattering the false distinction that many stubbornly clung to between a "reformist" president and the repressive mullahs. Until now, Europe in particular was pinning its hopes on President Mohammad Khatami to bring about internal change. A new approach is required, which provides another chance for Europe and the United States to forge a common plan.

It turns out that Pakistan, or more specifically the country's top nuclear expert, A.Q. Khan, and those who supported and protected him, were actively sharing nuclear technology with at least three nations—North Korea, Iran, and Libya. This ominous trade has been exposed and, if we are to believe news accounts, ended. Further, Khan is reportedly revealing to interrogators information about his global dealings, including facilitators in Asia, the Middle East, and Europe. Despite the obvious damage already done, with this data in hand, considerable progress can be achieved in the race to deny rogue states weapons of mass destruction and the means to deliver them.

And not least, the sustained post-9/11 focus on terrorist funding from Saudi Arabia and other Persian Gulf states, training, indoctrination, and state sponsorship has had some effect, though obviously not nearly enough, on the ability of groups in the region to operate effectively.

Sixth, the implosion of the Soviet Union and the demise of the Warsaw Pact continue to have overwhelmingly positive reverberations. While Jewish life was largely snuffed out in the Cold War and the anti-Semitic campaigns that took place in several eastern-bloc countries—notably the USSR, Czechoslovakia, and Poland—Israel's enemies found practically limitless diplomatic, political, and military support.

Fifteen new countries have emerged in place of the defunct USSR, some more democratic than others, some closely allied with the United States. Jewish communities have been reborn throughout these countries, and signs of communal life abound. Relations with Israel have been established and in some cases are flourishing, including with several predominately Muslim nations.

And in Central Europe today, in stark contrast to the situation just twenty years ago, Israel now has some of its closest friends anywhere, including Poland, the Czech Republic, Slovakia, Hungary, Bulgaria, Romania, Croatia, and the Baltic states. Several of these countries will shortly be joining the EU, where their pro-Israel voices hopefully will be heard. Moreover, each of these countries seeks ties with the larger Jewish world and is also witnessing the revitalization of long dormant Jewish communities.

Seventh, I alluded to Israel's ties with Turkey. Indeed, this is one of the most important developments for Israel in recent years, not least in the military-to-military sphere. It also serves as a model of Israel's ability to establish a close relationship with a predominately Muslim country. When a new Turkish government took office in 2002, concern was expressed that its pro-Muslim sympathies, in contrast to the fiercely secular nature of many other political parties, might damage the bilateral relationship, but this has not proved the case.

Speaking of allies, Israel's link with India, which has skyrocketed in the past twelve years, is another key factor in Jerusalem's global positioning. Israelis joke that India sought the tie so it could boast that the combined Indo-Israeli population constitutes one-fifth of the world's population!

India's booming economy, vast potential, and shared strategic concerns with Israel create a common agenda and a mutually beneficial working link.

Israel's other important ties shouldn't be ignored either, such as with Australia, Britain, Canada, Italy, Japan, Singapore, South Korea, and, above all, Germany, not to mention the Pacific island nations, which are often Israel's most stalwart allies in the UN (apart from the United States), and Costa Rica and El Salvador, whose embassies are in Jerusalem. Finally, while Israel maintains open or discreet contacts with a number of Arab countries, its relationship to date with Jordan is in a category all its own and therefore deserves special mention.

Eighth, the countries of Western Europe, however late in the day, are waking up to the danger of anti-Semitism. It took longer than it should have, but there's growing recognition of the need for decisive action, particularly in France. Various conferences have recently taken place, political leaders are speaking out with greater frequency and clarity, and law enforcement and judicial authorities appear to be stepping up their efforts. There is also increased monitoring of what's being beamed into European countries via satellite from the Arab world and what's being preached in mosques and taught in Islamic schools on European soil.

Moreover, there is now greater understanding in Europe of what some Jews have been saying from the onset of this current wave of anti-Semitism, namely that this should not be seen as an exclusively Jewish problem. Attacks on Jews are nothing less than assaults on Europe and its value system.

The multiple challenges faced by European countries with sizable and growing Muslim populations have no easy answers. Nor should anyone believe that the surge of anti-Semitism can be dealt with by a few well-chosen words from a politician's lips or an occasional prison sentence. But at long last a slumbering Europe is opening its eyes and seeing before it a problem that is both serious and unlikely to disappear on its own. In the scheme of things, that must be labeled progress.

Ninth, even as we concern ourselves with possible fallout from the Gibson film, we mustn't lose sight of the remarkable progress achieved in Christian-Jewish relations during the past fifty years, both with the Catholic Church and major Protestant denominations. In fact, it's no exaggeration to say that more progress has been made in Christian-Jewish relations in the past five decades than in the previous 1,500 years.

We have friends in the Christian world who don't want to see backsliding by their churches in attitudes toward Jews, and they oppose Gibson's whole retrograde approach to current theology and teaching.

In other words, we are not alone in this battle. As but one example, read the op-ed by Father John Pawlikowski of the Catholic Theological Union in the *Baltimore Sun* ("The Poison in 'The Passion,'" February 25).

And tenth, despite our small numbers relative to the world's population, Jewish voices still count in corridors of power and decision-making circles, and not just in the United States. Governments and other key institutions often consider the Jewish dimension as they deliberate policy. They may respect a Jewish viewpoint, they may worry about damage to their image, especially in the United States, or they may simply believe entrenched stereotypes of Jews as vastly more powerful than our numbers alone would suggest.

While we may not always succeed in our efforts, this image gives us a fighting chance to make our case, and that's a far cry from the powerlessness we experienced not so long ago in our history, with all its catastrophic consequences.

There they are—my list of ten factors, to which others could surely be added, that we ought to keep in mind these days. They might serve as an additional dollop of confidence to get us through this tumultuous period.

And what exactly is it that we should be doing? Three basic things, I believe.

Each of us has the capacity to do more. I'm a great believer in the power of individual initiative, creativity, and inspiration. Each of us has strengths. We should play to them as we ask ourselves how we can best help enhance understanding of Israel, combat anti-Semitism, and strengthen interfaith fellowship in our communities and beyond.

In addition to our individual actions, when we come together in groups, we leverage our voice and our reach. That's why organizations matter. But all organizations are not qualitatively equal, even if they share a commitment to Jewish well-being, any more than all colleges and universities are identical because providing an education is their primary objective. Through organizations with access to top leaders and savoir faire in dealing with complex issues—like the American Jewish Committee—our views can be expressed most effectively.

Plant for the future. Recent events should remind us again of the long haul we face to eliminate anti-Semitism and achieve peace and security for Israel. That's all the more reason why we must prepare our children and grandchildren for what lies ahead, starting in the home. But it must be done thoughtfully. Frightening children is not the most effective way. Rather, it's incumbent on us to inculcate in them pride in being Jewish, awareness of the vast riches of Jewish civilization, and connection to Jews everywhere, from Israel to Argentina to France.

In Ecclesiastes it is written, "To everything there is a season."

This is a season to remember our blessings.

It is a season to face our challenges squarely, courageously, intelligently, and in concert with our friends.

It is a season to recall that Jews have always been animated by hope, a belief that human action can make the world more just and harmonious.

And it is a season to remind ourselves, as Rabbi Tarfon taught us in the *Sayings of the Fathers*, that while we may not be required to complete the work, neither are we free to desist from it.

Letter from a Newspaper Junkie
March 23, 2004

From an early age I had a thing about newspapers. I began reading the *New York Times* every morning before I was ten, and the *New York*

Post was obligatory after-school reading. I always started with the sports section and then moved on to other parts of the paper.

I marveled at how newspapers could be put together overnight. I was fascinated by the window on the world provided by newspapers. I even enjoyed leafing through the Russian and Yiddish newspapers delivered daily to my grandparents in the apartment next door, though I could make little sense of the unfamiliar scripts.

Living in Munich during the seventh grade, I discovered the *International Herald Tribune*. It had two big advantages over its *New York Times* co-owner (with the *Washington Post*)—cartoons and Art Buchwald's column.

By high school I added to my reading list *Newsweek, U.S. News & World Report*, and the *New Republic*, plus, as a debater, I needed to consult a wide range of newspapers and magazines to research the annual topics of the National Forensic League and to prepare for Model UNs and Student Congresses.

To this day, I continue to have a fascination with newspapers—the real thing, not the Web site version. In fact, one of the great joys of my sabbatical year in Geneva (2000–01) was the morning ritual of going to our neighborhood kiosk and buying *La Tribune de Genève*, the local paper, *Le Figaro*, the right-of-center French daily, and *La Repubblica*, the left-of-center Italian daily. Taking these along with the *International Herald Tribune*, which was delivered to my home each morning, I would park myself on our balcony, weather permitting, and explore the world.

While always a newspaper and, more broadly, a news junkie, one thing changed for me over the years: Whereas I believed every word of what I read as a child, I gradually came to understand, long before the shenanigans of Jayson Blair, Stephen Glass, and Jack Kelley, that newspapers, even in democratic societies, need to be read with a degree of critical sense rather than the naive leap of faith I had once made.

For quite some time, influenced no doubt by the fact that my mother and her family had fled the USSR, I had simplistically assumed that because newspapers in Communist countries, as instruments of the state, made an art form out of distortion and deceit—there's no *pravda* ("truth") in *Izvestiya* ("news"), and no *izvestiya* in *Pravda*, the old Soviet joke went—the polar opposite was surely the case where freedom of the press reigned.

Moreover, it wasn't until I had developed personal knowledge about an issue or familiarity with a particular story that I could begin to separate fact from fiction and notice errors of omission or commission.

But I also discovered that it could be quite difficult to address these issues with the journalists concerned or their editors, and therefore battles had to be chosen very carefully. While some journalists were open, others were remarkably thin-skinned. I remember a syndicated column by Jack Anderson in the early 1980s that dealt with the plight of Jews in the USSR. Those of us in the Soviet Jewry movement always welcomed attention to the issue, but I found myself totally misquoted. I picked up the phone and called Anderson's assistant, complimenting the overall column and then pointing out what I thought might simply have been a transcription error. To make a long story short, I was told more than once that my call was presumptuous and that I wouldn't be interviewed for other stories because I was a "troublemaker." In fact, I was never again called.

In words attributed to Mark Twain, one should "never pick a fight with a person who buys ink by the barrel."

During the Palestinian intifada that began in 1987, I was struck by what seemed, in too many outlets, the simplistic urge to juxtapose a heavy-handed Israeli military battling freedom-seeking Palestinian youngsters. An example: An experienced *Washington Post* journalist called and said she had been asked by her editors to do a story on the local Jewish reaction to the uprising. I invited her to join me for an American Jewish Committee meeting in suburban Washington that was to focus on that very issue.

In my opening remarks, I said that Israel needed to defend itself against the violence that had broken out, which was no easy thing since Palestinian children were being deliberately placed in the front lines. At the same time, I added, I was pained by reports of possible Israeli military excesses and loss of innocent life. The next day, the paper carried on its front page a story that led with only the second half of what I said, completely ignoring the balanced context, and thereby suggesting that I had been unabashedly critical of Israel. I was astonished by the misrepresentation, particularly in such a respected paper.

Shortly afterwards, I had the eye-opening experience of reading *Beyond Belief: The American Press and the Coming of the Holocaust 1933–1945* by Deborah Lipstadt, an assistant professor of Jewish history at UCLA at the time. It's a book well worth reading. Let me quote a brief excerpt:

> Many years ago Alexis de Tocqueville praised the press in large and populous nations such as America for its ability to unite people who share certain beliefs about an issue but, because they feel "insignificant and lost amid the crowd," cannot act alone. According to Tocqueville the press fulfills its highest purpose when it serves as a "beacon" to bring together people who otherwise might ineffectively seek each other "in darkness."... There is no way of knowing whether the American people would have ever been aroused enough to demand action to rescue Jews. But we can categorically state that most of the press refused to light its "beacon," making it virtually certain that there would be no public outcry and no "common activity" to try to succor this suffering people.

A subsequent book, *Why Didn't the Press Shout? American and International Journalism During the Holocaust*, edited by Robert Moses Shapiro, sheds additional light on the role of the media.

Max Frankel, the former managing editor of the *New York Times*, writing of the paper's coverage of the Shoah, said in his contribution to the volume: "No single explanation seems to suffice for what was surely the century's bitterest journalistic failure." He adds: "Only six times in nearly six years did the *Times*'s front page mention Jews as Hitler's unique target for total annihilation. Only once was their fate the subject of a lead editorial. Only twice did their rescue inspire passionate cries in the Sunday magazine."

Among the reasons he cites for this state of affairs: "[P]apers owned by Jewish families, like the *Times*, were plainly afraid to have a society that was still widely anti-Semitic misread their passionate opposition to Hitler as a merely parochial cause." Arthur Hays Sulzberger, the paper's publisher, "went to great lengths to avoid having the *Times* branded a 'Jewish newspaper.' He resented other publications for emphasizing the Jewishness of people in the news."

Laurel Leff, an assistant professor in the School of Journalism at Northeastern University, went into further detail in her powerful essay, "The Holocaust in the *New York Times*," in the same book:

A newspaper can clearly demonstrate the significance it attaches to a news story. It can make the event the lead, day after day, and key several inside stories off it; it can run editorials and magazine pieces that reveal and reinforce the paper's judgment about its importance; it can highlight the story in weekly and yearly summaries of top news events. The *Times* never did this with the extermination of the Jews....

You could have read the front page of the *New York Times* in 1939 and 1940 without knowing that millions of Jews were being sent to Poland, imprisoned in ghettos, and dying of disease and starvation by the tens of thousands. You could have read the front page in 1941 without knowing that the Nazis were machine-gunning hundreds of thousands of Jews in the Soviet Union. You could have read the front page in 1942 and not have known, until the last month, that the Germans were carrying out a plan to annihilate European Jewry. In 1943, you would have been told once that Jews from France, Belgium, and the Netherlands were being sent to slaughterhouses in Poland and that more than half of the Jews of Europe were dead, but only in the context of a single story on a rally by Jewish groups that devoted more space to who had spoken than to who had died. In 1944, you would have learned from the front page of the existence of horrible places such as Maidanek and Auschwitz, but only inside the paper could you find that the victims were Jews. In 1945, Dachau and Buchenwald were on the front page, but the Jews were buried inside.

These studies provide a useful backdrop not only for understanding historical events, but also for grasping the media's unrivaled power to affect public opinion and, ultimately perhaps, the direction of policy formulation.

This brings us to the last three-and-a-half years of press coverage of events in the Middle East. During this period I've kept a file of some of the troubling reporting that has caught my eye. It's by no means systematic or comprehensive, nor is it meant—not at all—to suggest that *all* reporting by the outlets mentioned is somehow flawed or biased. I'm not a professional media basher. Covering the complex Middle East isn't an easy assignment, even for the most experienced journalists, and those of us caught up in the events may not always be the most dispassionate readers. Still, I've read enough problematic reporting in some papers, not to mention what we might see on television or hear on the radio, to prompt this letter.

Sometimes it's what's missing.

While the Israeli-Palestinian conflict is almost microscopically covered and, as an open society, Israel is inundated with more foreign correspondents per square foot than any other nation on earth, some stories taking place elsewhere are almost totally—and inexplicably—missing from the press.

Take Sudan. This past Saturday, the *New York Times* (NYT) carried an Associated Press (AP) brief on p. A5 quoting a senior UN official: "In my view, this is the world's greatest humanitarian crisis and possibly the world's greatest humanitarian catastrophe. There has been systematic burning of villages [by Arab militia] and displacement of the population." In fact, over the past decade, an estimated two million Sudanese have been killed in a war that casts Arab and Muslim forces against African Christians and animists. Why has this story been largely missing from our newspapers, and when it appears, merits only a paragraph at the bottom of page five? Will a future Deborah Lipstadt one day write a book examining the media's relative silence in the face of such an immense tragedy?

Sometimes it's the use of words.

Reuters announced shortly after 9/11 that it would not use the word "terrorist." Stephen Jukes, global head of news, explained: "We all know that one man's terrorist is another man's freedom fighter.... To be frank, it adds little to call the attack on the World Trade Center a terrorist attack." And if not a terrorist attack, i.e., the deliberate and, in this case, massive targeting of innocent men, women, and children, what exactly was it?

Most often, we are faced with such sanitized or ambiguous words as "activist" to describe those bent on doing harm: "'No comfort and no relief until revenge is taken,' one [Palestinian] activist cried through a loudspeaker. 'The Jerusalem Brigades are coming, all ready to blow themselves up and avenge the blood of martyrs'" (NYT, September 21, 2001). But "activists" can just as easily refer to those Democrats and Republicans trying to get their candidate elected who would be revolted by any association with suicide bombings or vengeance.

Or "militant." On November 6, 2003, the *Times* referred to "militants representing a wide range of causes" gathering in London to protest President George W. Bush's visit. But three days earlier, the same paper announced that "Saudi Arabia has started a crackdown on militants loyal to Osama bin Laden." Has the word "militant" become a one-size-fits-all term to be used for anyone from a peaceful demonstrator to a supporter of the mastermind of 9/11?

Sometimes it's the unspoken.

Remember the lynching of the two Israeli soldiers in Ramallah in 2000? Those camera crews that tried to tape the scene were either stopped or their tapes were confiscated by Palestinians. An Italian private television station was able to smuggle out its tape, which was later broadcast worldwide. Fearing that RAI, the Italian public station, would be blamed, Riccardo Cristiano, the local correspondent, sent a letter to the Palestinian Authority, later printed in a Gaza newspaper: "We respect the work arrangements between journalists and the Palestinian Authority.... Rest assured that this [broadcast of the lynching] is not our way, and we would never do such a thing."

Nearly a year later, the AP wire service protested to the Palestinian Authority about threats against a freelance cameraman who filmed Palestinians celebrating, *pace* Reuters, terrorist attacks in the U.S. "The videographer, on assignment for AP Television News, was summoned to a Palestinian Authority security office," AP reported, "and told that the material must not be aired. Calls in the name of the Tanzim militia, an armed group associated with Yasir Arafat's Fatah group, warned him he would be held responsible and made what he interpreted as threats on his life" (September 12, 2001). To date, AP has still not released the tape.

And ten days later, Stephen Jukes of Reuters noted: "We don't want to jeopardize the safety of our staff. Our people are on the front lines, in Gaza, the West Bank and Afghanistan. The minute we seem to be siding with one side or another, they're in danger."

How much attention has the media paid to a self-examination of the issues raised by these three revealing episodes? Are audiences being told that some stories in the Palestinian territories may not be pursued because of "work arrangements," or that threats to journalists may lead to suppression of stories or self-censorship? The answers, I believe, are quite obvious.

Sometimes it's the mainstreaming of fringe individuals.

On February 23, 2004, the day the International Court of Justice (ICJ) was to open its hearing in The Hague on Israel's security barrier, the *Times* gave its lead space on the prestigious op-ed page to none other than Noam Chomsky. It would be as if Charlton Heston were the only person asked to comment on gun control legislation. Chomsky is a fierce critic of Israel, so much so that he has called for a binational state in its stead. His paper trail on Israel is a long one and very much out in the open. Why would the nation's most highly regarded paper give Chomsky, of all people, the opportunity to offer his views on the hearing?

Two days later, the same page offered two op-eds with contrasting—and responsible—views on President Jean-Bertrand Aristide's future in Haiti. Why didn't the paper follow the same format and invite two differing viewpoints from "mainstream" sources to debate the issues before the ICJ?

To make matters still worse, on the same day the *International Herald Tribune* (IHT), now wholly owned by the *Times*, gave its lead op-ed space to Palestinian spokesman Saeb Erekat to discuss the ICJ case, without providing for an opposing Israeli position. And the next day, adding oil to the fire, the IHT reprinted Chomsky's piece.

By the way, some leading European newspapers make a regular habit of featuring fringe individuals from Israel and the U.S., like Uri Avnery or Norman Birnbaum, who can always be counted on to voice shrill criticism of Israel on any given issue. Readers, of course, have no way of knowing that these individuals are either barely known or represent only a small minority back home.

There's also been the mainstreaming of fringe organizations.

The Council on American-Islamic Relations (CAIR) is a case in point. There is a good deal of material in the hands of law enforcement as well as in the public domain to suggest that this group may be closely tied to the radical Islamic network, despite insistent denials to the contrary. Not only have the major papers failed to investigate the claims against this group, but they also quote it regularly. CAIR thus becomes simply "an advocacy group based in Washington" (NYT, June 16, 2003) or "a nonprofit civil rights group in Washington" (NYT, March 28, 2003), as if it were nothing other than the Muslim version of the NAACP.

And these groups have also been fiddling with Muslim population numbers in the United States for transparent political motives. Two scholarly studies conducted at the University of Chicago and the City University of New York Graduate Center estimated the Muslim population at roughly two million. A third academic study, "Religious Congregations and Membership: 2000," had a slightly lower figure— 1.5 million Muslims. All three studies were reported on in the *New York Times*. That hasn't stopped Muslim spokesmen from insisting on higher numbers, which are often reported uncritically in the media. For example, on December 28, 2002, the *Times* cited CAIR's estimate of "seven million Muslims in the United States" without comment, while another article (June 16, 2003) reported that various groups put the number "between four million and eight million," ignoring the findings of the three scientific studies which the paper had previously reported.

Meanwhile, the *Washington Post* (February 26, 2004) was declaring that "Muslims number 6 million to 7 million, or about 2.4 percent of the population," without even mentioning a source. And columnist Philip Bowring, writing in the *International Herald Tribune* (September 25, 2001), spoke of a "7 million strong [Muslim] minority in America's midst."

Groups like Hamas and Islamic Jihad, which are on the U.S. government's terrorist list, are often described as "militant" organizations who oppose Israeli "occupation," implying that the issue is the West Bank and Gaza, when, in point of fact, they openly assert that all of Israel, pre- and post-1967 is "occupied" land and call for Israel's total destruction. Seldom is their ultimate goal described in press accounts. In fact, in the *New York Times* front-page story (March 22, 2004) reporting on the Israeli assassination of Sheikh Ahmed Yassin, it is not until the fourteenth paragraph, on p. A15, that Hamas is identified as "officially committed to Israel's destruction," which, needless to say, was key to Israel's decision.

My "favorite" in this category was an interview with a Hamas leader in a top Italian daily, *La Repubblica* (May 19, 2001). Up front, he declares that Israel has no right whatsoever to exist. In response, the interviewer asks him for his views on the Mitchell Plan and other aspects of the peace process!

Sometimes it's double standards.

Take the issue of foreign troops in Lebanon. Here's how the *New York Times* (January 21, 2004) described the Israeli presence: "After Israeli troops withdrew from southern Lebanon nearly four years ago, ending two decades of occupation, the border was marked by the United Nations." The key word here is "occupation."

Compare that with an article in the same paper the previous day: "It also increased friction between Israel and Syria, which maintains a large military presence in Lebanon and supports Hezbollah." Notice the absence of any reference to Syrian "occupation" of Lebanon, though that is exactly what it is and precisely what the U.S. Congress called it when it passed the Syria Accountability Act late last year.

Sometimes it's the headlines.

In *Le Temps*, a leading French-language Swiss daily (April 18, 2001), the front-page headline read: "Israel reoccupies part of the Gaza Strip." It is not until page four, line 23, that readers discover the Israeli action was in direct response to a Palestinian attack.

In *La Repubblica* on the front page (May 8, 2001), the headline read: "Newborn killed in Palestine. The pain of the Pope." It is not until page three that readers learn that the Israeli military action referred to was in response to Palestinian mortar attacks on Jewish targets and that the Israeli military apologized for the accidental killing of the child. Incidentally, on page 23 of the same issue, a small story mentions that up to one hundred children were killed by guerrillas in Angola and another sixty were kidnapped. There was no reported reaction from the Vatican.

In *El Pais*, Spain's most prominent daily, the headline after release of the Mitchell Report (May 22, 2001) read: "United States demands of Israel a cease-fire and a halt to new settlements." It omitted entirely the fact that the very first step demanded by the report was a halt to Palestinian violence.

There was a particularly infelicitous headline on the front page of the *New York Times* (March 6, 2002): "Syria Chief Backs Saudi Peace Plan as Mideast Boils." It seemed to herald a breakthrough in the Syrian position, yet in the third paragraph readers discover that Syria "called for the right of return for Palestinian refugees," which would, of course, totally destroy Israel as a Jewish state and therefore is a negotiating nonstarter.

In the *New York Times* (March 13, 2002), the headline read: "UN Chief Tells Israel It Must End 'Illegal Occupation.'" It is not until the eighth and penultimate paragraph that we are told that the secretary-general also "condemned Palestinian terror attacks on innocent civilians as 'morally repugnant.'"

On April 30, 2002, while the *New York Times* carried the headline "Palestinian Chief Denounces Terror" and the subhead "Hours Later, Suicide Bomber Kills 2 Near Pub in Tel Aviv," the *New York Post*, by contrast, went with a far more straightforward headline: "Lethal blast mocks Abu's [referring to PA Prime Minister Mahmoud Abbas] no-terror vow."

And in the *International Herald Tribune* (August 29, 2003), an article appeared about the Israel Vocal Arts Institute's program in Tel Aviv, which prepares people from around the world for careers in opera. The headline read: "An Israeli settlement of opera hopefuls." There was nothing whatsoever about "settlements" in the story, other than the provocative headline. When queried about the choice of words, the paper's managing editor acknowledged that it was a poor choice. It was an unusual admission.

Sometimes it's the hype.

The story of Jenin is perhaps the best example. With Palestinian spokesmen referring to the events there in April 2002 as "Jeningrad" and claiming vast numbers of casualties at the hands of Israeli troops, some Western news outlets swallowed the claims hook, line, and sinker.

On April 14, the London *Independent* concluded its news story with these words: "Jenin has become a place etched in the consciousness of the Palestinians. What happened there will not go away, however hard Israel tries to keep the refugee camp away from the eyes of the world. This was an atrocity."

Two days later, the same paper carried another report under the headline "Amid the ruins, the grisly evidence of a war crime": "A monstrous war crime that Israel has tried to cover up for a fortnight has finally been exposed.... The sweet and ghastly reek of rotting human bodies is everywhere, evidence that it is a human tomb."

Not to be outdone, the London *Evening Standard* declared (April 15, 2002): "We are talking here of massacre, and a cover-up, of genocide."

And the *Guardian* went a step further in its April 17 editorial: "Jenin camp looks like the scene of a crime. Its concrete rubble and tortured metal evokes another horror half a world away in New York, smaller in scale but every bit as repellent in its particulars, no less distressing, and every bit as man-made. Jenin smells like a crime."

The facts about Jenin are now well-known and confirmed by outside groups. Rather than take a lesson from NATO in Serbia and wage war by bombing from the air, and thus risking the loss of innocent life, Israel chose the far more dangerous option of sending its troops into the narrow and booby-trapped streets of Jenin to conduct a house-to-house search for suspected terrorists and their workshops. As a result, twenty-three Israeli soldiers lost their lives in the operation, while fifty-two Palestinians, all but a handful armed gunmen, were killed. A "monstrous war crime?" "Genocide?" 9/11 redux? Hardly.

Sometimes it's the photo.

While I have a large collection, three in particular stand out for me.

The first appeared in the *New York Times* on September 30, 2000, and has since received considerable attention. Taken by an AP photographer, it shows a uniformed Israeli wielding a club and a young man beneath him with a bloodstreaked face. The caption read: "An Israeli policeman and a Palestinian on the Temple Mount." The only problem is that the "Palestinian" was in fact an American Jew, Tuvia Grossman, who was being protected by the policeman after a Palestinian mob had pulled him and his friends from a taxi and started beating them. The *Times* first published a correction, then, under pressure, reprinted the photo with the proper caption. And HonestReporting.com noted that in 2002 a French court "condemned the Associated Press for 'misrepresenting [Grossman] as a member of the Palestinian community.'"

The second appeared in the *Times* on May 6, 2002. Actually, there were three photos in all. They were taken at the annual Salute to Israel Parade in New York. The photo on the front page showed marchers carrying Israeli and American flags in the background and, in the foreground, two pro-Palestinian demonstrators with a Palestinian flag and a sign facing the camera that said: "End Israel's Occupation of Palestine." The caption read: "Hundreds of thousands of people lined Fifth Avenue in Manhattan yesterday for a parade commemorating Israel's 54th anniversary. The boisterous but peaceful event also drew several hundred protesters." There were two additional photos inside the paper, one of a group of pro-Israel supporters, the other of a pro-Palestinian group.

What was wrong? The *Times* devoted exactly fifty percent of its photos to the pro-Palestinian side despite the fact that, by the paper's own admission, there were as many as 800,000 pro-Israel supporters attending the parade and "several hundred protesters." Why was such disproportionate attention given to the latter?

While the damage couldn't be undone, the outpouring of complaints to the *Times* led the paper to issue what was in effect an apology to its readers, a relatively rare occurrence and a good object lesson.

And the third photo appeared in the *New York Times* earlier this year, again on the front page and above the fold. It showed Israel building a segment of the security barrier, part of the wall in this particular case (which constitutes less than five percent of the planned barrier, the rest being a fence), with a heavily armed Israeli soldier on one side and a 91-year-old Palestinian woman and her daughter on the other. The photo's message could not have been clearer. In fact, it was so transparently clear that it prompted some to ask whether the Palestinians had cleverly staged the scene by having the two fragile and bereft women there as the counterpoint to the tough-looking, gun-wielding Israeli soldier.

And sometimes, it's the cartoons.

By definition, political cartoons are meant to have an edge, but there are some that, in my judgment at least, have crossed a line and reveal something far more insidious. While there have been a few such examples in the American press, the worst have appeared in mainstream West European newspapers and magazines, and they touch on incendiary themes—Israelis as the new Nazis, Israelis as Christ-killers, and Israelis as child-killers.

Pope on the cross—full-page cartoon in
Panorama **(Italy), April 18, 2002**
The text reads: "… You shoot at the house where my God was born, at his sepulcher, at the statue of his mother. You terrorize my priests and nuns in order to extract four miserable Palestinians … and if I protest, you call me an anti-Semite?"

"Holocaust II," Eleftherotypia (Greece), April 1, 2002 (front page)

La Stampa (Italy), April 3, 2002
"Surely they don't want to kill me again?"
Caption at bottom: "Tanks at the Manger."

Ta Nea (Greece), April 2, 2002

The Independent (Great Britain), January 27, 2003
This cartoon was voted "Cartoon of the Year, 2003" by the British Political
Cartoon Society.

I could keep going. The subject is vast, and there are many cate-
gories worth exploring in far greater detail. In reality, I've only begun
to skim the surface, and there are many areas I haven't even touched
on, such as the almost obligatory description of Prime Minister Ariel
Sharon as "right-wing," "hawkish," "inflexible," or "hard-liner," while
largely avoiding any description when mentioning Chairman Arafat
other than his formal title. Or the antiseptic way the Six-Day War is

usually mentioned, during which Israel "seized" the West Bank and Gaza, implying aggressive intent on Israel's part, but without an accompanying explanation of what led to this war for Israel's survival. We can fight back when we see what we believe to be unbalanced, misinformed, or erroneous reporting. Commissioning serious studies of the treatment of the Israeli-Palestinian conflict in specific outlets is one way to document and present the record. Contacting editors and reporters is another, but always bearing in mind that broad-brush accusations are not likely to lead anywhere other than creating an enemy, whereas thoughtful and well-reasoned approaches may stand a chance of success. And alerting sympathetic advertisers to a recurring problem might also be helpful in some cases.

As for me, my lifelong fascination with newspapers continues, but I understand far better today the media's power to identify an issue, frame it, ignore it, or even misrepresent it. After all, it's about human decision-making and all the "baggage" that goes along with it.

Caveat lector. Let the reader beware.

Letter from a Changing America[*]
April 14, 2004

A couple of years ago, my son Michael was asked to play on a travel soccer team in Westchester. When I called the coach to learn more about the team, this was his memorable reply: "Look, it's an interesting group of kids. There are several old American types on the team. You know, Irish, Italians, and Jews. And there are several new Americans, like Latinos, Africans, and Asians."

We Jews may see ourselves as relative newcomers to this country, but clearly there are those who practically associate us with the Founding Fathers. I suspect the Irish and Italians would be equally surprised by their new establishmentarian status. Yet given the lightning speed of sociodemographic change in America these days, this should not be all that shocking.

---

[*] An abridged version of this piece appeared in a May 14, 2004, article in the *Forward*.

As we consider the challenges facing Jews, there are so many immediate and pressing issues—Israel's elusive quest for lasting peace and
security, the drumbeat of radical Islam, the menace of international terrorism, and the resurgence of anti-Semitism—that some may think it
an exercise in folly to talk about the long term, but we would be woe-
fully remiss if we didn't.

America is changing rapidly. If American Jews don't grasp the significance of these changes, then we just might be left in the dust one
day, notwithstanding our remarkable success to date. This would have
serious consequences for Jews worldwide. After all, America has
played a unique role in the life of the Jewish people, particularly in the
postwar era. That role, simply put, is irreplaceable, but it is by no
means guaranteed. We can never afford complacency, nor assume confidently that today's policy—say, toward Israel—will necessarily be
tomorrow's.

Change in and of itself is not something to fear. Go back fifty years
in American history. Some may wax nostalgic over what they believe
was a simpler and more harmonious period in our nation's life. In some
ways, perhaps, it was. But it was also a time when America was only
belatedly coming to grips with the shameful racial divide, as the
Supreme Court issued its landmark ruling in *Brown v. Board of
Education* declaring that segregation of public schools "solely on the
basis of race" denied black children equal educational opportunity. It
would be many more years, though, before the last vestiges of legal-
ized racial discrimination—the "Jim Crow" laws—were removed from
the books, especially in the Southern states.

(I remember vividly my parents' first trip to Florida, by car, in 1959.
When they returned to New York, practically all they could talk about
was their horror at the sight of separate drinking fountains, toilets, and
accommodations for whites and blacks all along the route south of the
Mason-Dixon line.)

In fact, it was only in 1954 that the Pentagon announced that all-
black military units, standard fare as recently as World War II, were a
relic of the past.

And consider some of these statistics compiled by the U.S. Census
Bureau:

Just 69 percent of black children ages five and six were enrolled in schools in 1954, compared to 96 percent in 2002.

Fifteen percent of blacks age 25 and over were high school graduates in 1954, compared to 79 percent in 2002.

And whereas only 2 percent of blacks age 25 and over were college graduates fifty years ago, the figure was eightfold more by 2002.

Meanwhile, in the United States Congress half a century ago, the roster was two black members of the House, one Latino senator and one congressman, and eleven Jewish members of the House and one Jewish senator. Today, by comparison, in the 108th Congress there are thirty-nine black House members (including two delegates), twenty-five Latinos (including one delegate), and eleven Jewish senators and twenty-six Jewish House members. And this is not to mention a meteoric rise in the number of women.

For Jews generally, the 1950s was a relatively good period, but only a decade or so earlier American Jews had discovered the severe limits of their political clout in their inability to persuade the Roosevelt administration to take earlier and more vigorous action to help Europe's Jews. And while President Harry Truman had shown great courage and devotion to principle in extending diplomatic recognition to Israel in 1948, the Jewish state would have to wait fourteen years before the U.S. authorized the first sale of military equipment. Moreover, it would only be in 1970 that the glass ceiling was shattered and a Jew was named to lead an Ivy League college (Dr. John Kemeny at Dartmouth). Many communities, including the town I live in today, were notorious for their vigorous efforts to restrict the purchase of homes by Jews. And it would not be until 2000 that a major political party would nominate a Jew to its presidential ticket—and an observant Jew with a wife named, not Hillary or Laura, but Hadassah at that.

To appreciate more generally the changes at hand, the total U.S. population in 1954 was just over 160 million, 87 percent of which was classified as white, 10 percent as black, and just under 3 percent as Latino. (Asians were statistically insignificant.)

In 2000, according to the U.S. Census Bureau, the population had risen to 282 million. Of this number, 69 percent were white, 12.7 percent black, 12.6 percent Latino, and 3.8 percent Asian. Quite a contrast!

So much, by the way, for the political philosopher Montesquieu's prediction, in 1721, that "the population of the earth decreases every day, and if this continues, in another ten centuries the earth will be nothing but a desert."

Not only is America's population growing, principally through immigration (11 percent of the current U.S. population was born in another country), but so is the world's. And since most of the global growth is taking place precisely in those countries least able to provide a promising future for their citizens, migration trends are likely to continue.

Thus, by 2050, according to current projections of the U.S. Census Bureau, the U.S. population is expected to reach 420 million. The breakdown will be 50 percent white, 24.4 percent Latino ("of any race"), 14.6 percent black, 8 percent Asian, and 5.3 percent "other."

Another way of looking at the changes at hand is through religious affiliation and practice.

We have come a long way from the America described in Will Herberg's 1955 classic, *Protestant-Catholic-Jew: An Essay in American Religious Sociology*. At the time, 67 percent of Americans identified as Protestants (primarily members of mainline denominations), 25 percent as Catholics, 4 percent as Jews, and 4 percent as "other" or "none."

Within the Christian population today, the number of Catholics has grown, largely due to immigration from Latin America. But many Latinos, nearly one-quarter according to a recent survey, identify with evangelical churches.

Indeed, evangelical Protestants now appreciably outnumber mainline Protestants. While American Baptists, Episcopalians, Lutherans, and Presbyterians are declining in number, groups like the Assemblies of God, Pentecostalists, and Southern Baptists have experienced rapid growth. So, too, have the Mormons.

Buddhists, Hindus, Muslims, Sikhs, and Taoists, barely visible in America twenty years ago, are today a presence.

Meanwhile, Jewish numbers are, at best, static.

The American Jewish Identity Survey of 2001, conducted by the City University of New York Graduate Center, estimated 5.5 million American Jews, of whom just 51 percent identified their religious affiliation as Judaism. Some 1.4 million indicated a religion other than Judaism, while another 1.4 million responded that they were secular or nonreligious.

The National Jewish Population Survey 2000–01, sponsored by United Jewish Communities, reported an estimated Jewish population of 5.2 million, of whom 4.3 million had "strong connections."

But it's not just about numerical trends.

America is an ever more religious country. According to Harvard professor Diana Eck, "'We the people' of the United States now form the most profusely religious nation on earth." Of course, religion has always been a key element in our culture and identity. As Alexis de Tocqueville astutely observed in *Democracy in America*, written more than 160 years ago, "On my arrival in the United States the religious aspect was the first thing that struck my attention."

Today, in the words of the *Washington Post*, "America is the most religious country in the developed world." While church attendance has fallen sharply in what some observers now call "post-Christian, secular" Europe, it continues to rise in this country. If only 4 percent of Swedes attend church weekly, the comparable number in the U.S., according to the paper, is 44 percent. (Another survey reported the overall weekly church attendance figure among Americans at closer to 30 percent.) And whereas just 13 percent of the French said religion was very important to them, more than half of Americans replied affirmatively.

New York Times columnist Nicholas Kristoff recently wrote that "a new Great Awakening is sweeping the country, with Americans increasingly telling pollsters that they believe in prayers and miracles, while only 28 percent say they believe in evolution."

In a National Opinion Research Center survey conducted in 2000, 35 percent of Americans, including 45 percent of Protestants and 53 percent of blacks, agreed that "the Bible is the actual word of God and is to be taken literally." Moreover, a Pew Research Center study earlier this month revealed that the number of Americans who believe that

Jews are responsible for the death of Jesus has risen to 26 percent today, and especially disturbing, that 42 percent of blacks and 40 percent of Latinos believe this to be true.

By way of comparison, a 2003 Harris (Lou, not David) survey found that "Protestants (90 percent) are more likely than Catholics (79 percent) and much more likely than Jews (48 percent) to believe in God." The same survey found that African Americans are more likely to believe in God (91 percent) than other ethnic groups, with Latinos second (81 percent).

A Pew study on religion (2002) reported that 67 percent of those surveyed believe that "the U.S. is a Christian nation," while 25 percent disagree, and 48 percent, including 71 percent of evangelicals, believe that "the U.S. has special protection from God."

At the same time, reflecting the depth of support for religious pluralism, "84 percent believe that a person can be a good American even if he or she does not have religious faith," according to the Pew study.

I suppose that includes the fellow in the *New Yorker* cartoon who says to a couple he meets at a cocktail party, "I don't belong to an organized religion. My religious beliefs are way too disorganized."

A third way of looking at the shifts in America over the past five decades, aside from the ethnic and religious changes, is through the lens of the Electoral College.

Americans move. On average, the experts say, we change our place of residence every five years, more often than not in the direction of the Sun Belt.

Whereas 62 percent of the U.S. population lived in either the Northeast or the Midwest in 1900, by the year 2000, according to the U.S. Census Bureau, 58 percent lived in the South or West. Many Jews, of course, have followed these trends, creating fast-growing communities in places like Boca Raton, Las Vegas, Phoenix, and San Diego.

In 1952, there were 531 votes in the Electoral College. New York had by far the largest contingent, 45. This elevated not only the state's importance in presidential elections, but also that of the Jewish vote, since Jews formed a markedly higher percentage of the state's population than they did elsewhere. Pennsylvania and California each had 32 votes. Illinois had 27, Ohio 25, and Michigan 20. (Florida had 10, the same number, incidentally, as Kentucky and Louisiana.)

Compare that with 2004. California has 55 of the current 538 votes, or more than 10 percent. Texas ranks second with 34. New York has decreased from 45 to 31 votes. Florida has jumped from 10 to 27 and will soon overtake New York. Pennsylvania, Illinois, Ohio, and Michigan have all dropped substantially. On the other hand, states like Arizona, Colorado, Georgia, Nevada, and Washington are growing in political strength.

And speaking of elections, what is the single best predictor today of a voter's political preference? Many say it's the degree of religious observance. The more likely an individual is to attend religious services, the more likely that person is to vote Republican, and, conversely, the less likely to attend religious services, the more likely to vote Democratic.

What does all this mean for American Jews?

First, our percentage of the American population, which peaked at nearly 4 percent, is declining and may not be much more than 1 percent by midcentury, barring unforeseen developments.

Second, other groups, whose numbers and political savvy are growing, will be seeking a greater share of what is ultimately a finite political pie. Eighteen-year veteran New York congressman Steven Solarz lost his seat in the 1992 primary, partially as a result of redistricting to create a new "safe" seat for the Latino community.

Third, the natural inclination of other groups, be they Latino, Asian, African, Arab, or Caribbean, will be to exert influence on those domestic and foreign policy concerns of greatest importance to them. As one example, there could well be some shift in our global orientation in the decades ahead, given the rapidly growing Latino and Asian populations here.

Fourth, whether Jews are entirely comfortable with the trend or not, the growing religiosity of Americans is a fact we must contend with, as it has profound political, social, and cultural implications for the country, and for minority communities like our own.

And fifth, the center of gravity of political power is shifting. Southern and Western strategies are increasingly the name of the game.

Our work is cut out for us in those states where our numbers are small or our organizations not as strong as elsewhere. As individuals, we need to be deeply involved in both political parties and at all levels. And if we once took pride when candidates for office, at least in the New York area, learned a few words of Yiddish, today and long into the future it's going to be Spanish.

Does all this mean that Jews are doomed to eventual political irrelevance? Absolutely not. Our impact on decision-makers and public opinion has never been determined by numbers alone, but by many factors. And our experience at the American Jewish Committee is that many ethnic and religious communities seek, for a variety of reasons, to collaborate with Jewish organizations.

Nevertheless, American Jews will have to become even more adept at the field of interethnic and interfaith diplomacy, building ties with other communities based on mutual understanding and mutual interests and, for our part, a high comfort level with Jewish values and issues. Coalitions are the name of the game, and they require both acute sensitivity and well-honed skills of negotiation and compromise.

While the American Jewish Committee has further bolstered its historically extensive intergroup engagement in recent years—including a series of regional training workshops, a Spanish-language Web site, new programs with the Haitian, Indian, Korean, and Turkish communities, and stepped-up links with a range of religious groups—the Jewish community overall appears to have pulled back from the field. That constitutes a strategic mistake. This work must be pursued, indeed intensified, on the national, state, and local levels, as we have interests to protect on all three levels.

Some American Jews contend that we've reached a point of such unprecedented success and access that we don't really need to be concerned about what other groups, especially those currently on the margins, think. That's shortsighted in the extreme.

We must constantly cultivate friends committed to such bedrock issues as the special U.S.-Israel relationship and the proper balance between religious freedom and church-state separation. And as the country's population surges and diversifies still more, we have an immense stake in ensuring that America's remarkable experiment in democratic pluralism and tolerance continues to prosper.

To borrow a phrase, forewarned is forearmed, or at least it ought to be.

Letter from Washington[*]
May 4, 2004

Welcome to our Annual Meeting, as we mark our ninety-eighth year. To quote the late Ed Sullivan, "We've got a really big show for you."

Members and friends of the American Jewish Committee, ladies and gentlemen—picture the scene. A stately synagogue in London, where elegance and decorum are the rule of the day. Top hats and tails can be seen. The rabbi begins his sermon. He speaks of the weekly Torah portion with eloquence and conviction. Every few minutes, his homily is interrupted by a woman from the balcony shouting "Amen" or "Hallelujah." Eventually, an usher approaches the woman and asks if anything is wrong. "No," she says passionately. "It's just that when I hear the rabbi speak, I get all filled up with religion." "Madam," the usher replies scornfully, "I'm sorry but there's no place for that here."

Here's the deal this week. We bring you the best possible program, and you bring us your passion, only not the Mel Gibson kind, please!

This week is meant to enrich and stimulate our minds as we face complex issues; it's also meant to stir our souls and reinforce our mutual links as we reaffirm that all Jews are responsible one for the other.

Some of you are seasoned veterans of these meetings; others are here for the very first time. Some of you drove here; others crossed oceans and countless time zones to attend. Everyone is welcome. Each of you, I hope, will take the opportunity this week to participate in the deliberations, make new friends, and get hold of our latest publications, which you'll find on the literature tables outside.

This evening started on an upbeat note. That wasn't by accident. It was intended to serve as a reminder of who our friends are and what

[*] This letter is an adaptation of the opening speech at the American Jewish Committee's Ninety-eighth Annual Meeting.

has been achieved, and there will be more of the same throughout the week.

I'm most grateful to Brigadier General Klaus Wittmann and Colonel Jochen Burgemeister for traveling from Germany to Washington especially to be with us. They symbolize for me one of the most exciting, forward-looking, and rewarding programs launched by the American Jewish Committee in recent memory.

When we began the relationship with the German armed forces a decade ago, Colonel Burgemeister was our very first partner. He believed in the importance of introducing German military officers and American Jews to one another, both to consider the painful past and to contemplate a brighter future together. While proud to wear the uniform of the Bundeswehr, he also fully understood the heavy responsibility resting on his shoulders.

Over the years, our relationship grew in a number of ways. More and more German military delegations visited AJC headquarters, making it an obligatory stop as part of their visits to the Pentagon, West Point, the UN, and various American military bases around the country.

And we had the opportunity to travel to several German military sites, including the Ministry of Defense, the two German armed forces universities in Hamburg and Munich, the officers' school in Hanover, the refugee camp run by the Bundeswehr in Macedonia for Kosovar Muslims fleeing Serbia's ethnic cleansing, and impressive programs for German high school students conducted by the German military.

We also had the chance to receive in New York delegations from the Führungsakademie, the General Armed Forces Command and Staff College, in Hamburg, and to visit the college and address the officers, who were largely German but included Americans and other Europeans as well. It was through this process that we had the privilege of meeting and befriending Dr. Wittmann, director of the faculty, who became an integral part of the AJC-Bundeswehr partnership.

The presence of these two officers tonight to mark the tenth anniversary of our collaboration speaks volumes about the possibilities of shaping history, if only we allow ourselves to dream dreams and commit ourselves to realizing their vision.

We dare not permit ourselves—not today, not tomorrow—to become immobilized by an inability to see beyond the moment. We must never allow the painful scars of our past to deprive us of the requisite strength to build a brighter future. And we cannot ever yield to a sense of helplessness or despair that saps our collective will to affirm who we are and the values that define us.

Brigadier General Wittmann, Colonel Burgemeister, with friends like you, we can look to the future with optimism and confidence. We salute you.

And I'm equally delighted that we had the opportunity this evening to pay tribute to one of our closest and most beloved coalition partners, Andy Athens. Much has been said about Andy. I would only add that our collaboration is proof positive of what can be accomplished when we work in tandem with our friends.

For our part, I know beyond the shadow of a doubt that the objectives of the American Jewish Committee, and for that matter of the Jewish community of Greece, have been substantially advanced, more than one might imagine, by Andy's steadfast devotion to those very same goals, which he always saw as entirely consistent with his abiding love of Greece and his devotion to enhancing Greece's ties with the world.

Andy, you've honored us tonight by allowing us to honor you.

Ladies and gentlemen, last week I had the privilege of addressing the conference of the fifty-five-nation Organization for Security and Cooperation in Europe, known as the OSCE, which was devoted exclusively to the subject of anti-Semitism and was held in Berlin.

Even after dozens of trips, each time I'm in Germany I feel like an emotional yo-yo. This time was no exception.

I try to imagine a twelve-year-old boy in Berlin in 1932 doing what boys of that age like to do—play sports, visit the candy store, build a model plane or ship, and wonder what the future holds.

And then, within a year, that boy was facing the abyss, as he and his parents, and hundreds of thousands of other German Jews, became the primary target of Hitler's Nazi regime that had just assumed power.

That boy was my father. The ensuing twelve years, until the war's end in 1945, were a far cry from what he once imagined his life would be.

Now here I am, that boy's son, traveling regularly to Berlin, visiting the American Jewish Committee's Lawrence and Lee Ramer Center for German-Jewish Relations on the rebuilt Leipziger Platz, calling on the German government as a friend to discuss issues of mutual concern, and looking to the German armed forces as partners.

And then I visualize the day in 1961 when the East German government began constructing a wall for the purpose, not of keeping unwanted people out, but rather of penning in its own citizens. Not long after that I read in the paper that two Americans had been detained in East Berlin for some alleged political transgression. To my dismay, one was my father, and the other was Daniel Schorr, now with National Public Radio. Both were on assignment for CBS. Fortunately, they were released rather quickly.

As a child of the Cold War, I make a point of walking through the Brandenburg Gate each time I'm in Berlin. I remind myself of what once was—a divided city, with repression on one side and democracy on the other, and many valiant attempts, some ending in tragedy, to cross that wall and savor the precious gift of liberty. And I'm reminded, no less, of what can be—in this case, the triumph of freedom over tyranny.

Last Wednesday, I was invited to a state dinner hosted by German President Johannes Rau in honor of Israeli President Moshe Katsav. Again, the yo-yo experience.

On the one hand, I couldn't help asking myself how Jewish history might have turned out differently had there been an Israel in the 1930s, when Jews could still leave Europe, if only they had a place to go.

On the other hand, the evening was one more reminder, if any were needed, of history's evolution, or perhaps revolution in this case, as Germany and Israel continue to develop their unique bilateral relationship.

And there was still more in Berlin.

Here was an intergovernmental conference on anti-Semitism and—you know what—it seemed entirely appropriate and fitting that it was held in Berlin. After all, it was Germany that, in the postwar years, went about the enormous task of creating a modern-day democracy, teaching unflinchingly about the past, establishing a special bond with Israel, and witnessing not only the rebirth of a Jewish community, but also the world's fastest growing Jewish community, at that.

And yet how painful it was that such a conference on anti-Semitism was even necessary in 2004, less than sixty years after the war's end.

Who among us would have imagined even five years ago that the nations of North America, Europe, and Eurasia would feel compelled to gather for two days—and for the second time in as many years—because of a growing realization that the cancer, which had largely been in remission, at least in Western countries, was now back?

And not only was it back, but we could identify three different malignancies: the racism and xenophobia of the extreme right; the virulent anti-Zionism mixed with anti-Americanism and anti-globalization of the extreme left; and the unalloyed vilification of Judaism and the Jewish people emanating, not from the Islamic world in its entirety, but certainly from important segments thereof.

If there was any good news, it came in the fact that of the fifty-five nations gathered, many, like the United States, were represented by their secretary of state or minister of foreign affairs. Indeed, it was Colin Powell who set the tone when he told delegates: "Today, we confront the ugly reality that anti-Semitism is not just a fact of history, but a current event."

I don't wish to spoil your evening and make you regret your decision to come to Washington, but it's important that we all come face to face with the kind of current event being spoken of. These days, ignorance is no excuse, denial no longer an option.

The first film clip you're about to see, which lasts three-and-a-half minutes, depicts a modern-day blood libel and comes from a twenty-six-part series courtesy of Hezbollah and Syria. It was first aired last fall. Importantly, it was also transmitted around the world via satellite technology. One of the countries where it could be seen was France. In fact, it prompted the French ruling party to introduce legislation into the parliament banning, as I understand it, shows that seek to incite religious or racial hatred.

We are grateful to MEMRI, the Middle East Media Research Institute, for permission to show the film.

The second film clip, which is about the same length as the first, comes from a longer film prepared by the Washington-based Investigative Project. It shows in graphic detail the Islamic radical threat right here on American soil.

And finally, regular readers of my monthly letters will be familiar with some of the grotesque cartoons that have been published in leading European newspapers and magazines. While I would never question the right to criticize Israel, or, for that matter, any other country, what you will see goes far beyond the bounds of legitimate criticism by touching on such incendiary themes as deicide and Holocaust role reversal, with the Jews this time portrayed as Nazi-like perpetrators. Again, please direct your attention to the screen.

It's painful viewing, isn't it? But if it doesn't serve as a wake-up call, what will?

We can't afford the luxury of the businessman in the *New Yorker* cartoon who's pictured in his house, talking on the phone, with his briefcase in hand. The caption reads: "I just got home. Can you call back tomorrow when I'm still at work?"

Friends, in a world

- in which the chief rabbi of France urges observant Jews not to wear a *kippah* at night while riding the metro and to travel in groups;
- in which synagogues, Jewish schools, and cemeteries have been the targets of terrorist attacks, while other attacks planned against Jewish institutions from Germany to Hungary to Spain were foiled by alert law enforcement;
- in which the *New York Times* carries a front-page story last month reporting on those Muslims in Europe who seek to impose Islam on Europe;
- in which a Belgian Arab leader presses the Belgian government to adopt Arabic as an official national language;
- in which, as the astute Fouad Ajami points out, Europe is attempting "false bonding with the peoples of Islam" in the vain hope that "the furies of radical Islamism" will pass it by;
- in which Israel is subject to nonstop demonization by those who see in the current circumstances a new opportunity to brand it a pariah state;

- in which Israel is declared the greatest threat to world peace in a European Union survey;
- in which Israel's very right to defend itself against terrorist groups, whose declared aim is Israel's destruction, is repeatedly challenged;
- in which the United Nations reveals its utter moral bankruptcy when issues pertaining to Israel are brought before it;
- in which jihadists openly and unabashedly announce their intention to target Jews anywhere and everywhere;
- in which terrorist links have been revealed right here in the United States, from Bridgeview, Illinois, to Richardson, Texas; from Tampa, Florida, to Herndon, Virginia; and from Lackawanna, New York, to Charlotte, North Carolina;
- in which AJC's many attempts—and we were not alone, though altogether we were few in number—to call attention to the domestic link to international terrorism in the decade prior to 9/11 too often fell on deaf ears, Democratic and Republican alike;
- in which some American universities, once considered oases of civility and reason, require warning signs for Jewish students, especially those supportive of Israel;
- in which an Oxford University professor rejects an Israeli applicant on the grounds that he served in the Israeli army, while his colleague in Manchester summarily dismisses two Israelis, both incidentally sympathetic to Peace Now, from the boards of two academic journals, solely on the basis of their citizenship;
- and in which a former Israeli prime minister is physically prevented from addressing students at a Canadian university by violent protests;

we have no choice, no choice whatsoever, but to face reality as it is.

Thankfully, we have a savvy and sophisticated organization, the American Jewish Committee, as a vehicle for confronting that stark reality.

AJC empowers us by sponsoring groundbreaking research and analysis, leveraging our voices, reaching the highest levels of decision-makers and opinion-molders, testifying before the United States Congress, the UN Commission on Human Rights, the Organization of

American States, and the OSCE, advertising in the media—including tomorrow's *New York Times* and Thursday's *Wall Street Journal*, and projecting our vision and values.

We need the American Jewish Committee today more than ever.

And the American Jewish Committee needs us no less. Not only does it need us, but it needs our friends, our colleagues, and, yes, our children and grandchildren, for we are in this for the long haul.

That's precisely why we've launched a Centennial Campaign to raise at least $60 million in new endowment funds, because we must have a financially secure agency to serve future generations. This is our responsibility to them. Let history show that we rose to the occasion.

For those of us immensely proud to be Jewish and incalculably enriched by our identity, who feel an unbreakable link to Jews around the world, who support Israel's right to live in peace and security, and who believe that the Jewish people, by dint of our history and heritage, have an important contribution to make to a world badly in need of repair, I know of no other organization that gives us a better chance to have an impact than AJC.

I know I'm preaching to the choir—you're here—but it's important to underscore that we are blessed with an institution that is particularly well-suited to the times.

We have a superb chapter, national, and international staff that just keeps getting better in every sector of our work. As my counterpart in another national Jewish agency said to me, "You guys are the Jewish organizational equivalent of the 1961 New York Yankees." We have talent galore among our lay leaders. And we have a smooth working partnership between the lay and staff leadership that provides a model for how an effective agency ought to be run.

We have proved again and again our ability to anticipate trends and adapt ourselves institutionally:

- from establishing a division on international terrorism years before 9/11, to creating a division on Latino and Latin American affairs;
- from instituting a model fellowship program for young people now in its fifth year, to developing a leadership program for

Russian Jews in the U.S. entering its eighth year, as well as a division on Russian Jewish affairs;

- from opening the Transatlantic Institute in Brussels, Europe's capital, to hiring a representative in India, the world's largest democracy;
- from creating a state-of-the-art multilingual Web site, to airing biweekly radio commentaries that reach 10–15 million listeners per cycle;
- from expanding our global reach to include twelve active partnerships with Jewish communities abroad, plus our five overseas offices, to substantially increasing our interfaith and interethnic outreach and diplomacy in this country;
- and from launching Project Interchange Europe eighteen months ago, to focusing on Israel advocacy in American high schools and teaching about Israel in colleges.

We have been there—early, well-prepared, and ready for the long run. And each of these initiatives, and many others, are yielding concrete results. Our efforts are making a difference in ways that are both seen and unseen.

Moreover, we aren't hampered by ideological blinders. We adjust our thinking to the facts, not the facts to our thinking. We resist labels in a society that loves to assign them.

Literally within the span of twenty-four hours last month, I received two letters. One was from a gentleman who said that he had never joined AJC because of "our ultra-liberal approach to things" and our failure to understand "the realities of the situation." The other was from a lady who asserted that, as a Democrat, she is finding it harder and harder to justify her membership in an organization that is widely seen, she claims, as "Republican."

Ah, it's not easy being a centrist organization that one day tilts in one direction on one issue, the next day tilts in another direction on another issue. It means being shot at from both sides.

By the way, it's not that we're centrists because we can't make up our mind. You know the story of the man who found himself equidistant from two glasses of water and died of thirst.

We're centrists because we value independent thinking and reject those who have one-ideology-fits-all explanations for everything that happens. History has taught us that no school of political thought has a perfect track record when it comes to major public policy challenges in democratic countries.

On a related note, shortly after Israel's creation, David Ben-Gurion warned his fellow Jews of "the danger of political blindness," "the naiveté with which we attempt to solve complicated questions," "the lack of talent to understand each other and appreciate each other's difficulties," and the "lack of talent to act as one entity in which a single member bends his will to that of the majority." We at AJC have taken those warnings to heart.

And there's another AJC strength I must mention. I like to think it's in our bloodstream. It's called integrity.

You've put your trust in this organization. We take our fiduciary responsibility seriously and are working night and day to justify the confidence you've placed in us.

Ladies and gentlemen, we've come a long way, a very long way, in the postwar years.

We have scaled one mountain peak after another, defied the odds again and again, and, in the process, written bright new chapters of our history.

We have seen Israel not only survive, but flourish. We have seen Israel defend democracy as fiercely as it defends its borders. We have seen Israel extend the frontiers of knowledge to the benefit of all humanity.

We have seen Israel stand tall as its enemies have repeatedly tried and failed to bring it to its knees. We have seen Israel achieve peace with two of its neighbors and aspire to peace with its other neighbors, but tragically to no avail, as yet.

We have seen the miracle of the return of millions of Soviet Jews to the Jewish people and the rescue of tens of thousands of Ethiopian Jews who yearned for two millennia to live in Zion.

We have seen the rebirth of Jewish communities in Western Europe after the war wrought its devastation, and in Eastern Europe since the Iron Curtain became a discarded relic of history.

We have seen vibrant, dynamic Jewish communities throughout the world that, whether big like the Canadian or small like the Costa Rican, look hopefully to the future.

We have seen Christian-Jewish relations achieve more progress in the past fifty years than in the previous 1,900.

We have seen the unspeakable tragedy of the Shoah etched on the consciousness of many nations, many people—never enough, of course, but far more than we might have imagined.

And we have seen the emergence of a remarkable Jewish community in this blessed country that has come a long way from the time, 350 years ago, when twenty-three Jews from Recife, Brazil, disembarked from the *Ste. Catherine*, a French ship, in the port of New Amsterdam, later New York, and established the first Jewish community in North America—over the objection of Peter Stuyvesant, I might add.

Yet, at the same time, we have challenges.

I've touched on some of them tonight, those that seem to me most immediate and ominous. They'll be explored in further detail in the coming days.

I've written about others, including, in my April letter, the long-term challenges we as a Jewish community face here in light of dramatic and accelerating sociodemographic changes.

And I've both spoken and written about what I believe to be the single greatest challenge of all—the challenge of instilling in our children and grandchildren a sense of joy, enrichment, and pride in being part of the Jewish people, a visceral link to fellow Jews and to the State of Israel, a belief that by our actions we can make a difference in improving the world around us, and a passion—yes, there's that word again—to participate in shaping the Jewish destiny.

Working together in this extraordinary organization, and collaborating with good friends at home and overseas, we can rise to any challenge, I believe, however great.

Am Yisrael chai.

Letter from Belzec[*]
June 3, 2004

We stand in a place that is at once sacred and accursed.

We bow our heads in loving memory of the hundreds of thousands of Jews whose lives were destroyed here over a ten-month period in 1942.

We recoil in horror and, yes, incomprehension, even after all these years, at the systematic annihilation of the Jewish people by the Nazis and their collaborators.

Imagine: Nearly one in ten Jewish victims of the Holocaust was murdered in the gas chambers of this tiny space, which measures less than fifteen acres.

We are here, above all, to declare that we have not forgotten, we cannot forget those who perished here, despite the meticulous Nazi attempt to erase every last vestige of this killing field.

We have not forgotten, we cannot forget, first, how our fellow Jews were murdered. But just as important, we have not forgotten, we cannot forget, how they lived their lives, contributed to world civilization, practiced their faith, and yearned for better times to come.

And we are here to declare that we shall never forget, we dare never forget.

We owe it to the martyred. We owe it to ourselves. We owe it to future generations.

We take to heart the searing words of Job (16:18) inscribed on the memorial wall here: "Earth, do not cover my blood. Let there be no resting place for my outcry."

This extermination camp, now finally demarcated, protected, and memorialized after decades of neglect and desecration, stands as a stark and permanent reminder of man's seemingly limitless capacity for inhumanity.

---

[*] Adapted from a speech given at a dedication ceremony in Belzec, Poland. Belzec, located in the southeastern corner of Poland, near the Ukrainian border, was one of the six most notorious death camps in Poland, together with Auschwitz-Birkenau, Chelmno, Majdanek-Lublin, Sobibor, and Treblinka.

Let no one ever seek to ignore, deny, trivialize, or underestimate that capacity for inhumanity. The fate of the world may hang in the balance.

But our presence here today, hundreds of Jews and non-Jews alike, including the Polish president and other leading dignitaries, also serves as a reminder, I trust, of man's capacity for humanity—for compassion, solidarity, and remembrance.

It stands as an object lesson in the unexpected and hopeful possibilities of history, against the backdrop of unparalleled tragedy.

Could anyone sixty years ago have imagined that three years after the war's end the sovereign Jewish state of Israel would be established, and that state would serve as home and haven to millions of Jews from around the world?

Could anyone sixty years ago have imagined an Israeli embassy in Warsaw, whose ambassador is with us for this auspicious occasion?

Could anyone sixty years ago have imagined that the Jews, defenseless in the Shoah, would create a military force in Israel, proudly represented here today by 150 officers who have come as a sign of homage and respect, that time and again would show unimaginable courage and determination in defeating those bent on destroying the state?

Could anyone sixty years ago have imagined a Poland free of occupation, at peace with its neighbors, now linked organically to twenty-four other democratic European nations, including Germany, and serving as a vital bridge between Europe and the United States?

And could anyone sixty years ago have imagined a Jewish community—only a tiny fraction of its former self, but proud and vibrant nonetheless—here in Poland, having reemerged from the ashes of the Shoah, followed by decades of Communist oppression, to carry on the rich Jewish tradition that has been an essential part of the Polish landscape for more than 800 years?

No, none of these striking developments can fill the void created by the Shoah. None can bring back the six million. None can return a childhood to the millions of youngsters denied one.

But they do underscore for us what is possible, if only we dare to dream dreams, unite in common purpose, and match our strength to our convictions.

Let us never forget that it is we—governments, civic institutions, faith communities, and individuals—who must remain vigilant in defense of the precious gift of liberty and united in opposition to any form of tyranny.

Belzec reminds us why.

It is we who must educate others, especially our youth, about the frighteningly short distance from dehumanizing a people to destroying that people.

Belzec reminds us why.

It is we who must affirm Israel's importance to the Jewish people worldwide as a beacon of hope and oasis of freedom.

Belzec reminds us why.

And it is we who must sound the clarion call about the danger of contemporary anti-Semitism, which demonizes the Jewish people and justifies violence against Jews and Jewish institutions, wherever they may be.

Belzec reminds us why.

We would not be here today dedicating this memorial site and museum were it not for the single-minded vision of one man, Miles Lerman, son of Poland, citizen of the United States. He made it his mission to create this memorial. He was ably assisted by the staff of the United States Holocaust Memorial Museum. He deserves our everlasting gratitude.

This historic project was implemented through an agreement between the government of Poland and the American Jewish Committee. We were honored and humbled to be asked to assume this historic responsibility. I especially wish to acknowledge the role of AJC's Rabbi Andrew Baker in bringing this project to fruition. And our Polish partners could not have been more cooperative, dedicated, and sensitive to our concerns. The results speak for themselves.

In the Jewish tradition, we are commanded to remember, *zakhor*.

We do so today—enveloped by haunting memories, excruciating pain, and overwhelming loss.

But we also do so, I hope, affirming an unshakable resolve to build and defend a more humane world. Let this be our enduring legacy to those whose lives we mourn in this sacred and accursed place.

Letter from Twentieth-Century History
June 14, 2004

The death of former President Ronald Reagan in the same week as the moving sixtieth anniversary commemorations of D-Day reminds us how close our civilization came to destruction twice during the twentieth century. If not for the determined and self-sacrificing efforts of U.S. and Allied forces, the Nazi juggernaut might have pushed the world back into a new Dark Age. And if not for the steadfastness of the Free World in the struggle against Communism—expressed so well and, ultimately, triumphantly, by President Reagan—half the world might still be living today behind an Iron Curtain of suppression and totalitarianism.

The key theme of twentieth-century history is the defeat of these two looming threats to liberal democracy, Nazism and Communism, a fact understood by those who rightly view Winston Churchill as among the truly outstanding public figures of the century. In his time many others in high places dismissed Churchill as an alarmist, but he turned out to be remarkably prophetic.

More than any other single individual, Winston Churchill saw the twin threats of the twentieth century emerge, repeatedly sounded the alarm, confronted the naysayers and skeptics, and brilliantly captured the perfect balance between clear-eyed realism and unshakeable optimism in his unmatched rhetoric.

As early as 1932, Churchill warned about Germany's intentions and urged his own country to step up defense expenditures in response:

Now the demand is that Germany should be allowed to rearm. Do not delude yourselves. Do not let His Majesty's Government believe, I am sure they do not believe, that all Germany is asking for is equal status.... This is not what Germany is seeking. All these bands of sturdy Teutonic youths, marching through the streets and roads of Germany with the light of desire in their eyes to suffer for the Fatherland are not looking for status. They are looking for weapons and when they have them believe me they will then ask for the return of lost territories or colonies.

In 1938, after the Anschluss, the Austrian union with Nazi Germany, Churchill spoke in the House of Commons:

> For five years I have talked to the House on these matters—not with very great success. I have watched this famous island descending incontinently, fecklessly, the stairway which leads to a dark gulf. It is a fine stairway at the beginning, but after a bit the carpet wears.... Now is the time at last to rouse the nation. Perhaps it is the last time it can be roused with a chance of preventing war, or with a chance of coming through with victory should our effort to prevent war fail.

And less than six months later, reacting to Prime Minister Neville Chamberlain's ill-fated meeting in Munich with Hitler, Churchill famously remarked in the House of Commons:

> They should know that we have passed an awful milestone in our history when the whole equilibrium of Europe has been deranged, and the terrible words have for the time being been pronounced against the Western democracies: "Thou are weighed in the balance and found wanting." And do not suppose this is the end. This is the beginning of the reckoning. This is only the first sip, the first foretaste of the bitter cup, which will be proffered to us year by year, unless by a supreme recovery of moral health and martial vigour, we rise again and take our stand for freedom as in the olden time.

Meanwhile, some other highly respected observers had a far less ominous take on Germany and its leadership, reminding us once again that vaunted job titles or academic pedigrees are not necessarily guarantors of uncommon wisdom or, for that matter, even common sense.[1]

While Churchill was sounding the warning about "sturdy Teutonic youth" as early as 1932, the legendary Professor Harold Laski offered a rather different view:

> The day when they [the Nazis] were a vital threat is gone.... [I]t is not unlikely that Hitler will end his career as an old man in some Bavarian

---

[1] I am indebted to Christopher Cerf and Victor Navasky, authors of *The Experts Speak*, for the following six citations.

village who, in the *biergarten* in the evening, tells his intimates how he nearly overturned the German Reich.... It is comforting to live on the memory of an illusion.

The next year, Walter Lippman, the famed American journalist, noted, after Hitler delivered a speech in the Reichstag denouncing war, that:

[T]he outer world will do well to accept the evidence of German goodwill and seek by all possible means to meet it and to justify it.

And Britain's *Daily Express*, reacting to Chamberlain's signing of the Munich Pact, confidently declared:

Britain will not be involved in war. There will be no major wars in Europe this year or next year. The Germans will not seize Czechoslovakia. So go about your own business with confidence in the future and fear not.

The next year, *Time* magazine offered the following assessment of French military strength:

The French army is still the strongest all-around fighting machine in Europe.

In 1940, exactly one day before the Japanese joined the Axis nations, General Douglas MacArthur predicted that "Japan will never join the Axis."

And not to be outdone, on December 4, 1941, Frank Knox, U.S. Secretary of the Navy, stated:

No matter what happens, the U.S. Navy is not going to be caught napping.

Once again with 20-20 foresight, it was Churchill who saw the Cold War evolve, grasping the essential point that Joseph Stalin, part of the wartime triumvirate, would turn on London and Washington as soon as the opportunity presented itself. The British leader, even in the heyday of the anti-Nazi alliance, never ignored or underestimated the true nature of Soviet Communism. His words, delivered at Westminster College in Fulton, Missouri, in March 1946, defined the new historical era:

> From Stettin in the Baltic, to Trieste in the Adriatic, an iron curtain has descended across the Continent. Behind that line lie all the capitals of the ancient states of Central and Eastern Europe. Warsaw, Berlin, Prague, Vienna, Budapest, Belgrade, Bucharest and Sofia, all of those famous cities and the populations around them lie in what I must call the Soviet sphere, and all are subject in one form or another, not only to Soviet influence but to a very high and, in many cases, increasing measure of control from Moscow.

His prescient remarks were not universally welcomed. Roy Jenkins, in his magisterial biography of Churchill, described it as "one of the most controversial … speeches of the post-war years." He went on to say about the speech:

> [T]he core message was hard and clear. Whether or not it was given that name, a Western alliance was necessary, and there should no longer be any pretence that the leading members of the United Nations stood in an equally close relationship with each other.... In 1946 ... it was strong meat, not least for the American press.

Jenkins points out that the *Wall Street Journal, New York Times, Chicago Sun*, and London *Times*, among others, were critical of the speech, the *Chicago Sun* referring to its "poisonous doctrines."

After the ferocity of the Second World War, it was entirely understandable that many in the West hoped for a respite from conflict, but it was not to be, and it fell to Churchill and, later, President Harry Truman to be the bearers of the sobering news.

The example of Winston Churchill has much to teach us today.

As a nation, however, we're not terribly keen on history. We've always defined ourselves as a country hurtling toward the future rather than tethered to the past. From conquering the frontier to exploring space, it's all about the possibilities of tomorrow. Sure, we invoke the past, but it's usually fleeting, mechanical, and superficial.

In many ways, this forward-looking attitude explains the genius of America—our pioneering spirit and can-do approach to life, unwavering optimism, staggering economic growth and development, and unrivaled social mobility. Given the choice, we'd much prefer to make history than study it.

But history, apart from its inherent interest and explanation of how we got to where we are, reveals lessons that we would be ill-advised to ignore. True, history seldom repeats itself in precisely the same form, but then again human nature and the behavior of state and nonstate actors don't entirely reinvent themselves in each generation, either.

Take our present situation. In response to the horrific events of September 11, our nation declared a global war on terrorism. But in the ensuing three years things have become quite complicated. The original story line of a nation at peace experiencing unprecedented loss of life from a fanatical terror group has yielded to a multidimensional tableau.

We are now witnessing a fierce debate over whether Washington overreached, launched an unnecessary invasion of Iraq, antagonized the Muslim world in the process, alienated many of our traditional friends, and trampled on civil liberties here at home, not to mention in Abu Ghraib and Guantanamo. This debate is necessary and emblematic of a thriving democracy. But, at the same time, it must not be allowed to distract us from the very real threat we as a nation continue to face from our declared enemies.

In a highly partisan era, further accentuated by upcoming U.S. elections, any discussion of these issues runs the serious risk of being interpreted as support for one side or the other. I intend no such thing.

My point is this: What happened on 9/11 was an attack on America and what we stand for as a nation; it would have happened no matter which political party was in power at the time. This may be precisely the right moment to remind ourselves of this one central fact, because, politics and partisanship aside, it could happen again at any time. And there are lessons from last century's history that we would be wise to absorb, most especially the danger of underestimating an emerging global threat or lulling ourselves into a false sense of security.

Voters in November will decide which party is better equipped to handle the national security challenge, and the many other challenges, our country faces. That is as it should be in any democratic society. But no one should believe the terrorist threat against America (or, for that matter, Israel) is linked to a particular party. History has amply demonstrated the opposite.

Let's face reality. We are at war, and our resolve as a nation is being tested. At the same time, there are those who would prefer to believe that the threat is exaggerated, or it is manufactured, or it derives from our own actions; therefore a change in our own behavior is the antidote. They are profoundly mistaken, I believe.

First, let's call the war by its real name. It's a war against—take your pick—Islamism, Islamo-fascism, jihadism, radical Islam, or militant Islam.

In other words, it's a war against an ideology, fueled by a combustible mix of theology, politics, self-righteousness, and fury, which has an unmistakable and airtight worldview and hasn't been shy to express it. Just as we fought fascism, Nazism, and communism in the twentieth century, today we are locked in a struggle with yet another variant of totalitarian thinking in possession of "absolute truth." Our semantic effort to cloak the true nature of the struggle by deliberately avoiding naming its source, lest we offend some Muslims, is misguided, if not downright disingenuous.

No, this is not a war on terrorism. It is a war on those who, in the name of their fanatical beliefs, employ terrorism to advance their aims, as well as those who give them succor and sanctuary. Terrorism is their weapon of choice, but if they had potent armies, is there any doubt those would be employed as well? Would we then have to rename the conflict as the "war on terror and armies"?

Second, this war will continue regardless of who is in power in Washington (or Jerusalem).

We need to remind ourselves that, whatever the very real differences among political candidates, to our enemies they are essentially all the same, representatives of "evil" or "illegitimate" regimes.

Radical Islamic forces declared the United States and its overseas interests targets during the Carter era. This continued unabated during the Reagan and Bush eras. And had Sheikh Omar Abdel Rahman and his cohorts succeeded in their goal, one World Trade Center tower would have been entirely destroyed in 1993, which was during President Clinton's first year in office. As it was, during Clinton's two terms in office there were fatal attacks against American targets in Kenya, Saudi Arabia, Tanzania, and Yemen, and foiled attacks in the United States, including plans to destroy significant New York landmarks.

Similarly, in the eyes of Hamas, Islamic Jihad, Hezbollah, and other groups committed to Israel's destruction—as opposed to those genuinely supportive of a negotiated settlement—it doesn't matter one whit who is in power in Jerusalem and what the prevailing attitude toward the peace process is. They're all the same—Israelis, Zionists, and Jews—and, therefore, they constitute the enemy.

Prime Minister Shimon Peres, committed to the Oslo process, learned this in the run-up to the 1996 elections, when a series of deadly bombings contributed to his defeat. So did Prime Minister Ehud Barak, who spearheaded an intense effort for a two-state solution five years later.

In fact, while much was made of the impact of the 3/11 bombings on the Spanish elections earlier this year, the plain fact of the matter is that terrorists have successfully wielded influence on other elections, including those in Israel.

Third, this war will not come to an end anytime soon. That ought to be painfully obvious.

Given the hydra-headed organizational nature of the enemy, its geographic dispersal, the nature of the weapon of choice—i.e., terrorism—the wide-ranging support structure of mosques, *madrassas* (Islamic schools), front organizations, satellite technology and the Internet, readily available funds, and the openness of democratic societies, there is no Berlin or Tokyo for us to target, no V-E or V-J day to signal when a formal end to hostilities is declared, and no Iron Curtain to raise or Berlin Wall to demolish as signifying victory.

We in the West have an attention-span problem that will be severely tested. We dare not be found wanting. The stakes are far too high.

Bear in mind the path of death and destruction to date. Imagine the frightening possibilities ahead, including the potential use of biological or chemical agents or even, one day, nuclear weapons, which Osama bin Laden has declared must be acquired as a "religious duty." Remember that this enemy insists that its love of death through so-called martyrdom matches our passion for life. In 1997, for instance, Bin Laden declared: "Being killed for Allah's cause is a great honor achieved only by the elite of the nation. We love this kind of death for Allah's cause as much as you like to live." And recall that for our adversaries everything and everyone is fair game—the more carnage the better. After all, spreading fear and anxiety is the name of the game. The traditional military field of combat has been extended to include every conceivable civilian venue.

Fourth, a sustained global challenge requires a sustained global response. The United States has unmatched resources, but it needs international cooperation at every level—and the diplomacy to match—to gain and maintain the offensive. At the same time, those countries that believe they can avoid involvement by keeping their heads low or their mouths shut, or by maintaining a certain distance from Washington, are likely to be in for a rude awakening. Some already have.

Fifth, we need to encourage and empower the forces of moderate Islam—and, yes, they most assuredly do exist—to assert themselves more forcefully in the battle for title to their religion. Easier said than done, I fully realize, and, to boot, the line between extremism and moderation is not always easily or neatly drawn. The world of Islam, and the Arab culture in particular, are still so alien, so impenetrable to most outsiders, even after all these years, that we must tread with great caution, avoiding the certitudes that too often have caused us to stumble in the region, yet not with such caution that we effectively paralyze ourselves.

At the same time, there are limits to the role outsiders can play in the struggle for control of a religion that claims the allegiance of one-fifth of the world's population and that forms the majority in dozens of African and Asian nations, plus Albania and Turkey on the European continent, a plurality in Bosnia, and a significant minority in many others.

And sixth, returning to the earlier theme, we need to remind our-selves of relevant twentieth-century history, especially the tendency by some to underestimate threats as they emerge, especially those posed by Hitler and the Third Reich or the Soviet regime.

In both cases, there were examples aplenty of a misreading of intent, failure of imagination, neglect of warning signs, inability to grasp the capacity for evil, childish projection of our values onto others (e.g., "Surely the Soviet Union wants the same thing for its people as we do, so how threatening can they be?"), naiveté, romanticization, self-fla-gellation, and, of course, appeasement.

History is lived forward, but studied backward. No, the current threat is not identical either to the Second World War or the Cold War, but surely the lessons of these two conflicts ought to have some applic-ability.

The challenge in both was to our way of life, our value system, and our view of global order and stability. It came about not because of any particular policy of ours, but rather because of who we were and what we represented. It was not directed at particular politicians or political parties. In turn, it required not a partisan but the maximum possible unified response. It necessitated an unprecedented demonstration of strength, power, courage, and resolve. In one case, it prompted war on a previously unimaginable scale; in the other, the ever-present threat of war and one daunting test after another, from the Berlin blockade to the Cuban missile crisis to the invasion of Hungary and Czechoslovakia.

There was room neither for the woolly-eyed or wobbly, nor the faint of heart or squeamish, much less the prophets of doom and gloom.

So, too, after the Cold War's end, there was a temptation to believe that conflict would not end entirely, perhaps, but henceforth it would take the form of internal and regional battles far from America's shores. Even when we were hit by terrorist attacks in the decade of the 1990s, only a few observers grasped the true nature of the menace, namely, a new global struggle between radical Islam and the world of so-called infidels, led by the United States. These observers were often derided as shrill or paranoid, even by some Jewish leaders who should have known better. The events of 9/11 drove home the point they were making with a vengeance.

But with the passage of time and the political fractionating of America, we run the risk of diverting our attention or downplaying the threat.

Winston Churchill, where are you?

Letter from Buenos Aires
July 27, 2004

Julio and Balbina Kupchik are an elderly Jewish couple who live in a quiet middle-class neighborhood in Buenos Aires.

He was born in Argentina, she in neighboring Uruguay, both to immigrant parents from Eastern Europe. Like many Jews of his generation, he worked in textiles and did reasonably well, at least until 2001, when Argentina was hit by a massive economic earthquake, the aftershocks of which are still being felt throughout the country. Still, they manage, in part by renting out a room to American college students who spend their junior year in Argentina's capital. They prefer Jewish students, they say.

For the last six months, my son Michael has lived with the Kupchiks. He asked to be placed with a Jewish family that spoke no English. He got his request.

It has been a wonderful experience for Michael. The Kupchiks are a loving and nurturing couple, and to top it off, Mrs. Kupchik is a terrific cook.

It has also been an unexpectedly emotional experience. When Michael first met the extended family, he learned that Luis, the Kupchiks' son, was killed on July 18, 1994. That was the day that the headquarters of the AMIA, the Jewish community's central welfare organization, founded in 1894, was destroyed in a terrorist attack that left 85 dead and 300 wounded. It was the single most lethal attack against a Jewish target outside Israel since the Second World War.

Luis, an architect, had gone to the AMIA in the morning to make the burial arrangements for his maternal grandfather, Isaac Schalit, who had died the previous day. He was accompanied by two first cousins, Fabián and Pablo Schalit, the only children of Mrs. Kupchik's brother, and by a close friend, Elías Palti, who insisted on joining him, despite missing work, because "a friend is a friend." All four were killed in the bombing.

And in a tragically surreal twist, Estefanía, one of Luis's two children, was to celebrate her tenth birthday precisely on that fateful day, July 18, 1994.

In fact, while a large American Jewish Committee delegation was in Buenos Aires to mark the tenth anniversary of the attack on the AMIA, Estefanía was in the United States. She couldn't bear to be in Buenos Aires on that day. As she told a reporter for the news magazine *Día 8*: "I decided to travel to Miami. I'm going to the home of Ariel, my father's best friend. His son was born the exact same day as I. This way I can avoid all the ceremonies and try to celebrate my birthday. It's not that I'm not in solidarity with the families of the victims. It's rather that I don't understand the meaning of justice.... All I know is that my father made me very happy. And now he's no longer here."

Julio and Balbina Kupchik do the best they can, but it's far from easy. They draw strength from one another, and from their remaining family members, friends, and a weekly support group.

Their effort to cope is rendered still more difficult by the notable lack of progress in the investigation of the AMIA case. In the competition between malfeasance and malevolence by Argentine authorities over the past ten years, it's hard to know which is ahead. Suffice it to say that it's a real horse race.

Actually, to be precise, it's the last twelve years, not ten. In 1992, the Israeli Embassy in Buenos Aires was also the target of a terrorist attack that killed 29 people and injured over 200. That investigation has gone nowhere.

While some families of the AMIA bombing victims have immersed themselves in public campaigns to pressure the government of the day to act, the Kupchiks have chosen not to. Instead, they live quietly with their searing pain and irreplaceable loss, and their pessimism about whether justice, however belated and inadequate, will ever be attained.

In that pessimism, they are not alone. Many Argentineans with whom we spoke, Jews and non-Jews alike, are doubtful the full truth will ever be revealed and the culprits placed behind bars. Too much time has passed, too many opportunities squandered, too much evidence lost, too much incompetence revealed, too much corruption exposed, and too many political skeletons in closets to protect.

In fact, at the commemorative ceremonies for the victims, speaker after speaker blasted government leaders going back to 1994, while also taking aim at judges, prosecutors, the intelligence services, the federal, regional, and local police, and a host of other targets for botching the investigation to date. Marina Degtiar, whose brother was killed in the attack, summed up the feelings of many: "This has been a decade of infamy. Those who covered up the truth are accomplices and should therefore be declared guilty."

Meanwhile, the same issue of *Día 8* that carried the interview with Estefanía Kupchik had a lead story entitled "Ten Years of Secrets and Lies," referring to the AMIA investigation.

For some, the only glimmer of hope is the current government, under the leadership of President Néstor Kirchner, which took office in 2003 promising to leave no stone unturned in the pursuit of justice.

As the president said at the American Jewish Committee's Annual Dinner earlier this year: "It is ... for us a source of shame that it has not been possible to clarify, arrest, and punish the culprits of this enormous affront against the Argentine people.... We will not give up our most firm commitment to historical truth, will not give up until we achieve justice in the case of the [Israeli] embassy and in the case of AMIA."

In his speech at the tenth anniversary ceremony, Abraham Kaul, head of the AMIA, looked directly at President Kirchner, who was standing together with his wife in the first row of a crowd estimated at 10,000–15,000, and said, "Mr. President, with you a candle of hope has been lit. Do not let it die."

The president's task is enormous. He must mobilize an entire government apparatus to implement his vision, which wouldn't be easy under the best of circumstances, and is made even more difficult by the ossified Argentine bureaucracy. He must overcome widespread incompetence and intrigue. He must defeat a "culture of impunity" in the country, a term we heard again and again. And, not least, he must find the diplomatic spine to follow the investigative trail wherever it leads, in all likelihood to Iran, Syria, and Hezbollah, and confront the real perpetrators of the two terrorist attacks, not just those who served as domestic accomplices.

In our ninety-minute meeting on July 19, President Kirchner reaffirmed the resolve he has expressed to us on previous occasions since taking office. He even went so far as to express frustration with certain otherwise friendly nations whose cooperation he needs in the investigation but who have not been forthcoming. He spoke of the "contradiction and hypocrisy" of those nations that condemn terrorism but do not "coordinate action" in the struggle "to isolate and destroy it." Clearly, the reference was to Switzerland, whose strict banking secrecy laws have blocked one important dimension of the investigation, and to Britain, whose courts have denied an extradition request from Argentina for a high-ranking Iranian diplomat believed to be connected to the AMIA case.

In the same meeting, the president revealed to us a breakthrough in the case—forty-five tape recordings presumed lost ten years ago had been found. This could shed light on an important aspect of the investigation. They were part of a larger collection of phone taps of Carlos Telleldin, a local car thief believed to be an accomplice in the terrorist attack.

Or so the thirty AJC and AMIA representatives present at the meeting thought. Hours after Abraham Kaul, the AMIA leader, announced the news at a press conference immediately following our meeting and in the presence of the president's chief of staff, the president's office denied that he had made such a statement, instead suggesting that he had said only that the "receipts" for the tapes had been found, not the tapes themselves. This set off a media firestorm. For days following the press conference, the story was front-page news in every major Argentine media outlet. Speculation about the cause for the misunderstanding was rife. For example, in a lead editorial, the English-language daily *Buenos Aires Herald* dubbed the episode "Kassettegate" and wondered aloud whether the problem was "a mania for news" by the government, with Kirchner "showing off to the AJC with a one-day wonder," or if Kirchner was "simply misinformed, whether maliciously or not."

I'd rather not speculate about motives. Perhaps it all stemmed from a genuine misunderstanding. All I know is that should President

Kirchner succeed in moving the investigation forward, he will provide a compelling reason for Argentines to begin to overcome their deep-seated skepticism and cynicism toward the state. But should he fail, Argentine confidence in the institutions that govern them will surely plummet still further.

Moreover, there is the very real danger that failure to investigate successfully the two attacks will only invite more such attacks against a country that may be deemed a "soft target." With a Jewish population numbering more than 200,000, hundreds of Jewish institutions scattered around Buenos Aires and other urban centers (e.g., Rosario, Cordoba, Santa Fe, La Plata, and Mendoza), inadequate foreign intelligence capabilities, long and penetrable borders, and a particularly worrisome border area with Brazil and Paraguay known as the Triple Frontier, where radical Middle Eastern groups have been known to operate and raise funds (see "Letter from Juan," January 12, 2004), the possibility of further attacks surely cannot be ruled out.

Meanwhile, it should come as no surprise that Jewish groups in Argentina are not necessarily of one mind about how to handle things. After all, if the last two Jews remaining in Afghanistan are not even on talking terms, as the *New York Times* reported in an article that would have been funny were it not so tragic, why should Argentina, or any other Jewish community for that matter, be different?

There is widespread anger with the DAIA, the Jewish group that is supposed to handle political representation for the community. Rubén Beraja, who was the DAIA's president at the time of the bombing and president of the Latin American Jewish Congress (and thus a vice president of the World Jewish Congress), is currently in jail for banking irregularities. Many in the community believe that he and his colleagues put their own financial interests ahead of the interests of the community—and of the AMIA investigation—in their dealings with President Carlos Menem, who led the country from 1989 to 1999. In fact, the DAIA speaker at the July 18 event publicly acknowledged that mistakes had been made and asked for forgiveness.

That didn't stop some DAIA representatives from earlier creating a false rumor that the American Jewish Committee, together with AMIA, our partner organization since 1998, was planning to honor President

Kirchner in May at our annual meeting. Decrying any award as premature, they rushed to the Argentine press with their comments and were assisted by a New York-based international Jewish organization that loves to fan the flames of controversy when it involves what are perceived to be rival Jewish groups, such as the American Jewish Committee. Of course, none of this was true, but the rumor took on a life of its own that was hard to squelch.

And at a different rally, this one organized by Memoria Activa, a group founded in the wake of the 1994 bombing by those unhappy with the position taken by the established Jewish groups, a Jewish attorney attacked Israel, and in particular the late Prime Minister Yitzhak Rabin, for alleged connivance with Argentina to suppress the presumed Syrian link because of Israel's interest in pursuing peace talks with Damascus. This set off another controversy within the Jewish community, mostly directed at the attorney for his lack of judgment in airing allegations as facts and thereby embarrassing Israel.

But beyond the divisive politics, there are the poignant individual stories. We met with representatives of six families, each of whom had a tragic story of love and loss to share with us. And we met with survivors of the attack. Like the accounts of 9/11, there was no rhyme or reason as to why some survived and others didn't. There was the young woman who came for the first time in her life to the AMIA building on July 18 to help her parents, both accountants, who were working there. They survived, she didn't. And on it goes.

And beyond the individual stories, there is a Jewish community, one of the world's largest and most vibrant, that, like the rest of Argentina, was battered by the recent economic collapse. In fact, the crisis for the Jewish community began three years earlier than for the country as a whole, when two Jewish-owned banks went belly-up, resulting in a loss to Jewish community institutions of an estimated $26 million.

The bottom fell out for many Argentine Jews, largely a middle-class community, and suddenly there was a whole class of "new poor" who couldn't make ends meet, could no longer afford the Jewish education that was such a prominent feature of communal life, and, whether just emerging from university or in their fifties, couldn't see any job prospects. This prompted stepped-up emigration to Israel, although a few have since returned, while others sought European citizenship, an American green card, or opportunities offered by Jewish communities seeking growth in Canada and New Zealand.

Yet the vast majority remain and, frankly, it's not all that hard to understand why. Argentina, despite its well-known and much publicized problems, is a magnificent country. On paper, it has all the ingredients to be one of the world's leading nations. In fact, as the *Economist* noted, ninety years ago Argentina's per capita income "was on a par with that of France and Germany, and far ahead of Italy's and Spain's," though its decline ever since has been stubbornly steady. And Buenos Aires has few rivals in its majesty and flair. Some call it the only truly European city in the world.

Paris captures the beauty of French culture, Rome of Italian culture, and Madrid of Spanish culture, but Buenos Aires, designed, built, and inhabited by Europe's great civilizations, embraces the best of all. True, the city is fraying at the edges, crime is up, street beggars can be found at practically every intersection, and Argentineans snatched defeat from the jaws of victory in the final match of the America's Cup soccer championship against Brazil, tantamount to the loss of a military war. But for many Buenos Aires residents, or *porteños* as they are called, Jews included, it remains a seductively attractive and stimulating life.

It's not perfect. The economy could go into yet another tailspin, especially given the country's extraordinarily high level of foreign indebtedness. The modern era of democracy is only two decades old. It follows a period of brutal dictatorship from 1976 to 1983, during which thousands of people "disappeared" and were never heard from again, a disproportionate number of them Jewish. Indeed, it was during this time that Jacob Kovadloff, director of the American Jewish Committee's office in Buenos Aires, was compelled to close shop and hurriedly leave the country for New York with his wife and children because of death threats by right-wing extremists.

The nostalgia for a strong populist leader like Juan Perón (or his wife, Eva) hasn't entirely disappeared. It was only ten years ago that the state ended the requirement that the country's leader must be a Catholic. Even so, the presidential conference room in which we met

President Kirchner displayed a large crucifix on the wall behind the president's chair. Pockets of anti-Semitism still exist. And who can forget that Argentina gave refuge to many Nazis, including Adolf Eichmann and Josef Mengele, after the war?

But, and there's always a but, the economy is on the rebound, other places have their problems too, few cities can compare with Buenos Aires, the nearby ocean, mountains, and countryside beckon, the community is strong, the Jewish schools are among the best anywhere, the synagogues, at least some of them, provide successful models for attracting young people and fostering a sense of belonging, and families have ever deeper roots in the country, extending in some cases to the fourth generation.

At the end of the day, though, overshadowing everything is the long memory of July 18, 1994, the day that has scarred the entire community. As the mother of one of the victims wrote in a moving eulogy to her beloved daughter five years later: "A part of me has died for all time.... No one could be the same person; I am missing a part of my heart.... Now that I have to watch over your children, my grandchildren [who were one year old and thirteen days old on the day of the bombing], I cannot wait for them to grow, so that I can tell them all about you, and in this way, they can keep alive your presence in their hearts."

Letter from an Admirer
August 18, 2004

Never in recent memory has Israel come in for more withering criticism than during the past few years, even if Israel has never lacked for relentless critics.

Never in recent memory have I been more proud to be a friend of Israel.

Ever since Yasir Arafat unleashed this latest round of terror, forsaking an historic chance for peace and—one would naively assume—revealing once and for all his true colors, the assault on Israel has only intensified.

Bizarre, isn't it?

Israel gives peace still another try in 2000, proposes a viable Palestinian state, agrees to divide Jerusalem, and, in the process, enjoys the active support of President Bill Clinton, a respected international statesman. And yet all is quickly forgotten by those ready to forgive the Palestinians anything and everything ... and to accuse the Israelis of anything and everything.

Meanwhile, the Palestinians reject the offer on the table, refuse to make a counter-proposal, deny any Jewish historical link to Jerusalem, seek to destroy the Jewish character of Israel through the so-called right of return, laud teenage suicide bombers as martyrs, teach incitement in the classroom, lionize Saddam Hussein to the bitter end, and turn corruption into an art form. And yet all is quickly forgiven by those ready to forget anything and everything that might taint their sacrosanct image of the Palestinians as the poster child of "oppressed people."

In the wake of Israel's spurned peace offer, the Jewish state has been mugged, mauled, and maligned in the international arena. Not so the Palestinians, mind you, who are unassailable in the UN and the precincts of Western Europe's intelligentsia, regardless of what they do or don't do. In these salons of spin, there's always a convenient rationale to explain the otherwise inexplicable behavior of the Palestinians, usually by turning the focus to alleged Israeli misdeeds, which can always find a receptive and uncritical audience.

Nor has Israel's latest announcement of a unilateral withdrawal from Gaza and the dismantling of at least four settlements in the West Bank had any discernible effect on the Israel-bashing crowd.

Inch for inch, pound for pound, no other nation on earth comes even remotely close to Israel in the assault it has experienced.

Think about it. There are refugee populations, unresolved territorial conflicts, and humanitarian crises galore around the world. Few merit the attention of the UN General Assembly, much less the media elites in Western Europe.

Why the selective outrage?

Why, for instance, are there so many demonstrations for the Palestinians by kaffiyeh-clad Romans or Parisians but not for Sudanese Christians, black Africans of Darfur, Saudi women, reform-minded journalists and students in Iranian prisons, occupied Lebanese, and, yes, Jewish victims of terror?

And why is there such an absurdly romanticized view of the Palestinians that willfully ignores any pesky fact—and there are many—that could get in the way of this airtight thinking?

Then again, I suppose, facts can't hold a candle to the psycho-political rush that comes with donning the kaffiyeh or dabbling in "liberation politics" in lockstep with one's ideological confreres. Friends of Israel have nothing comparable to offer.

But let's put this crowd aside. From my experience, if asked, many of them would challenge Israel's very right to exist. They won't be easily swayed because of the larger uniform they wear. Rethinking their views on Israel would probably risk shaking the foundation of their entire ideological construct.

In many places I travel, especially in Western Europe, it's anything but popular to be unabashedly pro-Israel these days. Germany is the notable exception, though some negative change is afoot even there. (Eastern Europe, by the way, is an altogether different, and far brighter, story when it comes to Israel.)

While some government, academic, and media interlocutors may be too polite to say it to my face, it's clear they regard me, and those who think like me, as having fallen on our heads, lost in the wilderness of Neanderthal thinking, oblivious to the diplomatically obvious, lacking in human compassion, or, to cut to the chase, captive to a right-wing mentality that they believe links the despised Ariel Sharon to the detested George W. Bush.

My European interlocutors frequently insist that that they are pro-Israel and have only Israel's best interests in mind. They all but say that they want to save Israel from itself. They would recoil in horror and hurt if they were accused of endangering Israeli security by their actions or words. And I believe that most are quite sincere, even if our thinking differs.

Where we part company is usually near the starting point of the discussion.

They tend to see the root of the conflict as Israel's (unsought) presence in the West Bank, Gaza, and the eastern half of Jerusalem. Their analysis stems from this basic premise, which helps explain the tone and tenor of much of what's being said in Western Europe.

My starting point, on the other hand, is that the root of the conflict today remains what it has been from the start—Israel's very presence, period.

When the right of the Jewish people to a sovereign state in the region is unambiguously recognized, when Palestinian children (and their Syrian and Saudi counterparts) are taught that Israel is a legitimate, bona fide neighboring country, and when Iranian Olympic athletes compete against their Israeli counterparts rather than withdraw from the competition, then the negotiating environment, I'm quite confident, will change rapidly and dramatically.

Let's face it. Had it been their real objective, the Palestinians could have had their state alongside Israel long ago. Opportunities abounded for the creation of such a state as far back as 1947 and as recently as 2002 when President Bush set forth his vision of a two-state solution. And had the Palestinians at any time emulated the laudable examples of Egyptian President Anwar Sadat and Jordanian King Hussein, they could have conquered Israeli public opinion and created a tidal wave of support for a negotiated settlement. Alas, rather than killing the Israelis with kindness, the Palestinians chose to kill the Israelis with nail-studded bombs.

Those who profess good will to Israel need to bear in mind that the nation's obsessive preoccupation with security is grounded in reality.

Israel's rough-and-tumble, arms-laden neighborhood is a fact, as is the striking absence of democracy and law-based societies among its neighbors.

Moreover, Israel's small size is often little appreciated, especially by those who have never visited and simply can't imagine a country so narrow and exposed at its population center.

In addition, the bulk of Israel's population counts Holocaust survivors, Jewish refugees from Arab lands, or Jewish refugees from the Soviet bloc in their immediate family. In other words, Israelis know from recent historical experience the ominous dangers that Jews face. Rampant anti-Semitism in the Arab world today only reinforces this point.

And finally, Israelis don't put all that much stock in outside assurances of security, other than the commitment of the U.S. government. In the 1973 Yom Kippur War, for example, it was only Washington that rushed to help Israel in its hour of dire need. And when the U.S. required landing and refueling rights in Europe for its cargo planes carrying vital weapons and spare parts to Israel, just one country, Portugal, came forward, and not before intense diplomatic pressure.

Some interlocutors ask if I've succumbed to an idealized view of Israel which allows for no fallibility on its part. Most assuredly not. The country has its share of problems.

I've never been a fan of the nation's self-flagellating extreme left or chest-thumping extreme right, both of whom live in their intellectual version of la-la land. Politicization of Judaism in Israel is bad for the state, worse for religion. Those rabbis and others who insist that their interpretation of faith trumps the authority of the state pose a clear danger to the common good. The constant demands of maintaining coalitions damage good governance. Too many Israelis live below the poverty line. Social tensions along religious and ethnic lines persist. Civility in daily life could use a big, and I mean big, boost. And I could go on, but none of these issues deters me from my central point.

I stand in admiration of Israel today, and I say so with unreserved pride.

While there are many reasons, let me highlight five.

First, like a kid in a candy store. I am simply thrilled to be witness to a sovereign Jewish state. For nearly 1,900 years, Jews yearned for a return to the cradle of Jewish civilization. Jerusalem was at the center of our prayers. How lucky we are to live in an era when Jewish national self-determination has become a living reality. How fortunate we are to see the formal reconnection of the Jewish people with Jerusalem and the historic land with which we have been inextricably linked from the very beginning of the Jewish journey.

To be sure, there are lots of unresolved issues in the task of nation-building, but given its relative youth as a country and the immense challenges it's faced from the day of its birth, Israel has traveled light-years.

Second, Israel was established as a democracy and has remained steadfast to the ideals of freedom, its critics' claims notwithstanding.

Examples of Israel's fierce commitment to democracy abound, but one in particular stands out that says it all for me.

Recently, a group of Palestinian villagers called on the Israeli High Court of Justice to review the placement of the security barrier, claiming that the route created hardships for them. The court ruled in favor of the plaintiffs, arguing that the barrier must be moved because in this case the humanitarian considerations of the Palestinians need to be taken into account, even if they create additional security risks for Israel. The Israeli Ministry of Defense promptly agreed to abide by the court ruling, and the prime minister's office said it would not challenge the decision.

If this isn't democracy at work, what is? How many other democracies would experience something similar in a time of what can only be described as war?

Third, the vast majority of Israelis remain firmly committed to the search for peace with the Palestinians and refuse to abandon hope, no matter how distant a dream it may seem at moments like this. In fact, I know of no other nation that yearns for peace, prays for peace, as much as Israel. The pursuit of peace is central to the tenets of Judaism and to Israel's quest from the day of its establishment.

Israelis know that the price for peace will be compromise, painful, risky compromise, but they know as well that there is no alternative in the long run. Otherwise, the Jewish, democratic, and humanistic character of Israel will suffer fatal wounds.

There is a vigorous debate in Israel on the best way to achieve that long-sought peace. That is as it should be. It befits Israel's democratic, multiparty character. It also reflects the recognition that in the unenviable situation Israel finds itself—without an obvious Palestinian peace partner as long as Arafat holds the reins of ultimate power, and with the threat of continued terror—there is no single foolproof remedy.

Fourth, faced with unrelenting violence, Israel has stood firm. This tiny nation, smaller than Belgium, has demonstrated a capacity and will to defend itself that is nothing short of awe-inspiring. An enemy that has resorted to the use of children as human bombs, that sees

Israel's open and democratic society as the country's Achilles' heel, that deliberately targets civilians, and that abuses ambulances, hospitals, mosques, and even schools to spread terror has utterly failed in its goals.

Israel has adapted to this form of unconventional warfare through a combination of superb intelligence-gathering and a policy of preemption that could serve as a model in the global struggle against those who use terrorism to advance their radical ideology.

Tragically, nearly one thousand Israelis have lost their lives in Palestinian terrorist acts. Many more have been physically and emotionally scarred. But the Palestinian aim of breaking Israel's resolve, demoralizing the population, and bringing the nation to its knees has not succeeded. To the contrary, despite all the differences and divisions in Israeli society, there is a unity of purpose to stay the course that can only be admired.

And despite the claims of Palestinians and their supporters about alleged Israeli "atrocities," it is precisely the determined Israeli effort to avoid unnecessary loss of life that is so striking. Are mistakes made? No doubt. The pressures on a nineteen-year-old Israeli soldier can be enormous in such a conflict setting. The margin of error is slim to none. And the Palestinians are determined, as a tactic of choice, to goad the Israelis into targeting civilians, thus hoping to provoke an international outcry against Israeli actions.

The lengths to which Israel will go to avoid unnecessary Palestinian casualties were illustrated in the terrorist stronghold of Jenin. There, two years ago, Israeli lost twenty-three of its own soldiers in house-to-house combat rather than bomb from the air and risk innocent Palestinian casualties, speaking volumes about the moral compass of Israeli society.

And fifth, Israelis refuse to stop living. Even when terrorism was at its height, in March 2002, Israelis didn't cower in their homes or otherwise give in. If the suicide bombers celebrate death, Israelis celebrate life. It can't always be easy to keep up a brave façade. How must parents feel when they send their children off to school in the morning, not knowing whether they'll return home safely that evening? Given the ever-present dangers, the simplest act of eating out, riding a bus, walking in a park, or partying in a discotheque can require nerves of steel, even if Israelis dismiss it as nothing special.

It's not just the daily routine of living that's worthy of admiration, though. It's also the determination to push ahead in every field of endeavor. Israel has a great deal to offer the world—from agriculture to science, from medicine to the arts, from nanotechnology to software—and it hasn't missed a beat in helping push back the frontiers of knowledge and development.

No, Israel isn't a perfect society. It still has a way to go to deal with the seemingly limitless challenges that constantly threaten to overload the national circuitry. But it is a remarkable society all the same. The words of President John F. Kennedy ring as true today as when he expressed them over four decades ago:

> Israel is the child of hope and home of the brave.... It carries the shield of democracy and it honors the sword of freedom.

Letter from Łódź
or
Ode from Oy to Joy[*]
September 28, 2004

It's in the nature of my work that I ride an emotional roller-coaster. There are moments of profound sadness, and others of sheer exhilaration.

This was once again the case recently.

First, I was invited to participate in the commemoration of the sixtieth anniversary of the liquidation of the Łódź Ghetto.

Łódź, a city southwest of Warsaw, was home to the second largest Jewish community in Europe on the eve of the Second World War. As

---

[*] This essay is dedicated to the memory of Alina Viera, a cherished American Jewish Committee colleague who died earlier this year after a courageous struggle against a pitiless illness. A proud daughter of Poland and the Catholic Church, Alina embodied the very best of her native land and reached out to the Jewish people in friendship throughout her life. Knowing that death was imminent, Alina requested that the Mourner's *Kaddish* be recited in her memory by the AJC staff. It was.

many as 230,000 Jews, one-third of the city's population, lived along-side Polish Catholics, Germans, Russians, and other groups in this thriving textile center. Jewish religious and cultural life was remarkably vibrant.

Immediately after the Nazi occupation on September 8, 1939, persecution of the Jews began. Jewish-owned shops were plundered, bank accounts frozen, synagogues destroyed, and Jews barred from using public transportation.

On April 30, 1940, a ghetto, known as the Litzmannstadt Ghetto, was established which measured no more than four square kilometers. (Łódź was renamed Litzmannstadt earlier that month, after the World War I German general Karl Litzmann.) According to the *Encyclopedia of the Holocaust*, approximately 164,000 local Jews were initially forced to live there. Jews from Austria, Czechoslovakia, Germany, and Luxembourg were also transported to the ghetto in 1941 and 1942.

(In November 1941, a subsection of the ghetto was established for more than five thousand Roma, i.e., Gypsies. Within three months, they were transported to a death camp.)

This ghetto was the second largest in Nazi-occupied Europe, after the Warsaw Ghetto, and turned out to be the longest standing. It remained in use until the last transport train left the Radegast Station on August 29, 1944. This station is referred to as the *"Umschlagplatz"* of Łódź. *Umschlagplatz* was the site bordering the Warsaw Ghetto from which hundreds of thousands of Jews were deported to the death camps, especially Treblinka.

Under strict Nazi control, a Judenrat, or Jewish Council, was established to administer the daily life of the ghetto. Mordechai Chaim Rumkowski was placed in the morally impossible position of chairman. From his appointment in 1939 until his deportation to Auschwitz on the last transport from Łódź, Rumkowski was variously seen as a Quisling by some Jews, a savior by others.

In the ghetto, the Jews, as best they could, continued to educate their children, organize health services, and conduct clandestine political activity.

The Jews also wrote. They penned diaries, chronicles, and poems about their plight, many of which were later discovered. Here's one segment of a much longer poem by Simcha Bunim Shayevitsh. It was written on the eve of Passover in 1942, two years before his death, and later published in *Łódź Ghetto: Inside a Community under Siege.*

And in an hour of good fortune
The miracle of rebirth occurs
And spring is here again.
But for us in the ghetto
No one any longer cares about hunger
Which cries out from every limb.
And everyone has forgotten
Death which visits everyone personally
And does not skip a house.
And like a desolate, trembling sheep,
One shivers and trembles
At the order for deportation
Into an unknown land.
One trembles and quakes
At Belshazzar's cryptic writing[*]:
　—Life or Death.
An old woman sees the hearses drive by;
Her eyes gleam with envy:
　—Yes, yes, the man was lucky.
And the young man lowers his head:
　—No, no, everything is hell anyway.
And the young girl spits three times:
　—Tfu, tfu, tfu, let the Angel of Death be my bridegroom, already.
And even the child trudges on the march,
Stammering with a plaintive weeping:
　—Mamele dear, Oh I don't have any more strength;
Oh, put me there on the black wagon.

From the Łódź Ghetto, the Jews were deported to Auschwitz-Birkenau and Chelmno. The latter camp is not widely known. Located

---

[*] A reference to the Book of Daniel. It was Belshazzar who saw the writing on the wall, which Daniel interpreted as a prophecy of doom.

forty-five miles west of Łódź, Chelmno was the first death camp in which mass executions were carried out by gas. In all, an estimated 320,000 Jews were murdered there.

Of the 150,000 Jews who were sent on the transport trains, only 5,000–15,000 survived. Additionally, more than 40,000 ghetto inmates died from hunger, illness, or exposure.

Jerzy Kropiwnicki, the current mayor of Łódź, was the force behind the commemoration. He credits Wladyslaw Bartoszewski, chairman of the Polish Council for the Protection of Memory, a former foreign minister, and a Righteous Gentile, with having inspired him to mark the anniversary date. Until this event, Łódź as a Holocaust site had largely been ignored since the war. No longer.

Explaining his decision, the mayor said:

I have been thinking a lot about the situation of a crime witness. When people analyze the question of crime, usually they think about the two sides: the executioner and the victim. We rarely realize that there is also a third party—the witness. In Łódź the perpetrators were the Germans, the victims the Jews, and the witnesses were those who were not shut in a ghetto, i.e., the Poles. In every crime the roles of the executioner and the victim are fixed forever. The witness stands before an eternal moral challenge—he can either be silent together with the executioner or cry with the victim. In my opinion, silence is morally unacceptable. The witness of the crime must cry out.

These are the dimensions of the tragedy which we recollect, a crime that has been perpetrated on innocent people, on the inhabitants of our city. And we must not be silent about it.

City officials expected about 1,500 to attend the commemorative events. In fact, more than 5,500 showed up, straining the city's ability to host them. They came from Israel, across Europe, and North America. Many were aging survivors, their children and grandchildren accompanying them. A few were non-Jews who came as an expression of solidarity. The city, to its credit, pulled out all the stops to create a solemn and moving program spread out over nearly three days.

A number of dignitaries participated, including the Polish prime minister, an Israeli cabinet minister, the mayor of Tel Aviv (Tel Aviv and Łódź are sister cities), the American, Israeli, Austrian, Czech, and German ambassadors to Poland, and distinguished cantors and musicians.

Among the most powerful moments was the memorial service at the Jewish cemetery, the largest in Europe. Established in 1892, it contains nearly 180,000 headstones or *matzevot*. Since the cemetery was located in the ghetto, many of those 40,000 Jews who died within the ghetto walls were buried in unmarked graves there.

From the cemetery, we marched a mile or so to the Radegast Station, the arrival point for Jews deported to the Łódź Ghetto and the departure point for Jews transported to the death camps. It is here that the mayor has embarked on an ambitious plan to create a memorial to the victims and a museum. Several boxcars of the Deutsche Reichsbahn used to carry Jews are placed on the adjoining tracks as part of the permanent exhibit. Much of the work has been done at city expense, but the project will require an infusion of outside funds to be completed.

The mayor has appealed to a number of sources, including the American Jewish Committee, for the one million dollars required to finish the work. As the survivors gradually disappear from our midst, the importance of preserving and protecting sites connected to the Shoah only grows.

The city of Łódź is not a wealthy metropolis, and, in any case, it shouldn't be expected to bear this responsibility alone. To state the obvious, the tragedy that befell the Jews was not of its making. The city deserves help.

I was deeply moved by my time in Łódź. Words become hopelessly inadequate in such situations to describe the welter of feelings—from grief to incomprehension to anger to resolve—that engulf me and give me no rest.

I was touched by the personal stories that I and others heard from many survivors. They wanted to talk. They needed to talk. Time was running out for them, they realized, and they prayed their stories would outlive them. Returning to Poland was not easy for some. Walking once familiar streets filled with suffering and anguish brought their nightmares back in even sharper relief.

How they picked up the pieces of their broken lives after the war, found their footing, and marched on to build new lives, new families, a new country, Israel, and new hope is beyond my ability to grasp, constantly shadowed as they were by the single greatest crime in human history, as well as the realization that anti-Jewish hatred did not end on May 8, 1945.

Think about it. It wasn't as if a contrite world suddenly begged for forgiveness at war's end and sought to make amends. Some survivors made their way home to their towns and villages, often to find nothing other than the enmity of their former neighbors who feared repossession of homes and belongings.

It is not widely known that hundreds of survivors, perhaps more, were killed in Poland and Hungary in the period just after the war. The pogrom in Kielce, Poland, was perhaps the most notorious example. In July 1946, forty-two Jews, all survivors, were murdered when the Jews were falsely accused of a blood libel.

Other survivors found Displaced Persons (DP) camps the only safe haven, and so they stayed on in Germany and Austria, of all places, though under the administration of the British and Americans. Those who tried to reach Palestine were blocked more often than not by the British and placed in internment camps on Cyprus. And the survivors, for a variety of complex psychological reasons, were mostly reticent to talk about what they had endured. Perhaps it was just as well, because at the time the world was largely uninterested in listening. The brutal, bloody war was over, and it was time to move on, to look forward, not backward. And, in any case, who wanted to be reminded of sins of commission and omission?

I was transfixed by the interaction between the survivors and their children and grandchildren—the younger generations struggling to imagine a time and place beyond their capacity to comprehend, yet knowing that it would soon fall to them to shoulder the responsibility for and protection of that memory.

I was struck, at the same time, by the many ways in which things had changed for the better.

After more than forty years of stultifying Communist rule, here we were in democratic Poland, now a member of NATO and the European Union. Polish troops are fighting side by side with American forces in Iraq. Poland is today one of Israel's staunchest allies in Europe. There's bilateral cooperation in just about every field of endeavor.

No, anti-Semitism hasn't been completely eradicated in Poland, but it's competing with a strong wave of what can only be called philo-Semitism, which seeks to reclaim the Jewish contribution to Poland as an integral part of the nation's history. This wave has led to any number of Jewish cultural festivals, academic institutes, exchange programs with Israel, volunteer efforts to care for Jewish cemeteries, Christian-Jewish initiatives, books, and museum exhibits.

Bear in mind that Jews have lived on Polish soil for nearly a thousand years, and that on the eve of World War II Jews comprised ten percent of the total Polish population and fully one-third of Warsaw's residents.

The mayor's laudable effort to commemorate the Łódź anniversary needs to be seen in this light. So, too, does the Polish government's exemplary cooperation with the American Jewish Committee to preserve and protect the site of the Nazi death camp at Belzec, where 500,000 Jews perished. The dedication ceremony took place earlier this year in the presence of the Polish president. (See "Letter from Belzec," June 3, 2004.)

And there was one other bit of good news on this trip. The timing was totally coincidental, but the symbolism couldn't have been more powerful. I was invited to speak at the Summer University of the European Union of Jewish Students. This was the twenty-first annual weeklong gathering of young people from across Europe, who get together to celebrate their Jewish identity, learn from one another and from guest speakers, and form lasting friendships.

This year's program was in a village an hour north of Berlin in what was the former East Germany (GDR). It turned out to be a nine-hour drive from Łódź. The drive, incidentally, helped me understand the ease with which Nazi forces attacked Poland in 1939. The land was flat as a pancake from one end to the other—not a hill in sight.

Maybe for the students, given their youth, the location was nothing exceptional. For me, though, it was. As a child of the Cold War, I still pinch myself every time I cross what was once the Iron Curtain and recall the stunning, and previously unimaginable, events that began in 1989 in Eastern Europe and culminated in 1991 with the implosion of the Soviet Union.

Until fifteen years ago, when these students were in elementary school, there were virtually no identified Jews in the GDR, and there certainly would have been no Jewish summer gatherings. To the contrary, the GDR was for decades an implacable enemy of Israel, a hotbed of anti-Zionism, a sanctuary for Middle Eastern terrorist groups, and run by a government that rejected any moral responsibility for the crimes of the Third Reich, not to mention that it was a viciously totalitarian regime that kept 17 million citizens in its iron grip.

(German reunification has proved far more difficult and costly than anyone imagined. That becomes immediately obvious even to the casual visitor. After fifteen years and a trillion dollars spent on economic development, the gap between West and East Germany remains wide, unemployment in the east is high, many young people have depopulated the former East Germany by moving to the western part of the country, and the potential for extremism, feeding off of widespread dissatisfaction and disillusionment, is quite serious.)

But most striking for me was the encounter with hundreds of young European Jews. If Łódź makes you cry, these young people make you smile. This is the future and, judging from the many individuals I spoke with, it's bright indeed. These are the Jews from Thessaloniki, Minsk, Warsaw, Amsterdam, Vienna, Berlin, and Moscow who weren't meant to be. Had Hitler fully succeeded, had Stalin after him, there might have been tiny pockets of Jews in neutral Sweden, Switzerland, Spain, and Turkey, but little more.

Spending Shabbat with these future leaders was a time I won't soon forget. The unadulterated joy in being Jewish, the determination to stand with Israel and against those who would delegitimize or demonize it, and the pride in being young Europeans embarked on the experiment of stitching together a continent-wide community all profoundly struck me.

In my conversations, I found the young people cognizant of the many daunting challenges they face as Jews—ranging from political to demographic—but undeterred.

At a time when many Jews are distressed about the state of the world, this encounter was cause for optimism. Our survival as Jews, we know, has never been due to sheer numbers alone, but rather to the power of tenacity, passion, and faith.

All three were very much on display in that most improbable of places—a village in the heart of the former East Germany, just an hour north of the Brandenburg Gate.

Letter on Darfur
October 1, 2004

Never again.

Those were the words expressed by the international community after the previously unimaginable magnitude of the Holocaust against the Jewish people became fully revealed. They were meant to give voice to the notion that such large-scale tragedies must not be allowed to recur.

And those words have been repeated over and over since. But their true test, of course, is not in their repetition but rather in their implementation. What's the record?

Some important steps have been taken since World War II.

Consider the precedent established by the Nuremberg trials and the adoption of the Universal Declaration of Human Rights and the Genocide Convention; or the emergent role of nongovernmental organizations as advocates for human rights protections; or the technological revolution that brings images from around the globe into homes in real time; or the priority that some governments, at least some of the time, attach to human rights in their foreign policy; and the democratic and civil rights revolutions that have swept major parts of the world. In sum, there's been a quantum leap forward from the situation that prevailed only sixty years ago. More people are free and secure in their rights than ever before.

But sadly, as we know all too well, the story doesn't stop there. These advances notwithstanding, the end of World War II didn't bring with it an end to crimes against humanity. Far from it. While some might have allowed themselves to believe that the world would finally come to its senses, alas, that wasn't to be. Instead, we've been witness to one unfolding tragedy after another.

Think of the incalculable human toll of Communist rule in the Soviet Union and China. Think of the killing fields of Cambodia. Think of the "disappeared" during Argentine military rule. Think of the ethnic cleansing in Bosnia and Kosovo. Think of the mass murder of Christians and animists in southern Sudan. Think of the genocide in Rwanda. I could go on at length.

In each case, the words "never again" didn't mean a whole lot, did they? Oh, there were excuses aplenty from those on the outside—claims of ignorance of what was going on, disputes over the facts on the ground, protestations of diplomatic or military impotence, assertions that national interests weren't involved, and arguments that these were internal, not international, matters. For the millions upon millions of victims of repression, war crimes, or genocide, however, the excuses rang rather hollow.

And now, we are confronted with yet another tragedy of immense proportions. In the western Sudan, tens of thousands of black Africans have been killed by Arab militias. Well over a million people have been displaced, and the end is not yet in sight.

While human rights and international relief agencies have done important work, many governments have dithered, the United States being among the few exceptions. The governments, you see, haven't agreed on whether it's genocide, as if the semantic argument were the beginning and end of the discussion; or they don't want to jeopardize their ties with the Sudanese government, which is unquestionably complicit in the tragedy; or oil interests have trumped humanitarian interests; or perhaps they're suffering from compassion fatigue.

The Holocaust should have taught us at least two things: Never underestimate man's capacity for inhumanity, and indifference in the face of such inhumanity is utterly indefensible.

Isn't it high time for the world to demonstrate that the words "never again" actually do have meaning in the twenty-first century?

Surely those entrusted with power in national governments and regional and global institutions could put into place a coordinated plan of action for western Sudan, if only they had sufficient political will and moral outrage. The time to act is now, not next week or next month, after still more lives are lost. Let's hope, as a first step, that recent encouraging statements from the African Union lead to concrete peacekeeping action.

And shouldn't each of us as individuals take to heart the words from Leviticus in the Hebrew Bible, "Neither shalt you stand idly by while your neighbor's blood is shed"?

The judgment of history awaits our generation. It's not going to let any of us off the hook, I fear, as Darfur becomes a name indelibly imprinted in the annals of mass atrocities.

Letter from a Friend of Israel
October 29, 2004

It has been coming.

Many in the Israeli settler movement believed that when push came to shove, Prime Minister Ariel Sharon wouldn't turn against them.

Many on the left were convinced that Sharon had a trick up his sleeve and, therefore, it was all a big bluff.

And those relentless critics of Israel outside the country, especially the ones who've made a living out of demonizing Sharon, argued that he wasn't interested in any compromise. To the contrary.

Everyone, it seemed, had conveniently forgotten that Ariel Sharon was never so much an ideological as a strategic hawk, and that the two are not the same. Moreover, it was Sharon, wasn't it, who had implemented Prime Minister Menachem Begin's orders to remove Israeli settlers from Yamit in fulfillment of the Israeli-Egyptian peace treaty.

The handwriting had been on the wall for some time, for anyone who cared to look. But, of course, by definition, those who opt to live in denial or are blinded by hatred can't see.

Sharon, the wily politician and strategist, had long been signaling a turnaround. The first Likud leader to acknowledge publicly the inevitability of a Palestinian state, he also came to understand the danger for Israel's democracy, Jewish character, and security of a continued presence in the Gaza cauldron, in particular. Unwilling to wait any longer for a credible Palestinian leader and partner to emerge, he chose to take matters into his own hands.

It could not have been an easy decision. Any such move is fraught with tremendous risk. But in his cost-benefit analysis, Sharon concluded that the rationale for staying in Gaza could no longer be justified and that time was not working in Israel's favor.

In an ideal scenario, of course, any change in the status of Gaza should have come about through formal talks between Israelis and Palestinians, but such was not to be. As long as Yasir Arafat is around, direct negotiations are impossible. Arafat could never make the transition from guerrilla leader to statesman. That's been amply demonstrated by now. It's only regrettable that the rules of the Nobel Peace Prize don't permit revocation of the award once given. Whether Arafat survives his current illness or not, the likelihood of a Palestinian leader being in a position to start serious talks with Israel anytime soon appears quite remote.

And so Sharon decided to act, and to act decisively. Yes, there are thousands of Israeli settlers who've lived in Gaza for more than three decades, often with the encouragement of Israeli governments (and Sharon himself). A whole generation has been born there, and some have been buried there, including victims of Palestinian terrorism. And yes, some settlers chose to live in Gaza because they believed they were fulfilling a higher goal for the State of Israel and the Jewish people, involving both religion and security. The impact of withdrawal on the settlers will be gut-wrenching and heartrending, and Sharon knows this.

Moreover, Sharon understands that such a unilateral step on Israel's part may be deliberately misinterpreted by the Palestinians as admission of military defeat at the hands of terrorists, even if this is clearly not the case. Hamas and others will surely try to exploit the moment to maximum advantage.

And Sharon grasps the essential fact that allowing a vacuum in Gaza, at Israel's southern doorstep, could complicate matters still further, unless Egypt, the United States, the European Union, and others cooperate to prevent a descent into chaos and a rebuilding of the terrorist infrastructure.

But Sharon also came face-to-face with the inescapable reality that the "greater good" required him to consider the interests of the state above those of several thousand settlers, and that those interests were being seriously undermined by a continued Israeli presence in Gaza.

In doing so, Sharon exhibited admirable leadership qualities. He was undeterred by the knowledge that he might split his own party, lose some members of his governing coalition, or even face death threats. And he showed that a leader's thinking can evolve in new and unexpected ways. His speech in the Knesset the day before the vote offers eloquent testimony to his vision and courage. It should be required reading for students of the Middle East.

It's interesting to consider the reaction to all this in various places.

In a rational world, the Palestinians should be delighted. After all, they may soon be rid of the Israeli military and civilian presence in Gaza, a presumed goal of their efforts. That would mean the opportunity to govern themselves—for the first time in their history, since even Egypt, which controlled Gaza from 1948 to 1967, never offered local residents a modicum of autonomy, much less full sovereignty—and thus the chance to prove to the world that they can deal responsibly with sovereignty. If so, a well-run, peaceful Gaza might eventually persuade the Israeli public that they have nothing to fear from a Palestinian entity emerging in the West Bank as well, creating a snowballing momentum toward a final settlement.

Alas, rational thinking doesn't always prevail in this part of the world, and so the Palestinians, by their negative reaction to date, could prove that the late Abba Eban's much cited comment—"The Palestinians never miss an opportunity to miss an opportunity"— remains relevant.

The attitude of some settlers and their supporters, including several dozen rabbis, is also noteworthy and profoundly disturbing.

Rather than limiting themselves to dissent through the channels of democracy, they self-righteously claim a higher authority as their sole guide. They threaten civil unrest, call on soldiers to disobey orders, and brand Sharon a traitor. Reality and their brand of messianic religious belief collide frontally. These individuals mistakenly equate the future of Gaza with the future of Israel. Yet how can they justify the long-term presence of 7,500 Jewish settlers living under Israeli sovereignty, and the soldiers needed to protect them, in a teeming population of more than one million Palestinians crammed into this tiny space? Israel's very being as a Jewish and democratic state is undermined with each day they stay there.

Importantly, as Sharon has noted, the Palestinian population in Gaza, which numbered 200,000 after the 1948 Israeli War of Independence, has practically doubled in each generation, which only portends a worse demographic situation in the years ahead.

And it's sobering to recall that this raw and heated internal debate is taking place against the backdrop of the ninth anniversary of Yitzhak Rabin's assassination. Before November 1995, few Jews believed that such a tragic crime, in the name of a blend of misguided faith and politics, was possible in the Jewish state. Today few doubt that it could repeat itself.

It is said in the Talmud that the destruction of the Second Temple in Jerusalem in 70 C.E. came about because of hate-filled divisions among the Jews. Have we really learned anything since? One begins to wonder.

In the meantime, reaction in Europe has been, by and large, all too familiar.

Having relentlessly criticized Sharon since he took office in 2001 and, for that matter, long before, Europeans find it all but impossible to suddenly change course and, by doing so, at least implicitly admit to faulty judgment. Such admissions are rarely a strong suit of elected officials.

Incidentally, more or less the same happened in reverse with Europe and Arafat. Having invested so heavily—diplomatically, politically, psychologically, and financially—in the Palestinian leader, many Europeans proved themselves unable and unwilling to acknowledge openly that the man was not all he was cracked up to be, no matter how much incontrovertible proof was assembled about his links to terrorism, incitement, and corruption.

Take, for example, the group of visiting European parliamentarians who were in the American Jewish Committee building in New York on the very day the Knesset voted to endorse the Sharon plan for withdrawal. They talked as if absolutely nothing was happening. It was the all-too-familiar rhetoric along the lines of "with Sharon peace is impossible."

Meanwhile, televised images showed the Israeli leader surrounded by a phalanx of sixteen security guards and zoomed in on graffiti invoking Rabin's assassination and calling for the same fate for Sharon. In other words, while Sharon was literally putting his life on the line to seek approval for a withdrawal from Gaza and four West Bank settlements, those who presumably should welcome these steps couldn't overcome their implacable hostility to even acknowledge them.

A more or less similar experience took place shortly before, in a meeting we had overseas with a European foreign minister. He was reciting the by-now predictable litany of complaints that Sharon was an obstacle to peace and nothing good could happen as long as he was in office.

We suggested that more than meets the eye was going on, citing the planned Gaza withdrawal, declared support for a two-state solution, and the construction of the security barrier, which could be seen as implicit, if not explicit, acknowledgment of the logic of an eventual territorial separation, all undertaken by a Likud-led government. But the minister looked at us as if we had fallen on our heads, though he was too polite to say as much.

This attitude of "don't confuse me with the facts" was also on display a few weeks earlier when a delegation of German television and radio news editors came to the American Jewish Committee. A few were particularly aggressive in their approach to the meeting. It was as if the fact that we were Americans and friends of Israel put us on a lower moral plane and required us to justify ourselves from the get-go to our accusers.

As but one example of the tenor of the conversation, an editor, barely concealing her contempt for Sharon, demanded to know why "a wall" was being built "on Palestinian lands." When I tried to explain that the wall was in reality a fence in all but a few built-up areas (and that this structure was not even remotely akin to the hated Berlin Wall), and that Palestinian lands were in point of fact disputed lands, she grew even more testy and pushed back, insisting on knowing why the wall, not the fence, wasn't built on the Green Line.

I asked her what the Green Line was. There was a moment's silence, and then she blurted out that it was "the internationally recognized boundary between Israel and Palestine." I replied that this was not the case and asked the other eleven guests if they knew what the Green Line was. Not one could respond, though surely their jobs required nuanced understanding of current events. I explained that it was simply the 1949 Armistice Line, that there had never before been a state called Palestine, and that a final demarcation of any border between Israel and a Palestinian state must await the outcome of peace talks and the resolution of competing claims. It's doubtful that I made even the slightest dent in the thinking of those whose minds were clearly made up long before the meeting took place.

Not for the first time, I left struck by several things: the sheer ignorance of those who came on so strong, the unwillingness of members of the group who disagreed to speak out (after the meeting ended, a few quietly expressed embarrassment about their colleagues' behavior), and the absence of intellectual humility in offering advice on resolving a complex conflict about which they knew little, and on which the very survival of the State of Israel depended.

In the same spirit, I must recount an exchange with a moderate Arab foreign minister that took place during our annual diplomatic marathon in September, when the American Jewish Committee meets separately with leaders of nearly sixty countries.

Having known this minister for many years, we began with an exchange of pleasantries and reminiscences. Then things turned more serious when he told us that, while recognizing the terrorist threat faced by Israel, he was deeply concerned about the construction of Israel's "wall" and the grave damage it posed to peace prospects.

Aware of the fact that the minister represented a country that had no love for Arafat and the Palestinians, we asked what advice he would offer Israel in dealing with terrorism. He thought for a moment or two before responding: "I would tell the Israelis to tear down that wall and instead build a fence. It's less humiliating."

Overcoming our astonishment, we told the minister that a miracle must have occurred because his advice had been followed to the letter by the Israelis, who built a fence, not a wall. It was clear from his reaction, though, that he didn't believe us and never would, regardless of what we said, at least until Al-Jazeera or whoever was his primary source on these matters changed their tune, however improbable that might be.

In sum, the cumulative effect of years of vilification of Sharon and automatic-pilot criticism of Israel in the media, rarefied intellectual circles, and the UN have all led to a situation where, even when Israel takes a bold step toward disengagement, which deserves credit, it instead continues to get raked over the coals. The comments range from "it's all a sleight of hand" to "it's too little, too late" to "it's designed to suffocate Gaza" to "it's only meant to strengthen Israel's hold on the West Bank."

Well, let's see. Time will tell. Facts will speak for themselves. Much can interfere with the process, and few things in the Middle East skip along merrily in the way we might hope. But what's abundantly clear is that Sharon is dead serious and has staked his political life, in fact his very life, on moving the process forward. This creates a new opportunity in the region, which, if played right, can reduce tensions and over time open up possibilities for further peacemaking. There's no guarantee, far from it, but it's worth the attempt and merits international support.

Whoever wins the U.S. presidential elections on November 2 (and I pray that whoever is declared the winner will win decisively enough so that there's no question in anyone's mind about the integrity of the electoral process), the American role will be critical in the months ahead, as it has been throughout. Fortunately, both leading candidates have expressed their support for Sharon's plan.

And, as always, the role of American Jews will prove consequential. In particular, the voices of those who support the bold decision of Prime Minister Sharon to begin disengagement will need to be heard above the din. A great deal is at stake in Israel's quest for peace and security, for the preservation of a Jewish and democratic state. We dare not be silent or indifferent at this critical juncture.

Letter from Sofia
November 30, 2004

Here's a quiz.

Can you name the European country that protected its 50,000 Jews during the Second World War, despite Hitler's determined efforts to have them deported to the death camps?

Let me give you a hint.

It's the very same country that was allied with Hitler as one of the Axis nations, just as it had joined with the Central Powers during World War I.

The country? Bulgaria.

Located in southeastern Europe, Bulgaria, about the size of the State of Tennessee, isn't exactly a household name for much of the world. It spent a good part of the last thousand years trying to assert its independence, more often than not unsuccessfully. For five centuries it was dominated by the Ottoman Empire, and before that by the Byzantine Empire. It gained its full freedom from the Ottomans in 1878, only to choose the losing side in both world wars, and then to fall into the Soviet orbit for four decades.

Moreover, with no significant diaspora in the West, with little tourism from outside the region until recently, and with little known about its culture, people, or products, the usual response I've encountered to Bulgaria is something akin to a blank stare. When asked to place it geographically, most people say that it's somewhere in the Balkans, but few know exactly where.

In fact, it is in the Balkans, and its location is strategically important. Its neighbors to the south are Turkey and Greece, to the west

Serbia and Macedonia, and to the north Romania. On the east, it borders the Black Sea, together with Romania, Ukraine, Russia, Georgia, and Turkey.

Bulgaria's population numbers 7.5 million. Like an increasing number of European countries, its population is expected to decline in the coming years due to a low birthrate. Ethnically, the country is 84 percent Bulgarian, 9.4 percent Turkish, and 4.7 percent Roma (Gypsies). Religiously, 83 percent of the population is Bulgarian Orthodox, 12 percent is Muslim, and there is a smattering of Catholics and Protestants. Jews number approximately 6,000–8,000, though estimates vary.

Having been to Bulgaria several times on behalf of the American Jewish Committee, most recently this fall, I believe the country deserves much more attention than it has received to date. Here's why:

Bulgaria's history of religious tolerance, symbolized by the placement of the central synagogue, mosque, and metropolitan church all within a few hundred yards of each other in Sofia, the capital city, needs to be studied and its lessons applied elsewhere, especially in these turbulent times.

A *Los Angeles Times* article, which appeared on February 12, 2001, stressed the point:

> During a decade of ethnic and religious wars that devastated the neighboring former Yugoslav Federation—including the conflict between Muslim ethnic Albanians and Orthodox Christian Serbs that engulfed the province of Kosovo—Bulgaria has been a model of peace.

No doubt, anti-Semitism reared its ugly head every so often in modern Bulgarian history, but it never developed the kind of traction it did elsewhere in Europe.

And, while outside forces have apparently sought to radicalize Bulgaria's Muslim Turkish community, they've reportedly had little success to date.

The one notable recent exception to this policy of tolerance and mutual respect came in the mid-1980s, during the Communist era, when Todor Zhivkov, the longtime ruler, launched a campaign of persecution against ethnic Turks. The policy included compelling them to adopt Slavic surnames and restricting the use of the Turkish language in public. In the summer of 1989, just months before Communism and Zhivkov both became history, Turks were encouraged to leave the country, and over 300,000 fled to neighboring Turkey. In the ensuing years, many returned to their former homes.

Bulgaria's principled and courageous protection of its Jewish community, resulting in the truly startling fact that at the end of the Second World War there were actually more Jews in the country than at the beginning, deserves greater attention and acclaim.

A letter from Karl Hoffman, a representative of the (Nazi) Reich Security Main Office in Bulgaria, dated April 5, 1943, and cited in the *Encyclopedia of the Holocaust*, helps explain why.

> The Jewish Question does not exist in Bulgaria in the sense that it does in Germany. The ideological and racial prerequisites for convincing the Bulgarian people of the urgent need for a solution of the Jewish Question as in the Reich are not to be found here.

It must be said, however, that the record is not perfect. Bulgarian troops actively participated in the deportation of nearly 11,400 Jews from Macedonia and Thrace (areas of Greece annexed by Bulgaria), principally to Treblinka. Only a handful survived. Thus, the Bulgarian record is viewed quite differently among the remnant Jewish communities in Macedonia and Thrace than it is among Bulgarian Jews. Also, though they were not deported or killed, able-bodied Bulgarian Jewish men were forced to participate in hard labor under poor conditions during the war.

The Bulgarian king, the church, members of parliament, professional associations, and others were all involved in the defense of the Bulgarian Jewish community, who, like the Jews of Denmark, were considered an intrinsic part of the Bulgarian nation, not a separate community. While heated debates persist to the present day among the various parties as to who was primarily responsible for the rescue, the bottom line is that 50,000 Jews who otherwise would have been deported to the camps were saved.

For those interested in learning more, several books on the rescue have been written, including *Beyond Hitler's Grasp: The Heroic Rescue of Bulgaria's Jews*, by Michael Bar-Zohar, a Bulgarian-born historian.

And at least one documentary film has been made, *The Optimists: The Story of the Rescue of the Bulgarian Jews from the Holocaust*, by the Israeli filmmaker Jacky Comforty. It was shown at the AJC-sponsored Westchester Jewish Film Festival two years ago to rave reviews.

Bulgaria has rapidly emerged as one of America's best friends in Europe. In fact, there's currently discussion about establishing U.S. military bases in Bulgaria, and the Bulgarians are eager to see this happen. Moreover, this summer the U.S. and Bulgarian militaries conducted joint exercises. And when Bulgaria sat on the UN Security Council for a two-year term in 2002–03, the United States could count on support and understanding, which, as we know all too well, wasn't necessarily the case with every other European country.

Bulgaria has been playing an active and responsible role in the international arena. In the 1990s, for example, while much of the former Yugoslavia was in turmoil, Bulgaria pursued a constructive policy that helped calm the regional waters rather than seek to exploit the situation to national advantage.

Today, 480 Bulgarian troops are serving in the Karbala region in Iraq, under Polish command. When two Bulgarian civilian truck drivers were taken hostage in July by terrorists in Iraq who demanded the removal of Bulgarian troops from the country, President Georgi Parvanov and Prime Minister Simeon Saxe-Coburg Gotha refused, urging other affected countries to do the same. This stance prompted Secretary of State Colin Powell to describe the Bulgarian position as "an example to all of the nations of the world, and especially the nations within the coalition" in Iraq.

Bulgaria has also deployed peacekeepers to Afghanistan, Bosnia, and Kosovo, and agreed to train twenty Iraqi policemen at the police academy in Sofia.

In March, Bulgaria became a member of NATO and, having completed its entry talks with the European Union after more than four years of negotiation but several months ahead of schedule, is on track to join the EU in January 2007.

During the year 2004, Bulgaria occupied the chairman-in-office of the Organization for Security and Cooperation in Europe (OSCE), the fifty-five-member governmental body that monitors human rights and elections. In this capacity, Bulgarian Foreign Minister Solomon Passy, who has earned widespread international respect, served as the head of the timely and important OSCE Conference on Anti-Semitism, held in Berlin in the spring.

Bulgaria has had an increasingly close bilateral relationship with Israel since ties were reestablished in 1990 following the break in 1967. At that time, in the wake of the Six-Day War, all the Warsaw Pact nations except Romania severed links with the Jewish state.

Contact flourishes in every field imaginable. There is much good will toward Israel in Bulgaria, and the nearly 45,000 Bulgarian Jews who, shaped by a long Zionist tradition as well as fear of Communism, made aliyah in the early years of the Jewish state—and who have contributed significantly, if quietly, to Israel's growth and development—help form a natural bridge between the two countries.

The Jewish population is only a fraction of its former size, largely due to the aliyah, and is rapidly aging. Even so, it's drawing some newcomers who wish to be identified with the community or have only belatedly discovered a Jewish connection in the post-Communist era.

The community, centered in Sofia and with a smaller concentration in Plovdiv, is overwhelmingly Sephardic, having largely arrived in the wake of the Spanish Inquisition and as a result of the Ottoman welcome. But the first traces of a Jewish presence in what is today Bulgaria date back to the first century.

The Organization of Jews in Bulgaria, with which the American Jewish Committee has a formal and fruitful relationship, is very open to affiliation.

In contrast to some other European Jewish communities, which make conversion to Judaism all but impossible and even refuse to recognize liberal congregations as full members of the formal communal structure, the Bulgarian community does not apply rigorous standards of Jewish law in determining eligibility for membership.

To the contrary, it takes a relaxed view of who is a Jew. Without such an approach, the community's numbers would be substantially diminished, though I don't believe this to be the main reason for adopting such a position. Rather, it's driven by the feeling that whoever wants to be part of us is welcome, and it's not our business to ask too many questions.

Not the least of its attractions, for those looking for a new travel destination, Bulgaria offers a beautiful Black Sea coast, opportunities galore for winter sports, interesting and unusual folklore, and the lure of the unbeaten path.

As a little-known historical aside, in the 1980s Bulgaria became a place where Jews living in the Soviet Union could arrange to meet their relatives who had immigrated to Israel. Since there was no tourism permitted between the USSR and Israel, it was necessary to find a third country to which residents of both countries could travel. It wasn't that hard for Soviet citizens to get permission to vacation in Bulgaria, as it was considered a trustworthy ally, and Israelis, even absent formal diplomatic ties with Sofia in that period, could often manage to get visas, providing much-needed Western currency for the struggling Bulgarian economy.

Is everything perfect? Not at all.

For one thing, Bulgaria still has some serious catching up to do to achieve a Western standard of living and a modern, efficient infrastructure. During its more than four decades behind the Iron Curtain, Bulgaria had even less exposure to the West than other Communist countries, due both to its location and to a regime that was quite suffocating in its pro-Soviet orientation and ideological Marxist orthodoxy.

It should be noted that Bulgaria long felt a special connection to Russia, though that is no longer the case. The languages are similar, and both have used the Cyrillic alphabet, created by Bulgarians in 815 C.E., for well over a thousand years. Orthodox Christianity is the dominant religion in both countries. And Bulgarians remember with gratitude Russian help in freeing them from the yoke of Ottoman rule.

That's why, even when Bulgaria sided with the Nazis in World War II, it never declared war on the Soviet Union. (In September 1944, however, the Soviet Union declared war on Bulgaria.)

And it helps explain why during the Communist period, Bulgaria was often referred to as the sixteenth republic of the USSR, since its ties to Moscow were perhaps closer and less fraught with tension than those of any other Warsaw Pact nation. As one result, the Soviet KGB relied rather heavily on its Bulgarian counterpart to undertake clandestine work around the world.

Moreover, Bulgaria suffers from some of the very same social ills experienced by several other post-Communist nations, namely, corruption, organized crime, and the need for administrative reform. The current government is seeking to tackle these problems head on, with the encouragement of the European Union, but, to state the obvious, there is no overnight solution.

At the end of the day, though, I'm bullish on Bulgaria, because I've been impressed with the striking progress I've witnessed on each of my visits, beginning in the early 1990s.

It's also because I've seen a nation trying to establish itself as a responsible regional and global citizen.

Moreover, I place a very high premium on Bulgaria's current pro-American and pro-Israeli orientation, which are not universally popular in Europe these days and are not cost-free, either.

Bulgarian diplomats assigned to the UN, for example, came under unrelenting pressure from several European nations and, in particular, the Arab League during the country's two-year stint on the powerful Security Council. Some of the encounters, I am told, were not pleasant, with Arab diplomats attempting heavy-handed tactics, but the Bulgarians held their ground. By the way, Bulgaria has actively pursued good political and commercial relations with the Arab world, yet not at the expense of its ties with Jerusalem.

And, above all, I don't for a moment take for granted Bulgaria's protection of its Jewish community during the war, which was an act of extraordinary and all-too-rare courage and humanity. In recent years, I might add, the Bulgarians have been among the most forthcoming nations in returning property that once belonged to the Jewish community.

In other words, Bulgaria is a country worth getting to know. One might say that its time has come.

Letter from Istanbul
December 21, 2004

The European Union's invitation to Turkey last week to open negotiations for membership is truly momentous. No, this isn't hyperbole.
If anything, it's an understatement.

After more than four decades of hemming and hawing about what
to do regarding Turkey, the EU has finally decided to take the plunge.
The path ahead isn't likely to be short, much less simple. Many things
can still happen that could complicate, even derail, the process, but a
threshold has been crossed, and there's really no going back.

Since the founding of the Turkish republic in 1923, on the rubble of
the legendary Ottoman Empire, by Mustafa Kemal, known to the world
as Atatürk, the goal he established has been to anchor this strategically located nation, straddling two continents, firmly in Europe and the
West.

But even as Turkey has largely embraced Atatürk's bold vision of
modernity, separation of religion and state, and democracy, the overall transition from an agrarian, traditional, and relatively poor society
hasn't been easy. How could it be otherwise, given the nation's size
(larger than Texas) and the distance to travel? And, despite truly
impressive advances on many fronts, there's still work to be done, as
Brussels has pointed out, to meet the high political, economic, and
legal standards set by the EU, a process that will take a minimum of
ten years, and possibly longer.

In its October 2004 report on Turkey's progress toward EU accession, the Commission of the European Communities took note of many
positive steps since its last report in 2002, including enacting political
reforms, increasing civilian control over the powerful military,
strengthening the judiciary, adopting anti-corruption measures, abol-
ishing the death penalty, ending the ban on the use of Kurdish and
other minority languages, and lifting the state of emergency. On this
basis, the commission recommended to Europe's leaders that "accession negotiations" be opened.

At the same time, the report found that: (i) "corruption remains a
serious problem in almost all areas of the economy and public affairs";

(ii) "non-Muslim religious communities continue to experience difficulties connected with legal personality, property rights, training of clergy, schools, and internal management"*; (iii) "the situation of women is still unsatisfactory ... discrimination and violence against women, including 'honor killings,' remain major problems"; and (iv) "there are still considerable restrictions (in cultural rights), in particular in the area of broadcasting and education in minority languages."

Turkish leaders are clearly determined to meet the stringent criteria for admission imposed by the EU.

For Europe, Turkey's membership would mean many things.

First, it would formally extend Europe's borders to the Middle East, specifically to Iran, Iraq, and Syria. The implications of this one fact alone are staggering.

It would also extend those frontiers to the Caucasus and Central Asia. As a result, Europe is likely to be drawn deeper into thorny issues that until now have been largely kept at arm's length, including the Turkish-Armenian dispute and the domestic instability in Georgia, as Turkey shares borders with both Armenia and Georgia.

Second, on the day of formal accession, Turkey would likely be the single most populous country in the EU, giving it considerable influence under the power-sharing arrangement.

Currently, Germany, with 82 million inhabitants, is the largest nation, but its median age is just under forty and it faces negative population growth, while an estimated 70 percent of Turkey's population is under the age of thirty. Thus, from nearly 70 million current inhabitants, its population could reach as high as 90 million over the next few decades.

Third, it would end the notion of the EU as a so-called "Christian club," since more than 99 percent of Turkey's population is Muslim. Indeed, the current prime minister, Recep Tayyip Erdogan, a devout Muslim, leads a political movement, the Justice and Development Party (AKP), which is far more sympathetic to religious values than many of his secular predecessors, though he insists there is no hidden agenda lurking in the wings.

---

* The concern expressed by the commission was not directed at the status of the Jewish community, but of other minority religious communities, including the Greek Orthodox Church.

Fourth, Turkey's current per capita gross domestic product is less than one-third the average for the twenty-five EU member nations, which suggests that for some years to come after membership, Turkey would be a net recipient of EU funds. (Bulgaria and Romania, slated to enter the EU in 2007, are in quite similar positions.) At the same time, Turkey's vast market and economic dynamism mean that European companies will find in it ever increasing business opportunities, and Turkey's youthful population could, in theory at least, provide much-needed workers for Europe's rapidly aging societies.

Fifth, it would finally end Europe's longstanding ambivalence toward Turkey. On the one hand, Turkey has been a NATO member since 1952, as well as a member of the Council of Europe and the Organization for Security and Cooperation in Europe (OSCE). Yet Europe has in the past shown reluctance to open itself fully to Turkey, with some nations attempting to hide behind others in the hope that they themselves would not be accused of blocking full entry, while in fact seeking precisely that.

One striking change in recent years has been the position of Greece. Previously, it could be counted on to oppose Turkey's entry into the EU. No longer. Athens has reversed course, arguing that having Turkey in the EU makes far more sense for achieving calm in the Aegean Sea, resolution of the Cyprus standoff, and containment of Islamic fundamentalism than having Turkey forced to fend for itself outside the EU's borders.

And sixth, Europe would once again be challenged on internal migration issues, just as occurred with the recent accession of the ten newest members, only more so given Turkey's size and relative economic position. When will Turkish workers and their families enjoy free movement within the EU? And when that happens, what will be the social impact on the countries where they settle?

Let's remember that the invitation to open membership talks, scheduled to begin in October 2005, does not itself guarantee a positive outcome. There are those in Europe who strenuously oppose Turkey's entry, pushing instead for a "privileged partnership." They're not likely to give up the battle anytime soon.

Should the German Christian Democratic Party return to power in the next national elections, for instance, the current German position strongly favoring Turkey's entry is almost certain to be reversed. In neighboring Austria, there isn't much enthusiasm for Turkey's admission, either. Surveys of voter opinion in other countries reveal a mixed picture. If the issue is put to a referendum, as President Jacques Chirac has proposed for France, at the end of the membership talks, no one can predict the outcome. But were that referendum held today, two-thirds of the electorate would vote against, according to a poll published last week in a leading French newspaper.

Suffice it to say that there's unease in some quarters surrounding what is euphemistically referred to as the "values" or "cultural" issue, or, to put it more bluntly, the religious question. The perceived difficulty of integrating Muslim migrants into Europe, including many Turks who came to Germany as guest workers forty years ago and stayed, as well as growing fear of Islamic radicalism, fuels this thinking.

A symbol of opposition has been former French president Valéry Giscard d'Estaing, who, in a widely quoted column in *Le Figaro* two years ago, declared that Turkey's admission to the EU "would be the end of Europe." He went on to note:

> The European convention sought to define the foundation of what brings us together: the cultural legacy of ancient Greece and Rome, the religious heritage which infused European life, the creative zeal of the Renaissance, the philosophy of the Enlightenment, the contribution of rational and scientific thought. None of these elements was shared by Turkey.

Chris Patten, the EU's outgoing external affairs commissioner, rejects the argument:

> The proposition that Europe can be defined by religion is a false one, not to mention dangerous. In many ways the EU is a reaction against the idea that we can define ourselves by religion or ethnicity.

For other nations in the Muslim world, the example of Turkey formally joining Europe could be salutary. It challenges Professor Samuel Huntington's thesis of the "clash of civilizations." It underlines the tangible benefits of embracing democratic reforms, a market economy, and human rights protections. And it could eventually spur the nations of Central Asia with close historical, linguistic, and political ties to Turkey, including Azerbaijan, Kazakhstan, Turkmenistan, and Uzbekistan, to move closer to Europe through the "Turkish connection."

For the United States, Turkey's accession to the EU has been a longtime foreign policy goal. Although publicly rebuked by President Chirac for interfering in Europe's internal affairs, President George W. Bush has affirmed America's interest in seeing Brussels take the leap and open membership talks with Ankara.

Earlier this year, President Bush said:

America believes that, as a European power, Turkey belongs in the European Union. Turkey's membership would also be a critical advance in relations between the Muslim world and the West, because it is part of both.... Fifteen years ago, an artificial line that divided Europe— drawn at Yalta—was erased. And now this continent has the opportunity to erase another artificial division—by including Turkey in the future of Europe.

Of course, Washington is gambling that Turkey's traditional pro-American posture wouldn't be weakened inside a Europe where some member nations are determined to build up the regional body as a counterweight to what's seen as America's unchecked global power and influence.

In the Turkish Jewish community, with which the American Jewish Committee has a very close affiliation, last week's news from Brussels will be enthusiastically received. The 22,000-member community has long taken the view that Turkey's future anchored in Western institutions is the best guarantee of national security, stability, and prosperity.

And, in Israel, the EU's announcement will also be welcomed. Israel has publicly declared its support for Turkey's accession. Even though, like Washington, Jerusalem runs the risk of slippage in its thriving bilateral ties with Ankara should Turkey's foreign policy become "Europeanized," it believes the overall benefits for Turkey and the eastern Mediterranean make the risk well worth taking.

In a recent American Jewish Committee visit to Turkey, the European Union was issue number one (and two and three) on the agenda of government officials, including the prime minister and foreign minister. The October EU Commission report had just been released, and the ensuing two months were seen as the last chance to persuade European leaders to do the "right thing" at their fateful meeting in Brussels on December 16–17.

Turkish leaders view the AJC as important to the political equation. Not only have we been consistently regarded as a steady and reliable voice for the Turkish-American relationship, but also, because of AJC's wide-ranging contacts throughout Europe, the Turks have counted on our support when we meet with French, German, Greek, and other European leaders. Lacking a well-organized diaspora community, they've looked to American Jews to fulfill that role. They've had a rather good case to make.

Jews have lived in what is today Turkey since the fourth century B.C.E.

When the Jews of Spain were faced with the Inquisition during the rule of King Ferdinand and Queen Isabella, the leader of the sprawling Ottoman Empire, Sultan Beyazit II, issued a decree welcoming the refugees. The Jews were treated well, and their communal life flourished throughout the empire.

To mark the 500th anniversary of the decree, a Turkish Jew wrote an effusive poem entitled *Canto in Praise of the Noble Turks*. Here's an excerpt:

We were ejected,
by all rejected,
only by Turks respected.
You asked of us nothing;
we, in turn, demanded nothing;
together we lived loving

and mutually respected.
Oh, blessed Turkish brethren:
We were ejected,
by all rejected,
only by Turks respected.

Fast-forward to the Second World War. Turkey adopted a position of neutrality. As was the case with other neutral nations, its history during this period was not uncomplicated. But a number of Jewish scholars and artists fleeing the Nazis found refuge in Istanbul and, it should be added, contributed significantly to Turkish intellectual and cultural life.

There were a few Turkish diplomats, among them the intrepid Selahattin Ülkümen, who risked their own lives to save Jews. Ülkümen, the thirty-year-old Turkish consul general on the Nazi-occupied Greek island of Rhodes, rescued several dozen Jews, for which he was later honored by Yad Vashem. He paid a high price for his courage, however. His residence was strafed by the Nazis, and his wife was killed.

And it's noteworthy that, until 1944, Angelo Giuseppe Roncalli, who later became the widely admired Pope John XXIII, was the Apostolic Delegate in Turkey, where he assisted in protecting Jews. At the same time, the Jewish Agency, headquartered in then Palestine, mounted major operations from Istanbul to help Jews in Nazi-occupied Europe.

Although Turkey voted in 1947 against the UN Partition Plan, two years later it became the first predominantly Muslim nation to recognize the fledgling State of Israel.

In the 1990s, the bilateral relationship took off in dramatic fashion, including defense cooperation, joint military exercises, counterterrorism measures, intelligence-sharing, a free trade agreement, and tourism. And when earthquakes killed more than 20,000 Turks in 1999, Israeli rescue teams and field hospitals were among the first on the scene. Subsequently, Israel, with the help of the American Jewish Committee, built a complete village in Adapazari for earthquake survivors who had lost their homes. More recently still, Turkey, a water-rich country, has signed an accord with Israel to sell much-needed water to the Jewish state.

Today, Israel regards its links with Turkey as vitally important and mutually beneficial. Moreover, it helps make the case to other predominantly Muslim countries that there shouldn't be any obstacles to establishing ties with Israel.

During our most recent visit to Ankara, there was concern in Jerusalem over statements by Turkish leaders critical of Israeli actions in Gaza. In addition, our visit came against the backdrop of Seymour Hersh's widely discussed article in the *New Yorker*, claiming that Israel was training Kurdish independence fighters in northern Iraq, a red flag for Turkey. Israel categorically denied the allegations.

In our sessions with the prime minister and foreign minister, these and related issues came up, including Turkish anxiety about Israel's security barrier. I'm not sure we achieved a full meeting of the minds, but it was clear that our interlocutors, mindful of the priority we attach to robust Turkish-Israeli ties, were eager to reaffirm the importance of the link, their desire to help advance the peace process, and their plans to visit Israel sooner rather than later.

Indeed, since our trip, we've been advised by Turkish officials that the foreign minister may travel to Israel this month, and the prime minister a few months later.

And not least, Turkish Jewry, though diminished in size, largely due to aliyah, continues to prosper and enjoy a full communal life, including keeping alive the Judeo-Spanish language of Ladino. Anti-Semitism exists, but is not regarded as a major threat, according to communal leaders.* What is a threat—and not only to Jews—is terrorism.

Just over a year ago, four deadly terror attacks in Istanbul, including two targeting the Neve Shalom and Beth Israel synagogues, were another reminder of just how serious the threat is. These were not the first such attacks, either. In 1986, the Neve Shalom synagogue, the largest in Istanbul, was attacked by Palestinian terrorists. Twenty-two

---

* To enhance understanding of Judaism in Turkey, the Turkish Jewish community and the American Jewish Committee collaborated on a project to publish a Turkish-language edition of AJC's *Children of Abraham: An Introduction to Judaism for Muslims* by Reuven Firestone. The book was released prior to our visit in October 2004.

worshipers were killed during a Shabbat service. Six years later, a planned terrorist attack against the same synagogue was thwarted by alert security personnel.

The authorities' response in November 2003 was immediate, and the official statements emphasized that an attack on a synagogue was an attack on Turkey.

Our visit to Istanbul was timed to coincide with the rededication ceremony of Neve Shalom. In addition to presenting a Torah scroll, made possible through the generosity of Ambassador Alfred Moses, AJC's honorary president, at the Shabbat service preceding the ceremony by two days, we wanted to express our solidarity with the Jewish community and our gratitude to Turkish officials for their steadfastness.

Particularly heartwarming for us was the presence of many Turkish dignitaries, as well as representatives of other faith communities, including the Greek Orthodox ecumenical patriarch, with whom we had met the day before in his Istanbul offices.

Also, we were deeply moved that the U.S. ambassador to Turkey and his family made a special trip from Ankara for the Shabbat service, and that the U.S. consul general in Istanbul attended both the service and the rededication event.

I only wish that diplomats from countries other than the U.S., Israel, and Britain had been present, just as I would have hoped to see other Jewish organizations from abroad stand with Turkish Jews at this emotion-laden moment in their history.

Before ending, I must put in a plug for Istanbul, the city with one foot in Europe, the other in Asia. It's unquestionably among the world's most spectacular and intriguing metropolises. In fact, the very same adjectives could be applied to the entire country.

Not only is Turkey a sightseer's paradise, but it's also a fascinating showcase of a nation's effort to find the right balance between respect for its heritage and the promise of the future.

Eighty years after Atatürk first charted that future direction, Turkey has now taken a giant step forward. The history of Europe will never again be the same.

Letter from Thessaloniki
January 27, 2005

This is the story of a city that most assuredly deserves telling. Somehow, for too many Jews, it seems to have fallen through the cracks of Jewish history, though the city was at the epicenter of that history for centuries.

Named for the sister of Alexander the Great and variously referred to as Thessaloniki, Salonika, Saloniki, and Salonica, it was at the crossroads of great civilizations—principally the Hellenistic, Roman, Byzantine, and Ottoman—for much of its history. Indeed, one could argue that the fault line between East and West ran through the city and the surrounding region, known as Macedonia.

The first Jews, probably hailing from Alexandria, Egypt, settled there before the Common Era and came to be known as Romaniote Jews.

The Apostle Paul, according to the Acts of the Apostles, preached on three occasions to the Jews of Thessaloniki around the year 50 C.E., perhaps, scholars believe, at a synagogue called Etz Ahaim, "Tree of Life."

The noted rabbi and writer Benjamin of Tudela (Spain) visited Thessaloniki in the twelfth century and wrote in his travelogue:

> After a two-day sea voyage, we arrive at Thessaloniki, a big coastal town, built by Selefkos, one of Alexander's four heirs. Five hundred Jews live here, headed by Rabbi Samuel and his sons, well-known for their scholarship. Rabbis Sabetal, Elias, and Michael also live there as well as other exiled Jews who are specialized craftsmen.

It is the story of a city where the first Ashkenazi Jews, fleeing persecution in Central Europe, arrived in the fourteenth and fifteenth centuries.

An estimated 15,000–20,000 Jews from Spain settled there to escape the Spanish Inquisition, thanks to the warm welcome accorded them by the Ottoman Empire, the ruling power from 1430.

Jews from other European countries, including Portugal—which, following the Spanish example, in 1496 ordered the Jews either to convert to Catholicism or leave—also found both haven and opportunity in Thessaloniki.

In 1537, the poet Samuel Ushkue of Ferrara (Italy) famously described Thessaloniki as the "City and Mother of Israel."

It is the story of a city, second only to Safed, where Kabbalah was studied with particular fervor and intensity, and where Solomon Alkabetz, who wrote "*Lekha Dodi*," the beautiful Shabbat hymn, spent time.

As many as 30,000 Jews lived in Thessaloniki by the start of the seventeenth century, fifty years before the first Jews, also of Sephardic origin and fleeing the Portuguese Inquisition from Recife, Brazil, set foot in what is today the United States.

Shabbatai Zevi of Smyrna (today Izmir, Turkey), the self-proclaimed seventeenth-century messiah and king of Israel, attracted as many as 300 Jewish families to his religious bandwagon in this city. To save his life, Zevi converted to Islam, and his followers, who came to be known as Donmehs (apostates), became a curious Muslim-Jewish hybrid.

It is the story of a city whose Jewish community counted as many as thirty synagogues, mostly named for the towns and regions where Jews originally hailed from (e.g., Provencia, Castilla, Aragon, etc.), and became a model of Jewish communal life, with centers of religious study, schools, a hospital, orphanages, an asylum for the mentally disabled, and an old-age home, as well as many newspapers, including the first to be introduced in the city, *El Lunar*, published in Ladino, in 1864.

Ladino, the Judeo-Spanish language, was widely spoken after 1492 (Greek was the lingua franca for Jews until then) and helped define the overwhelmingly Spanish character of the Jewish community right up to the twentieth century.

Jews came to be an innovative and dynamic, if not dominant, force in the commercial and cultural life of the city.

The bustling port was closed on Shabbat and Jewish holidays, given the number of Jews who worked there, principally as stevedores.

Interestingly, many Jewish stevedores from Thessaloniki who immigrated to Palestine played a leading role in developing the port of Haifa.

In a display of interfaith coexistence that shouldn't be forgotten, least of all these days, Jews, Muslims, and Orthodox Christians lived in relative harmony and mutual respect, though not without the occasional flare-ups, especially by the Christians against the Jews.

It is the story of a city where, in 1900, the Jews numbered approximately 80,000 (of a total population of 173,000) and, according to *Jewish Heritage in Greece*, in addition to thirty synagogues, "there were ten (Jewish) clubs, a college, four high schools, and fifteen grade schools."

At that time, Greeks, Turks, Albanians, Bulgarians, Armenians, and Jews all gave the city a bustling and polyglot atmosphere, further enhanced by the popularity of several French schools, but its unique character was about to be challenged. In a book on the city, family life and the historical backdrop, *Farewell to Salonica*, Leon Sciaky, a Jew of Spanish origin, poignantly captured the moment:

> The century was drawing to a close. Stealthily the West was creeping in, trying to lure the East with her wonders. Almost inaudible as yet was her whisper. She dangled before our dazzled eyes the witchery of her science and the miracle of her inventions. We caught a glimpse of her brilliance, and timidly listened to the song of the siren. Like country folk at a banquet, we felt humble and awkward in our ways. But vaguely we sensed the coldness of her glitter and the price of her wooing. With uneasiness we gathered tighter the folds of our homespun mantles around our shoulders, enjoying their softness and warmth, and finding them good.

It was in Thessaloniki that Mustafa Kemal, later known as Atatürk, was born, and where the movement of Young Turks developed to challenge what they viewed as the authoritarian and arbitrary rule of the Ottomans, eventually ousting Sultan Abdul Hamid II.

Zionism developed strong roots that came out into the open after the end of Ottoman rule in 1912, since until then Jews were hesitant to speak publicly about a Jewish state while the Ottomans controlled both Palestine and Thessaloniki. David Ben-Gurion, Itzhak Ben-Zvi (Israel's president from 1952 to 1963), and Ze'ev Jabotinsky were among the early Zionists to visit and come away impressed by the vitality and sophisticated organizational structure of the Jewish community.

Thessaloniki was formally incorporated into Greece in 1913. King George, the Greek monarch at the time, made a point of affirming that the Jews, like all minorities, would be treated as full and equal citizens of the state.

In the interwar period, Jews for the first time began to leave in large numbers, as many as 30,000 departing. The city's economic difficulties and the devastation wrought by a fire of unknown origin in 1917 that destroyed much of the infrastructure—including virtually all of the synagogues—and left 50,000 Jews homeless, contributed to the exodus. Jews headed for Palestine, the United States, other European countries, and South America.

In 1931, false rumors circulated that Jews were conspiring with Bulgarian nationalists to separate Macedonia from Greece, resulting in physical violence against Jews and an outcry from extremists that Jews were not "pure Greeks" and therefore could not be trusted. Hundreds of Jews fled their homes, and some Torah scrolls were desecrated, according to a report prepared for the American Jewish Committee by an eyewitness in the city. Greek officials, led by Prime Minister Eleftherios Venizelos, promptly condemned the attacks and sought to restore order.

On the eve of the Second World War, Thessaloniki still had a Jewish community numbering 50,000 and was considered to be the world's greatest center of Sephardic Jewish culture and civilization.

It is the story of a city that, in 1940–41, contributed many of the nearly 13,000 Jews who fought in the Greek army, 343 as officers, against the Nazi invaders and their allies. More than 500 were killed in battle.

Thessaloniki was occupied by the Nazis on April 9, 1941, and severe restrictions were immediately placed on the Jews.

The Nazis attacked not only the living but also the dead. They destroyed the vast Jewish cemetery dating back two millennia, looting it and using the headstones for construction purposes.

In 1942, all Jewish men ages 18 to 45 were conscripted by the Nazis into forced labor in Greece and then released, though only temporarily, when the Jewish community paid an enormous ransom. To date, despite repeated approaches to the German government, the Thessaloniki Jewish community has been unable to receive restitution of the funds. The German position has been that all wartime claims with Greece were settled in the 1960s. The Jewish community has now taken the matter to the Greek judicial system and a decision from an Athens court is expected within the next few months. Whether the German government would recognize any court decision in favor of the community remains to be seen.

Shortly thereafter, in a matter of months in 1943, 46,000 Jews from Thessaloniki—overwhelmingly the descendents of those Jews exiled from Spain almost exactly 450 years earlier—were deported in cattle cars to Auschwitz-Birkenau.

Only 1,950 Jews survived. In other words, 96 percent of the community was wiped out, the highest fatality rate of any major Jewish community in Nazi-occupied Europe.

In Greece, a few brave individuals, most notably Archbishop Damaskinos and the Athens police chief, Angelos Evert, sought valiantly to protect Greek Jews against deportation. In a remarkable letter to the Greek prime minister, the archbishop wrote: "Our Holy Faith recognizes no distinction, superiority or inferiority, based on race or religion, holding as doctrine that 'There is neither Jew nor Greek,' condemning therefore any tendency to create any discrimination or racial or religious distinction."

After the war, some survivors struggled to rebuild their lives in their cherished city, despite innumerable obstacles, while others preferred to move on, mostly to Palestine.

Those Jews who remained gradually reestablished a semblance of Jewish communal life, but had to cope on a daily basis with an overwhelming and wrenching sense of loss. Where once there had been pulsating Jewish energy in every nook and cranny of the city, after the war the community was defined above all by empty spaces, recurring nightmares, irretrievable loss, lingering fear, and only the occasional dim echo of glorious times past.

It is the story of a city where, in 1997, a striking public memorial, the first of its kind in Greece, was dedicated to the victims of the Shoah in the presence of the Greek president, Konstantinos Stefanopoulos, and other dignitaries, including a delegation from the American Jewish Committee. The monument has since been defaced more than once.

King Juan Carlos of Spain visited a year later and was astonished to encounter Jews who continued to speak Ladino 500 years after their forced exile. As a memento, the community head gave the king a silver box engraved with a key, a reminder that those Jews forced to leave Spain kept the keys to their homes and passed them on from generation to generation.

Some 1,000 Jews currently live in Thessaloniki, somehow valiantly managing to maintain a school, two synagogues, a home for the elderly, a small museum, a cemetery, and, above all, a proud heritage.

It is the story of a city where the Jewish community has engaged in protracted on-again, off-again negotiations with governmental authorities for compensation for the land once occupied by the vast Jewish cemetery destroyed by the Nazis and now used as part of a local university. Resolution of this problem is long overdue.

There was a telling comment about the city from Professor Ari Goldman of Columbia University, writing in the *International Herald Tribune* last year about his shock at the attitude toward Jews he encountered traveling in Europe: "After all the hatred I've heard from European academics, I would like to bring a few here to Salonika to show them what Jews without political power look like."

Today, while attention is focused on the dramatic gathering of world leaders and camp survivors in Auschwitz, Greece marked its second annual observance of a national Holocaust Remembrance Day. The German foreign minister, Joschka Fischer, was the keynote speaker and struck just the right tone, and not for the first time, I might add. Again and again, he's proved himself to be an unusually good friend of the Jewish people. The American Jewish Committee, which strongly supported the Greek Jewish community's effort to have the day designated, was represented at the memorial events in Thessaloniki, as were many Greek dignitaries and diplomats from the United States, Germany, Spain, France, Canada, and, of course, Israel.

As I scanned the audience in Thessaloniki, regrettably, I didn't see any of those European academics Ari Goldman referred to. I can't say I was surprised, though. Their intellectual and moral certitudes might have been called into question, and we wouldn't want that to happen, now would we?

In the final analysis, the wartime tragedy that befell Thessaloniki is a permanent reminder of the ultimate evil perpetrated by the Nazis and their collaborators. To think of what was lost is to be overcome by a crushing weight, a deep and dizzying descent into a hellish mix of grief and rage.

But we must struggle to remember that it is also the story of a city that stood as a towering symbol of the glory that was Jewish civilization here for 2,000 years. And yes, the determination of a tiny cluster of Jews—the heirs of that tradition—to find the strength to carry on, to keep the flame lit against all the odds, in this sparkling city on the Aegean Sea, cannot help but serve as an inspiration.

Letter from a Centrist
February 28, 2005

There was an eerie familiarity to the story: Israelis getting together at a nightclub on a Friday evening and once again being targeted by the purveyors of the cult of death and destruction. The attack on the Dolphinarium, another beachside Tel Aviv club, also took place on a Friday evening, not quite four years ago.

This time it was Islamic Jihad. Or was it Hamas? Or maybe Hezbollah? Or possibly the Al-Aksa Martyrs Brigade?

Did it have a Syrian angle? Or possibly Iranian? Or was it homegrown?

In a way, these are all distinctions without a difference. What these groups share in common is far more important—they seek the destruction of the State of Israel, one murdered Israeli at a time.

And since they strive for Israel's annihilation, they seek to sabotage any peace process that could, at the end of the day, acknowledge Israel's permanence in the region, whatever its final borders.

This latest attack, coming after a brief lull, presents a major challenge—actually two—to the new Palestinian Authority leadership. First, their reaction not only in word but especially in deed will say a great deal about their true colors. Moreover, it represents another reminder that for Mahmoud Abbas to succeed, he will have no choice but to confront the terrorist groups in his midst. He cannot hope to move ahead without dismantling the terrorist infrastructure, and he cannot delude himself—or others—into believing that a *hudna*, a temporary ceasefire, will do the trick. No one suggests it will be easy for him, but there is no alternative. In the process, he will have the support of outsiders with a stake in his success, including the expected pledges of financial assistance from an international donor conference hosted by British Prime Minister Tony Blair in London this week.

There are those on the Israeli right, and among its friends abroad, who are now quick to write off any peace prospects as foolishly illusory at best, potentially fatal at worst. They point to Friday's attack as one reason why. I don't dismiss their fears—far from it—but I'm not so quick to rule out the possibility of progress.

On Israeli national security matters, I've always been stubbornly centrist. There are, of course, centrists and centrists. One kind is simply frozen on the fifty-yard line, unable or unwilling to make a decision, like the fellow who finds himself equidistant from two glasses of water and dies of thirst. And then there's the centrist who believes that the ideological purists residing on the left and right possess, at best, partial truths, and that the answer lies somewhere in between.

That's why I admire Prime Minister Ariel Sharon. Improbable as it may seem to those who have made a career of demonizing Sharon as the poster politician of the right, he has come to define the Israeli political center. To his credit, he has questioned some of his own most cherished earlier assumptions and reached the conclusion that, for the sake of maintaining a Jewish and democratic state, the country must make painful territorial adjustments. In his strategic analysis, there are no risk-free policy options. The choices are not between good and bad, but rather between bad and worse.

While some on the left will gloat, arguing that Sharon has finally awakened to the realities they've been speaking about for years, it's not that simple.

If the right lived in the la-la land of a Greater Israel, in which Israel would somehow maintain forever its presence in the territories while preserving its Jewish and democratic character, and, at the same time, enjoy unwavering American support, the left wasn't any more rooted in reality. In their dreamworld, Oslo had essentially brought to an end the culture of hate against the Jewish state and ushered in a new Middle East, with Israel as a charter member.

Sharon has grasped the flaws in both camps' thinking. He's quite literally put his life on the line to chart a new course that, spoken or not, essentially embraces the logic of a two-state solution, while refusing to be seduced prematurely by the siren song of an end to hostilities, when none has yet occurred.

Of course, what offers us a glimmer of hope these days, above all, is the change in Palestinian leadership. After all, if there is the oft-discussed window of opportunity, it has largely been due to Yasir Arafat's demise and the election of Abbas. The other key players, including Prime Minister Sharon, President George W. Bush, President Hosni Mubarak of Egypt, and King Abdullah of Jordan, remain the same (though the winds of democratic change may have begun to have a positive effect on the attitudes of some of the regional players).

Now this would seem obvious, yet it is anything but. In a perfect world, the many people who kept Arafat politically alive to the very end, practically genuflecting before their kaffiyeh-clad hero, even after it became crystal clear that this father of modern-day terrorism had no interest in peace and every interest in armed struggle, should offer an apology—at least those among them who purport to be on the side of a peaceful settlement of the conflict.

The fact of the matter is that, as far as Arafat was concerned, both Prime Minister Sharon and President Bush got it right. They reached the inescapable conclusion, after the laudable peace efforts of Prime Minister Ehud Barak and President Bill Clinton, that Arafat would never be part of the solution, only part of the problem, so it was time to stop coddling him and instead start marginalizing him. The sooner Arafat was sidelined, they reasoned, the greater the likelihood of restarting peace talks.

In the meantime, Israel and the U.S. would hold fast against those elected officials, UN bureaucrats, media commentators, and members of the intelligentsia who wanted to give Arafat just one more chance, or gloss over his historic failure at Camp David, or ignore his complicity in the *Karine-A* affair, or pretend that his signature wasn't found on documents authorizing funds for those who committed terrorist acts against Israelis, or look the other way when *Forbes* in 2003 listed him sixth among the world's wealthiest kings, queens, and despots, or argue that, as the Palestinian leader, he was the only game in town.

What explains this Arafat "defense industry"? Is it, as some in the Jewish community believe, nothing more than old-fashioned anti-Semitism, which created a virtual cult around the Jewish state's principal foe? Is it the romanticizing of a "revolutionary" leader, who, for some inexplicable reason, is deemed off-limits to mainstream scrutiny or criticism? Or is it simply wholesale political prostitution, a kowtowing to the Arab world for political, commercial, or personal gain?

And if Arafat's life didn't offer enough reasons to raise questions, then surely his last days and death did. In a way, he died as he lived—in mystery, duplicity, and contradiction.

Does anyone know the cause of his death? If not, why not? Why did French authorities list Jerusalem as his birthplace on the death certificate when Arafat is known to have been born in Cairo? How much money did he have at the time of death? Why were all these funds everywhere but where they should have been—stashed in overseas banks rather than invested in Palestinian schools, clinics, and housing? What deal was struck between Suha Arafat, referred to by some as the "widow of opportunity," and Palestinian leaders regarding the bank accounts and allocation of funds?

These are not simply idle or academic questions, meant to beat a "dead" horse. Something went terribly wrong. Critical judgment in too many circles was suspended.

And it's not as if the situation has entirely corrected itself, either.

I recall the year 2000, when Clinton and Barak were eagerly seeking an agreement with Arafat. The contours of the deal are well known. The point is that the anti-Israel crowd was on automatic pilot and, therefore, totally blind and deaf to the fact that Israel was offering a two-state solution, partition of Jerusalem, and settlement of the refugee question. To sit in the UN in the fall of 2000, as I did, was to believe that Israel adamantly refused to consider any compromise whatsoever.

Now fast-forward to February 2005.

Next month, we'll see whether the UN Human Rights Commission, which begins its annual six-week session, continues merrily along the familiar path of singling out Israel for every alleged sin on earth, irrespective of the rapidly changing facts on the ground, while blithely ignoring truly egregious human rights violations in countries with more diplomatic muscle than Israel. And, if this is the case, we'll also have the chance to observe whether the European Union member states find the moral and political spine to stop going along with this charade, rather than endorsing it or hiding behind abstentions, which they seek to portray in hagiographic terms. Once again, France will be in the limelight—the same France that, while lately seeking to bolster bilateral ties with Israel, has managed to block the EU from adding Hezbollah to its terrorism list and went way over the top in its handling of Arafat's last days in Paris.

In the meantime, we already have the first reaction to current events from those who claim to seek nothing more than peace in the region, but can't overcome their natural instinct to take a potshot at Israel whenever possible.

Take the World Council of Churches. At a time when Prime Minister Sharon has formed a coalition with Shimon Peres and the dovish Labor Party, risked his political career on an early withdrawal from the Gaza Strip and four settlements in the northern West Bank, shifted the security barrier closer to the 1949 Armistice Line, is engaged in productive talks with Mahmoud Abbas, just released hundreds of Palestinian prisoners as a goodwill gesture, ended the practice of retaliatory house demolitions, been described as a partner for peace by no less than President Mubarak, been invited to visit Tunisia, and faces potentially violent dissent from Israelis opposed to what they see as dangerous—and unilateral—concessions to the Palestinians, what did the Geneva-based World Council of Churches decide to do at its Central Committee meeting earlier this month?

The WCC, representing 340 churches, denominations, and church fellowships in over 100 countries, with a combined membership of 400 million, endorsed the decision last summer of the Presbyterian Church (USA) to initiate "a process of phased, selective divestment from multinational companies involved in the occupation" and urged member bodies with investment funds to consider "economic pressure" against Israel.

By the way—in case anyone is wondering—the WCC did not take up the timely issue of Syria's continued occupation of neighboring Lebanon, or its suspected involvement in the assassination of Rafiq Hariri, the nation's former prime minister, though it was meeting at the time of his murder, much less call for economic pressure against Syria. And, needless to say, it couldn't endorse the Presbyterian Church (USA) decision to initiate "a process of phased, selective divestment against multinational companies involved in the occupation" of Lebanon, because that church had never adopted such a position against Syria.

The differences between the Israeli and Syrian "occupations" ought to be abundantly clear, but they are apparently not to the WCC constituency. While democratic Israel took possession of the West Bank and Gaza Strip in a war for its very survival, and has shown its readiness more than once to negotiate the decades-long dispute over land with the Palestinians, autocratic Syria remains in Lebanon to control its destiny, send otherwise unemployed Syrians to find work, ply the lucrative drug trade, and use Hezbollah as a proxy to keep the pressure on Israel.

Let's see whether the UN Human Rights Commission surprises us for once and recognizes the new Israeli-Palestinian reality, or, like the World Council of Churches, reverts to form. Any bets?

But the key arena to watch is what actually happens on the ground between Israelis and Palestinians, and the supporting roles played by the United States, Europe, Egypt, Jordan, and other interested parties.

It's clear, even with the best of will, that the road ahead will resemble a minefield.

If one assumes for a moment his commitment to living side-by-side with Israel, Mahmoud Abbas will have to contend with those terrorist-sponsoring countries and violent groups that have no interest in seeing any peace accord with Israel. Moreover, he will have to deal with the consequences of decades of the teaching of incitement and hate against Israel and the Jewish people, whether in mosques, schools, refugee camps, or the media. And he'll have to prepare the Palestinian people—something Arafat, of course, never did—for the compromises necessary to achieve peace with Israel, such as abandoning the so-called "right of return," accepting the fact that no Israeli government, for compelling security reasons, can accept final borders along the 1949 Armistice Line, and agreeing to a final end to the conflict.

And Israel faces enormous hurdles as well. Internally, while a clear majority of the Israeli people supports Sharon's approach, a determined minority can create one headache after another for the Israeli leader. The atmosphere is already highly charged. Gaza settlers compare themselves to victims of the Shoah. Rabbis urge soldiers to disobey orders to remove settlers. Claims are heard that Sharon is a traitor and will bring on a second Holocaust. Mass demonstrations are planned to prevent dismantling of the settlements.

Meanwhile, some Palestinians are already declaring that Israel's planned withdrawal from Gaza reflects a Palestinian triumph and an Israeli defeat, similar to what Hezbollah claimed after Israeli forces were withdrawn from southern Lebanon. Whether Egypt controls its border with Gaza and effectively prevents the smuggling of weapons remains a major question. The future of Gaza, after Israeli withdrawal, is difficult to predict. Will it emerge as a Hamas-controlled terrorist mini-state, or will it begin to focus less on the eradication of Israel and more on the education of its children? What success will the PA have in establishing security control in those areas for which it has responsibility?

While the term "secure and defensible borders" is often used to describe Israel's needs in any peace process, it's far easier said than done, given the small physical space, topographical challenges, range of available and prospective weapons, and tricky neighborhood—factors that are often inadequately appreciated in the international community. (The threat posed by Iran requires separate discussion.) At the same time, we should never forget, history has amply demonstrated the remarkable skill, strength, and adaptive capacity of the Israel Defense Forces.

Before closing, let me go into my own la-la land for just a moment and offer what some may consider an off-the-wall thought.

What if the Palestinian Authority announced that it understands the religious connection between, say, the few hundred Jews in Hebron and the Jewish faith and would welcome a Jewish presence in a new Palestinian state? Whether they would stay is another matter, but wouldn't it serve as an important test of any Palestinian state's commitment to pluralism, not to mention respect for Jewish biblical tradition, something Arafat regularly pooh-poohed? And why is it accepted as perfectly normal that Israel has a sizable Arab minority and is judged, in part, by its treatment of that minority, while it is assumed that any new Palestinian state will be totally *Judenrein*, free of Jews, even as it controls some of the holiest sites in Judaism, to which Jews have been spiritually and, when possible, physically attached for millennia?

As we go forward, to state the obvious, the U.S. role will remain absolutely indispensable, since no other nation has shown the same willingness to stand by Israel through thick and thin, and, at the same time, no other nation has the same clout with such key Arab players as Egypt, Jordan, and Saudi Arabia.

The fledgling discussions about a closer relationship between Israel and the European Union, and Israel and NATO, are also highly significant and bear watching. Both frameworks—the EU and NATO—offer intriguing possibilities for anchoring Israel more firmly in key international institutions.

And the larger Arab world should now step up to the plate and begin to send tangible signals of its readiness to normalize relations with Israel, following the examples of Egypt, Jordan, and Mauritania. Such action would provide a major boost by strengthening the hand of those committed to peace, while isolating those who are not. That will be the message carried by the American Jewish Committee to three Arab capitals in scheduled meetings coming up shortly.

One potential opportunity to send such a signal comes next month when the Arab League convenes in Algiers. Another chance arises shortly thereafter, should the Arab bloc and its friends decide to reconsider some of the harshly worded resolutions they ritualistically introduce each year at the UN Human Rights Commission.

Surely, this is a time that cries out for statesmanship and the daring thinking that goes along with it. Yet, as Friday's tragedy in Tel Aviv reminds us, it's also a time to ensure that wishful thinking doesn't entirely lose touch with reality.

Letter from Rome
March 28, 2005

In a way, it all began for me in this magnificent city thirty years ago to the month, so please indulge me as I take a walk down memory lane.

It was here that I started working in the Jewish world. Initially, I thought it might be the equivalent of a Peace Corps experience—two or three years devoted to helping Jews overseas before moving on to a different career track. It's now been three decades and, if ever there was another possible career track, I've long since forgotten what it was. Smitten by the experience I had in Rome, I have just kept going.

All of this was anything but predictable. I grew up in a proudly Jewish home, but full of content it wasn't. It's somehow assumed these days that a Jewish civil servant probably had a different upbringing than most other American Jews—day school, Jewish summer camp, religious training, ritual observance, Hebrew study, year in Israel, etc. In my case, it was none of the above.

I've written elsewhere about what were, for me, the earthshaking events of the early 1970s—shortly after I graduated from college—that prompted me to think more about my identity, particularly the 1973 Yom Kippur War and the Soviet Jewry movement. Indeed, it was the latter that led me to seize the opportunity to participate in an official U.S.-Soviet teachers' exchange in 1974, one of the early fruits of détente. Apart from giving me an unusual look from the ground up at a country largely off-limits to foreigners, this program afforded me the chance to meet a number of Soviet Jews eager to emigrate and, in many cases, forbidden from doing so.

During the time I was in Moscow and Leningrad, the Jews I met gave me an immersion course in courage, identity, yearning, and determination. I was also given an education in state-sponsored anti-Semitism and anti-Zionism. In addition, I came face-to-face with the power of Communist oppression and the suffocation of any vestige of intellectual or physical freedom. And I came to realize just how lucky I was that my maternal grandparents, with two small children in tow, had succeeded in leaving the Soviet Union in 1929, after experiencing twelve years of Leninist and Stalinist rule, though it would be another twelve years before they arrived in the U.S.

Nearly three months after arriving in the USSR, I was forced to leave by Soviet authorities. They weren't thrilled by my repeated efforts to look behind the facade of the Potemkin village they had so diligently constructed for the benefit of foreign visitors.

By December 1974, I was out of that nightmarish country, having lost fifteen pounds from an already thin frame and admittedly shaken by the rough nature of my expulsion. But I was also on fire. I was determined to do something. I owed it to the people I had met in the schools where I taught, in the synagogues I frequented, and in the homes I visited.

After brief stays in Norway and England, I traveled to Rome. I knew that Soviet Jews able to get out went first to Vienna and then, if they were headed for countries other than Israel, to Rome for processing. I quite literally knocked on the door of HIAS—the Hebrew Immigrant Aid Society—at their offices in Viale Regina Margherita and told the first person I met that I was a Russian-speaking American Jew who had just spent time in the USSR and was eager to assist Jews who managed to get out. To make a long story short, I was given a job as a caseworker. That job began exactly thirty years ago this month.

I was in heaven.

The work was anything but easy, but that was just fine with me. The days were long, the pressure unrelenting, and the work all the more taxing because it was almost exclusively in Russian. These Soviet Jews were, in a real sense, living betwixt and between—in a state of suspended animation—as they waited for months in a strange and wondrous land until their visas came through and they could depart to start a new life. In some cases, past criminal records or Communist Party membership made obtaining a visa, especially for the United States, difficult if not impossible. And while a few other countries, particularly Australia and Canada and, to a lesser extent, New Zealand, were theoretically open, the selection process was generally far more rigid and prolonged than for the U.S.

While waiting in Rome, the refugees were entirely dependent for their support on Jewish agencies. They were unable to work legally, unfamiliar with the local language, and uneasy about their children's loss of education. Tensions often ran high, as many would not passively accept that their fate rested entirely in the hands of others—just months or years after they had taken fate into their own hands by challenging the Soviet system in seeking to leave—and as the caseworkers, too few in number, sought to cope with an inherently difficult situation.

There were lots of surprises along the way.

For the refugees, a big surprise was the strength of the Italian Communist Party. In the mid-1970s, the PCI, as it was called, was at the peak of its power. Party offices, newspapers, posters, and flags emblazoned with the hammer and sickle were everywhere. The party, under the leadership of Enrico Berlinguer, referred to itself as Eurocommunist, implying a less doctrinaire ideology than what could be found behind the Iron Curtain or, for that matter, in the French Communist Party, which, headed by Georges Marchais, was patterned along Stalinist lines. Even so, Soviet Jews had little good to say about anything remotely connected to Communism, and could not believe that some Italians—beneficiaries of democracy, civil liberties, and a market economy—might actually be willing to chuck it all in pursuit of a Marxist utopia.

And to remind themselves of just how bad things were in the USSR, the Soviet Jews would tell jokes—the same jokes they had heard back home, only in Italy they could be told without fear of reprisal.

A couple of examples:

The *Moscow Evening News* advertised a contest for the best political joke. First prize was ten years in prison; second prize, five years; third prize, three years; and there were six honorable mentions of one year each.

Who were the first Communists in history?
Adam and Eve. They walked around naked, had one apple between them, and thought they lived in paradise.

What's meant by an exchange of opinions in the Soviet Communist Party?
It's when I come to a party meeting with my own opinion, and I leave with the party's.

What's the difference between Catholicism and Communism?
In Catholicism, there's life after death. In Communism, there's posthumous rehabilitation.

Italy, at the time, also had its neo-fascists—the Movimento Sociale Italiano, or MSI, led by Giorgio Almirante. They were essentially the ideological heirs of Benito Mussolini. Though fewer in number than the Communists (and Trotskyites, anarchists, and others on the extreme left), they were no less vocal or visible. Again, for Soviet Jews coming from a country that had been invaded by the Nazis and lost millions of its citizens, Jews and non-Jews alike, the notion that such a party could operate openly and attract support was difficult to swallow.

And there were other surprises.

For me, perhaps the biggest—and the most unexpected—was the fierce battle over the country of destination for emigrating Soviet Jews. It was waged among Israel, the United States, and American Jewish organizations, and also involved the Dutch and Austrian governments. (Holland represented Israeli diplomatic interests in Moscow, while Austria was the first country of arrival for exiting Soviet Jews.) This is a much longer story. Suffice it to say that Israel wanted desperately to ensure that all Jews able to leave the USSR would resettle in the Jewish state. Israel saw this influx as a once-in-a-lifetime way to advance nation-building. It also argued that, since Jews were officially leaving the USSR with exit visas for Israel, any large-scale defections to other countries could endanger the Soviet rationale for letting Jews go.

I'd been rather naive. I simply assumed that all of us involved in any aspect of the Soviet Jewry effort were playing on the same team, trying to assist Jews in need in whatever ways we could. I wasn't at all prepared for the knock-down-drag-out battles, during which Israeli officials assailed the motives of agencies like HIAS and the American Jewish Joint Distribution Committee, and tried to get the American government to restrict entry of those Soviet Jews who wanted to live there but had left the USSR with visas for Israel.

I learned a great deal in this period, and not only about the Soviet Union or the complex politics of the Soviet Jewry movement.

I met a group of people in Rome, mostly but by no means exclusively Jews, who worked tirelessly to assist the refugees. They were unsung heroes, their names barely remembered today, but their devotion made all the difference in the lives of those helped.

And I must say a word about the Italian people, who showed exceptional kindness and sensitivity to the thousands of Soviet Jews living, at any given moment, in transit in the Rome region, and about the Italian government, which went out of its way to ease their traumatic journey and ensure their safety.

I saw the astonishing degree to which the Jewish world went to assist the refugees every step of the way—from the moment they first set foot in the West until they were able to stand on their own two feet in their new homes.

I became acutely conscious of the threat posed by an amalgam of Arab and European left-wing terrorists who had in their crosshairs Israeli and Jewish targets across Europe (and other targets, as well).

Two years before I began working, terrorists were arrested in Austria following a foiled attack against an Austrian transit center for Soviet Jews. A few weeks later, three more terrorists were arrested while crossing the Italian border into Austria, again with the aim of attacking a transit center housing Soviet Jews. Later that year, terrorists boarded a train crossing Czechoslovakia en route to Vienna and carrying Soviet Jews, in an effort to force the Austrian government to shut down transit facilities for the refugees.

And the list goes on and on, including: attacks on Jewish and American offices in Rome in 1976, which fortunately caused no casualties; in 1981, a bomb detonated outside a gathering place for Soviet Jews in Ostia, near Rome, which injured four people; bombs at the HIAS offices in Rome in June 1982; an attack on the main Rome synagogue four months later, which killed a child and wounded nearly forty others; and an attack, in 1985, at the El Al counter at Rome's Fiumicino Airport, which killed sixteen people and injured dozens.

I had my first exposure to the coming Jewish demographic crisis. Intermarriage, which had been rare in my slice of the Jewish world, was rampant in the HIAS office in Rome, with the notable exception of the Libyan Jews employed there. Interestingly, almost all the Jewish employees had themselves been refugees, mostly from Central and East Europe, who came to Italy after the war. Only a few of the children of the intermarried considered themselves Jewish. Moreover, both among this group and the Soviet Jews, the number of children per family was strikingly low.

Coming from an Ashkenazi milieu in New York, I knew virtually nothing about Jews from Arab countries. In Rome, I encountered a small community of Jews from Libya. For several decades in the twentieth century, Libya had been an Italian colony. When these Jews were compelled to leave, many went to Israel; others resettled in Rome or Milan. I came to know this community well. In fact, I married into it.

I learned about their rich history, fierce pride in being Jewish, strong attachment to Israel and Zionism, distinctive religious traditions, and their expulsion from ancestral lands where they predated by centuries the Arab conquest. I realized that while I had heard an unending stream of commentary about Palestinian refugees, I had barely known that the Arab-Israeli conflict produced two sets of refugees, but that the world seemed entirely uninterested in the fate of Jews from Arab countries. Perhaps it was because these refugees—rather than being turned into political pawns like the Palestinians, and encouraged to languish endlessly in refugee camps as wards of the international community—had quickly rebuilt their lives.

I also had known nothing about the distinctiveness of the Roman Jewish community, which is described as the oldest continuous Jewish presence in Europe, dating back to the second century B.C.E. Thousands more Jews were brought to Rome as slaves after the destruction of the Second Temple in 70 C.E. Some of the scenes of the Roman victory over the Jews are to be found on the Arch of Titus, near the Coliseum. By tradition, Jews to this day give the arch a wide berth.

How a tiny Jewish community (neither Ashkenazi nor Sephardi, by the way), today numbering no more than 15,000, managed to survive is a separate—and remarkable—story. And, of course, we're talking about a community that didn't always have it easy, far from it, whether during the reign of certain popes or in the Second World War. Remember that "ghetto" is an Italian word, first used in Venice in 1516. In Rome, the ghetto, near the Tiber River, was established in 1555. A conquering Napoleon rescinded the ghetto laws in 1809, but with papal rule reestablished by 1814, the ghetto was not truly dismantled until 1870. In an historical twist, today it's considered a trendy residential area for Romans.

And there were other, less weighty things I discovered during my years in Italy.

For instance, I learned that a red traffic light can be an opinion, not a command. As an example, when I had to go to Naples with a Soviet Jewish family, we took a taxi from the train station to the American Consulate. The driver went through every red light. Finally, he came to a screeching halt at an intersection though the light was green. When I asked in my halting Italian why he went through the red lights but stopped for the green light, he turned to look at me as if this were the dumbest question he'd ever been asked, before replying: "How do you expect me to go through the intersection on the green light when all the cars from the other direction are going through on the red light?"

I learned that ALITALIA stands for "Always late in take-off, always late in arrival."

I learned that FIAT stands for "Failure in automotive technology," even though I consider the original Fiat 500—the Cinquecento—the most adorable car ever designed.

I learned that what passed for Italian food in New York was anything but. And I discovered not only the perfect pizza in Rome, but also a way of making ice cream—"*gelato*," as it's called—that should put others to shame.

I learned the limitations of my Italian. Shortly after I arrived and needing a place to live, I was told to walk the streets of residential neighborhoods and look for signs with the word "*Affitasi*," meaning "for rent." Finding one such sign attached to the entrance of a lovely building, I rang the bell of the *portiere* (i.e., the super). In my primitive Italian, I tried to ask if I could see the apartment for rent. She said no. I persisted, so she gave in and took me to the underground garage, pointed to a parking spot, and told me that's what was being advertised.

I learned not to take some things too seriously. When I finally rented a place to live, I looked for a laundry and dry cleaner. Finding one down the block, I entered. When the owner, wanting to give me a receipt for the items I'd brought in, asked my name, he was baffled by the response. The letter "h" doesn't exist in Italian and, in any case, few surnames end in a consonant, so "Harris" wasn't going to fly with this fellow, no matter what I said. Instead, with that wonderful Italian flair, he announced that henceforth I would be known to him as Signor X, and indeed I was.

In the last thirty years, Italy has changed dramatically from a country that exported its citizens to one with a rapidly growing immigrant population, including an estimated one million Muslims, as well as many Asians and East Europeans, who make up for the negative population growth—due to low birthrates—among Italians themselves. I doubt the name Harris would be considered exotic today.

I learned that if you want to increase your self-esteem, spend time in Rome. Titles are ubiquitous. Dress nicely, and the chances are pretty good that in the course of a day you'll be referred to as "Dottore" or "Professore."

I learned—and this was disorienting for me at first, coming from a world of, let's call it, "résumé conversationalists"—that Italians can sit and talk for hours, even days, without ever once referring to alma mater or place of work. Once you get used to it, it can be quite refreshing, if not downright healthy.

And I learned that there's a method to the madness. Though it may seem otherwise, there are rules of the road, and Italians, I found, are superb drivers. Despite claims of inefficiency, periodic strikes, and the tug of *"La Dolce Vita,"* the country works remarkably well. What's more, Italians have an infectious charm that can take the edge off otherwise trying situations.

During a visit to Rome earlier this month with an American Jewish Committee delegation, at a time when Italy is governed by a markedly pro-U.S. and pro-Israel right-of-center coalition led by Prime Minister Silvio Berlusconi, I reminded myself how far Italy had traveled in the last thirty years.

Italy today is one of the leading industrialized nations in the world. Its political system is more stable now than at any time in its postwar history. As a founding member of the European Union—the original treaty of the first six member countries was signed in Rome in 1957— it can be justifiably proud of the dramatic way in which European integration has evolved. It is increasingly multicultural in its outlook. And Italian troops are serving with distinction around the world in a variety of peacekeeping operations, including the fourth largest contingent of foreign forces in Iraq, though opinion polls reveal overwhelming public opposition to the Iraq deployment.

As a related aside, in these thirty years, the Vatican, which our delegation also visited for meetings, has taken a giant step forward in its attitude toward Jews and Israel. Building on the adoption of *Nostra Aetate* by the Second Vatican Council in 1965, which ended the deicide charge against the Jewish people and whose fortieth anniversary we celebrate this year, Pope John Paul II was the first pontiff to pay an official visit to both a synagogue (the main synagogue in Rome) and to Israel, including the Western Wall. Moreover, under his leadership, diplomatic ties between the Holy See and Israel have been established, and anti-Semitism has been vigorously fought.

And I reminded myself how far I had traveled, thanks to that fateful decision to seek a job in Rome in 1975.

I embarked on an immensely fulfilling professional career. I came to appreciate more fully the enriching connective tissue linking Jews across time and space. I began a three-decades-long love affair with

Italy. And, speaking of love, I fell in love with my future wife. Luckily, much of her family lives in Rome, meaning we always have a ready-made excuse to spend time in this endlessly captivating city. They call Rome the eternal city. I understand why.

Letter from Prague
April 28, 2005

The only critical comment about this spectacular city I've heard in recent years has to do with the taxi drivers. Everyone who has visited seems to have a story about them. Notorious throughout Europe, they've been known to engage in violence, charge exorbitant fares, and, in at least one documented case, administer a shock, through electrodes wired to the backseat, to a passenger who protested his treatment. Fortunately, these taxis can be avoided. Otherwise, Prague appears to be on everyone's list of favorite cities. Mine, too.

Variously known as the "city of a hundred spires" and "Golden Prague," the city just keeps getting better, ever since the end of Communism in 1989 and a growing prosperity that has permitted, among other things, the restoration of many Baroque and Art Nouveau buildings in the central district.

Emblematic of the city's special qualities are two striking features.

First, the single most visited site is the Jewish Museum, which, in fact, is a series of four remarkable synagogues (Maisel, Spanish, Pinkas, and Klausen), the legendary old Jewish cemetery, the ceremonial hall, and an educational and cultural center, all within a few blocks of each other. More than 600,000 visitors tour this site each year, many of whom have their first, and perhaps only, encounter with Jewish religion, history, culture, and, not least, the story of the Golem, which, after all, originated in Prague. (The Old-New Synagogue, built in the thirteenth century and the oldest functioning synagogue in Europe, is in the same district but is not part of the Jewish Museum.)

Second, Prague is a mecca for classical music. There are concerts galore. I don't know of another city where people hand out flyers on the street not for salacious nightclubs or "closing" sales, but rather for nightly concerts featuring the music of Wolfgang Amadeus Mozart, Johann Sebastian Bach, and Antonio Vivaldi, not to mention such Czech composers as Antonin Dvorak, Leos Janacek, and Bedrich Smetana.

By the way, it was Smetana's "Moldau" that inspired the melody of "Hatikvah," Israel's national anthem.

And speaking of music, the national philharmonic plays in a hall overlooking the Vltava River in Prague. The roof is ringed by busts of famous composers. During the war, Adolf Hitler ordered Felix Mendelssohn's bust removed because he was of Jewish origin. His troops climbed to the roof, but couldn't figure out which one was Mendelssohn, so they removed the bust with the largest nose. It turned out to be that of Richard Wagner, Hitler's favorite composer!

The city pulsates with history. So does the country. Indeed, if one were looking for a place that defines the epicenter not only of European geography but, even more, of its turbulent history, this might be it. In fact, the history is so multilayered, so staggeringly complicated, that it is one of the reasons why I, for one, could never quite get it right. There were just too many border adjustments, rulers, outside occupiers (including, of all people, the Swedes), nationality questions (Czechs, Slovaks, Moravians, Bohemians, Silesians, Ruthenians, Jews, Hungarians, Roma, Germans, Poles, etc.), name changes, and conflicts.

Let's focus only on the twentieth century. Even just skimming the surface takes time.

The architects and mapmakers of the 1919 Paris Peace Conference—U.S. President Woodrow Wilson, British Prime Minister David Lloyd George, and French Prime Minister Georges Clemenceau—dealt with the aftermath of World War I, including the collapse of the centuries-old Austro-Hungarian Empire. Among other notable decisions taken in a six-month period that was to shape (and misshape) the world for decades to come, they endorsed an entirely new—and some would say artificial—country called Czechoslovakia, which included Bohemia, Moravia, Slovakia, and parts of Silesia and Ruthenia (the Subcarpathian region), with Prague as its capital. In this new country, according to a 1921 census, there were 354,352 Jews.

As Margaret MacMillan notes in her magisterial work, *Paris 1919*, the leading Czechs of the day, Tomas Masaryk and Edward Benes, who in succession became the country's first two presidents, were among the most popular and admired of the many political figures who came to Paris to make their claim for self-determination. "Benes and Masaryk were unfailingly cooperative, reasonable, and persuasive as they stressed the Czechs' deep-seated democratic traditions and their aversion to militarism, oligarchy, high finance, indeed all that the old Germany and Austria-Hungary had stood for," she wrote.

In the ensuing twenty years, Czechoslovakia embraced democracy and quickly emerged as one of Europe's leading industrial economies. Prague was a city infused with the energy and vitality of three dominant cultures—Czech, German, and Jewish. Franz Kafka—born in Prague in 1883, a Jew, and most at home in the German language and culture—came to symbolize the genius emanating from this cultural crossroads, as well as the complicated psychological make-up of Jews of this milieu and generation. Assimilation, rejection of religion, and high rates of intermarriage were all quite prevalent at the time.

Then came the notorious events of 1938. In the name of protecting the German-speaking population of Sudetenland, a Czechoslovak region abutting the German and Austrian borders, which Hitler claimed was the target of persecution and discrimination, the Third Reich demanded annexation.

In what became the quintessential act of appeasement, British Prime Minister Neville Chamberlain and French Prime Minister Edouard Daladier, in September 1938, agreed to Hitler's terms at a meeting in Munich.

(In 2001, Israeli Prime Minister Ariel Sharon warned Western nations, including the U.S., not to "appease the Arabs at our expense ... Israel will not be Czechoslovakia." Sharon's remarks were strongly criticized by the White House.)

In March 1939, the Nazis occupied what were known as the Czech Lands and renamed them the Protectorate of Bohemia and Moravia. Slovakia, declaring its independence, established a pro-Nazi regime under Father Jozef Tiso. Nazi troops were allowed to occupy Slovakia in August 1939. The rest of the country was also dismembered—

Ruthenia was handed over to Hungary, the Silesian region given to Poland.

In other words, by the time the first shot of the Second World War was fired, when German troops invaded Poland on September 1, 1939, what had been Czechoslovakia was already under total Nazi domination.

The war took a terrible toll on the entire nation. One story, perhaps, dramatized the times.

In September 1941, Reinhard Heydrich was named as the *reichsprotektor*, the top Nazi in the Protectorate of Bohemia and Moravia. (Heydrich was also one of the architects of the Nazi Final Solution.) Eight months later, he was assassinated by Czech resistance fighters. In retaliation, Nazi forces wiped out two entire villages—Lidice and Lezaky. In Lidice, 339 men were murdered, the women and children sent to concentration camps. In Lezaky, 54 men, women, and children were killed. In both cases, the villages themselves were destroyed, including churches and cemeteries. And the reprisals didn't stop there; hundreds of others were arrested and killed.

For the Jewish community, the war exacted a massive toll. There were approximately 118,000 Jews in Bohemia and Moravia, including Jewish refugees who had fled the German-dominated Sudetenland. Of these, 26,000, mostly those with family members abroad or sufficient financial resources, managed to leave. Eighty thousand of the remaining 92,000 Jews were deported to Terezin, a fortress town an hour's drive from Prague that was built by Emperor Josef II in the late eighteenth century. (Incidentally, Josef II, the son of Empress Maria Teresa, was considered a hero by Jews, as he allowed them to leave the ghetto, avail themselves of free education, and practice Judaism without interference.) The town itself was turned into a ghetto and transit camp, first for Czech Jews, later for Jews from other countries as well. In Terezin, 30,000 Jews died, mostly of hunger, disease, and exposure. The rest were eventually deported. Only 10,000 Czech Jews returned home from the camps after the war.

Importantly, Terezin was the camp that the International Committee of the Red Cross visited in 1944. The Red Cross delegates were completely fooled by the extensive Nazi preparations to hide the true nature of the site and to present the inmates as well-treated, with practically all the amenities of a summer camp.

Terezin is where many paintings, letters, notes, and poems were hidden by the inmates in the hope that they would one day be found. Here is an excerpt, displayed at Terezin today, from the poem of a fourteen-year-old boy, Hanus Hachenburg, who was killed in 1944:

> I was a child once—two short years ago.
> My youth was longing for another world.
> I am a child no longer....
>
> But I also believe that I am only sleeping,
> That I shall see my childhood once again,
> Childhood like a wild, wild rose
> Like a bell to wake me from my dreams.
>
> And one day perhaps I shall understand
> That I was just a tiny creature,
> As small as that chorus
> of thirty thousand.

The Pinkas Synagogue in Prague lists the names of 78,000 Czech Jewish victims of the Shoah on its walls: Stangel, Tandler, Frankel, Koch, Koppel, Bergmann, Ornstein, Hoffenberg, Kohler, Heilbrunn, Koch, Luria, Grossman.... The names go on and on.

The places where they were sent, twenty-four in all, are listed on an adjacent wall: Terezin, Auschwitz, Treblinka, Chelmno, Lodz, Dachau, Mauthausen....

And nearby, there are these words from Lamentations (1:12): "Let it not come unto you, all ye that pass by! Behold, and see if there be any pain like unto my pain."

For three years after the war's end, Czechoslovakia, having become whole once again, sought to rebuild itself under the leadership of its president, Edward Benes. He had succeeded Tomas Masaryk in 1935 and served until the ill-fated Munich agreement in 1938, to then become leader of the government-in-exile, headquartered in London, in 1940.

Benes was best known in the postwar period for the decrees that bear his name and resulted in the expropriation of property and expulsion of more than three million German-speaking residents of the Sudetenland, insisting that all who could not prove their loyalty to the state during the war must leave. To this day, the consequences of those decrees cast a shadow on German-Czech bilateral ties and affect the domestic political life of Germany, since the expellees and their families have organized themselves politically. Similar action was taken against the Hungarian minority, whose members were compelled to leave their homes and move to neighboring Hungary.

At home, Benes presided over a National Front government that included members of the Communist Party. By 1948, the Communists were in complete control, after the president accepted the resignation of the non-Communist ministers, paving the way for a Communist seizure of power, with Klement Gottwald at the helm. It was also the year that Jan Masaryk, the son of Czechoslovakia's first president and himself a popular foreign minister, was found dead. The Communists claimed he committed suicide; others suspected foul play.

While some Jews stayed, either because of their involvement in the Communist Party or their attachment to their native land, an estimated 20,000 Jews from across Czechoslovakia left for Israel by 1950, after which emigration became almost impossible.

Until 1989, Czechoslovakia was in the hands of the Communist Party. It was a loyal Soviet client state. It was a member of the Warsaw Pact and Comecon, the Soviet-dominated regional economic group. It had its secret police, show trials, kangaroo courts, gulags, listening devices, snitches, censors, jamming of Western broadcasts, heavily fortified borders, and all the other accoutrements of a highly repressive society. The country's prewar cultural and intellectual vibrancy was extinguished in the name of Marxist-Leninist orthodoxy, its art in the name of Socialist Realism.

And Jews had a rough time as well, particularly in what came to be known as the Slansky Trial, when fourteen leading Communist Party members, eleven of them Jewish, were arrested and put on trial in 1952. Rudolf Slansky, the most prominent member of the group, had been the secretary-general of the Czechoslovak Communist Party after World War II. The trial was characterized by historian Meir Cotic as "the first anti-Zionist show trial in the communist bloc." The defendants were accused of high treason and linked to an alleged international Jewish conspiracy involving Israel and the American Jewish Joint Distribution Committee (JDC); confessions were extracted from them. All but three were executed. It may well be that this trial set the stage for the infamous Doctors' Plot in the Soviet Union, which took place the next year and had strikingly similar parallels.

Fifteen years later, in August 1967, the New York-based director of the JDC, Charles Jordan, was found dead in Prague. The death caused alarm in the Jewish world and speculation as to its cause, but for years the Czechoslovak government stonewalled. Only recently, files from that era have been opened, at least those files that did not disappear along the way. The longstanding theory that Arab terrorists operating on Czechoslovak soil were linked to his murder was given a boost.

But then there was that brief period in 1968 that came to be known worldwide as the Prague Spring and was led by Alexander Dubcek. While never renouncing Communism, Dubcek and his colleagues insisted that its true spirit entailed "socialism with a human face."

Tragically, like spring itself, it couldn't last. In August 1968, the Soviet Union, together with a number of Warsaw Pact allies (Romania refused to participate), sent in an estimated 600,000 troops to crush this challenge to tyranny. Their force was overwhelming. But during a brief window of opportunity, tens of thousands of Czechs, including more than 3,000 Jews, left the country and resettled permanently in the West.

Perhaps the best-known protest came from a twenty-year-old student named Jan Palach. As a student at Prague's prestigious Charles University (the oldest university in Central Europe), he participated in demonstrations and strikes against the occupation. When this proved to no avail, on January 16, 1969, after writing a letter intended for publication, he went to Wenceslas Square and set himself on fire. He died three days later. An estimated 500,000 people attended his funeral. One of the slogans scrawled on the Wenceslas Statue before the police removed it read: "Do not be indifferent to the day when the light of the future was carried forward by a burning body."

In the ensuing three months, an estimated twenty-five people sought to emulate his example of suicide to protest the repression; six succeeded.

In 1977, the voices of protest and reform could again be heard. They came in the form of a remarkable human rights statement called Charter 77. But those involved paid a heavy price. Daniel Kumermann was a good example. In a lengthy profile of him in the *New Yorker* (November 1990) entitled "The Window-Washer," Janet Malcolm wrote:

> In 1977, he had a job as a computer programmer on a six-month trial basis, and not wanting to immediately wreck his chances for a permanent position, he had placed himself in a special category of signers, whose names were kept secret. He lost the job anyway and, after failing to find permanent work in the field, openly re-signed the Charter in the summer of 1978. Thereafter, only menial work was available to him. During the next twelve years, he was arrested five times and was taken in for interrogation more often than he can remember....
>
> Kumermann said: "I always had two [interrogators]. There was the one who dealt with the political side of it—the Charter—and the other, who dealt with the Jewish side of it.... They had an anti-Jewish department. They called it the Anti-Zionist Department, actually.... Most of the Charter signers were accused of working with the C.I.A., and I was accused of working with the Israeli Mossad. They thought in James Bond terms. Also, they believed that America was ruled by the Jews.... They really believed it. They had persuaded themselves of these conspiracy theories.

Finally, the Communist scaffolding came tumbling down in 1989. One after another, the countries of Central and Eastern Europe imploded, to be replaced by post-Communist societies. In the case of Czechoslovakia, it was dubbed the Velvet Revolution, and the country's most prominent dissident during the hard times, poet and playwright Vaclav Havel, was elected president. He quickly emerged as one of the world's leading statesmen and moral voices. And in a sign of things to come, his very first overseas trip was to Israel.

Havel, like a number of his counterparts in the region, understood that one of the most despicable aspects of Communist policy was the anti-Israel, anti-Zionist, and anti-Semitic policies of the previous regimes. Under instructions from the Kremlin, countries like Czechoslovakia had actively assisted Israel's enemies by providing weapons, training, sanctuary, and financing to terrorist groups, not to mention active support at the UN and other international bodies for every conceivable anti-Israel and anti-Zionist measure.

Having said this, it's important to acknowledge the special role played by Czechoslovakia in Israel's founding. This would require a separate essay, but suffice it to say that weapons provided by Czechoslovakia to the fledgling Jewish state were absolutely crucial to the ability of the Jews to defend themselves, and that political and diplomatic support was also forthcoming. And rumor has it that, while the government was also willing to sell weapons to the Arab countries at the time, none of the shipments actually arrived, while cash payments were always demanded in advance. Mysteriously, Jewish fighters were able to get wind of each of the planned deliveries and prevent their arrival.

Needless to say, this sympathetic policy changed rather quickly, as the Communist bloc realized that Israel was not likely to become a socialist ally in the Middle East. Czechoslovakia fell into line behind the increasingly pro-Arab, anti-Israel policies of the Kremlin. But Czechoslovak assistance made a huge difference in 1948, a fact that should never be forgotten.

Since democracy's return in 1989, some things have moved at lightning speed.

On January 1, 1993, in what became known as the Velvet Divorce, the country that was put together at the Paris Peace Conference separated into two nations—the Czech Republic, with a population just over ten million and a landmass slightly smaller than South Carolina, and Slovakia to its east and southeast.

According to the CIA's *World Factbook*, the ethnic breakdown of the Czech population is Czech 81.2 percent, Moravian 13.2 percent, Slovak 3.1 percent, Polish 0.6 percent, and German 0.5 percent. In terms of religious affiliation, the Czech Republic may have one of the highest percentages of declared atheists anywhere in the world—39.8 percent. Roman Catholics comprise 39.2 percent of the population, Protestants 4.6 percent, and Orthodox 3 percent.

The Federation of Jewish Communities, with which the American Jewish Committee has a longstanding relationship, estimates that there are 3,000 registered Jews in the country, about half of whom live in Prague. (Prague's prewar Jewish population was about 52,000.) The majority are wartime survivors. Their care and maintenance represent a challenge for a small community. And the younger people are all the children or grandchildren of this Holocaust generation. To meet any local Jew is to know that there is quite a story—or perhaps several stories—that help explain the family's survival, first through Nazism, then through Communism.

And as in Hungary, Poland, and other neighboring countries, there is inevitably a question about how many more Jews there are outside the self-declared community. In some cases, people are only now discovering their Jewish roots, which were deliberately hidden from them by their families in the postwar era, just as Madeleine Albright and Tom Stoppard, both born into Czech Jewish families, did recently. And there are also, it is believed, a few thousand mostly American and Israeli Jews who've settled in Prague in recent years, attracted by the lifestyle and business opportunities.

In 1999, the Czech Republic, together with Hungary and Poland, and with support from the American Jewish Committee, joined NATO. And in 2004, the Czech Republic entered the European Union. In essence, the country had officially moved from East to West—from the Warsaw Pact to NATO, from Comecon to the European Union. The Czech Republic was finally at home. It had been a long journey.

Of the post-Communist societies, there's little doubt that, other than Slovenia, the Czech Republic has made the most successful transition. Drawing on its legacy of democracy, advanced economy, and vibrant culture, the country has quickly become a magnet not only for tourists but also for investors from elsewhere in Europe, especially neighboring Germany, which is also by far the Czech Republic's major trading partner. Lower labor costs than in Western Europe and a well-educated work force have been big pluses when it comes to investors. Today, just about all the leading indicators in the Czech Republic point upward, except one. Like many other European countries, it's experiencing negative population growth due to a very low birthrate (1.2 children per woman).

Politics in this country are anything but gentle. During a recent visit to Prague by an American Jewish Committee delegation, the government was, not for the first time, in turmoil, with three cabinet ministers having submitted their resignations and the prime minister, Stanislav Gross, under a cloud of suspicion for alleged financial misdeeds. The immediate future was uncertain, with various political parties, including a surprisingly strong Communist Party (whose base of support rests largely on pensioners and former apparatchiks), angling for advantage. Nonetheless, signs of growing prosperity abound—new and restored buildings, factories, boutiques, upscale restaurants and bars, shopping malls, and an improving infrastructure. Having traveled to the country many times, I find that the changes are clearly visible from visit to visit.

But what's most striking from a Jewish perspective is that the Czech Republic today is one of the top tourist destinations for Israelis and Jews from around the world.

There's a great deal to see, beginning with Josefov, i.e., the Jewish Quarter in Prague, and Terezin.

Moreover, there are few countries anywhere better disposed toward Israel. To hear the Czech president, Vaclav Klaus, or foreign minister, Cyril Svoboda, on the subject of Israel is to be reminded of steadfast friends willing to speak out.

In doing so, they carry on a remarkable tradition of friendship first epitomized by Tomas Masaryk. He was appalled by the Czech version of the Alfred Dreyfus affair, known as the Leopold Hilsner affair, which occurred in 1899 and involved a false accusation of ritual murder. He didn't hesitate to speak out vigorously against this blatant anti-Semitic act. Later, as president, Masaryk became the first head of a modern state to visit Palestine and did so specifically to meet with the Jewish community there. No wonder there are a kibbutz and a forest named after him in Israel.

He was followed by Edward Benes, the country's second president, and Jan Masaryk, the son of Tomas and foreign minister in the 1940s, both of whom strongly advocated for the creation of a Jewish state. After the Communist period ended, President Havel resumed this tradition, immediately reaching out to Israel and frequently speaking out against anti-Semitism.

To understand the uniqueness of this support—can any country match it both for passion and constancy?—consider the words of Tomas Masaryk expressed in 1918:

> The Jews will enjoy the same rights as all the other citizens of our State. Furthermore, I wish to stress that we wish to abolish the unmoral Austrian system of oppression by the clerical state which exploits Church and religion for political ends. As regards Zionism, I can only express my sympathy with it and with the national movement of the Jewish people in general, since it is of great moral significance. I have observed the Zionist and national movement of the Jews in Europe and in our own country, and have come to understand that it is not a movement of political chauvinism, but one striving for the rebirth of its people.

Or those of Jan Masaryk, writing in 1942 as foreign minister of the government-in-exile:

> Twenty-five years ago, the Balfour Declaration gave the Jewish people hope for the future. None of us could ever have dreamt then what was in store for them. My Government and myself want to assure you of our deep sympathy and understanding. I personally shall never rest till human dignity is returned to those sons and daughters of Israel who will escape alive out of the Teutonic Beelzebub's clutches. Palestine is almost the only star in the stormy sky of present-day iniquity. I hope and pray that the United Nations will succeed in destroying Hitler before his devilish plan of annihilation is realized. There is not a minute to be lost. There are too many graves already.

Or those of President Benes, expressed in 1947 at a conference of European Zionist Federations in Czechoslovakia:

> It will, first of all, be necessary to put a radical and permanent end to racism and anti-Semitism. At the same time, your aspirations for an independent homeland should be fulfilled. I regard the creation of a Jewish state in Palestine as the only just and possible solution of the world Jewish problem. I promise that whenever and wherever an opportunity offers itself, I shall help promote this solution.

And this principled support for Israel and the Jewish people, as I've suggested, continues to the present day. It deserves greater awareness and appreciation.

Finally, anti-Semitism in the Czech Republic is not seen as a major problem today, certainly not in comparison with some other European countries. To the contrary, visiting Jews generally find a warm reception.

Even so, it's impossible to ignore the gaping hole in the Czech landscape. Where once Jews were counted in the tens and hundreds of thousands, where once Jews were a major presence in the commercial, scientific, cultural, and civic life of the country, and where once Jews argued incessantly over religion, politics, and culture, today the Jewish community, despite its valiant efforts to preserve memory while looking to the future, is a bare shadow of its former self.

By the way, if nothing else, the arguing hasn't stopped. During a recent visit, the community was wracked by conflict, so much so that on Shabbat a fistfight broke out at the synagogue, sending at least one person to the hospital. This was not the first time, either. Depending on the person you're speaking with, the issues seem to involve an allegedly autocratic communal leader who was recently deposed, a rabbi who was dismissed and later rehired, conflict between Chabad and other Jewish groups, Israelis with local business interests, disputes over restitution funds, and personality clashes. And all of this, by the way, has made its way into the general media.

In the final analysis, however, there is something profoundly inspiring about witnessing the rebirth and renewal of a nation that endured the one-two punch of Nazism and Communism. And, even with the squabbling, the reemergence of a Jewish community in the very city where Hitler planned his museum of religious and cultural artifacts of an annihilated Jewish people is testament to the determination of Czech Jewry to continue its proud 1,000-year history.

Oh, I almost forgot. Remember the earlier reference to Daniel Kumermann, who, after signing Charter 77, was subjected to countless arrests and interrogations? Guess what became of him in this new era? He was appointed the Czech Republic's ambassador to Israel and recently completed a wonderfully successful term there. Yes, hope really does spring eternal.

Letter from Down Under
August 15, 2005

I can't be sure which came first.

I may have learned about Australia from my paternal grandmother, Rela, who lived a few blocks from us on Manhattan's West Side and who often mentioned her love of the country. In fact, every time she got angry at her husband or son (my father)—which was rather frequently—she'd brandish her Australian passport, obtained after settling in Melbourne following a harrowing wartime experience, and threaten to return to a city she described in idyllic terms. Melbourne, she said more than once, was a wondrous European metropolis with one big bonus—it was on the other side of the world from blood-soaked Europe.

Actually, she had never wanted to leave Melbourne, but her husband and son, separately, had ended up in the States after the war. When all three finally connected, they must have put the decision about where to live to a vote. My grandmother, to her everlasting regret, was on the losing end. New York wasn't ever her cup of tea. Living alone for decades in a first-floor apartment, after being widowed, with gates on the windows and an array of locks on the front door, fearful of going out after dark, she never really found happiness.

Or maybe it was because of the 1956 Summer Olympics in Melbourne, when I was seven years old. I remember being fascinated by the pageantry and competition, and making a vow that one day I'd be an Olympic athlete. It didn't matter what the sport was, although I began playing kickball and dodge ball with greater fervor than ever.

Not only did I associate the Olympics with Australia, but I also had my first lesson in the Cold War thanks to those games—the by-now legendary Soviet-Hungarian water polo match. Just as my family made clear to me, in 1956, that we supported Adlai Stevenson in his second presidential bid against Dwight Eisenhower, so I got the message that we were rooting for Hungary in a rough-and-tumble match that was less about sports than about Soviet occupation and repression.

In other words, Australia loomed large in my life from an early age.

Years later, it was off to London for a graduate degree and my first chance to meet Australians in large numbers. Both my university and the city in general, especially the neighborhood known as Earl's Court, which had been dubbed Kangaroo Court, were filled with Australians. Generalizations may be a bad habit, but since we all make them any-way, here's mine: The Aussies I met were uniformly friendly, outgoing, and without airs. The same, quite frankly, couldn't always be said of the host Britons. The only things I couldn't quite get used to were Australian parties. The volume of beer, the tendency of men and women to separate along gender lines for conversational purposes, and the preoccupation of men with sports about which I, a bit sports-crazed myself, was nonetheless clueless—Australian Rules football, rugby, and cricket—made me feel like an outsider. Unfortunately, given the whims of British weather, I never got to a "barbie," the famous Australian barbecue usually held in backyards or parks, which I had hoped to experience.

A few years later, stationed in Rome, I was working with Soviet Jews in transit awaiting visas from various countries for permanent resettlement. Australia was one of those countries. It wasn't an easy place to enter, in contrast, say, with the U.S.—the wait was much longer and the criteria for acceptance far more stringent. But those obstacles didn't deter Soviet Jews from applying, especially, for some reason, refugees from Ukraine.

Without having been to Australia, I could intuitively understand those who sought to resettle there. The country, from a distance, seemed immensely appealing—democratic, prosperous, lush, and secure, with strong Jewish communities in Sydney and Melbourne. I imagined a place that blended the best of Britain and California.

It also turned out to have another advantage, at least for some Soviet Jews. When I asked one fellow—from Odessa, I believe—whether he was concerned about Australia's distance from other countries, he said that was precisely why he wanted to go there. He determined that Australia was about as far away as he could get from Moscow, the Kremlin, and the KGB. That was reason enough for him, he declared.

Apropos, one day a young Roman Jew came to our office seeking help to immigrate to Australia. He said Italy didn't offer much in the way of a future for young people. I told him we would need parental permission, since he was just seventeen. His mother showed up a week later. I asked whether she would let him move. I'll never forget her reply: "He can go wherever he likes as long as he comes home every Friday for Shabbat dinner."

It wasn't until twenty years later, in 1997, that I had my first chance to visit Australia. Spending a week in Melbourne, Canberra, and Sydney, I wasn't disappointed. If anything, I had underestimated the impact the country would have on me.

And a second trip to the same three cities this summer reminded me why. I'll skip the book-length explanation and limit myself to three reasons.

First, to cut to the chase, Australia has it all. And that's British understatement, not California hyperbole! Australia is a thriving, dynamic, picturesque, and alluring multicultural country, where nearly one in four citizens was born abroad. It's a country that works hard and plays equally hard.

To be precise, Australia is a continent, not just a country. Its size is roughly equivalent to that of the continental United States, but its population, just twenty million, is only about seven percent of ours. The population density is just over six inhabitants per square mile. (By comparison, Israel's is more than one hundred times greater.)

It is a democratic nation par excellence, where citizens are actually fined if they don't vote on election day. The head of state is the Queen of England—after all, the country's full name is the Commonwealth of Australia. The prime minister, John Howard, who has won four consecutive national elections since 1996 as leader of the Liberal Party, presides over a parliamentary form of government.

It has one of the most successful economies in the world. As the Australian ambassador to the U.S., Michael Thawley, noted in a speech last year at the University of Virginia, "We have a very strong economy. We have grown faster than the United States and the G8 in the past twelve years."

In the most recent United Nations Human Development Index (2004), Australia ranked third in the world, after Norway and Sweden. The index measures life expectancy, adult literacy, school and university enrollment, and Gross Domestic Product per capita. (The United States was eighth.)

Religious freedom flourishes in Australia, as befits a democratic country. There's an old Australian belief that a proper intersection should have a church on one corner—and a pub on a second and a betting parlor on a third. (I was never told what was expected on the fourth corner.)

At the same time, unlike the United States, private faith is not a significant factor in public life. God is largely kept out of the political debate. In fact, there was a buzz in Canberra, the nation's capital, because a senator had been elected who was a self-described Evangelical, a rare occurrence for the national parliament.

Interestingly, though, the line of separation between church and state is drawn differently in Australia than in the U.S. For instance, parochial schools, including Jewish day schools, are recipients of public funds, and the national census includes a (voluntary) question on religious affiliation.

Sydney, helped by its spectacular harbor, is one of the world's great cities. A century ago, the Polish-born author Joseph Conrad described Sydney harbor as "one of the finest, most beautiful, and safe bays the sun had ever shone upon." And Melbourne, with its beachfront, cultural treasures, gardens, commercial energy, and unparalleled athletic facilities, doesn't take a back seat to any place, least of all its urban rival, Sydney.

It's not as if everything was always perfect. There have been some stains on the Australian record.

To this day, the country continues to grapple with moral, legal, and social questions related to an earlier history of mistreatment of the indigenous people, who now comprise barely one percent of the population, but cast a long shadow on the nation's conscience.

In the years leading up to the Second World War, Australia's immigration policy, like those of Britain, Canada, and the United States, was restrictive with respect to European Jews seeking refuge. At the thirty-two-nation Evian Conference, held in July 1938 to discuss the plight of Jewish refugees, Australia's delegate, while expressing sympathy for the Jews, stated that his country was reluctant to accept large numbers because of fear of creating a "racial problem" at home. Only about 7,000 Jews, principally from Austria, Germany, and Czechoslovakia, entered Australia in 1938–39, before wartime conditions made any further immigration impossible.

Moreover, from the year of its independence in 1901, Australia had a "whites only" immigration policy. Discrimination based on race or nationality was not formally abolished until 1973. The government of Prime Minister Gough Whitlam took the historic step. Today, Australia is a bustling multiracial, multiethnic society.

Even now, however, there remain some controversies about immigration. Specifically, while I was in the country, a fierce debate raged around the government's tough mandatory detention policy for asylum seekers.

And it wasn't long ago that a politician named Pauline Hanson from Queensland, one of Australia's six states, triggered national attention with her movement, One Nation, which was accused by critics, including Jewish community leaders, of being racist and xenophobic.

Among the recent immigrants, I should add, are a few hundred thousand Muslims from South and Southeast Asia, as well as from the Arab world. Politically, their presence is felt principally in the Sydney area, where in a few electoral districts candidates for public office are starting to take their views into account.

While the majority of Muslims are regarded as moderate, there have been serious problems. Several homes were raided in late June, after security officials uncovered evidence that Islamic extremists were planning attacks on landmark buildings, including the world-famous Sydney Opera House. In addition, incendiary material has been found in some Islamic bookshops—one police raid on a shop in Melbourne took place shortly after I left the city—and there are also a few radical Muslim groups, like Hizb ut-Tahrir, and clerics, like Sheikh Mohammed Omran, who warrant close scrutiny.

Dr. Colin Rubenstein, the widely respected executive director of AIJAC (Australia/Israel and Jewish Affairs Council), AJC's partner organization in Australia, writing in the *2004 American Jewish Year Book*, noted that anti-Semitism remains a problem, citing 481 anti-Semitic incidents in 2003, including physical violence, face-to-face harassment, and threats to Jews. Further, he noted:

> Examination of the anti-Semitic material in the [Australian] media indicated that older racist imagery of Jews, associated with the extreme right, was now supplemented by the anti-Jewish rhetoric of Islamists and the political left, for whom opposition to Israel spilled over into hostility toward Jews.

Still, the overall climate for Jews has been highly favorable. Jeremy Jones, director of AIJAC's office in Sydney, who closely monitors anti-Semitism and other forms of extremism, noted in an article last year in *Jewish Political Studies Review*:

> According to the strong national ethos of modern Australia, what matters is not the country, society, or community a person comes from, but whether he or she is willing to contribute to and be part of Australian society. For most Australians, whether or not a person is Jewish is completely irrelevant or certainly far less relevant than his or her societal contribution.

Second, Australia plays an eminently responsible role in seeking to advance freedom, peaceful conflict resolution, and stability and security not only in its region—from East Timor to the Solomon Islands, from Indonesia to Papua New Guinea—but well beyond.

It may not be widely known, but Australia is the only country that has fought side by side with U.S. soldiers in every major war over the last hundred years, from the First World War—when the commander of the Australian Corps was the admired Lieutenant General Sir John Monash, a Jew—to Iraq. (For those wondering, Britain did not join U.S. forces in Vietnam.)

Incidentally, the Australian involvement in the Iraq war has not been without controversy. The Labor Party candidate, Mark Latham, who ran against Prime Minister Howard in the last national elections in October 2004, called for the withdrawal of Australian troops from Iraq.

The bilateral relationship between Washington and Canberra, formalized in the ANZUS treaty pact signed in 1951, has become even closer since 9/11, when Prime Minister Howard was visiting Washington, having met President George Bush the previous day. The two leaders are reported to get along famously.

(Speaking of Australians and Texans, here's an example of Australian humor: A Texas farmer travels to Australia on vacation. He goes to a farm and meets the owner, who proudly shows him the corn fields. "Our corn fields yield twice as much," the Texan boasts. Then the Aussie shows him his herd of cattle. "Our cattle are at least twice as big," the Texan states. All of a sudden, a kangaroo comes hopping toward them. "What's that?" the Texan asks. Without missing a beat, the Aussie farmer replies, "Don't you have grasshoppers in Texas?")

The Australian government is clear-headed and steely in its response to the global terrorist threat. As it happened, Prime Minister Howard was in London on July 21, the day of the four failed terrorist bombings there. He appeared at a press conference with Prime Minister Tony Blair, and here are excerpts of what he said:

> No Australian government that I lead will ever have policies determined by terrorism or terrorist threats, and no self-respecting government of any political stripe in Australia would allow that to happen.

Can I remind you that the murder of 88 Australians in Bali took place before the operation in Iraq; and could I remind you that the 9/11 attack occurred before the operation in Iraq; can I also remind you that the very first occasion that Bin Laden referred to Australia was in the context of Australia's involvement in liberating the people of East Timor. Are people, by implication, suggesting that we shouldn't have done it?

We lose sight of the challenges we have if we allow ourselves to see these attacks in the context of particular circumstances, rather than the abuse through a perverted ideology of people and their murder.

On the military front, there is broad Australian-U.S. cooperation and coordination, including growing interoperability between the two force structures and collaboration on missile defense projects.

On the economic front, the annual volume of trade between the U.S. and Australia is an impressive $28 billion. Last year, a free-trade agreement was implemented. And as Ambassador Thawley pointed out, "Australia is now the eighth largest direct investor in the United States and has more direct investment in the United States than the United States has in Australia."

On the political front, other than the United Kingdom (and Israel), the United States has no closer or more consistent ally. The only potential cloud on the horizon is the China factor. Australia has a rapidly increasing economic link with China. In fact, a study published earlier this year by the Association for Asian Research (AFAR) concluded that "China is now as critical for Australia's economic security and prosperity as the U.S. is for its military security." Given U.S. concern about an eventual confrontation with Beijing over Taiwan, Australia fears it may be asked by Washington to take sides. The AFAR study also asserted: "Beijing has put Canberra on notice that China expects Australia to remain neutral should a conflict break out. For their part, several Bush administration officials have emphasized their expectation of Australian support for American forces involved."

Australia's close ties with Israel are also noteworthy. Indeed, Israel today has few better friends than Australia. This is true both in the bilateral sphere and in multilateral settings, particularly at the United Nations, where Australia has shown increasing impatience with one-sided resolutions that single out Israel for condemnation. Earlier this year at the UN Human Rights Commission in Geneva, for example, it stood alone with the United States, among the fifty-three member nations, in opposing several such resolutions.

Australia voted for the original UN partition plan, which led to the creation of the State of Israel and, in 1949, was one of the first countries to establish diplomatic links, as well as to support Israel's candidacy for UN membership. It has been among the most outspoken nations in asserting not only Israel's right to exist as a Jewish state, but also its need to take appropriate measures to defend itself against the terror and violence it has faced.

Emblematic of this longstanding, bipartisan friendship were the eloquent comments of Prime Minister Howard in 1998 on the occasion of Israel's fiftieth anniversary:

> By any measure, it has been a remarkable 50 years for Israel—years of struggle, years of wars, and the terrible price of senseless terrorism. It has also been 50 years of democracy, of fighting for principle, of survival in the face of constant attacks on Israel's very right to exist. For the Israeli people, and Jewish communities all over the world, there is much in the first half-century of Israel's statehood to celebrate. It is a history of which there is much to be proud and to take heart for the future of the Israeli nation....
>
> Like Australia, Israel is a nation strengthened by immigration.... Building on the traditions of centuries of adversity and exile for the Jewish people, Israel epitomizes indomitable spirit and fortitude....
>
> Since Israel's foundation, Australia's support for Israel's right to exist within secure and recognized borders has been unswerving. I have long been personally committed to Israel and its people. I assure you of the continuing strength of that commitment for the future.

The prime minister has kept his word.

When he and I shared the podium earlier this summer at a gala dinner in Sydney for the Jewish Communal Appeal, he moved the audience with his unswerving commitment to Israel:

> For an Australian of my generation, to watch as a very young boy the beginning of that country [Israel] from afar, to see its heroic struggle

against impossible—so it seemed—prejudice and opposition, and to watch the double standards of many around the world toward the status and the role of Israel and its right to exist as a free and independent homeland for the Jewish people, has certainly been one of the amazing national stories of the post-World War II period.

And third, Australia has one of the world's most vibrant Jewish communities. Again, no overstatement. From its earliest origins in 1788, when at least eight Jews were part of the first fleet of ships that brought 827 convicts from England to Australia, to the present day, Jews have been part of the fabric and fiber of this nation, both in its earlier incarnation as a British colony and, since 1901, when the Jewish population numbered just over 15,000, as citizens of an independent country.

In the American Jewish community, we spend a lot of time talking about, researching, debating, and anguishing over our future. In particular, we worry about Jewish illiteracy, weakening ties to Israel, high levels of intermarriage, and fraying links to the community.

It's not as if these problems are unique to us. But in Australia, for a variety of reasons, they aren't quite as acute as here, even if everything isn't always hunky-dory.

Jewish day schools attract as many as 65 percent of Jewish youth. In both Melbourne and Sydney, several of the schools have facilities to match the best private schools anywhere. Test scores place the students from these day schools at or near the top in state examinations for their age groups. And there is a range of school options reflecting the pluralistic nature of the Jewish community, i.e., something for everyone.

Israel looms large in the consciousness and identity of Australian Jewry. It may be distant geographically, but it figures prominently in how Jews relate to the larger Jewish world. According to statistical data, the percentage of Australian Jews who have visited Israel is twice that of American Jews.

Whereas the intermarriage rate in the United States is currently estimated at roughly 50 percent, in Australia the figure is 22 percent.

But the situations of Australian and American Jewry are not identical.

While there is a rather robust Jewish community in Perth, in Western Australia, and smaller communities in Adelaide and Brisbane, the overwhelming majority of Australia's 120,000-plus Jews live either in Melbourne or Sydney. Surely, this is a contributing factor to the overall strength of the community. At the end of the day, most young Jews, after their seemingly obligatory stint abroad as students, backpacking travelers, or professionals—a rite of passage they share with their Australian non-Jewish peers—come home and settle. Unlike the United States, there is not a great dispersion of Jews across the country. This helps ensure a critical mass for the communities in Melbourne and Sydney, and their institutions.

Importantly, it also creates a connective thread from generation to generation. Extended families tend to live in the same city, often in the same neighborhood. As a great believer in the role of the extended family, and especially grandparents, as a transmission belt for Jewish identity and values, I've often worried about the impact in the U.S. of the geographic break-up of the family. But when grandchildren see grandparents twice a week rather than twice a year, it can have a lifelong positive effect.

Moreover, though the first Jews arrived in Australia in 1788, and for nearly 150 years thereafter originated primarily from Britain, a significant percentage came from Central and Eastern Europe after the Second World War as survivors of the Holocaust. In fact, apart from Israel, Australia has the highest number of survivors per capita of any country in the world, primarily concentrated in Melbourne. This proximity to history, if you will, has contributed not only to Holocaust consciousness in the younger generations, but also to a greater understanding of the meaning of Israel and the importance of community participation. Thanks in large measure to this influx, the number of Jewish day schools and synagogues grew rapidly.

Speaking of synagogues, there is another important difference between Australian and American Jewry. There are no Conservative or Reconstructionist movements to speak of in Australia. The bulk of those affiliated with a congregation are connected to an Orthodox rather than a Reform or Liberal institution (although it doesn't always translate into daily Orthodox practice).

In addition, even at the risk of simplification, for decades the United States focused on the "melting pot" theory of social integration, which many American Jews, rightly or wrongly, interpreted as an "either-or" proposition—either they were Americans or they were Jews. Australia, on the other hand, adopted a multicultural approach. Jews by and large understood their country's approach as a "both-and" invitation—you are welcome to affirm your identities as Australians and Jews.

Lastly, Australian Jewry has benefited in the past four decades from a large inflow of Jews from South Africa, who have brought with them a highly developed sense of Jewish identity and involvement, and whose impact can be felt today throughout the entire communal structure.

For all the differences, however, the Australian and American Jewish communities share several characteristics in common.

For one, both are exceptionally well-organized. Most striking, perhaps, is the degree of political access that our respective communities enjoy. When I was in Canberra, I was impressed by the breadth and depth of relationships that had been nurtured by AIJAC, our Australian partner.

In the course of just one day, we met separately with four cabinet ministers, were invited to a state luncheon hosted by Prime Minister Howard for visiting Pakistani President Pervez Musharraf, saw three "shadow" ministers, and had dinner with members of the Australia-Israel parliamentary group. A few days later, we had a private meeting with the prime minister. In each case, it was obvious that there were longstanding friendships between Australian Jewish leaders and elected officials of the major political parties.

For another, both communities have faced challenges integrating two recent waves of arrivals—Israelis and Soviet-born Jews. As elsewhere in the Diaspora, the Israelis, who in the case of Australia number several thousand, essentially remain a group apart. They don't identify easily with the Diaspora model centering around the synagogue, community center, and federation. And those from the former Soviet Union, who experienced decades of oppression, atheistic indoctrination, and separation from Jewish life, have also, with some notable exceptions, found absorption into the larger established Jewish community quite difficult.

Finally, whatever the differences, Australian and American Jews have remarkably compatible outlooks and organizational structures. I was particularly struck by the degree of pride and gratitude that Australian Jews feel for their country, very much as American Jews do for ours. There isn't that unsettling phenomenon that exists in some other countries, where Jews may still not feel fully accepted, instead being viewed as the "other" or the "outsider," irrespective of how deep a community's roots in the land might be.

And if I still had any doubts about the similarities between us, seeing the familiar chicken—Jewish "comfort food"—sitting on my plate at one community dinner after another certainly dispelled them.

Letter from Caracas
October 20, 2005

Hugo Chávez is a household name throughout Venezuela, the oil-rich nation at the northern tip of South America, and increasingly throughout Latin America.

If his is not yet a household name throughout the United States, it ought to be, if perhaps for somewhat different reasons.

Chávez took office as president of Venezuela in 1999, after his election in December 1998. Since then, to put it mildly, he has proved himself a controversial figure, and not only in his own country.

To his defenders, he is a forward-looking leader, difficult to define in a word or two—a combination of nationalist, populist, preacher, socialist, pragmatist, and Robin Hood.

To his critics, he is using democracy and a social agenda as tools to attain authoritarian goals. In the process, the traditional watchdogs of democracy—the media, advocacy groups, and other actors in civil society—have been weakened by a bullying government.

He has emerged, according to the school of admirers, as a staunch defender of the nation's poor and disenfranchised, who form the overwhelming majority of the country's 25 million inhabitants. He has placed health care, land reform, literacy, education, and affordable food at the center of his political agenda. Drawing on Venezuela's bonanza in oil wealth, he has launched a long overdue political and social revolution. By reaching out to the marginalized in what had been a typically bifurcated South American nation—concentrated power and wealth in the hands of the minority, at the expense of the vast majority of impoverished urban and rural, largely black and mestizo citizens—he has charted a new path, one that will serve as a model for other nations afflicted by the legacy of colonialism, the long arm of imperialism, and the most recent menace, American-inspired economic "neoliberalism," as he dubs it.

Along the way, his supporters proudly note, he has deftly outflanked his formidable adversaries, who've been unable to unseat him over the past nearly seven years, despite two national elections (1998, 2000), a short-lived coup d'état in 2002, a crippling nine-week strike in the oil industry a few months later, and, most recently, a national referendum seeking his ouster (2004).

He has raised his sights high, so high in fact that his ambitions go far beyond the borders of his sizable country, which is twice the area of California and has a 1,500-mile coastline on the Caribbean.

Drawing on the inspiration of Caracas-born Simon Bolivar, who, nearly two centuries ago led the independence struggle against Spain and dreamed of South American integration, Chávez seeks to link left-of-center regimes and movements all across the continent.

Described by his fans as charismatic and a fiery orator, who, they acknowledge, never says in a word what he can say in ten, he builds on an oft-expressed solidarity with Fidel Castro's Cuba, periodic assaults on U.S. "hegemony," and an influx of petrodollars that permits influence-seeking, at times tantalizingly irresistible, offers of subsidized energy, barter arrangements, arms purchases, and medical assistance to countries in Central and South America.

Chávez's aims go far beyond the Western Hemisphere. He has forged close ties with Iran and Libya, fellow OPEC members. In fact, Venezuela was the only nation among the thirty-five member countries on the governing board of the Vienna-based International Atomic Energy Agency to reject, last month, a European resolution critical of Iran's nuclear intentions. And Chávez was a recipient in Tripoli last year—prepare yourself—of none other than the Muammar Qaddafi Human Rights Prize.

Until Saddam Hussein's downfall in 2003, the Iraqi leader could count on the support of Chávez, who, in 2000, became the first national leader to break the international isolation imposed on Iraq after the 1991 Gulf War by traveling to Baghdad.

More recently, Chávez has focused his attention on India, and even more so on China, which has itself been showing interest in boosting its reach in South America, including substantial investments in Venezuelan oil fields.

In other words, Chávez is seeking to create a new international alliance built on the strength of those nations he believes either have, or need, key natural resources and, for one reason or another, resent America's—and, to some extent, Europe's—dominant role in the world.

Global dependence on oil, coupled with sky-high prices, has given Chávez the means to advance his goals. After all, he leads a country that is the world's fifth leading producer of oil, may have the largest oil reserves in the world, has the second largest gas reserve in the Western Hemisphere, and, incidentally, is the fourth leading supplier of oil to the United States (in addition to owning 14,000 Citgo gas stations and eight oil refineries in the U.S.).

Chávez works on the assumption that, both literally and figuratively, he has countries like the United States—I can't resist—"over a barrel." Oil, and the revenue and influence it generates, are his weapons of choice in what he views as an asymmetrical battle with otherwise more powerful countries.

There's been an escalating war of words with the Bush administration. Chávez sees this as a big boost to his popularity, given his view that America fails to grasp the widespread resentment throughout Latin America, never far from the surface, that its "strong-armed" methods generate. At the same time, he claims to separate the U.S. government from its people, emphasizing his love of Americans, especially the downtrodden, to whom he's also offered financial assistance, and his ability to get along with Presidents Bill Clinton and Jimmy Carter.

Chávez loudly asserts that George W. Bush has secret plans to invade Venezuela and assassinate him. He told Ted Koppel's *Nightline* last year that the U.S. code name for the project is "Balboa," and he offered to share with Koppel documentary proof about it. He added: "What I can't tell you is how we got it, to protect the sources, how we got it through military intelligence."

More recently, he cited Pat Robertson's call to "take him out," referring to Chávez, as additional evidence of American intentions. After all, Robertson, who later retracted his comment, is viewed in Caracas as a right-wing Evangelical, representing a key constituency of the Bush administration.

In response, he has brandished the oil weapon. "Ships filled with Venezuelan oil, instead of going to the United States, could go somewhere else," he declared. He has dubbed President Bush as "Mr. Danger" and Secretary of Defense Donald Rumsfeld as "Mr. War," while dismissing Secretary of State Condoleezza Rice as a "true illiterate" for her views on Latin America.

Talking tough and standing up to the *yanqui,* he believes, will win him friends at home and beyond.

Then there are his detractors.

They see a demagogic leader who figured out that attaining power was more easily accomplished through the democratic process than by revolutionary means, and thus made the switch from seeking, as a military officer, to overthrow the democratically elected government led by Carlos Andres Perez in 1992, which landed Chávez in jail for two years, to leading a political party to victory in the 1998 election. (Incidentally, Perez was ousted on charges of corruption in 1993, and imprisoned in 1996 after being found guilty of embezzlement.)

Once in power, they assert, Chávez has incrementally set about consolidating authority, rewriting the constitution, packing the courts, limiting the media's right to criticize, intimidating opposition groups, and planning to expropriate private property. Meanwhile, contrary to his stated goals, poverty has actually increased since he took office over six years ago.

He has invited as many as twenty thousand Cuban doctors and other medical personnel to come to Venezuela, together with Cuban teachers and sports trainers. They are ostensibly there to provide needed services to previously neglected communities across the country, but also to win friends for his mentor, Fidel Castro.

He is helping fund left-wing movements throughout Latin America that could bring to power potential allies in Bolivia, which has the Western Hemisphere's third largest reserve of gas, and Nicaragua, while supporting Fuerzas Armadas Revolucionarias de Colombia (FARC), the notorious terrorist group at war with neighboring Colombia's pro-American regime, and seeking to find common cause with left-of-center governments in Argentina and Brazil, South America's two largest countries.

To further extend his influence, earlier this year Chávez launched Telesur, a round-the-clock South American Al Jazeera wannabe, to combat what he called the "cultural imperialism" of the Western electronic media.

Further complicating matters, and underscoring his mercurial thinking, Chávez also drew inspiration in the past for what he calls his "Bolivarian Revolution" from some extreme right-wingers, most notably an Argentine Holocaust denier, Norberto Ceresole.

Ceresole, according to a study by the Madrid-based think tank Real Instituto Elcano, believed that "the [political] leader guaranteed power through a civil-military party, based on a model denominated 'post-democracy.' In the long term, 'Bolivarian' integration of the continent would lead to a Confederation of Latin American States in which the armed forces would hold the reins of economic, social and political development and the security of the continent." In also calling for closer Arab-Latin American cooperation against the U.S., Ceresole warned that "the Jewish financial mafia" posed a potential challenge to the success of the Chávez movement. Ceresole died in 2003.

By aligning himself with some of the world's nastiest regimes, President Chávez is putting Venezuela in an untenable position, his critics contend. Are Iran, Libya, North Korea, and Syria the natural global partners for a country aspiring to greater progress and development?

And, conversely, why put the country on a collision course with the United States, Venezuela's leading trading partner (59 percent of Venezuelan exports go to the U.S., 33 percent of its imports come from the U.S.), a major source of tourism and investment, and a reference point for many Venezuelans, especially these days when the

Venezuelan-born manager of the Chicago White Sox has led the team into the World Series and generated excitement throughout Venezuela?

The Venezuelan leader has visited Tehran frequently, and the bilateral relationship is deepening. Iranians have established a beachhead in Venezuela, with growing investments and joint ventures, supposedly for peaceful, civilian purposes, though rumors of more pernicious goals are rife. As one foreign diplomat commented, when an Iranian embassy starts expanding in any capital, there's reason to worry, and, guess what, the staff of the Iranian embassy in Caracas has been growing.

There is also fear in some quarters that Chávez's deep-rooted sympathy for "anti-imperialist" forces and unbridled antipathy for the Bush administration, as well as a major Arab presence in Venezuela, might have led him to provide funding, training camps—Venezuela's Margarita Island is often named in this connection—and even Venezuelan passports for Middle East terrorist groups, though government spokesmen heatedly deny these charges.

And finally, domestic foes of Chávez worry that he has established such an iron grip on the country that changing political course may be difficult, if not impossible, in the near term.

Whether because of disarray and division within the political opposition, or because Chávez has successfully appealed to the majority on a platform of what is in essence class warfare, or because he is strangling the democratic process, adversaries don't see much light at the end of the political tunnel. Their main hope seems to be that one day oil prices will fall, which in turn would limit Chávez's ability to deliver on his far-flung promises and spark widespread disenchantment with his leadership. After all, according to the CIA's *World Factbook*, the petroleum sector accounts "for roughly one-third of [Venezuelan] GDP, around 80 percent of export earnings, and over half of government-operating revenues."

Meanwhile, among those trying to sort out these starkly contrasting views of the current situation and seeking to understand what the future is likely to hold are Venezuela's Jews.

It is in many ways a remarkable community. Largely centered in Caracas, with a smaller concentration in Maracaibo, most of its current members are either first or second generation. But the earliest Jews settled in the first half of the nineteenth century and came largely from Dutch-controlled Curaçao, where Bolivar found refuge among the settlement's Jews during the struggle for independence against the Spanish occupiers.

Some Curaçao Jews went to Coro, located on the Venezuelan coast northwest of Caracas, but in 1855 the entire community there, 168 people, was forced to leave due to intolerance and returned to Curaçao. As the Jewish Virtual Library notes, "It was the first time that Jews had been driven out of an independent nation in South America." Later, a few returned, but today the city, as least as far as Jews are concerned, is best known for housing the oldest Jewish cemetery in South America.

The Jewish community is roughly evenly divided between those of Ashkenazi and Sephardi origins. Their overarching sense of unity could well serve as a model for other Jewish communities fragmented along ethnic or other lines. They have developed an impressive communal infrastructure built around a central umbrella organization, La Confederación de Asociaciones Israelitas de Venezuela (CAIV), with which the American Jewish Committee signed an association agreement last year, fifteen synagogues (all but one Orthodox), and, perhaps most striking of all, a Jewish all-in-one campus, Hebraica. Combining Jewish nursery and day schools, a country club, cultural center, a verdant setting, and wide-ranging sports activities, Hebraica serves as the focus for much of the community.

The results of these communal efforts speak for themselves. The community is close-knit, an overwhelming majority of Jewish children attend Jewish schools, the level of participation is high, identification with Israel is intense, and intermarriage rates are low compared to the United States or Britain.

What is equally striking in talking with Venezuela's Jews, to the extent that generalizations are ever possible, is an obvious pride in being Venezuelan. Not only do they continue to appreciate the refuge the country provided—the Jews having come in search of safety and opportunity—but they also recognize the country's postwar record of tolerance and relative absence of anti-Semitism, as well as its support of the 1947 UN resolution calling for the establishment of a Jewish state.

On the whole, Jews have done well in Venezuela—and for Venezuela. They have built successful careers in a range of fields and have served as government ministers and ambassadors. In meeting with a number of Venezuelan Jews during a recent American Jewish Committee fact-finding and solidarity visit to Caracas, we heard the same comments over and over: "We love this country." "We feel welcome and at home." "There is little prejudice here." "There is no better climate anywhere in the world." "You must visit the magnificent beaches—better than those of any Caribbean island—and see the lush jungle." "Look at the magnificent mountains surrounding our beautiful city of Caracas. Can you imagine a more perfect setting for a city?" "We have an unparalleled community life here."

But intermingled with these comments were others, far less upbeat, essentially centered on three themes.

Crime and violence are serious problems. I was shocked at a dinner table to learn that of the three Venezuelan couples with whom I sat, two had suffered from what has been labeled *secuestro express*, a kind of mini-kidnapping, where an individual might be grabbed for a few hours and taken to his home and a few ATM machines before being released, always without the car he began his journey in. In fact, a local movie entitled *Secuestro Express* has been a box-office hit in Venezuela and was recently released in the United States to critical acclaim. By the way, in the case of the third couple, robbers had recently entered their home. The young adult daughters were in the house at the time, and they locked themselves in a bedroom with guns at hand, but due to a stroke of luck didn't have to use them.

Traveling through any reasonably nice neighborhood in Caracas, it's impossible not to notice the high—and I mean high—walls and fences, concertina wire, gates, bars, windows, cameras, and sometimes body-guards meant to protect private homes. Apartment buildings can also resemble fortresses. And in less affluent areas, the bars and gates on windows and doors are also quite ubiquitous.

Job opportunities for young people are another problem. Many of the children of Venezuelan Jews go abroad, often to the United States, for undergraduate or graduate studies. Upon completion of their degree, they may feel that their education is best put to use in a dynamic, technologically advanced country like the U.S. more easily than in Venezuela. And, in the current climate, the fear of nationalizing businesses, expropriating property, eliminating private medicine (there are quite a few Jewish physicians), stifling creative expression, and replacing meritocracy with quotas all put a damper on thoughts of a future in Venezuela.

And this brings me to the third point.

There have been some disturbing incidents affecting the Jewish community. The most notable one took place last November 29, when the police launched an early morning raid at the elementary school on the Hebraica campus, ostensibly in search of a weapons cache linked to the assassination of a federal prosecutor and, to boot, with an alleged Israeli connection. The three-hour search produced nothing, but did send shock waves through the community. Was this simple bumbling on the part of law enforcement? Or was it more calculated and intended to intimidate? Eleven months later, no one knows the answer for sure, though theories abound. It must be added that Venezuelan civil society reacted almost as one in expressing outrage at the incident.

There have been some worrisome political and government-controlled media references to Jews and Zionism, which of late seem to be growing both in intensity and frequency. The fear is that this could rapidly accelerate at any time.

For one thing, the administration is on friendly terms with governments and groups hostile to Israel and the Jewish people, including Iran and Islamic extremists, and Chávez himself wrote an admiring letter shortly after taking office to "Carlos the Jackal," the notorious terrorist imprisoned for life by a French court. At the same time, strange as it may seem in light of everything else going on, there is an active Israeli embassy in Caracas and modest but growing bilateral trade.

For another, there is a lurking concern that anti-Semitism is, if you will, being held in reserve, to be used to cast the Jews in the historically familiar role of scapegoat should things turn sour in the Bolivarian Revolution and an easy explanation be needed by its supporters to mobilize the collective wrath of the nation.

Surprise of surprises, there isn't a uniform assessment about the situation among the Jews with whom we met, but, needless to say, all are closely monitoring developments and trying to keep their options open. In most families we met, among the adult children at least, a few are now abroad. Whether they return home remains uncertain. In fact, population estimates for the Jewish community, as well as day school enrollment, reveal a steady recent decline—perhaps by as much as one-quarter in the past six or seven years.

The thought of possibly leaving was wrenching for those with whom we spoke, all the more so because this is a relatively young community. Many members still harbor memories of their journey as refugees—or their parents' journey—from Egypt, Bessarabia, Morocco, Hungary, and other places of origin.

In their view, replicating elsewhere the life the Jewish community has led in Caracas would be next to impossible. There is a deep love of country. And there's also vibrant, intergenerational family interaction. The extended family forms the foundation of the social network. Some Americans might view this as claustrophobic or limiting, but not in Caracas. There's a sense that this closeness could well be lost in another country, such as the United States, where families tend to drift apart over a vast territorial expanse.

The same is true for communal life. My jaw dropped when I first saw Hebraica. I've been to a lot of Jewish settings around the world in my travels, but this one takes the gold medal. It would be hard to find anything remotely approaching this breathtakingly beautiful soup-to-nuts center of Jewish educational, cultural, and social life. Leaving all this—and so much more—behind would be excruciatingly painful.

History has a mind of its own. As we know, it doesn't necessarily move in a linear direction. That's why it makes eminently good sense, in thinking about Venezuela and its Jewish community, to be ambidextrous—on the one hand, preparing for tough sledding ahead, while, on the other, ensuring that we don't create, or contribute to, self-fulfilling prophecies.

Letter from Lima
November 28, 2005

Here's a political trivia test:

Name the one country today—outside Israel—where the president, speaking before the Israeli Knesset in a special session earlier this year, began his remarks with the words, *Am Yisrael Chai* ("the people of Israel live").

Name the one country today—outside Israel—where the first lady is Jewish, was a member of a left-of-center Zionist youth movement, studied in Israel, and raised her daughter to speak Hebrew.

Name the one country today where the vice president is an active member of the Jewish community.

Name the one country today where the current prime minister, a distinguished economist, practically commuted to Israel as an investment banker, over a span of six or seven years, to advise it on privatization efforts.

And name the one country in South America today that is included in every list of Israel's closest friends in the world.

As you would have guessed from the title, the answer to all five questions is Peru, though the information may come as a surprise to many. After all, Peru seldom surfaces in discussions of world Jewry or Israel's global standing. It deserves greater attention, as befits a friend.

An American Jewish Committee delegation met with Alejandro Toledo, Peru's president since 2001, in September, one of several opportunities we've had to chat with the Peruvian leader. After a bit of bantering, he turned to us and said, "Let's get down to *tachlis*." In that spirit, let's focus, first, on the nuts and bolts.

Geographically, Peru is located along the Pacific Ocean, and is bordered on the north by Ecuador and Colombia, on the east by Brazil and Bolivia, and on the south by Chile. After Brazil and Argentina, it is South America's third largest country, slightly smaller than Alaska. Its population of 28 million places it fourth among the most populous South American nations, following Brazil, Argentina, and Colombia.

On the UN's 2004 Human Development Index, Peru ranks #85 of the 177 countries measured, well behind Argentina (#34), Chile (#43), and Uruguay (#46), but ahead of Paraguay (#89), Ecuador (#100), and Bolivia (#114). (For the curious, Norway tops the list, the U.S. is #8, and Sierra Leone comes in last.)

Historically, Peru was famed as the home of Inca civilization. Spanish explorers in search of gold and silver, led by Francisco Pizarro, arrived in the sixteenth century, ravaging the Incas through superior weapons and the deadly impact of imported diseases. The occupiers remained for nearly three centuries. They finally left in defeat in 1824, three years after the country declared its independence under the leadership of General José de San Martin, and four decades after a failed revolt led by the legendary Tupac Amaru, who claimed to be descended from the last Inca leader. Striking remnants of both the Inca Empire and the Spanish presence are still found in the country, making such places as Machu Picchu and Cuzco coveted destinations for travelers from around the world.

Of Machu Picchu, the British author Sacheverell Sitwell wrote:

> This is the most stupendous approach there has ever been, to something which in its own right is perhaps the most startlingly dramatic archaeo-logical site in either the Old or the New World. For the setting is enough, is almost too much in itself. It is nearly too good to be believed that there should be something to see here.

And of Cuzco, Christopher Isherwood, the Anglo-American writer, said:

> There is no sense in my trying to describe Cuzco; I should only be quot-ing from the guide-book.... What remains with you is the sense of a great outrage, magnificent but unforgivable. The Spaniards tore down the Inca temples and grafted splendid churches and mansions on to their foundations. This is one of the most beautiful monuments to bigotry and sheer stupid brutality in the whole world.

Politically, Peru is a democracy, but, like many of its neighbors, has had a topsy-turvy history, bouncing back and forth from elected leaders to military strongmen, with some extra dollops of corruption and scandal thrown in along the way.

The cynical view of Peru's political history was perhaps most succinctly expressed by the noted Peruvian writer Manuel Scorza who, in 1970, said, "In Peru, there are two kinds of problems: those which will never be resolved and those which will resolve themselves."

Possibly Peru's best-known—or most notorious—leader in recent memory was Alberto Fujimori, who served as president for ten years before seeking asylum in Japan rather than face corruption charges in his native land. Elected in 1990, when he ran against the famed Peruvian novelist Mario Vargas Llosa, the mathematician-turned-politician and son of Japanese immigrants promised to tackle the country's three most pressing issues—the hyperinflation that reached 400 percent under his predecessor, Alan Garcia; widespread corruption; and the devastation wrought by the Sendero Luminoso, or Shining Path, whose armed struggle in the name of a "utopian" communist vision cost tens of thousands of lives.

Fujimori was reelected in 1995, thanks to the adoption of a new constitution that allowed the president to serve more than one consecutive five-year term. (As a result of the Fujimori experience, the constitution was changed back to prevent an incumbent president from running for a second term.) During his decade in office, he succeeded in curbing inflation—with the help of his prime minister and finance minister, Efrain Goldenberg Schreiber, who was a member of the Jewish community—and dealt a near fatal blow to the guerrillas, capturing Abimael Guzman, the leader and ideological sparkplug of Sendero Luminoso. Among the many arrested was a young Jewish woman from New York, Lori Berenson, who, in a closed court, was found guilty of treason for collaborating with the guerrillas and sentenced to life imprisonment. Later, after pressure from Washington and a public campaign by her family, her sentence was reduced to twenty years.

Along the way, Fujimori was accused of human rights violations and embroiled in political and financial scandals. As a result, the Peruvian Congress, in 2000, declared him "morally unfit" to lead the country. An interim president was named, prompting Fujimori to flee to Japan and seek asylum in his parents' native land, which has no extradition treaty with Peru.

In June 2001, Alejandro Toledo was elected president, with 59 percent of the vote. In an improbable and inspiring political journey, Toledo became the first Peruvian of indigenous descent to lead the nation. Born in an impoverished Andean village, he was one of sixteen siblings, seven of whom died in early childhood. By age seven, he was shining shoes to help his family, who had moved to Chimbote, a coastal town, where their home had neither electricity nor running water. With the assistance of Peace Corps volunteers, he was able to obtain a scholarship to the University of San Francisco. After graduation in 1971, he went on to earn a doctorate at Stanford University and began a career as a respected economist and professor.

At Stanford, he met Eliane Karp, a naturalized U.S. citizen, who was born in Paris to Belgian Jewish parents with a strong Zionist background. After high school, she worked on a kibbutz, did her undergraduate studies at the Hebrew University in Jerusalem, and went to Stanford for a master's degree in anthropology. They married in 1979.

Regarding her Jewish identity, she said in an interview published in the *Jewish Journal of Greater Los Angeles* (June 9, 2000): "My vision of Judaism, although it is not religious, is one of enlightenment and justice. This is how I was brought up. My commitment as a Jew and a human being is to fight against dictatorship and injustice wherever it exists."

Returning for a moment to the subject of political trivia, as I learned four decades ago when researching a high school paper, Karp was not the first Jewish woman to marry a South American who would go on to lead his country; she was at least the second. Chicago-born Janet Rosenberg married Dr. Cheddi Jagan, a Northwestern University-trained dentist, who spearheaded Guyana's independence struggle against Britain, served as prime minister from 1961 to 1964, and as president from 1992 to 1997. In fact, after his death in 1997, she was elected head of state, a post she held for two years. Thus, not only was she the pioneer Jewish first lady in South America, but also the first Jew elected in her own right to lead a country in the Western Hemisphere.

In a case of "exquisite timing," Fujimori arrived by private plane in Chile earlier this month, precisely on the day our delegation was in Santiago to honor the country's president, Ricardo Lagos, and announced his wish to return to Peru to run for the presidency in the April 2006 elections. In reality, he is legally barred from doing so until 2011, and could face possible imprisonment. At the time of writing, Fujimori is being held by Chilean authorities, while Peru seeks his extradition. This adds to an already full bilateral agenda. Currently, there is a war of words between Chile and Peru over a disputed maritime boundary.

With or without Fujimori's return, Peru faces its share of challenges. It's true that there's been good news on the economic front. The U.S. Department of State earlier this year described the Peruvian economy as "well managed ... and one of the most dynamic in Latin America, showing particularly strong growth over the past three years." The nation's Gross Domestic Product (GDP) has grown at a healthy clip over the past several years, inflation has been curbed, foreign reserves have increased, and the external debt has declined as a percentage of GDP.

Even so, as a developing country, Peru still has a long way to go in attracting foreign investment, diversifying its economic base, raising the standard of living, addressing widespread poverty, boosting health care, and improving the educational system, including lagging high school graduation rates.

This may be why, according to one survey cited during our visit, as many as 80 percent of Peruvian young people think about leaving the country, most mentioning the United States as a desired destination, where an estimated two million Peruvians currently live. They contend that there are too few opportunities in their native land, although by any objective standard Peru, at least on paper, has all the ingredients—from vast size to abundant natural resources, from fertile farmland to extensive coastline—to become the continent's next Chile, in other words, a democratic country with solid institutions and a rapidly expanding economy. This fairly widespread sense of pessimism helps explain President Toledo's stubbornly low approval ratings in the polls—in the 10–15 percent range—notwithstanding the impressive economic performance of recent years.

And the lack of confidence in the Peruvian future is just one more reason why Americans need to be reminded of the importance of understanding—and engaging—the political, economic, and social issues affecting our Western Hemisphere neighborhood. At the moment, the United States is in negotiations with Peru, Colombia, and Ecuador for an Andean Free Trade Agreement, to replace the soon-to-expire Andean Trade Promotion and Drug Eradication Act. The aim is not only to spur increased bilateral trade, but also to promote investments and job creation for the three South American countries—an important objective both for these countries and the United States, as we have a profound stake, more than some seem to realize, in the success of hemispheric development.

The talks with Peru, whose principal trading partner is the U.S., are running ahead of those with its two neighbors. It could be that we'll see a bilateral deal before the quadrilateral agreement is completed. Any trade treaty would need Congressional approval, which is less certain today because of the unraveling of the consensus on free-trade issues in Washington that existed just a few years ago. As it was, the Central American Free Trade Agreement, which AJC supported, was barely able to make it through Congress before President George W. Bush signed it into law earlier this year.

It should be added that not everyone in Peru supports a free-trade agreement either. In a meeting we had with a number of church leaders, several voiced concern that such an accord would hurt, not help, the nation's poor. This echoes the views of Venezuelan President Hugo Chávez and others who decry what they insist is the negative social impact of Washington's promotion of "neoliberalism."

Moreover, Peru has a major fight on its hands with illicit drug cultivation, drug trafficking, and organized crime. As the Colombian government makes headway in its own struggle with the same problems, there's been a shift of focus by the underworld to Peru. The drug issue has been a major priority of the Peruvian government and a matter of close cooperation between Lima and Washington. Fortunately, relations between Peru and the U.S., which began with formal American recognition of the Republic of Peru in 1826, are excellent. To his credit, President Toledo has made strong ties with the U.S. a centerpiece of his administration's foreign policy. This pro-American orientation will assume even more importance starting on January 1, 2006, when Peru begins a two-year term as one of ten nonpermanent members of the UN Security Council.

By the way, there are as many as twenty Israelis currently serving jail time in Peru for violations of drug laws, many of them young people who traveled to South America for a break after their military service.

This is among the few issues clouding the work of the new Israeli ambassador—a member of the small Israeli Druze community and former ambassador to Vietnam—in an environment that otherwise could not be friendlier today. Another troublesome matter is an arms-trafficking case involving an Israeli, Moshe Rothschild, who's under investigation in Peru on suspicion of corruption, bribery, and illegal association for arms deals in the 1990s and is the subject of an international arrest warrant.

Ethnically, Peru's population is overwhelmingly comprised of Indians and mestizos, with a noticeably smaller European population than in the other countries we visited during this trip—Chile, Argentina, and Uruguay. Like other Latin American countries, the population is overwhelmingly Catholic, and the Catholic Church remains a privileged institution in the state's eyes, though Evangelical churches have been making significant headway in attracting congregants. There are also rather sizable Chinese and Japanese communities, whose origins in the country date back to the nineteenth century, and a smaller Arab, largely Christian, population. And there is, of course, a Jewish community, almost totally concentrated in Lima.

The first Jews arrived in the sixteenth century, fleeing the Spanish Inquisition and, as *Conversos*, practicing their religion in secret. But when the Spanish learned of their presence, they brought the Inquisition to Peru. The goal was to root out and destroy any religious "heresy" or "blasphemy." Torture and murder were the favored methods. Today there's a museum on the Plaza Bolivar in Lima—Museo de la Inquisición—devoted to this grisly history. In the same building that was used by the ecclesiastical court of the Inquisition from 1570 to 1820, the museum displays the dungeons. It was from here that those found guilty were taken to be publicly burned at the stake.

The modern community began about a century ago, with the arrival of both Ashkenazi and Sephardi Jews. According to Leon Trahtemberg, the principal of the Jewish day school in Lima, by the end of the 1920s, there were one thousand Jews in Peru; ten years later, the number had risen to 2,500. In 1938, however, the government banned further Jewish immigration. During this period, synagogues, youth movements, Zionist organizations, and benevolent institutions were established.

In the 1940s, the Jewish population reached 4,000, despite the restrictions on immigration. The León Pinelo Day School was founded, and an umbrella organization for the community was created.

In the 1960s, the population peaked at nearly 6,000 Jews. Communal life was thriving. More than 80 percent of Jewish children attended the Jewish day school in Lima, considered one of the nation's top schools, the three synagogues were in good shape, and the community enjoyed prosperity. Ties with Israel were strong, and there was a steady trickle of immigration to the Jewish state that eventually numbered over one thousand Peruvian Jews.

But the next decade witnessed the start of a thirty-year decline in the Jewish community's fortunes. First came a military coup, an economic crisis, a surge in street crime and kidnappings, and an unfriendly attitude toward Israel. (For instance, Peru, which had been a strong supporter of Israel's establishment, abstained on the infamous "Zionism is racism" resolution adopted by the UN General Assembly in 1975.)

This was followed by the terrorism and hyperinflation of the 1980s, and the severe jolts of the Fujimori period, all of which contributed to the emigration of Peruvian Jews, a rapid decline in enrollment at the Jewish school—from over one thousand students in 1970 to just 400—and a shortage of funds to maintain the extensive network of communal institutions.

Intermingled with these developments, sad to say, were several high-profile cases of alleged embezzlement and corruption by prominent Jews, including bankers and owners of newspapers and television stations.

One countervailing demographic trend during this period worthy of mention was the case of the B'nai Moshe, or Inca Jews. Numbering several hundred, they abandoned their Catholicism and began practicing a form of Judaism in the 1950s. After years of being ignored or dismissed, they were converted by an Israeli religious court in 1989 on condition that they leave their homes and move to Israel. All told, there are nearly 400 members of this community currently living in Elon Moreh, a settlement to the east of Nablus (Shechem), where it is believed that God first said to Abraham, "To your descendants will I give this land."

A second community has been seeking recognition as Jews, but so far unsuccessfully. Known as "Amazon Jews," they are descendants of Moroccan Jews who came to the region in the nineteenth century and settled in the country's interior, a thousand miles from the coast. They number no more than a few hundred and practice a faith that has been described by visitors as part Judaism, part Catholicism, and part supernaturalism.

Barring unforeseen developments, today's Jewish community, which includes a Chabad congregation, is determined to stay put. In fact, as a commitment to their future, the umbrella body, Asociación Judía de Perú, and the American Jewish Committee signed an association agreement during our recent stay in Lima. As the local Jewish leaders see it, the current government could not be friendlier, the economy has turned a corner, the community's roots run deep, and the likelihood is that the next government, to take office in July, will be well-disposed (and, according to current polls, could produce the first female president of Peru)—though, given Peru's history, political earthquakes can never be entirely excluded.

Each time I travel to a Jewish community like the Peruvian, I fantasize about bringing large numbers of American Jews with me. There are three reasons.

First, I'd like them to see the resolve of a population, in this case numbering fewer than 3,000, to maintain a full, active, and meaningful Jewish life. It just might have a salutary effect, particularly on the complacent or indifferent in our midst.

Second, the American visitors might gain a greater appreciation of the vital role that American Jews—and organizations like the American Jewish Committee—can, indeed must, play in enhancing the political and communal well-being of numerically smaller, and at times far more vulnerable, Jewish communities.

And finally, they might also understand, at a deeper level, the stake that we have, as proponents of democracy, pluralism, and economic development, in the direction that emerging countries like Peru take, not to mention the positive influence that we can exert through our active involvement in the field of international relations.

Letter from a Prisoner of Hope
December 27, 2005

This is a time of year to affirm hope. But since the news around us doesn't necessarily cooperate by respecting holidays, there's good reason for despair.

At the top of my list of concerns is the relentless challenge posed by Iran. The prospect of marrying the bone-chilling anti-Israel and anti-Semitic rhetoric of the extremist Iranian president with an undeniable quest for nuclear weapons should awaken even the most complacent among us. And those who seek comfort in the belief that the faulty intelligence on Iraq's weapons program could be repeated with Iran should think twice. There is no dispute among American, European, and Israeli intelligence agencies on Iran's nuclear intentions; to the contrary, there's a convergence of views.

What's not as clear is what to do about the challenge. Until now, Iran appears to have had the upper hand in talks with the EU3— Britain, France, and Germany. To date, every effort to strike a deal has been spurned by Tehran. Recently, Russia entered the picture with what it thought was a tantalizing offer of its own, supported by the EU3 and the United States, but so far Iran hasn't shown much interest.

There have been various "carrots" offered to Iran over the past eighteen months, including a green light to membership in the World Trade Organization, the supply of spare parts for its Boeing aircraft, acknowledgment of its right to peaceful nuclear energy, and closer economic ties with Europe. None has produced the desired result.

Conversely, there's been no consensus on the range of proposed "sticks," including military strikes, referral to the Security Council, public censure, economic sanctions, trade disruption, withdrawal of ambassadors, isolation of Iranian leaders, more aggressive support of opposition groups, and dismissal of Iran from the World Cup and Olympic movements.

Yet action is necessary; the passage of time only works in Iran's favor.

The coming months will be decisive in determining, first, the degree to which multilateral cooperation can be sustained (and, in the cases of Russia and China, achieved), and second, how far nations are prepared to go, even at cost to themselves, to prevent Iran from mastering the nuclear fuel cycle, after which the Rubicon will have been crossed. For starters, keep an eye on what happens at the next meeting of the International Atomic Energy Agency (IAEA), to be held in Vienna in March, where Iran will loom high on the agenda.

Let's not kid ourselves. If Iran is successful, all bets are off. An Iran with nuclear weapons—and the missiles to deliver them—would pose a clear and present danger to any nation within a 1,000-mile range of its borders, including, especially, Israel. Could Israel simply accept this new strategic reality? Would any of Iran's neighbors react by embarking on nuclear programs of their own? Might Iran one day arm its proxies, most notably Hezbollah, which today has a presence in dozens of countries worldwide, with nonconventional weapons? Outlandish? It was, after all, the tag team of Iran and Hezbollah, with Syrian complicity, which was behind the terror attacks in Argentina in 1992 against the Israeli embassy and 1994 against the AMIA building.

Iran is not the only reason for concern. My list is a rather long one.

North Korea, the "Hermit Kingdom," remains an enormous problem, both for the permanent threat it poses in Asia and its role as a global proliferator par excellence, including to Iran. Here, too, all outside attempts to change North Korean behavior have come up short.

While I believe that Israel was right to disengage unilaterally from Gaza, tragically, there has been little reason for short-term optimism on the peace front. Palestinians are far busier rearming than rebuilding, the Palestinian Authority is in disarray, and terror groups operate largely unchallenged by the PA. Where is Israel's partner to negotiate a durable two-state peace that brings to an end, once and for all, the claims of both sides?

Some observers, I fear, continue to underestimate the intractability of the root causes of this conflict—a refusal by many Palestinians to acknowledge an historic Jewish connection to any part of the land; a widespread belief that, from the start, Jews "stole" and "occupied" Palestinian land; entrenched and unvarnished anti-Semitism and Holocaust denial; a cult of martyrdom that accords heroic status to suicide bombers and other agents of murder and mayhem; and a sense of humiliation that the Jews, "sons of monkeys and pigs" in the vernacular heard in some mosques, somehow defeated the great Arab nation in 1948, and continue to retain the upper hand even after nearly sixty years.

I don't for a moment underestimate the ongoing dangers, divisions, and dilemmas we as a nation face in Iraq. At the same time, the growing clamor for withdrawal at this stage could create a scenario that would only make a bad situation worse. If the U.S. leaves under fire while the Sunni Triangle, in particular, remains a war zone, the impression that terrorists defeated the world's most powerful nation will incalculably damage American credibility. Generations to come will pay a heavy price, as Islamic radicals—and perhaps others with a cause—will take a page from Iraq in their efforts to bring the U.S. and like-minded nations to their knees.

Moreover, the prospect of an Iraq that could one day revert to old form is, to say the least, frightening. Remember the war it launched with Iran, resulting in one million casualties? The invasion and occupation of Kuwait? The mass killings of Iraqi Kurds using chemical weapons? The free hand given by Saddam Hussein to his sadistic sons, Qusay and Uday? The deliberately triggered environmental disasters? The harsh treatment of the Marsh Arabs and Shiite Muslims? The Scud missiles launched at Israel and Saudi Arabia? The hefty payments to the families of Palestinian terrorists for suicide bombings?

Yet today, in their blind rage at American policy, some may be forgetting what the Saddam Hussein era was really like, or allowing themselves to believe that withdrawal from Iraq can take place without damage to the undeniable progress hitherto achieved or danger to the larger region.

The tragedy of Darfur continues while the world dithers. So much for all the hot air about "never again." Massive murder, rape, pillage, and displacement go on. When will it end? How will it end? Who will end it? Crocodile tears and highfalutin rhetoric don't save lives or send shivers down the spine of the Sudanese government, much less the state-supported Arab militias perpetrating the attacks.

Meanwhile, consider these mind-boggling statistics: Nearly three billion people live on less than two dollars a day; the same number have no access to sanitation; 1.3 billion people have no access to clean water; nearly a billion people are unable to read a book or sign their name; 20 percent of the world's population consume 86 percent of the world's goods; and more than 800 million people, including 300 million children, go to bed hungry every night.

Or put another way, the combined GNP of the world's forty-eight poorest nations is less than the wealth of the world's three wealthiest individuals, according to the Paris-based *Le Monde Diplomatique*.

Closer to home, I've just returned from an AJC mission to hurricane-ravaged New Orleans. I was overwhelmed by the magnitude and intensity of the devastation, even four months after Katrina, which disproportionately struck the poorest and most vulnerable of the region's inhabitants. I am concerned lest our country falter in its commitment to a massive rebuilding effort that will take years to complete.

Our nation's failure to embark on a full-court press to reduce dependence on imported oil remains for me among life's biggest mysteries. For the past twenty years, we've dreamily lived as if cheap and plentiful oil were our God-given right and as if the consequences of transferring billions of dollars to such retrograde countries as Saudi Arabia had no impact on our national security, political independence, or economic well-being.

My list of concerns goes on. I've only scratched the surface. But wait a second—isn't this letter guilty of "bait and switch" tactics by mentioning the word "hope" in its title, you might ask?

As a matter of fact, I'm a great believer in the power of hope—"the last thing ever lost," according to an Italian proverb—as is the agency I work for, the American Jewish Committee, whose credo is "Choosing hope."

It was the prophet Zechariah who used the term "prisoners of hope," if in a different context. I proudly admit to being one of those prisoners. Were it not for my unwavering belief in the possibility of change, I couldn't do the work I do.

There are, of course, other, less sanguine views of hope. François de La Rochefoucauld, the seventeenth-century Frenchman known for his pessimism, remarked, "Hope, deceitful as it is, serves at least to lead us to the end of our lives by an agreeable route." The English novelist Charles Dickens defined hope as "that very popular trust in flat things coming round!" And the German philosopher Friedrich Nietzsche wrote of hope, "the worst of evils, for it prolongs the torment of man."

Yet I've seen enough examples of the realization of hope to convince me, precisely at moments such as this, that we mustn't abandon it or allow ourselves to succumb to a debilitating sense of despair, that maintaining unflinching resolve, purpose, and faith can pay off. And that, even with all its inevitable zigs, zags, and reversals, history in the end moves forward.

Perhaps William Faulkner expressed it best in his speech accepting the Nobel Prize in Literature in 1950:

I decline to accept the end of man. It is easy enough to say that man is immortal simply because he will endure: that when the last ding-dong of doom has clanged and faded from the last worthless rock hanging tideless in the last red and dying evening, that even then there will still be one more sound: that of his puny, inexhaustible voice, still talking. I refuse to accept this. I believe that man will not merely endure: he will prevail. He is immortal, not because he alone among creatures has an inexhaustible voice, but because he has a soul, a spirit capable of compassion and sacrifice and endurance.

To illustrate my viewpoint, let me go back to 1975, the year I entered the Jewish professional world.

I had just been on a three-month-long teachers' exchange program in the Soviet Union, before being expelled. Subsequently, I began working in Rome with Jewish refugees, primarily from the Soviet Union.

I was immersed in an all-consuming vocabulary: Union of Soviet Socialist Republics, Cold War, Mutual Assured Destruction, Berlin Wall, Warsaw Pact, COMECON, Politburo, Gulag, samizdat, refuseniks, dissidents, informers, Prisoners of Zion, OVIR, *vyzovs* (i.e., affidavits from Israel), Communist Party of the Soviet Union, Komsomol, Pioneers, KGB, Soviet Anti-Zionist Committee, and so forth.

There had been no Israeli embassy in Moscow since 1967. There were no Jewish organizations operating openly in the USSR. There was only one synagogue, closely monitored, in all of Moscow; the same was true in Leningrad. The Soviet Union was arming Israel's enemies and helping spearhead the worldwide anti-Zionist campaign.

Who, in 1975, could have imagined that in our lifetimes the entire Cold War vocabulary would essentially go out the window? That, instead of one USSR, with fifteen republics, there would be fifteen independent countries? That the three Baltic nations would become members of NATO and the European Union? That the Israeli embassy in Moscow would be reopened? That a Russian president, Vladimir Putin, would establish a close personal tie with the Israeli prime minister? That Jewish organizations would participate in a veritable renaissance of Jewish life throughout what is now euphemistically referred to as the Former Soviet Union?

Who could have guessed that more than one million Soviet Jews would resettle in Israel, giving a huge lift to the nation in every sphere? That Natan Sharansky, political prisoner for nine years in the Gulag, would serve in the Israeli cabinet? That Germany would become the fastest-growing Jewish community in the world because of the influx of Jews from the FSU? That nearly one-quarter of the New York Jewish community would be comprised of Jews born in the USSR?

When I was an undergraduate at the University of Pennsylvania, I took a Russian history course with a very popular professor, Alexander Riasanovsky. He told a story of a relative—I believe it was his father—who was summoned to the Soviet secret police in the 1930s and questioned.

"Where were you born?" he was asked by the interrogator.

"St. Petersburg," he replied.

"Where were you educated?"

"Petrograd."

"Where do you currently live?"

"Leningrad."

"And where do you want to live?"

"St. Petersburg."

For that answer, he was sent to prison.

Who could have conceived in the 1930s, or even the 1970s, that, had he lived long enough, he might have realized his wish to live again in St. Petersburg?

In 1975, Israel had no formal peace treaty with any Arab nation.

That's changed. While, thirty years ago, an eventual peace accord with Jordan didn't seem impossible to imagine, given the history of quiet cooperation, the same couldn't be said for Egypt, the Arab world's largest and most influential nation and Israel's most implacable enemy. Yet today we speak of peace with both Egypt and Jordan. No, not a perfect peace, but peace nonetheless.

And Israel maintains contact, more or less openly, with at least half the Arab world, including full diplomatic ties with Mauritania and links with Morocco, Tunisia, Qatar, Oman, Bahrain, and the United Arab Emirates.

As I noted earlier, huge regional challenges still face Israel, but there can be no denying that previously unimaginable progress has been achieved.

And, in the same thirty-year period, Israel's population has doubled, its armed forces have maintained their qualitative edge, Israel has become a world leader in high technology, and its per capita GNP places it well within the West European range.

Meanwhile, the implosion of the Soviet bloc has meant, among other things, a new reservoir of political support for Israel from such countries as Poland, the Czech Republic, Bulgaria, Romania, Hungary, and Slovakia. And these very countries which, during the Cold War, supplied arms to Israel's foes and havens for anti-Israel terrorist groups, have turned a dramatic new page.

In 1975, Israel's ties with India and Turkey were chilly. Today those bilateral relationships are linchpins of Israel's foreign policy—defense cooperation is substantial, trade is booming, and human contacts are ever more numerous.

Remember the infamous UN General Assembly resolution, adopted in November 1975, which defined Zionism as a form of racism and racial discrimination? Its defamatory impact could be felt around the world. Where is it today? Repealed by the very same body that adopted it, one of the rare instances when the UN actually reversed itself. It took sixteen years of hard work to accomplish, but people of vision and iron will made it happen.

In 1975, South Africa was governed by apartheid. Minority rule prevailed. People were classified by color under the 1950 Population Registration Act. Where they could live was determined by race. Artificial "homelands," or Bantustans, were created to further restrict movement and rights. Eighty-seven percent of the land was in the hands of less than twenty percent of the population. Nelson Mandela had already been in prison for thirteen years. The African National Congress was banned.

That South Africa is now in the dustbin of history, replaced by a new, democratic South Africa, whose first president, in 1994, was none other than Nelson Mandela of the governing African National Congress.

When I began working in 1975, the Jewish community in Ethiopia was largely unknown to the outside world. There were only a few Ethiopian Jews in Israel and limited contact between Jewish groups and this ancient Jewish community in Ethiopia's Gondar Province.

In an extraordinary chapter of Jewish history, tens of thousands of Ethiopian Jews began streaming out of the country, mostly on foot and at great risk, fulfilling their age-old dream of "going up" to Zion. Several thousand died en route, victims of marauding bandits and harsh conditions, but the bulk eventually made it to Israel, thanks to exceptional courage and ingenious rescue schemes. I have seen first-hand the villages whence they came, and appreciate the vast cultural bridge they had to cross. Their integration into Israeli life, even with all the reported difficulties, has been awe-inspiring.

In 1975, Greece was getting rid of the right-wing colonels who had ruled the country for eight years; Generalisimo Francisco Franco, Spain's fascist leader for nearly four decades, was departing the scene; Portugal, just embarking on democracy after decades of repressive government, was finally letting go of Angola, Mozambique, and other African colonies; Germany was geographically divided; and Ireland was perhaps the poorest country in Western Europe.

Greece, Spain, and Portugal are now all thriving members of the European Union; Germany is reunited; and Ireland has become one of Europe's wealthiest nations.

In 1975, France still rejected responsibility for the wartime crimes of Vichy; Switzerland was stonewalling on the bank accounts of Holocaust victims; Austria refused to come to grips with its own central role in the Nazi period; East European concentration camp inmates and slave and forced laborers didn't receive a penny in compensation from West Germany; and the United States Holocaust Memorial Museum didn't exist.

Today France has acknowledged its past; Switzerland has sought to make financial amends; Austria has admitted that it wasn't the first "victim" nation of the Nazis, as it sought to portray itself for decades; hundreds of thousands of East European Jewish and non-Jewish survivors are receiving monthly stipends in recognition of the unimaginable suffering inflicted on them; and year after year, millions of visitors, mostly non-Jewish, come to the museum on Washington's National Mall to learn about the history of the Shoah.

In 1975, the Vietnam War was just coming to an end; Pol Pot became the prime minister of the "Democratic Republic of Kampuchea" in Cambodia, which in turn led to the horrific genocide of as many as two million Cambodians; and Augusto Pinochet was in charge of a right-wing dictatorship in Chile, responsible for thousands of murders.

Today Vietnam, while still Communist, is a popular destination for American tourists; Cambodia is no longer in the clutches of the madmen who created the "killing fields" and instead has become another popular tourist destination; and Chile has emerged as the number-one success story in Latin America—with solid democratic institutions and a strong economy.

And speaking of democracies, according to Freedom House, forty-one countries, representing one-quarter of the world's population, were classified as "free" in 1974, whereas, in 2004, the number of free countries was eighty-nine, representing nearly half of the global population.

I could go on to mention the remarkable advances in medicine, health care, technology, agriculture, and science; the rapidly growing importance of nongovernmental organizations that serve as watchdogs for monitoring human rights protections; and the great strides made in empowering women and minorities in many societies.

In saying this, I'm not seeking to paint a black-and-white picture, either of 1975 or of today. All wasn't bad then; all is far from good today.

We have immense challenges before us—as Jews, Americans, democrats (not Democrats), and pluralists.

And as the prospectus for any mutual fund indicates, past results are not necessarily a guarantee of future results. There's always the risk that "the future isn't what it used to be."

My point is simply this: It seems rough now, whether looking at the larger world or our Jewish world; it was no less rough before.

There were those who believed the sky was falling thirty years ago; their counterparts today give voice to the same message of gloom and doom.

There were those who chose to underestimate the enemies or, still worse, to attempt to pacify or appease them; their ideological descendants can be heard today making essentially the same arguments.

Then there were the steadfast and resolute—"prisoners of hope"— who, whatever their own differences, believed that values like democracy, human rights, equality before the law, a world free of racism and anti-Semitism, and religious freedom were worth fighting for and defending. They fixed one eye on the ground before them, while the other never stopped gazing at the stars.

May we always dare to be prisoners of hope.

2. SPEECHES AND TESTIMONY

Center for International Relations
Warsaw, Poland
February 4, 2004

I would like to thank you, Ambassador Janusz Reiter [president, Center for International Relations], for the opportunity to speak at this prestigious forum.

I know I'm in the company of experts and practitioners in the field of diplomacy and foreign policy, and I must say it's a humbling experience for me. But not humbling enough for me to sit down yet!

I've been traveling in Europe for the last week, and the one question I've been asked in foreign policy circles more than any other has been: Who will be the next president of the United States? Perhaps I can dispose of that question by recounting a joke from the Cold War era.

Two officials—one from the KGB, the other from the CIA—debate which country has the better espionage service. The KGB official declares: "We have managed to penetrate the vaults in Washington. We've found the results of the presidential elections for the last one hundred years. And now we have all that data safely stored in the Kremlin." The CIA official responds: "Oh, that's nothing. We have managed to penetrate the Kremlin's vaults, and we've found the results for the next one hundred years of Soviet elections. They are now sitting in the White House."

At the American Jewish Committee, we don't have access to anyone's vault. More seriously, all I can say at this point is what I believe to be rather obvious. First, the election could prove to be very close. It will certainly be vigorously contested and could get nasty. And second, the key issues are likely to be national security and the state of the economy.

I'm joined in Warsaw by nine colleagues from the American Jewish Committee, including Stanislaw Krajewski, our director here and a person known to many of you. Our visit is part of a long-term investment in the new and democratic Poland that has taken shape in the last fifteen years. Our investment, as a nongovernmental organization, is not in the commercial sector; rather, we seek to invest in the political, diplomatic, and human sectors. Our institutional philosophy is driven by the belief that we must be students of history, but never its prisoners. Some view the relationship between Poland and the Jewish people only through the complicated prism of the past. Others, including ourselves, study the past as a guide, but never as an excuse for paralysis or inaction.

The American Jewish Committee has sought to participate in the writing of a promising new chapter in relations between Poland and the Jewish people. Starting in the late 1980s, this became possible in a way that few might have foreseen. In fact, the past fifteen years have been extraordinarily exciting, with many pleasant surprises along the way. For our part, we at the American Jewish Committee were privileged to stand foursquare in support of the first round of NATO enlargement, including, of course, Poland, and to testify before the United States Senate in this regard. This was, I must tell you, one of our proudest moments. We are delighted to have a presence in Warsaw, which facilitates daily contact between the American Jewish Committee and a broad range of Polish governmental and nongovernmental institutions. And we are struck by the changing nature of the agenda that informs these daily contacts, as we talk more and more about the future, about possibilities for collaboration, and about bringing young people together.

When we decided to support Poland's NATO candidacy, there were those who wondered if our confidence was misplaced. No more. Poland's demonstration of solidarity with the United States in the war on global terrorism speaks volumes about Polish values and priorities. The commitment of Polish troops to Iraq and the leadership your troops have shown in the district under your control demonstrate exceptional courage, resolve, and friendship. Permit me to use this occasion to express our admiration and appreciation. You can be certain that we shall do our utmost in the United States to ensure that Poland's role is understood and recognized.

We know that our visit to Warsaw comes on the eve of a defining moment for Poland and Europe. On May 1, Poland, together with nine other countries, will join the European Union, bringing its membership to twenty-five nations. The anchoring of Poland in NATO and the European Union seemed only a distant dream just a few years ago. We fully understand, even as outsiders, the many-tiered significance of these two developments, both of which augur a bright future for Polish security and well-being. We will be with you in spirit on May 1 in Dublin, when EU accession becomes official. I only wonder if the visionary architects of European integration, who began the process by seeking a formula to end war between France and Germany, could have imagined how far their initiative would go. Of course, the process of enlargement is still not completed. Other countries, including Bulgaria and Romania, wait in line, and some further hint as to the fate of Turkey's candidacy is expected before this year ends.

Another striking development in recent Polish history has been the rapidly growing bilateral relationship between Warsaw and Jerusalem. Indeed, this link has become a pillar of Polish foreign policy. In that context, I'm delighted that the new Israeli ambassador to Poland is here this evening. For those who have not yet met him, permit me to introduce my close friend and a distinguished diplomat, David Peleg.

I also see Ambassador Maciej Kozlowski in the audience. Ambassador Kozlowski, whom I first met when he was posted to the Polish embassy in Washington, recently completed service as Poland's ambassador to Israel and is currently at work, if I understand correctly, on assessing the impact of EU accession on Poland's policy in the Middle East.

If I may be so bold as to express a view on the matter, I hope that at the end of the day the EU's Common Foreign and Security Policy will more closely resemble Poland's position, and not the other way around. I know that there is already pressure on Poland to realign its posture toward Israel in order to bring it closer to the position of certain influential EU member countries. Poland has amply demonstrated its strong will on matters of principle and its refusal to give in easily. I trust that in relation to Israel the same will hold true. Poland and Israel have nurtured a relationship that serves the interests of both nations. By dint of historical experience, the two countries share an understanding of the dangers of hostile neighbors. And the cultural and human bridges forged are deeply rooted and quite unique.

It is no secret that within the European Union there are differing viewpoints with respect to Israel and the Arab-Israel peace process. We count on Poland to associate itself with those most understanding of Israel's real and unenviable challenges in achieving peace and security in a volatile neighborhood. And we believe that many of the other new EU member states will be looking to Poland, as the largest of the ten new countries, for guidance, whether they say so openly or not.

I cannot overstate the importance we attach to this issue or, I'm certain, that Jerusalem and Washington do. It will have profound and lasting repercussions.

In his generous introduction, Ambassador Reiter suggested that we had some concerns about EU policy in the Middle East. Indeed, we do. While I have the greatest admiration and respect for the EU, I believe that on Arab-Israeli issues the EU has, to some degree, dealt itself out of the game by its tilt toward the Palestinians and away from Israel. German foreign minister Joschka Fischer made this point when he told his EU colleagues that they could not have it both ways—frequently criticizing Israel while expecting, at the same time, to enjoy Israel's confidence as a peace facilitator. This is most unfortunate, because the EU can play an important role in a number of spheres, not least by virtue of its own example.

The foundation of the EU, its common denominator among member states, is a profound commitment to democracy and its core values— freedom, human dignity, and the rule of law. And that, of course, is what most clearly differentiates Europe today from the Middle East, with the exception of Israel.

We at the American Jewish Committee are unabashed advocates of democracy and its guiding principles. Through democracy, the human spirit is unleashed. Through democracy, the frontiers of inquiry and knowledge are pushed to their limit. Through democracy, all citizens, whatever their race, religion, ethnicity, or gender, are invited to share in shaping their collective and individual destinies. Through democracy, wars between nations become obsolete and are replaced by peaceful conflict resolution.

I am very conscious of the fact that we are meeting this evening in the city that launched the Community of Democracy Initiative several years ago and propelled it forward to Seoul and next to Santiago. For this reason—and many more—Poland has become associated with the struggle for democracy and the rejection of any form of tyranny.

Yet when we look at the roster of the Community of Democracy Initiative, one group of countries is strikingly missing. There are countries from all the world's continents, but how many members of the twenty-two-nation Arab League? Why is this bloc of nations so resistant to democracy? In recent years, we have seen the welcome winds of change here in Central and Eastern Europe, in South Africa, in much of Latin America and Asia, but only marginally in the Arab world. Hence the remarkable 2003 Arab Development Report that spoke of the three deficits—the freedom deficit, the knowledge deficit, and the women's deficit. This was an unusual exercise in unflinching self-examination; its lessons need to be taken seriously.

Call me a dreamer, but I believe the EU can play a vital role in encouraging the democratic process and, with time, the lessons of European integration in the Middle East.

The European Union, I fully understand, seeks a larger role in the Middle East. Eager for an Israeli-Palestinian settlement, it does not want to be sidelined or relegated to a backseat role. But, as I noted, Israel and its friends do not have full confidence in the impartiality of the EU as a collective body on issues related to Arab-Israeli peacemaking.

That does not mean that within the EU there are not countries that have achieved a level of trust and confidence. Germany and Israel, for instance, do have a special relationship. But somehow when the EU comes together, it's too often driven by a lowest-common-denominator foreign policy regarding Israel. Hopefully, however, with Poland's help, that may begin to change.

I watch the UN very carefully both in New York and Geneva. I can count on one hand the number of times the EU as a bloc has voted with Israel on an issue. More often the EU abstains; at times it votes against Israel.

Moreover, from my perspective, the EU, for whatever reason, does not fully appreciate the security dilemma that Israel faces.

Let me put my own cards on the table. I believe in a two-state solution to the conflict. There is no other peaceful settlement possible. The majority of Israelis fully share this view. They have no interest whatsoever in occupying or dominating another people, even in a situation not of Israel's making. This is simply antithetical to the deeply rooted moral tradition of the Jewish people.

Israel today faces an overwhelming challenge—with whom shall it reach that two-state solution? The answer is anything but obvious, I'm sorry to say. The diplomatic conundrum we face is that a negotiated peace cannot be achieved with Yasir Arafat at the helm of not one but three entities: the Palestinian Authority, the PLO, and Fatah. Arafat has proven beyond the shadow of a doubt that his goal is war against Israel, not peace with Israel. But peace cannot realistically be achieved without Arafat, either. In truth, without Arafat's blessing, who in the Palestinian community has the authority or credibility to negotiate a lasting peace with Israel?

There are those in the European Union who have invested so heavily in Arafat over the years that they cannot face the reality that Arafat is not the partner for peace many had hoped for. I was among those at the White House in 1993 for the signing of the Oslo Accords. Whatever doubts some of us may have privately harbored, we nonetheless hoped and prayed that we were bearing witness to an historical turning point. And yet in the ensuing ten years, we learned that Arafat was not prepared to make the "peace of the brave," as he liked to call it. Rhetoric was one thing, reality quite another.

Not only do we have this diplomatic conundrum, but we also face another, equally daunting challenge. Things on the ground in this region don't simply stand still. The Middle East is not the divided island of Cyprus, for example, where, while the status quo may not be acceptable to one or both sides, neither views terrorism or other forms of violence as the answer to the standoff.

No, in the Palestinian-Israeli conflict, it is quiet different. The status quo is unacceptable. Rather than negotiate in good faith, the Palestinians have used terror to advance their goals. Hundreds of

Israelis riding buses, drinking coffee at cafés, attending a bar mitzvah, or participating in a Passover Seder have paid with their lives.

What is Israel to do under the circumstances? With no credible negotiating partner and with Palestinians plotting terror attacks just a few hundred meters from where Israelis live—few outside the region can appreciate the tiny dimensions of the space we're talking about—does Israel not have the right to defend itself? What would any other country do under similar circumstances? And do we not know by now that there is no clean, neat, and surgical method for Israel to combat terrorism? Do we forget that the terrorists are prepared to use children as shields, hide in mosques, and place their weapons-making workshops in apartment buildings, precisely to portray Israel as callous in its response? Coalition forces have learned the same realities in Afghanistan and Iraq.

But being compelled to adapt to such gritty circumstances does not blur the clear moral distinctions between the two sides—the side representing democracy and freedom, and the side representing tyranny and terror. Yes, mistakes have been made by Coalition forces in Iraq, as they have been made by Israeli troops. Yes, they are unfortunate, sometimes tragic. And yes, every effort must be made to avoid such mistakes. But to set the bar too high, given the nature and tactics of the enemy, is to separate oneself from the reality of armed combat.

Somehow, I have the feeling that these points occasionally get lost in Brussels. Instead, there is the "if only" approach: If only Israel had a different prime minister, if only Israel de-emphasized military responses, or if only Israel eased the conditions for Palestinians, then terror would abate and peace would approach.

This is an illusion. Both Ehud Barak from the left and Ariel Sharon from the right faced essentially the same set of issues—Palestinian terrorism and the absence of a credible Palestinian partner. Israel has tried a variety of responses, including attempts to de-escalate the conflict, open the borders to Palestinian workers, and relinquish control over the daily governance of Palestinians, as provided for in the Oslo Accords. Tragically, the results speak for themselves.

I wish for nothing more in my lifetime than a genuine accord between Israelis and Palestinians that provides for two states living side by side in peace. I refuse to give up hope, though the situation at the moment surely does not lend itself to much optimism. But if France and Germany could discard decades of enmity and war, and if the Berlin Wall could fall, leaving the Iron Curtain a fading memory, then anything becomes possible, with vision and the will to match.

There is one final subject I'd like to touch on—Europe and the United States. At the end of the day, whatever the differences *du jour*, Europe and the United States need each other today as much as ever. By the way, I fully understand the difficulty of speaking about Europe as a monolithic bloc, given the striking internal differences that have been revealed on subjects ranging from Iraq to the European constitution.

That said, I profoundly believe that the transatlantic partnership is the world's best hope for trying to ensure global stability, advancing the reach of freedom, protecting human rights, and vanquishing those enemies who are out to destroy the foundational values that define our societies.

We face two epic battles. The first is on the battlefield, though these days as often as not in the form of nonconventional warfare against terrorists and their sponsors. And the second battle, to which I made earlier reference, is to extend the reach of peace, freedom, tolerance, and economic advancement.

Winning only one of the two battles will not suffice. Both must be won, and decisively. Easier said than done, I know. But what is the alternative, to bury our heads in the sand and hope that the problems will simply disappear, or to fool ourselves into believing that there are band-aid solutions that will prove lasting?

Truth be told, neither Europe nor America acting alone can succeed. Sure, differences in strategy and tactics will surface within Europe or between Europe and America. This is only natural. But if, heaven forbid, we operate on separate, or still worse, competing tracks, then the dangers multiply and the chances for success recede.

We are facing transnational challenges, and therefore the response must be multinational. Saudi Arabia, we are told, has spent tens of billions of dollars to export its radical and medieval interpretation of Islam to the four corners of the earth, building schools and mosques as modes of transmission and staffing them with exponents of Wahhabism. Pakistan, incidentally one of the principal recipients of this Saudi largesse, is exporting its nuclear know-how and missile technology to states that aspire to global disorder.

Can any of us sit back comfortably knowing that millions of young men in Muslim religious schools are being fed a daily fare of Koran, martyrdom, and jihad? Is it unrealistic to believe that one day they will join the legions of veterans of the Afghan war against the Russians and the other so-called holy wars, from Bosnia to Chechnya to Kashmir, who are ready at a moment's notice to show up at the next battleground or to blow themselves up in the belief that seventy-two virgins await them?

Can we really draw airtight national boundaries and say that those issues affect you, but not me? These are transnational threats, every bit as much as are the environment, migration, and AIDS. None of these issues respects borders.

How do we achieve the best chance for success in facing these daunting challenges? Again, it's only by the United States and Europe working in partnership. And within the EU, come May 1, there will be added one significant country, the size of Spain and the size of the other nine new member states combined. That country, of course, is Poland. Poland has the opportunity very quickly to establish itself as a bridge country—between East and West, between Europe and the United States, and between Europe and Israel. I know that when the Polish people put their mind to something, their determination becomes practically legendary. We count on your determination. A great deal is resting on it. In turn, you can count on our continued friendship and support.

Dziękuję bardzo. Thank you very much.

Opening of the Transatlantic Institute
Conrad Hotel
Brussels, Belgium
February 12, 2004

Dr. Javier Solana, high representative for the common foreign and security policy of the European Union; Belgian Foreign Minister Louis Michel, Spanish Foreign Minister Ana Palacio, French Minister of European Affairs Noëlle Lenoir, U.S. Permanent Representative to NATO R. Nicholas Burns, U.S. Ambassador to the European Union Rockwell Anthony Schnabel;

Distinguished diplomats accredited to the European Union, NATO, and Belgium;

Dignitaries from the European Commission, honored members of the European Parliament;

Leaders of European Jewish communities, who have come from near and far;

Friends of the American Jewish Committee from governmental and nongovernmental institutions across Europe and the United States, including Susan Berresford, president of the Ford Foundation;

Members of the American Jewish Committee's Board of Governors and other members of the AJC delegation who are present this evening;

And Rhoda and Jordan Baruch, who turned our dream of a Transatlantic Institute into reality through their exceptional vision and generosity, together with members of their family representing three generations,

Good evening and welcome. *Bon soir* and *bienvenues.*

Sometimes I consider myself an endangered species. I am, you see, a committed transatlanticist. Until just a short time ago that was a rather unexceptional thing to be; most people I knew on both sides of the Atlantic were, to varying degrees, in the same club. Now, however, in some places, it could get me in big trouble, though not here at the Conrad Hotel this evening, I trust.

Call me hopelessly, irredeemably naïve, but, as a son of America and grandson of Europe, I remain convinced that Americans and

Europeans are joined at the hip by common foundational values and common existential threats, and thus by a common agenda.

Our shared values emanate from the very building blocks of our respective societies: democracy, the rule of law, and respect for the dignity of the individual.

The ties that link this precious fraternity of kindred nations must never be permitted to fray, for they represent the best—indeed, I would argue the only—hope for the ultimate realization of a genuinely peaceful and prosperous world.

After all, the democratic nations have renounced war as an instrument of resolving policy disputes among themselves. The weapons of choice when disagreements arise between democratic nations are diplomats and lawyers, not armies and suicide bombers.

The challenges facing our countries are, to a large degree, transnational—from terrorism to weapons proliferation and from failing states to fanaticism in the name of faith, not to mention the growing economic and technological divides between rich and poor, the unrelenting march of migration, the fragility of our environment, and the merciless spread of the AIDS virus.

None of these challenges is unique to any one nation. Rather, they are overarching and demand our collective attention.

In other words, even at the risk of stating the obvious—though I've learned that the obvious isn't necessarily obvious to all—the United States and Europe need each other now as much as ever.

At the end of the day, together, we must prevail in two battles, not one. We must win the war against those who threaten the fabric and fiber of our democratic societies. And we must win the peace to extend the reach of freedom, religious and ethnic tolerance, conflict resolution, and economic empowerment. Winning one battle without the other will prove a Pyrrhic victory.

Both of us have a profound stake in unleashing the forces of genuine democratization, equal protection before the law, and robust civil society in countries that by and large have been remarkably resistant to the breathtaking political and economic revolutions of recent times. Some of those countries are practically at Europe's doorstep; others, though more distant, nonetheless cast a long shadow.

No one should underestimate the enormity of the challenge, but those who cynically argue that the real choice in such countries is between tyranny and turmoil need to be proved wrong. A third way can be found; it must be found. Our belief in the indivisibility of human dignity demands no less. And transatlantic cooperation increases the likelihood of success.

Take Pakistan, for example. Imagine for a moment the catastrophic consequences if it descended into civil war or fell into the hands of the Islamists.

Here's a country of 150 million with 40 percent of its population under the age of fifteen. Not only does Pakistan possess weapons of mass destruction, but the world was on edge not long ago when India and Pakistan engaged in nuclear brinkmanship.

Moreover, there are nearly one million youngsters studying full-time in *madrassas*, private religious schools, where the Koran and jihad, and not physics and biology, are the principal educational fare, and Osama bin Laden could win his share of popularity contests. What's the future for these young people, and how will their future impact on us? Yet many of them, we are told, are in those schools not for reasons of ideology but simply in search of a hot lunch and a roof over their heads.

The unraveling of Pakistan would hit the jackpot on the political Richter scale and send massive shock waves throughout its neighborhood. Moreover, it would have staggering reverberations for both Europe and the United States.

The case of Pakistan, I would argue, is only Exhibit A indicating the need for greater transatlantic policy coordination.

The United States, by dint of its size, influence, and global reach, brings a great deal to the table. So does the European Union.

Working together, we increase the chances of success; working on separate tracks or, heaven forbid, at cross purposes, we only embolden our common enemies.

Let me digress for a moment. I am a longtime admirer of the European Union. The more I understand the inventive genius of Jean Monnet, the Frenchman called upon by Robert Schuman, the postwar French foreign minister, to conceptualize a structure that would prevent future wars with Germany, the more in awe I am and the more I appreciate the need for similarly bold thinking today.

The European Union's evolution over the past fifty years, based on the vision of political giants, has been nothing short of breathtaking. In fact, I believe the European Union to be the most ambitious and successful peace project in modern history.

A European Union of fifteen nations, soon to be twenty-five, with Bulgaria and Romania poised to join a few years hence, has much to teach other regions about institution-building and integration.

I am unwilling to accept the proposition that some other regions, including vast swaths of the Arab world, have no choice for the future but to live under corrupt, autocratic, suffocating regimes—with their striking deficits of freedom, human rights, women's emancipation, and academic inquiry.

Once again, as in the postwar period, these times require the vision of true statesmen. We must dare to dream and have the courage to act.

Ladies and gentlemen, leaders on both sides of the Atlantic Ocean need to emphasize our common values, common concerns, and, yes, common objectives. Some of those leaders are here this evening, and I salute their farsighted and principled leadership.

To be sure, there are, and inevitably will always be, differences between Europe, or at least some European nations, and the United States rooted in political rivalry, economic competition, and divergent assessments. In the larger scheme of things, however, and with a measure of good will, these differences ought to be quite manageable. In any case, they must never be permitted to overshadow our commonalities.

The American Jewish Committee has for decades been a trailblazer in building bridges between Europe and the United States. And at moments such as this, when cracks in the foundation have been revealed and younger people in particular may question the ties that bind us, the work of bridge building becomes still more important.

That is precisely why we chose to launch this initiative at this time. Talk, as they say, is cheap. It's action that is needed, and we want to do our part.

It means for us never losing sight of the larger picture of Europe and America as the likeliest of strategic allies.

It means never succumbing to the notion that Europeans and Americans may still live in the same solar system but no longer on the same planet.

It means resisting the temptation to declare that we Americans have gravitated irreversibly toward Hobbes, hard power, unilateralism, and the tug of faith, while Europeans have been hypnotized by Kant, soft power, multilateralism, and secularism, as if such sweeping generalizations could withstand close scrutiny.

And it also means facing the inevitable, tough issues where we may not necessarily find a complete convergence of views, but always doing so in ways that befit friends.

For us at the American Jewish Committee, those tough issues today include, above all, Israel's standing in the community of nations, which has come under frequent and repeated assault by too many who fail to understand that genuine peace cannot be achieved absent a credible and committed Palestinian partner.

No nation on the face of this earth yearns for peace more than the nation of Israel, which has not known a single day of true peace since its founding fifty-five years ago.

No nation has demonstrated a greater willingness to take tangible territorial risks in pursuit of peace than Israel, a country barely two-thirds the size of Belgium.

And yet peace cannot occur in a vacuum. Tragically, for Israelis and Palestinians alike, such a vacuum does exist. What is most glaringly missing is a Palestinian leadership prepared to foreswear terror and incitement and negotiate in good faith a two-state solution that is the only viable answer to this heart-wrenching conflict.

The tough issues also include our dismay at the rise in global anti-Semitism, and especially within the Muslim world. The rise is real, it is demonstrable, and it is chilling.

Troublingly, there are some who have sought to deny or minimize this ominous development; others who have attempted to rationalize it; and even those who have tried to lay blame for the problem on the Jews themselves.

We should be absolutely clear. Yes, anti-Semitism is a non-Jewish disease that directly threatens Jews. But history has amply taught us that anti-Semitism never stops with Jews. Ultimately, left unchecked, it will enter the bloodstream of otherwise civilized societies, and eventually damage, if not destroy, them.

And history has also taught us, or at least should have taught us, that anti-Semitism must be fought tenaciously, and not just by Jews. Whatever the source of the anti-Semitism, all well-meaning people need to join in the struggle. Political leaders have a special role to play, as do law enforcement and judicial authorities. The voices of civic, religious, human rights, and intellectual leaders must never be silent. And in the long term, there can be no substitute for the role of education in inculcating in young people the values of mutual respect and social harmony.

We count on the European Union, the United States, other democratic nations, and the nongovernmental organizations represented here this evening to stand strong and resolute in the struggle against what has been called the world's most enduring hatred.

The Transatlantic Institute will, we hope, quickly become an important new venue for addressing these and other pressing issues, such as the challenges posed by migration and acculturation, fanaticism and fundamentalism, bigotry in all its insidious forms, the relationship between religion and state, and dialogue among faiths, that affect Europeans and Americans alike.

Indeed, earlier today we held our first public trialogue among European Christian, Jewish, and Muslim leaders here in Brussels.

Our overriding goal is not simply to identify common problems but, even more importantly, to help pinpoint constructive, forward-looking solutions. In this effort, we shall seek the collaboration of like-minded individuals, trusted friends, on both sides of the Atlantic, many of whom are in this ballroom tonight.

Ladies and gentlemen, you honor us by your presence here this evening. Thank you for joining us in celebration of the opening of the Transatlantic Institute.

And once again, a very special word of appreciation to Rhoda and Jordan Baruch, the wonderful parents who gave birth to this beautiful new child.

"The Role of Education"
Organization for Security and Cooperation in Europe
Conference on Anti-Semitism
Berlin, Germany
April 28, 2004

Mr. Chairman, distinguished delegates,

Permit me to commend the fifty-five OSCE member nations for holding this timely conference on anti-Semitism. Your concern sends a powerful message about the importance you attach to the current struggle against what has been accurately described as the world's most enduring hatred.

How appropriate that Bulgaria now occupies the chair of the OSCE Permanent Council, given its laudable wartime efforts to protect its Jewish community against the tragic fate that befell six million of their coreligionists. There is much to be learned from the Bulgarian experience.

And allow me to express appreciation to the German government for hosting this gathering. It is entirely fitting that we assemble here in Berlin, which has emerged, after the infinite darkness of the Shoah, as a bright ray of light in the global campaign against anti-Semitism.

Our target audience in this session is youth. In 2000, I led a graduate-level seminar on post-Holocaust issues in Bologna, Italy. As part of the yearlong course, I encouraged my students, who came from Europe and the United States, to help me develop an action plan for dealing with contemporary anti-Semitism and other forms of bigotry—one example of the potential role of students as partners in this process.

Ten components of a comprehensive plan were identified. It is worth sharing them with you in outline form:

(i) building democratic societies based on the principles of equality before the law and respect for pluralism;

(ii) recognizing anti-Semitism when it manifests itself, whatever its source, and facing it squarely, without seeking to diminish it through rationalization or justification;

(iii) emphasizing the absolutely indispensable role of political leadership—and political will—in educating and mobilizing a nation;

(iv) ensuring that there are adequate laws to deal specifically with hate crimes, and that law enforcement and the judiciary are up to the task of apprehending and appropriately punishing offenders;

(v) utilizing the UN Convention on the Elimination of All Forms of Discrimination, the International Covenant of Civil and Political Rights, and other pertinent covenants, together with regional and global forums, such as the OSCE and UNESCO, as legal and diplomatic weapons to combat the purveyors of hatred;

(vi) encouraging responsible media outlets to focus the spotlight of exposure on acts of hate, and simultaneously ensuring that these outlets are never used, advertently or inadvertently, as vehicles to propagate bigotry and intolerance;

(vii) building a coalition of conscience in civil society that deems an attack on any group to be an attack on society itself—a kind of nonmilitary collective security pact, if you will;

(viii) urging religious leaders to emphasize the commonalities that unite the human family, even as each faith defends its distinctiveness, but never by denigration of other religions;

(ix) developing educational programs for children from an early age that introduce them to historical awareness, mutual respect, social responsibility, moral clarity, and moral courage;

(x) and celebrating the role of individuals who have made a difference in combating anti-Semitism and other forms of bigotry, and encouraging others to emulate their example.

Each of these ten components, I believe, is essential to building a multifaceted campaign against anti-Semitism and its related diseases. We must work on parallel tracks and summon the resolve to sustain our efforts. After all, talk is important but only as a first step. It is our action—or inaction—by which we will be ultimately judged. And history has surely taught us that there is no overnight or "wonder-drug" solution for ending the scourge of anti-Semitism.

In a world buffeted by seemingly endless challenges and plagued by a short attention span, it may prove difficult to focus on a particular issue—in this case, anti-Semitism—but failure to do so could prove calamitous not only for Jews, but also for the larger well-being of democratic societies.

Anti-Semitism, we must always remember, is like a localized cancer that, if not properly treated in time, runs the risk of metastasizing and ultimately destroying the entire body.

While each of the ten elements is essential, the key in the long run is education, the subject of this plenary session.

When all is said and done, it is really about the inculcation of a set of civic values in children that teaches them right from wrong and encourages them, as they grow up, to exercise what Jean Piaget, the child development expert, called their "autonomous" morality.

These civic values should include the essential propositions that all children, and their families, are full members of society deserving of respect; that differences arising from such factors as race, religion, or ethnicity are sources of strength, not shame; that hatred based on group identity is inimical to a society's self-definition; and that society values moral courage.

There are many laudable educational models that have been developed in the United States and Europe to help achieve these worthy, if daunting, objectives. In this regard, I wish to pay special tribute to the work of the member nations of the Task Force for International Cooperation on Holocaust Education, Remembrance, and Research, launched by the Swedish prime minister in 1998, chaired by my fellow panelist, Ambassador Franchetti Pardo, and advised by this session's chair, Prof. Yehuda Bauer.

I earnestly hope that additional countries represented here at this conference will consider joining the sixteen-nation task force in the coming months.

Another noteworthy initiative is a new European workshop, cosponsored by the American Jewish Committee and entitled "Education on Anti-Semitism," which just released a document detailing results of a conference of NGOs and educators here in Berlin. The conclusions emphasize the importance of dealing not only with historical anti-Semitism, but also current trends, including the attempt by some to use anti-Semitic language and images to demonize and delegitimize the State of Israel.

At the American Jewish Committee, we first developed a school-based program two decades ago entitled "Hands Across the Campus." It is currently being used in many American schools and has recently been adapted for use here in Germany. Its principal objectives are to increase student awareness of the importance of democratic values, civic participation, and diversity, as well as to train student leaders to take an active role in strengthening intergroup relations in their schools.

From our experience with this and other tolerance-building and prejudice-reduction, as well as Holocaust education, programs, we have drawn several lessons that may be helpful to this conference.

First, to maximize the possibility of long-term success, programs must be introduced early on, before a child's mind is fully shaped, and need to be continued throughout the educational process.

Second, these programs should be woven into the larger curriculum, whether through literature, history, or culture, so that messages are channeled and reinforced from many vantage points.

Third, success depends, above all, on the abilities of teachers themselves, regardless of how well conceived the written material might be. Thus, considerable attention must be paid to teacher training, including clear guidelines on how to deal with those students who resist learning about the Shoah or even deny its existence, as has been the case in some European schools.

Fourth, as the prominent philosopher of education John Dewey emphasized, students learn best when they are active, not passive, participants in the process. It is necessary but insufficient to convey to students the raw facts of the history of anti-Semitism, culminating in the Shoah, or the more generalized danger of group hatred.

Encounters with victims of hate crimes and survivors of the Shoah, field trips to memorial sites and museums, learning not just about victims' deaths but also their lives, becoming involved in hands-on projects to counter prejudice and strengthen respect for diversity, and several other vehicles can help translate the abstract or remote into the here and now, without oversimplifying, much less trivializing, historical events.

Jane Elliott, an American teacher, introduced the "Blue Eyes, Brown Eyes" program in her class in 1968 after discovering that many of her pupils harbored racist views of African Americans. She divided the class in two—those with brown eyes and those with blue eyes, and gave the former rights and privileges that were denied the latter. The exercise worked. The children came to understand the principle of discrimination based on characteristics they had no control over, in this case eye color. They grasped that it could just as easily have been skin color or religious affiliation.

This program has been used extensively, including by a Dutch antiracism group in South Africa a few years ago. After participating, a fifteen-year-old girl remarked, "A racist environment is very easy to create, much more easy than I thought. And the effects for the minority are much worse than I could ever dream of."

Fifth, emphasis needs to be placed on role models who, by their principled actions, have made a difference. A New York educator was recently honored for her lifelong effort "to eradicate hatred and bigotry through education." She explained her goal in teaching about the Shoah: "I'm trying to prepare children to be able to deal with racism and bigotry, and give them the tools to speak out, to take the role of the rescuer and not the bystander."

And sixth, all school-based programs need to be examined periodically to determine if, in fact, they are achieving their desired results. Good intentions, as we know, do not always necessarily translate into good results. There are various ways of determining this—regularly surveying students' attitudes, designing control groups, and sponsoring longitudinal studies.

Distinguished delegates,

Your commitment to addressing the resurgence of anti-Semitism through education is vital and deeply appreciated. I hope that, as a result of this conference, more countries will introduce curricula devoted to Holocaust education and civic values into their school systems, and that an OSCE-wide mechanism for reporting and sharing experiences will be developed. But even as we meet here in Berlin to explore what more the OSCE nations can do—and there is much more to be done—we dare not ignore the fact that elsewhere millions of children are actively being taught to hate those who do not share their identity, including, centrally, Jews.

From the schools of Saudi Arabia (a full study of the content of Saudi textbooks is available at www.ajc.org) to the *madrassas* of Pakistan, schoolchildren are presented with a world divided between the so-called "believer" and the "infidel," and are instructed to abhor the "infidel."

And evidence of similar teachings has even been found in some religious and educational institutions within the OSCE community of nations.

Not only must the OSCE nations do their utmost to monitor what is being taught within their borders at private schools and academies—I know that some countries already are—but many nations represented here also have ample diplomatic opportunities to express concern to those governments that, directly or indirectly, encourage and fund the poisoning of young people's minds.

If we are to mount a truly effective campaign against anti-Semitism, we ignore at our peril this dimension. The widespread use of satellite technology and cyberspace to transmit anti-Semitic motifs to Europe and elsewhere only heightens the danger still further.

We rightly want our young people to develop the capacity for moral clarity and moral courage in their own lives. We can expect no less of our own governments.

The very same moral clarity and moral courage must be brought to bear in dealings with those nations and groups that actively seek—through the teaching of incitement and hatred, the publication of anti-Semitic materials, and the spawning of grotesque conspiracy theories—to undermine our shared objectives here in Berlin. We let them succeed only at our collective peril.

Thank you, Mr. Chairman, for the honor today of addressing this distinguished body.

Presentation of the Jan Karski Award
to Per Ahlmark
AJC 98th Annual Meeting
Washington, D.C.
May 5, 2004

This occasion gives me double pleasure.

First, Jan Karski was one of my heroes, and I'm thrilled that we have a new award in his memory.

I knew Jan Karski quite well. Indeed, I was asked to give a eulogy at the Polish embassy here in Washington on the day of his funeral. Permit me to quote from my remarks.

Jan Karski—son of Poland, son of the Catholic Church, and son of the human family—devoted his life, indeed risked his life again and again, so that the cries of Polish Jews during World War II would not go unheard.

This courier of courage took to the world community—to presidents and prime ministers, to foreign ministers and supreme court justices, to famous writers and Jewish leaders—his eyewitness accounts of the systematic extermination of the Jews by the Nazis.

Many found his stories of gruesome activities in the ghettos and camps hard, even impossible, to believe, but Jan Karski told them and retold them to anyone who would listen.

Jan Karski modestly referred to himself as a "human tape recorder," replaying the messages he was asked to deliver. In actuality, he was a trumpet; a man who heralded the harsh tones of human indifference and cruelty so loudly that no one could deny hearing them, while at the same time personifying the softest melodies that make up the indomitable spirit and inherent goodness that mankind can still possess.

It is for Jan Karski's remarkable courage; his lifelong commitment to combating evil, first Nazism, later Communism; his friendship for the Jewish people and his unwavering dedication to the struggle against anti-Semitism until his last breath four years ago; his love of the State of Israel, which was so evident to those of us who heard him speak when we honored him in 1993; and his determination again and again to bear witness to the darkest moment in human history that we have named this award for him.

May we always cherish the memory of Jan Karski as near to our hearts as he cradled the souls of the millions of Jews he never knew but tried to rescue.

I can think of no one more worthy of being the first recipient of this prestigious award than Per Ahlmark. No one I know comes closer to embodying the spirit, the courage, and the commitment of Jan Karski than our honoree today.

Per Ahlmark has been a prominent political personality in his native land of Sweden, rising to serve as member of parliament, leader of the Swedish Liberal Party, minister of labor, and deputy prime minister.

He has been an equally well-known author of several widely discussed books—most recently, *It's the Democracy, Stupid*, which came out last month—not to mention being a columnist in Sweden's leading newspapers for decades, as well as an author of three books of poetry and a novel.

But what's most impressive about this man is not *what* he is but *who* he is. Per Ahlmark, you see, has devoted his life, his every waking moment to the very same values that defined Jan Karski.

He has stood with Israel in ways too numerous to enumerate. He has visited the country more than seventy times. When Israelis feared missile attacks from Saddam Hussein's Iraq last year and began preparing gas masks, Per Ahlmark boarded a plane for Israel and spent weeks in the country because, he said, that was the only place in the world he wanted to be at that perilous time. That was quintessential Per Ahlmark.

As you know, in today's Europe it is not exactly fashionable, to say the least, to stand up and defend Israel, but that's exactly what Per Ahlmark has done repeatedly and effectively across the length and breadth of his country, and far beyond as well.

He has spoken out, again and again, on the danger of resurgent anti-Semitism. He has also not hesitated to confront those who use anti-Zionism as a convenient mask for anti-Semitism. Indeed, he has warned that if the Nazis sought a world that was *Judenrein*, then the modern anti-Semites seek a world that is, in the first place, *Judenstaatrein*, free of a Jewish state.

Ladies and gentlemen, democracy has no more determined friend, and tyranny no fiercer enemy than our honoree today.

Per Ahlmark has stood foursquare in defense of human rights, whether for Soviet Jews or Bosnian Muslims, and in steadfast opposition to those in the international community who would practice double standards or selective moral indignation.

Fortunately for us at the American Jewish Committee, Per Ahlmark has channeled some of his seemingly limitless energy through United Nations Watch, the Geneva-based NGO founded by the late Ambassador Morris Abram to hold the UN to the noble standards of its own charter. He is cochair of this AJC affiliate.

Read his writings to get a feel for this truly remarkable man. Not all of them, you'll be pleased to know, are in Swedish. Some are in English.

Or better yet, sit back now and listen to this brave man with a mission and a message, who flew from Stockholm to be with us today.

Take in the profound wisdom of his words, feel his deep passion, admire the unflinching courage of his convictions, and observe the friendship for the Jewish people and Israel that oozes out of every pore of his skin.

Like Jan Karski, Per Ahlmark is the real thing—that all too rare righteous individual. To the Jewish people, he's an authentic hero of our age and, believe me, I don't use the word "hero" lightly.

In these trying times, I miss Jan Karski, but I'm ever so grateful that Per Ahlmark is here and by our side.

Ladies and gentlemen, on behalf of the American Jewish Committee, it is now my privilege to present the first Jan Karski Award to a moral giant, a profile in courage, and, not least, a dear friend, Per Ahlmark.

Presentation of the Madeline and Bruce M. Ramer
Diplomatic Excellence Award
to Ana Palacio
Foreign Minister of Spain, 2002–04
Washington, D.C.
May 7, 2004

Our first meeting with Ana Palacio was in September 2002, barely two months after she was appointed foreign minister of Spain.

We plunged right into a fascinating conversation.

I'm a veteran of many meetings, but seldom do I recall such a feeling of almost instant chemistry, certainly on our part. We felt we were in the presence of someone quite special.

Here was a foreign minister willing to speak openly and candidly, and not according to a predetermined script.

Here was a foreign minister who clearly wrestled in her own mind with difficult issues and wasn't afraid to acknowledge it.

Here was a foreign minister animated by an unmistakable sense of purpose and guided by a deeply held set of principles.

And here was a foreign minister who was a keen listener, eager to hear other points of view and to engage in the give-and-take of lively discussion.

With the press of everyone's schedule, we didn't have nearly enough time together that day. Fortunately, however, it turned out to be only the first in a series of meetings, including long lunches and dinners late into the night—and with Spaniards "late" takes on a whole new meaning—that took place between Minister Palacio and the American Jewish Committee in Madrid, New York, Washington, and, most recently, Brussels, not to mention numerous phone calls in between.

Our discussions ranged over many topics—from the search for Arab-Israeli peace to the war in Iraq, from the menace of global terrorism to Israel's treatment at the UN, and from the state of transatlantic relations to the challenge of European integration, including Turkey's possible accession to the EU.

One thing was abundantly clear each time we spoke with Minister Palacio: We were in the presence of a statesman, not a politician.

The difference is more than just semantic.

As Charles de Gaulle said, "The true statesman is the one who is willing to take risks."

Risks for Minister Palacio meant fulfilling the statesman's duty, according to Henry Kissinger, of bridging "the gap between his nation's experience and his vision."

All true, but being just a bit uncomfortable with this male-oriented language, I was pleased to discover that Abigail Adams, the highly acclaimed wife of this country's second president, John Adams, voiced sentiments tailor-made for Ana Palacio and today's occasion. "If we mean to have heroes, statesmen, and philosophers," said Abigail Adams, "we should have learned women."

Minister Palacio is Exhibit A.

Led by a government headed by Prime Minister José María Aznar, whom we had the privilege of hearing from at last year's Annual Meeting, and by Minister Palacio, Spain was catapulted into a leadership position on the global stage.

Spain, which has long understood the true meaning of terrorism, unhesitatingly joined with the United States and like-minded nations after 9/11 in the struggle to defeat this global cancer. Subsequently, notwithstanding strong domestic opposition and pressure from several heavyweight EU countries, Spain steadfastly supported the Coalition of the Willing in Iraq, sending troops and suffering casualties in the process.

And Ana Palacio did not hesitate to speak out publicly to explain Spain's position.

Here's what she wrote in a *Wall Street Journal* op-ed a year ago:

A European foreign policy cannot be focused on the maintenance of a balance of world power, but rather on the values and objectives we share with the United States, summarized in the notion of freedom. As our Cervantes had Don Quixote say, liberty is "one of the most precious gifts heaven has bestowed upon Man. No treasures the earth contains or the sea conceals can be compared to it. For liberty one can rightfully risk one's life."

And at the opening of our Transatlantic Institute in Brussels in February, Minister Palacio, who flew especially from Madrid to be with us and who has agreed to serve on the institute's board, said:

> To meet the challenge in the Middle East, we have to understand that we Europeans must do so by going hand in hand with the United States, with whom we share principles and values which, in the end, come to this: the idea of the value of the human being as the center of our political and social system.

Powerful thoughts, aren't they?

Ladies and gentlemen, Spain has traditionally had excellent relations with the Arab world. Without sacrificing those ties, Minister Palacio devoted herself to enhancing Spain's bilateral link with Israel, a country she visited several times during her term as foreign minister.

She showed particular understanding for Israel's battle with terrorism, recognizing that terrorism is terrorism, pure and simple. It can never be rationalized, much less defended.

This, as we know, is not a universally held view, but she pressed the point, especially in Brussels, and as a result helped place Hamas on the EU terrorism list. We are grateful for her successful efforts.

There is much more to be said about Minister Palacio, but time permits only one additional comment.

As foreign minister, she made a special effort to reach out to world Jewry, even, gasp, to those of us, like me, who are of Ashkenazi and not Sephardi origin! Seriously, against the backdrop of Spanish history, this was, of course, an especially meaningful gesture.

Ladies and gentlemen, our own beloved Madeline and Bruce Ramer of Los Angeles share in common with our honoree a sense of vision. In their case, it was the vision to create a special award for diplomatic excellence. This is the second year we present it.

In bestowing this award upon Minister Ana Palacio, the American Jewish Committee wishes to recognize her "principled and courageous leadership in advancing the transatlantic relationship, defending the cause of freedom and human dignity, and deepening the ties of friendship between Spain and the Jewish people."

An individual of exceptional valor and courage, she is a most worthy recipient of this coveted award.

Closing Remarks
AJC 11th International Leadership Conference
Washington, D.C.
May 9, 2004

Just what you need is one more speech.

Before saying a final word to those who participated in the Annual Meeting and the International Leadership Conference, I want to express my appreciation to this morning's four panelists, not only for being here today—especially on a Sunday, and, no less, Mother's Day—but also for what they represent and who they are. At the risk of singling out two of them, I feel I must say a few additional words about Chris Smith and Francois Zimeray.

I first met Congressman Chris Smith when he was practically a kid, elected to Congress in 1981. He looks young now, so do the math, and subtract twenty-three years. Here was a congressman who came from New Jersey—though I'm not sure that his district was heavily Jewish—and brought with him a passion for human rights and human dignity. The cause that captured much of his attention was Soviet Jewry, and we became very involved in it together. He traveled to the Soviet Union, and he took a leadership role, working at this cause, often unheralded, for many years. Chris, I want you to know that attending this Leadership Conference are dozens of people from the former Soviet Union, many of whom today live in Israel, Germany, the United States, and, of course, those who have chosen to stay in what is now, happily, the Former Soviet Union. They and we owe you a debt of gratitude that includes, but goes beyond, the words of Deuteronomy, "Justice, justice, shalt thou pursue," that we have just given you [engraved on a gift] for your more than two decades of steadfast support for a cause dear to us and dear to human rights. I want to thank you for that.

I also want to reiterate what was said a little earlier about François Zimeray, a member of the European Parliament from France, because I want to be sure that everyone understands it exactly. François Zimeray stood in what was, and I believe remains, a very lonely environment, in actuality, a hostile environment. And he stood firm, because he believed that his position was a matter of principle. Israel is a democratic country, and the European Union was founded on democratic values. The notion that history and reality could be turned on their head, and that Israel could be sacrificed on the altar of political expediency—and I choose my words very carefully—was something completely unacceptable. Whether François Zimeray was one of one, or one of the majority, he was determined to exercise the political will that we have all spoken about as absolutely necessary in the struggle against anti-Semitism.

It is all about political will and, no less, political courage. It's all about putting larger interests ahead of your own immediate electoral interests. François Zimeray paid the ultimate price for insisting on what should have been a no-brainer for the European Parliament and the European Commission: that they examine where their money was going. In transferring ten million euros a month or more to the Palestinian Authority, they have every right, as they would were they transferring money to anywhere else in the world, to know where that money is going and how it's being used, and to be certain that the use of the money is consistent with the core values and mission, in this case, of the European Union. That he had to pay the ultimate political price for something as seemingly obvious and self-evident is nothing short of tragic. All friends, not only of Israel, but of truth and principle and democracy, owe François Zimeray a tremendous debt of gratitude, and we're happy to acknowledge that here today. And though it's easy for me to say, François, there must be life after the European Parliament.

For those of you who were here Tuesday evening and still have some vague recollection of what happened through the fog of the last five days, I referred to the fact that, having just come back from Berlin, where I attended the OSCE meeting with our four panelists, I felt like an emotional yo-yo. I must confess to you that I have felt like an emotional yo-yo these last five days as well, from the heights of ecstasy to the depths of despair, as I see these issues of anti-Israelism, anti-Zionism, and anti-Semitism once again dominating our agenda. At one point in my life, I was naïve enough to actually believe that my mother, a survivor of the Holocaust from France, would be able to live the rest of her life without ever again hearing the three words *mort aux juifs* ("death to the Jews"), having heard them enough times during the war.

It is chilling to know that my relatives who still live in France, who fought in the Resistance but who chose once again to reaffirm their love of France, to know that my own children who lived with me in Geneva—heard the words *mort aux juifs* on European soil, at the height of democracy, at a time when we all somehow thought that the Shoah had been etched on the consciousness of the world, that anti-Semitism could—no, never be totally eliminated—but, yes, could be marginalized, could be disgraced.

To know that we've had to devote the last five days once again to addressing diagnostic strategies for dealing with the virus or the cancer of anti-Semitism; to know that the young people here—the Goldman Fellows, the interns, those from the European Union of Jewish Students, our own children—are going to have to face the battle once again that we have been fighting for nearly sixty years, since the end of the war, is as profoundly disturbing to you, I'm sure, as it is to me.

The notion that fifty-six years after the creation of the State of Israel by an act of the United Nations we still have to talk about Israel's legitimacy is equally dismaying. Can you imagine for a moment traveling to, say, Islamabad and sitting in a meeting with General Pervez Musharraf and beginning the meeting by saying, "General Musharraf, I want you to know that we recognize Pakistan's right to exist"? The man would laugh. "Who the hell are you to tell me that I have the right to exist? My right to exist is a fact. It's been a fact since 1947. I don't need you to come in the year 2004 and tell me I have the right to exist."

And fifty-six years after the creation of the state, fifty-five years after its entry into the United Nations as a member in good standing, we are meeting in Washington at the 98th Annual Meeting of AJC once again to address the question of Israel's very right to exist and to discuss strategies for how to return to our respective countries to defend its legitimacy. At the same time, we have to address how to fend off the efforts to vilify and to demonize the State of Israel. Can you imagine?

Israel, a democratic country that shares the same foundational values as Europe and the United States, is put to trial in the court of public and governmental opinion, while its neighbors, among the most egregious violators of human rights, for whom the word "democracy" does not even exist in their vocabulary, are given a pass?

Can you imagine that we live in a world in which the United Nations Commission on Human Rights, having already selected Libya as its chair, last week reelected Sudan as a member? Sudan, having just heard what Congressman Chris Smith said about two million people being slaughtered? Sudan, by a vote of what? One dissenting vote—the United States. Where is the moral compass of the rest of the world? Or is it all about power politics? Sudan has been elected to the Commission on Human Rights, and you know something? Today, by contrast, Israel, a democratic country, doesn't have a chance in a million of being elected to sit on the Commission on Human Rights.

I don't want to have to add what seems like an almost obligatory addendum, that Israel isn't perfect and, yes, there are differences within Israel and, yes, criticism of Israel is legitimate. I almost feel that it's kind of an admission of weakness. Of course, Israel isn't perfect. Of course, France isn't perfect. Of course, Germany isn't perfect. Of course, the United States isn't perfect. Why do we have to keep saying it? We know it. We feel we almost have to apologize, even in defending Israel, by always adding this language.

Israel has the same right to sit on the Commission on Human Rights as it does to sit on the Security Council, as it does to sit as an equal member of the International Red Cross Movement. We don't have to apologize for these rights. It should be a matter of fact. Those countries, especially in Europe, but the democracies of the world in general, shouldn't be standing for it. They shouldn't be standing for the shameful treatment—and not because it's about Israel, but because it ought to be about the way these institutions and nations define themselves. Do these democratic countries really want to be associated with a Commission on Human Rights chaired by Libya? In their vocabulary of justification and rationalization, can they really find satisfactory explanations, when they go to bed at night, to persuade themselves that they did the right thing? I don't believe it. I don't want to believe it, just as I don't want to believe that, even as anti-Semitism has come out once again into the open, it took years for countries that should have known better, that professed to know better, to respond.

Do you know that we went to Brussels shortly after the recent outbreak of anti-Semitism in Europe and spoke with the European Union commissioner in charge of this area? She looked at us and said, "Anti-Semitism? What anti-Semitism?" How many times did she have to hear the words, "Death to the Jews"? How many times did she have to see the role reversal whereby Jews were being depicted as perpetrators in Nazi-like images? How many times did she have to see references to deicide charges, especially after the Church of the Nativity, for her to wake up and realize that Europe was, yes, a zone of prosperity and harmony, but at the same time, was menaced by anti-Semitism? And if there were any region in the world that should understand anti-Semitism, it is Europe. If there's anyone who should be taking the lead in the struggle against anti-Semitism—God bless the United States, Israel, and the American Jewish Committee—but Europe should be taking the lead, because there is no part of the world that understands better the slippery slope of anti-Semitism, and how words turn into deeds, than Europe.

Europe should be taking the lead, and it shouldn't have had to be Ambassador Stephan Minikes and Congressman Smith and the others who had to push, prod, nudge, urge, pressure, and lobby most of the countries of the OSCE to have the first conference on anti-Semitism in Vienna and then the second conference in Berlin. It should have been Europe urging the rest of us to do so. Thankfully, the conference did take place, and a strong statement was adopted, and now the challenge will be its implementation.

The American Jewish Committee will be there every step of the way, working with our friends, to ensure that deed matches word.

One final thing: It's very easy, as we go through this roller-coaster of ecstasy and despair in the course of a week, to focus more on the bad news than the good. But I hope that you, like me, will walk away from this week empowered, inspired, and even more determined. Our strength was expressed last night in the *ruach* [spirit] that filled the room as we sang and danced, especially by the Israelis. Let me tell you, if Israel is a country on its knees, I didn't see it last night. We are a people that has been around for a very long time and that will be around for a very long time to come. I hope all of us take away from these meetings that sense of strength from our collectivity. Whatever our differences may be, they are minimal compared to our commonalities.

I hope as well, in addition to the inspiration that we took from each other, that we also drew strength from the friends who joined us for this six-day meeting: friends like the people on this panel; friends like the other speakers who have come and been with us throughout these days. We are far from being alone.

At the end of the day, what we are struggling for is not simply Jewish well-being and the right to be able to practice our religion as we wish. Unfortunately, we have become the litmus test for whether the world is prepared to defend values that not only respect Jewish rights, but the rights of all religious groups, the rights of all minorities. It's not a role we sought at Sinai, but one that we somehow acquired along the way, as part of our job description. The opportunity—and privilege—to work together with Jewish communities around the world, linked in common purpose, and with friends like those on this panel, should give us all renewed strength as we now go our separate ways.

A Decade of Bundeswehr-American
Jewish Committee Cooperation
Bundesakademie für Sicherheitspolitik
Berlin, Germany
November 22, 2004

Minister of Defense Peter Struck, Federal Academy President Rudolf Adam, members of the German Parliament, Israeli Ambassador Shimon Stein and other distinguished diplomats, officers of the Bundeswehr and NATO armed forces, American Jewish Committee colleagues, ladies and gentleman,

I am deeply moved by the high honor presented to me by Dr. Struck.

I would like to dedicate it to the memory of my father, who was a thirteen-year-old boy in this very city when the Nazis came to power, and who spent the ensuing twelve years as refugee, soldier in the French Foreign Legion, concentration camp inmate, soldier in the British Eighth Army, and espionage agent behind enemy lines for the U.S. Office of Strategic Services (OSS), and to my mother, who spent seventeen months, together with her family, fleeing the Nazis in occupied France until they were able to board a ship from Lisbon for New York in November 1941.

That their son could be standing here today on such an occasion speaks volumes about the possibilities of history. It also serves as eloquent testimony to something they both taught me by their example—the need to understand and remember the past, but never to abandon hope in the chance for a better future.

Ladies and gentlemen, it is a privilege for me to be with you today at the Federal Academy for Security Policy to mark the tenth anniversary of the unique relationship between the German armed forces and the American Jewish Committee. What an auspicious occasion this is! Allow me to pay tribute to my founding partner in this effort, Colonel Jochen Burgemeister, who is in the audience. I would also like to acknowledge the presence of General Klaus Wittman, who was a great believer in expanding our partnership.

Relations between Germany and the Jewish world have come a very long way in the postwar era, especially relations between Germany and Israel.

Indeed, next year we will mark the fortieth anniversary of the establishment of diplomatic ties between the two countries.

The needs of statecraft required Israel rather early on to make painful but necessary decisions regarding links with Germany that Jews elsewhere in the world were not compelled to do.

Jews in the Diaspora could choose to ignore Germany if they wished, boycott its products if they so desired, and avoid travel there. Israel, on the other hand, faced with the Herculean challenge of building a state while defending its borders against those who sought its destruction, could ill afford to reject out of hand relations with West Germany, however painful those links might have been for many Israelis.

The special relationship forged between Berlin and Jerusalem has been a matter of great consequence to Israel and of benefit to both countries. We trust that this special relationship will continue to grow and develop in the years ahead, even as the process of integration of European foreign and security policy advances.

Diaspora Jewish groups, with one notable exception, were several steps behind Israel in their policy regarding Germany.

From the start, the one exception was the American Jewish Committee. Not only did it not lag behind, but, to the contrary, it took the lead in its understanding of Germany's dynamic postwar history.

Grasping the enormity of the Shoah, the American Jewish Committee began to follow the wise counsel of Confucius, who said, in another era, "Better to light a candle than to curse the darkness."

Germany would not suddenly disappear, the American Jewish Committee reasoned; it would always be a major presence in the heart of Europe and, sooner or later, it would reemerge from the shambles of defeat and the occupation.

The only question was whether this postwar Germany would evolve in a positive or negative direction. History had taught us that we could ill afford to sit on the sidelines and wait for the question to resolve itself; we had to seek a role, however modest, in ensuring that light prevailed over darkness.

Our contact, it must be said, began quite tentatively. We Jews were apprehensive, and, truth be told, few Germans were interested. But it has grown dramatically over the span of decades. Thousands, actually tens of thousands, of people in Germany and the United States have been directly touched. And a high point in the relationship came for us in 1998, when we opened our office in Berlin, today headed by Deidre Berger.

For me personally, given my family history, the opportunity once again to plant Jewish roots in the soil of Berlin was one of the more moving moments of my life.

Yet, even as the comfort of light has, over time, replaced the terror of darkness, the past remains with us. The wounds have not fully healed, nor are they likely to anytime soon. The ghosts and shadows and cries of anguish continue to torment us. The questions, ultimately unanswerable perhaps, nevertheless persist.

The perfected industrialization of genocide still awakens us from our deepest sleep, fifty-nine years after the machinery was silenced.

Besides we Jews, who else today agonizes so much over the history of the Third Reich, sees the films, reads the accounts and memoirs, seeks out the survivors, visits the fields of ashes, the museums, and memorials, and attempts to connect this information to the contemporary world?

The answer, I believe, is that the struggle persists here in Germany more than anywhere else. This remains the case, even as we have left behind the twentieth century, and even after a new generation of German political leaders, largely born after the war, has assumed the mantle of national responsibility.

Not so among all Germans, to be sure. There are those who feel the time has long since come to close the history books, and even those who find false comfort in the writings of relativists who seek to challenge the singularity of the Nazi crimes.

But I have met an impressive number of Germans—in schools and universities, in churches and clubs, in the government and military— for whom the intellectual and emotional struggle goes on, for whom it is not yet possible to turn the page and put the past fully behind them.

For them and for us, the result is to bring us closer together. We might come at the issues from very different starting points, but, in fact, we are drawn nearer to one another than might at first seem obvious.

There is, then, much that we can do, that we should do together.

Let me suggest that our common agenda today, as Germans and as Jews, comprises at least four parts: (a) preserving memory; (b) building a world respectful of democracy and human rights; (c) serving as an early warning system against extremism and xenophobia; and (d) standing firm against those in the international system who flout the rule of law and threaten the precepts of peaceful coexistence and conflict resolution.

Why preserve memory? The answer is really very simple—or is it? It is to ensure that those who were consumed in the flames of the Shoah did not die in vain. It is about them, but also, truthfully, it is about us.

Unless we are somehow able to understand how a demented, anti-human ideology could take root in an otherwise advanced nation's soil, leading so many to participate so energetically in genocidal policies without parallel in human history, what world will await our children and grandchildren?

And this brings me to our second joint responsibility: building a world respectful of democracy and human rights.

In this endlessly complex world, one thing is abundantly clear from even a brief glance at history, and it offers the ray of hope we so desperately need.

It is the simple, irrefutable fact that democratic nations do not, as a matter of habit, declare war on other democratic nations; they resolve their differences peacefully.

Democratic nations don't deliberately starve their populations as an instrument of state terror, as the Soviet Union did in Ukraine, with devastating results, in the 1930s, or as North Korea has done more recently.

They don't use poison gas against their own citizens, murdering them by the thousands, as was the case against the Kurds in Saddam Hussein's Iraq.

They don't assassinate dissidents, or imprison journalists who expose the failings of the state, or silence protesting students, as has been the case in Iran.

They don't subjugate women, denying them education, employment, and even health care, as we witnessed in Afghanistan under Taliban rule.

They don't indoctrinate their children from the earliest grades to despise and distrust people of other faiths, as the Saudi school system systematically does.

They don't limit access to the Internet out of fear of the impact of unauthorized sources of information, as Syria has done.

And they don't seek to murderously suppress religious or ethnic minorities, as has taken place on a massive scale in the Sudan against Christians and animists, or as has occurred in the Darfur region, where widespread murder and rape have gone unchecked.

By nature, democracies may be imperfect, but, as Winston Churchill famously said in the House of Commons in 1947, "Democracy is the worst form of government, except for all those other forms that have been tried from time to time."

Democracies are a permanent work in progress and, yes, let's admit it, many remain deeply flawed.

Some democracies have been associated with slavery, colonialism, racism, anti-Semitism, costly military misadventures, and abuse of political power and legal authority.

And some democracies have not been immune to violence themselves. Indeed, today we mark the forty-first anniversary of the assassination of President John F. Kennedy, an American leader inextricably linked with this city at the height of the Cold War.

But one notable strength of a democratic system lies in the fact that when things go off track, corrective mechanisms are triggered.

Democracy has formed the cornerstone of the Federal Republic since 1949. Democracy is the common denominator of the twenty-five members of the European Union. The newest EU members knew full well that the price for admission included an unquestionably democratic system of governance. Earlier, Greece, Portugal, and Spain made the successful transition to democracy; others, no doubt, will follow suit....

National rivalries are now played out on the football field, not the battlefield. This is something worth celebrating, regardless of the outcome of the match, though you might not agree that it's almost beside the point who wins and who loses.

Our governments are answerable to the people, not the reverse. It is the rights of the individual, not the exaltation of the state, which forms the foundation of our societies.

President Adam, you quoted from a speech of mine just a couple of years ago in which I described myself as a committed transatlanticist, and thus a potentially endangered species. I am pleased to tell you that, for my part, nothing has changed. I remain absolutely stubborn and steadfast in my views....

Our shared values emanate from the very building blocks of our respective societies: democracy, the rule of law, and respect for the dignity of the individual.

The ties that link this precious fraternity of kindred nations, including, of course, Israel, must never be permitted to fray, for they represent the best—indeed, I would argue the only—hope for the ultimate realization of a genuinely peaceful and prosperous world.

Europe and the United States may face battles over Airbus versus Boeing, or over currency values; disputes over global warming, genetically modified foods, or the death penalty; tensions over the respective roles of NATO and the new European defense initiative; and differences over concepts of preemptive military action and unilateralism versus multilateralism.

I don't for a moment minimize these challenges, far from it, especially after the experience and mutual disappointments of recent years.

Yet, no matter how serious, these divisive issues must never be allowed to overshadow the commonalities that link us as nations, as peoples, and as societies. We must stand together. Our fates are intertwined because our overarching vision and values are intertwined. Our foes despise precisely what unites us—a bedrock commitment to open, democratic, and pluralistic societies.

It means for us never losing sight of the larger picture of Europe and America as the likeliest of strategic allies, as we are today in Afghanistan, to cite but one example....

We look to our partners in Berlin to emphasize on this side of the ocean the vital significance—and contemporary relevance—of the transatlantic partnership.

You can be assured that, on the other side of the Atlantic, the voice of the American Jewish Committee will continue to be heard, as it has been consistently, in support of the partnership and, more broadly, of an active and enlightened American role in world affairs.

Democracy is a strategic necessity, not a tactical option. It represents the best chance we have to transform the conduct of interstate relations and human behavior, the best opportunity to ensure that the Bundeswehr, NATO, or a European Rapid Reaction Force will always be underemployed, not overemployed. Please note that I did not say unemployed, just underemployed.

Our third common agenda item is to serve as an early warning system. This is an essential element of what militaries do to guard against armed threats to the security of a nation.

By virtue of our historical experiences and rather acute understanding of human nature, Jews and Germans today can serve as an early warning system when challenges to a spirit of tolerance and mutual respect occur, when extremist political parties seek to infiltrate the political mainstream, and when the prospect of ethnic cleansing or genocide looms.

We know from the past that menacing words and threats cannot be ignored. Adolf Hitler quite revealingly laid out his plans when he wrote *Mein Kampf* while in the Landsberg fortress, but how many took him and his book seriously?

We know that demagogues may test the waters to see how far they think they can go, just as Hitler first moved into Sudetenland, then paused, and just as he gradually imposed restrictions on Germany's Jews over a span of years.

More recently, we saw Saddam Hussein confidently conclude that the world would look the other way while he seized Kuwait in 1990, and Slobodan Milosevic similarly assume that his international critics did not have the stomach to translate words of condemnation into a tough-minded plan of action against his thuggish rule.

And most recently, there has been the unfolding tragedy in Darfur—murder, rape, pillage, and dislocation—while the Sudanese government and the Janjaweed militia leaders concluded that the world simply didn't have the will to confront yet another colossal man-made human tragedy.

We have witnessed a range of responses to such catastrophic events, including denial, appeasement, and silence. History should have taught us the devastating consequences of a failure of will and resolve. Inaction, for whatever reason, only invites more acts of evil. And remember, in particular, Churchill's definition of an appeaser as "one who feeds a crocodile, hoping he will eat him last."

There is no such thing as moral neutrality in these situations. No one can be let off the hook and permitted to argue that it is someone else's problem alone or, as we sometimes hear, that economics trumps morality.

Nor, in the final analysis, can there be any Faustian bargains or backroom deals. Tempting though these have been to some nations, the record shows that not only do they not work, but they almost always backfire.

In the face of manifestations of hatred, whether as governments, nongovernmental organizations, or individuals, our opposition must be loud and clear, and our presence felt. This is all the more important for us these days as anti-Semitism has been given new life in the extremist precincts of right and left and in vast swaths of the Islamic world.

That is precisely why, in 1999, when Milosevic began driving Kosovar Muslims out of their homes in a policy of ethnic cleansing, we at the American Jewish Committee felt it important to set an example by our actions—words alone are insufficient at such moments—in a region where hatreds have a tragically long life span.

We raised funds from our members to help the refugees. Before disbursing the money, however, we visited several refugee camps in Macedonia and a field hospital run by the Israel Defense Forces to assess the situation on the ground.

We were deeply touched by what we saw. The Israeli field hospital was superbly run. Today, as a sign of hope, there are a number of Kosovar Muslim children with Israeli names, in gratitude to the doctors and nurses who helped bring them into this world.

Of the four refugee camps we visited, one in particular impressed us. It was a German military operation. There was a special effort to provide a measure of dignity to the refugees by serving hot meals and building wooden floors for the tents; these amenities existed nowhere else. It may not sound like a lot, but, believe me, it was. And we were also moved by the medical assistance being provided by Die Johanniter, the German humanitarian organization.

When we returned to the States, we contacted our friends in Germany and proposed a joint humanitarian operation to assist the refugees. The response was immediate and enthusiastic.

The result was a pioneering effort, jointly sponsored by the American Jewish Committee and Die Johanniter, with cargo planes provided by the Bundeswehr, to bring relief supplies to thousands of refugees.

Our goals were three, and I believe we accomplished all of them:

First, to assist people in need, in this case Muslims, who were victims of intolerance, and thereby to underscore the sacred notion of one human family;

Second, to send a symbolic message that history could move forward and enhance the human condition, using our German-Jewish project as an example;

And third, to give shape and form to our belief that the German-Jewish relationship was at a sufficiently mature stage that we could act together in times of humanitarian crisis.

This brings me to the fourth and final part of our common agenda.

There are, as you well know, dangers to the international system to which we must remain alert.

Let me mention briefly just a few of those most pertinent to our discussion today, leaving aside for now such consequential matters as demographic trends; ecological threats, including global warming, the depletion of water resources, deforestation, and desertification; growing gaps between rich and poor nations; and the spread of infectious diseases.

I am particularly concerned about several developments.

Iran's quest to develop nuclear weapons and the means to deliver them with ever greater range and precision ranks at the top of my list.

For a while, many in the West thought that Iran had turned a corner, that the arrival of President Mohammad Khatami on the scene had shifted the balance of domestic power in the direction of the so-called moderates.

It is now abundantly clear that, much as some had hoped for an improvement in the internal situation, it has not occurred. To the contrary, the fundamentalists firmly hold the reins of power. They are determined to wage their struggle against perceived enemies within the country and beyond, including, of course, Israel, or the "Zionist entity" as they call it, and also against the West more generally, although sometimes their policy in this regard is subtly cloaked.

Temporary or short-term agreements may at times seem useful—and I recognize the efforts by Britain, France, and Germany in this regard—but painful experience, yours and ours, has taught us that countries like Iran or, for that matter, North Korea, cannot necessarily be expected to keep their word and fulfill their commitments.

The United States, by dint of its size, power, and global reach, brings a great deal to the table. So does the European Union.

We must find and sustain a common approach to Iran. I believe this to be the preeminent test of the transatlantic relationship in the months ahead. If we can, not only does it increase our chance of success in halting Iran's nuclear program, but it also proves the resilience of the relationship. Conversely, working on separate tracks or, heaven forbid, at cross-purposes, we only embolden what in the final analysis are our common enemies.

Let's face reality. Since 9/11 but even before, we have been confronted with a global threat. There are those who choose to believe the threat is exaggerated, or is only episodic, or derives from our own behavior, especially American (or Israeli). They assert that a change in American (or Israeli) attitudes is the needed antidote. They are deluding themselves.

Let's call the threat by its real name. Take your pick—Islamism, Islamo-fascism, jihadism, radical Islam, or militant Islam. It is not—I repeat, it is not—a war against Islam per se. In fact, it is a war to defend Islam against those who would kidnap its good name.

In other words, we are faced with an ideology, fueled by a combustible mix of theology, politics, self-righteousness, and fury, which has an airtight worldview and hasn't been shy to express it. Just as we fought fascism, Nazism, and Communism in the twentieth century, today we are locked in a struggle with yet another variant of totalitarian thinking in possession of "absolute truth." Our semantic effort to cloak the true nature of the struggle by deliberately avoiding naming its source, lest we risk offending anyone, is misguided, if not downright disingenuous.

No, this is not a war or, if you prefer, a campaign against terrorism. Rather, it is against those who, in the name of their fanatical beliefs, employ terrorism to advance their aims, as well as those who give them succor and sanctuary. Terrorism is their weapon of choice, but if they had potent armies, is there any doubt those would be employed as well?

At the same time, we need to encourage and empower the forces of moderate Islam—and, yes, they do exist—to assert themselves more forcefully in the battle for title to their religion. We must strengthen their hand through political support and social and economic development programs.

Easier said than done, I fully realize, and, to boot, the line between extremism and moderation is not always easily or neatly drawn. The worlds of Islam and of Arab culture in particular are still so alien, so impenetrable to most outsiders, that we must tread with great caution, avoiding the certitudes that too often have caused us to stumble in the region, yet not with such caution that we effectively paralyze ourselves.

Then there is Iraq.

Whatever one's starting point on the war itself, it is absolutely essential, I firmly believe, that the United States and its coalition partners press ahead in their current complex and dangerous mission.

If even a modicum of success is achieved in bringing about greater security and political stability, the positive repercussions will be felt far beyond Iraq's borders.

If not, the negative consequences will reverberate for generations to come and, make no mistake about it, impact on all of us. No one should underestimate what is involved here. And no one should take any perverse pleasure in observing the daily challenges faced by American forces and their partners.

And last but by no means least, there is the possible dawning of a new era in the Middle East. With the passing of Yasir Arafat, a potentially brighter new chapter will be written, though judging from the attendance at the Cairo funeral service and the statements of some political leaders and editorial writers, it would seem that the world lost a second Mother Teresa.

It is far too soon to predict the chapter's contents, but, in theory at least, it could usher in a new, more moderate and pragmatic Palestinian leadership, committed to peace with Israel and determined to move the negotiating process forward. Only time will tell.

We should not, however, fall into the trap of unrealistic expectations. The new team must emerge, establish its authority, and persuade Israel and the world of its determination to reverse Arafat's corrupt, dictatorial, duplicitous legacy and unblinkingly confront the twin evils of terrorism and incitement.

If so, it will find an eager and willing partner in Jerusalem. Prime Minister Sharon has already confounded his critics by accepting the principle of a two-state solution, calling for withdrawal of Jewish settlements from Gaza and the northern West Bank, and implicitly acknowledging the logic of territorial separation on the West Bank by the construction of the security fence.

But Israel must not be pushed farther and faster than it can responsibly go by the international community to satisfy the desire of those outside the region who seek a rapid solution.

No one—I repeat, no one—seeks peace for Israel more than the people of Israel, who have been denied that peace for fifty-six years.

No nation, faced with repeated wars for its very survival, has been more forthcoming in its willingness to compromise territorially for peace than Israel. And when else in history have the defeated nations, i.e., Israel's enemies, sought to set the terms for peace?

Peace cannot be built absent a credible negotiating partner. Peace cannot be built on empty promises. And peace cannot be built by simply talking about Israel's "legitimate security concerns," but not actively understanding and addressing those concerns, which begin with the basic proposition that the country is no larger than Wales or, put another way, is two-thirds the size of Belgium. Unlike Wales and Belgium, though, Israel's neighborhood is, shall we say, rather rough and tumble, and thus its margin for error is small to nil.

In other words, let no one ever seek to place Israel's security on the altar of political or diplomatic expediency.

Ladies and gentlemen, together, I hope, we will do all that we can to ensure Israel's security in the context of a Middle East where peace one day replaces war, where prosperity replaces poverty, and where harmony replaces hatred. It will not be easy, but the objective is worth the struggle, and the alternative is simply too frightening to contemplate.

In sum, we, Germans and Jews, have a full plate and a daunting agenda. But I am persuaded that our efforts can make a profoundly positive difference.

Our shared experience in the second half of the twentieth century, and during the past decade of cooperation between the German armed forces and the American Jewish Committee that we mark today, offers a glimmer of hope, perhaps even a metaphor for hope. It reveals what can be if only we dare to dream dreams and have the courage and determination to match.

For our part, we at the American Jewish Committee eagerly look forward to our next decade of collaboration.

Testimony to the
Committee on Foreign Relations
French National Assembly
Paris, France
April 14, 2005

Mr. Prime Minister, distinguished members of the Committee on Foreign Relations:

I am deeply honored to have this opportunity to appear here today. I wish to express my heartfelt appreciation for extending me an invitation.

I am joined in this chamber by a delegation from the American Jewish Committee that has been visiting several European capitals this week to broaden and deepen the transatlantic dialogue.

Permit me a few words at the outset about the American Jewish Committee.

The organization was founded nearly a century ago in response to pogroms against Jews in Eastern Europe. From its earliest days, it pursued two complementary tracks. The first was to help ensure the security and well-being of Jewish communities around the world and in the United States. The second, inspired by the Jewish prophetic tradition, was to contribute to improving the political and social health of societies at large.

As a consequence, our institution has been deeply involved throughout the twentieth century and until this very day in seeking to protect and extend the frontiers of human freedom, human rights, and human dignity.

In doing so, we have drawn strength from the enduring values emanating from the French Revolution. We recall that France, when it turned to democracy, did not hesitate to accord to Jews the full rights of citizenship, setting an example for the rest of the world.

It will come as little surprise, therefore, that we passionately advocate building a world based on democratic values, mutual respect, and pluralism.

But we are in a race against time.

On the one hand, there are those who seek to build a more harmonious world, in which political, economic, technological, and social development prospers both within nations and across ever more open and inconsequential borders.

But, on the other hand, there are those who would use violence, particularly in the name of religion, to keep us in a state of permanent tension. If conflict in the twentieth century was largely defined by political ideology, I fear that in the present century it will be principally determined by religion or, I should say, its abuse.

Professor Samuel Huntington of Harvard University wrote a much-discussed book entitled *The Clash of Civilizations*. While I understand the point he was seeking to make, I believe the more appropriate title would have been "The Clash within Civilizations."

Isn't the fault line every bit as much *within* certain religious civilizations? Some groups have members who reject the validity of other faiths, claim an exclusive link to a Supreme Being, insist on the centrality of religion for the exercise of state power, and justify violence for the realization of their vision, and other members who respect divergent beliefs while adhering to their own, view religion as a matter of individual conscience and not state policy, and have no need to deny someone else's beliefs in order better to affirm their own.

What makes this discussion particularly compelling is the inescapable fact that we are entering an era when weapons of mass destruction may become more readily available to those who would impose their obscurantist views on others. We have already had a taste of the lengths to which such forces are prepared to go, and only a failure of imagination could prevent us from seeing the ominous possibilities that might lie ahead.

And this is precisely why we are in that race against time and why the stakes are so high.

We at the American Jewish Committee believe that there is no simple, much less single, way of responding to the challenges before us. No individual, no nation, has a monopoly of wisdom on how to proceed. We, people of good will, must all listen to one another with open ears and open minds, and, yes, learn from one other. Nonetheless, certain things seem obvious to us.

The democratic nations of the world have created something well worth defending.

Pierre Mendès-France wrote in *La République moderne*, "*La démocratie est d'abord un état d'esprit.*" He was, of course, right.

There may be those so culturally and morally relativist as to be incapable of distinguishing between freedom and tyranny, or opportunity and oppression. And there may be others who, wracked by unending guilt and embarrassment about the blessings of their lives in democratic nations, idealize every society and leader antithetical to their own. We must never yield to either instinct.

It is unacceptable in a free society that members of parliament must live in hiding; or that women can be treated in an inferior manner; or that teachers fear discussing certain mandated topics in the classroom; or that religious figures can preach incitement and violence against the societies in which they live, while wrapping themselves in the mantle of constitutional protection; or that individuals demand the respect of the state while failing to recognize their own reciprocal obligations to the state; or that any group can be singled out and attacked on the basis of its religious, ethnic, racial, or other distinctiveness.

Democracy, whatever its imperfections, has unleashed the human potential in an unprecedented manner. It has demonstrated the proposition that human freedom and dignity are indivisible for all. When democracy falls short, it has self-corrective mechanisms. And yes, democracy has constructed vast zones of peace and prosperity....

As Europe has proven over the last fifty-five years, we maximize our chances of success in confronting global challenges when the democratic nations work in common purpose, not at cross-purposes. Of course, national or regional interests are not always entirely convergent—how could they be?—but we should never lose sight of the larger stakes involved. Only our common adversaries benefit from our division and discord. Conversely, when united in our objective, there is no limit to what we can achieve.

At times, there may be no alternative to projecting force, or applying it, as we did together in 1991 in ousting Iraqi troops from their brazen occupation of Kuwait or, more recently, in freeing Afghanistan from the grip of the Taliban and ending its role as a terrorist haven par excellence. Force must always be the last option, but there are times when it becomes unavoidable, for the alternative is still more unpalatable. Should the enemies of our common way of life and our value systems judge us to be weak, irresolute, or conflicted, they will not hesitate to challenge us, and we shall pay a heavy price.

At other times, diplomatic suasion rather than military might may be adequate to the task, but here again the key is unity of purpose. When the United Nations Security Council, led by France and the United States, spoke with one voice in calling on Syria to end, once and for all, its military and intelligence presence in Lebanon, it appears to have had an impact.

And we must, at long last, seek to encourage, in a sustained manner, the political, social, and economic development of those countries that have lagged behind because of the legacy of colonialism, or endemic corruption, or authoritarian rule, or inadequate attention and support from the more developed countries, or a combination of these factors.

If I may say so, such development is in these countries' interests; it is no less in ours. But it will only be achieved if, like the great postwar statesmen, we think boldly and act collectively, and resist the tendency to think only of the short-term gain to be acquired by acquiescing to the status quo.

There are some today who question the value of the transatlantic partnership or, for that matter, cast serious doubts on the viability of the Franco-American relationship. Those on both sides of the Atlantic Ocean who believe in these links—and not simply for reasons of historical nostalgia, though there is a rich history between us—need to stand up and be heard.

The American Jewish Committee is, in this sense, a true believer. Some will call us naive or, worse, out of touch with reality. So be it. We shall continue to speak out in favor of the closest possible links between Europe and the United States, as serving the highest interests of a world at peace and the best hope for the realization of a democratic, interconnected, and bountiful world.

This is precisely why, just over a year ago, in the presence of Javier Solana, Ana Palacio, Noëlle Lenoir, and other leading European personalities representing the European Union and national governments, AJC opened our Transatlantic Institute in Brussels. We wanted to demonstrate by our actions at this critical moment in world history that we recognized the looming dangers of drift and discord—and understood our obligation to help preserve the democratic alliance.

We know that differences have arisen in the past. Consider this comment from a review (in *Commentary*, an American Jewish Committee-sponsored monthly journal) of Luigi Barzini's *The Europeans*:

> Is the Atlantic Alliance breaking up? The signs are certainly ominous. A common defense policy remains elusive.... Monetary affairs are a continuing source of dispute. Outside the Atlantic region proper, in crucial areas such as the Middle East, ... the supposed allies often find themselves working at cross-purposes.... The United States, Europeans say, has been impulsive and unpredictable in foreign affairs.... From the American viewpoint, the Europeans seem unwilling to shoulder their

share of the common burden and are all too willing to spend money on welfare programs rather than on defense.

The year? 1983.

Optimists would say that, notwithstanding the differences, the alliance has largely held together, even surviving the end of the Cold War. Pessimists would probably reply: *Plus ça change, plus c'est la même chose.* On balance, I prefer to side with the optimists.

We fully recognize that there have been serious differences of views on a number of matters in recent years, including the Arab-Israeli conflict. While we may be united in seeking a peaceful solution to the conflict based on a two-state solution, this cannot fully mask areas of tension, although I hope that the tension has been reduced in recent months. Indeed, the death of Yasir Arafat and the election of Mahmoud Abbas as chairman of the Palestinian Authority have, we hope, created a new window of opportunity. Also, we believe, it has revealed the utter bankruptcy of the Arafat period, during which Israel and the United States came to the realization that peace without new Palestinian leadership was not possible, though others, including France, differed in their assessment.

We believe that no nation seeks peace more than the nation of Israel, and no nation has taken more tangible risks to achieve peace with its neighbors than Israel. We also recognize that it takes two to make peace.

When a genuine partner emerged in Egypt and Jordan, peace with Israel became a reality. And if a partner emerges in the Palestinian Authority, as we hope Chairman Abbas will prove to be, then peace will again become a reality. But we must never allow our wishful thinking to race so far ahead of observable facts that the two lose all connection. Time and performance will tell if Chairman Abbas has not only the will but also the ability to exert authority, especially regarding extremist and armed Palestinian factions. If so, it could augur well for the future of Israelis and Palestinians alike.

Mr. Prime Minister, distinguished members of the Committee on Foreign Relations:

I come before you as a son of the United States and a grandson of Europe, above all of France. My parents, born elsewhere, both found refuge in France, my mother from Communism, my father from Nazism. Their only common language was French. Like the other members of my family, they adapted quickly to the republican values of this great nation. They embraced France in the same manner as France embraced them.

But then came the war, the invasion and occupation, the Vichy regime, the arrests and deportations, the flight, and the Resistance, and when it was over, my family, most of whom had thankfully survived, were scattered in France, the United States, and what became Israel.

Though divided among these three countries, they all felt fortunate. After all, they were living in democratic nations, linked by a common commitment to basic foundational values. This allowed them and their fellow citizens to flourish in an atmosphere free of the long shadow of persecution, even if Israel faced continuous challenges to its very existence from hostile neighbors and still does from countries like Iran and terrorist groups like Hezbollah, Hamas, and Islamic Jihad.

But today, there are storm clouds gathering that are cause for concern. In particular, the growth in both verbal and physical incidents of anti-Semitism, not limited to any one country but certainly evident in France as well, gives pause. The impression of this growth is borne out, in a telling example, by recent statistical reports indicating the highest number of anti-Semitic incidents here in France since 1990, when the first government study was conducted. It is reinforced by many conversations with individuals who have been directly affected by incidents of intimidation or verbal and physical violence.

Whatever the source, be it from Islamic extremists who speak in genocidal terms; or from anti-Zionists who seek uniquely to deny the Jewish people the right of national self-determination and make this world, as the former Swedish deputy prime minister, Per Ahlmark, has said, "*Judenstaatrein*," free of a Jewish state; or from the extreme right that, not for the first time, casts the Jew as the "other," the "conspiratorialist," or a "lesser human"; or from those who seek to deny or trivialize the Shoah, hoping perhaps that, as the survivors and eyewitnesses disappear from our midst, they will have a better chance of capturing the allegiance of younger generations; or from those who, driven by an overriding obsession, depict Israel and, by extension, its supporters abroad only in the most grotesque terms, the threat is real.

And considering as well the ready availability of satellite technology, cyberspace, and porous borders, we are reminded that what may once have been seen as national problems are increasingly transnational in nature, requiring, in turn, international cooperation.

Through our repeated visits, meetings with officials, contacts with leaders of Jewish institutions, and reestablishment of a presence here, we are well aware of the measures taken in recent years by France, under the leadership of President Chirac and Prime Minister Raffarin, as well as other European countries and the Organization for Security and Cooperation in Europe, to cope with the growing problems. We commend these efforts, including the decision to ban the racist and incendiary broadcasts of at least two Middle East-based television stations. Such measures are necessary both to defend Jewish communities against the dangers that lurk and to protect societies at large against the very real risk that what starts as anti-Semitism will end with an assault on all the core values that define these societies. We must never forget that anti-Semitism may begin with the Jews, but history surely teaches us that it never ends with the Jews.

We urge you continued strength and vigor in combating anti-Semitism, whether in the school system, on the streets, in the media, or wherever else it rears its ugly head. We fully understand that the battle is neither easy nor won overnight, but we count on the fact that today France appreciates the high stakes involved and has the will to persevere.

For our part, we stand ready to assist if asked. We have nearly a century of experience in dealing with anti-Semitism and other forms of bigotry both at home and abroad, which has afforded us the opportunity to understand what political, civic, law enforcement, judicial, educational, and other approaches are more (and less) likely to succeed.

While this is a much larger and longer discussion, permit me to mention just two basic things we have learned in seeking to combat anti-Semitism.

First, it is absolutely essential that political leaders be seen and heard. They must be strong and steadfast, both in their words and actions. No one should ever doubt their resolve to stand against anti-Semitism.

Second, documented cases of anti-Semitism should never be met with denial, delay, or rationalization. In this regard, I must say, frankly speaking, that the reaction of some French officials in the years 2000 and 2001 was disappointing. For whatever reason, they failed to grasp the significance of what was going on and, while the perpetrators allowed themselves to believe that they could act with impunity, the victims experienced isolation and fear. The change in official recognition of the seriousness of this problem—its threat to France's Jewish citizens and to France itself—is striking, and appreciated.

In closing, may I say that we believe the dialogue between our two countries, as well as between France and the American Jewish community, to be both important and timely. As a participant in such dialogue for many years, I can personally attest to its value.

Be assured that we at the American Jewish Committee are committed to broadening and deepening the points of contact between us. Indeed, we believe it vital to create more opportunities for increasing mutual understanding, exploring issues of difference, and identifying areas for mutual cooperation.

And we shall also continue to help American audiences understand that we all have a stake in your success in the domestic challenges you face and in ensuring the most robust possible link between Paris and Washington.

In saying this, I am aware of the fact, as I noted earlier, that there has been a serious perception gap between France and the United States. This is no less true between France and the American Jewish community. From the perspective of American Jews, our national surveys reveal, there is a widespread belief that, among the major European countries, France has by far the chilliest attitude toward Israel. Moreover, the same surveys reveal that France is regarded as facing the most serious problem of anti-Semitism in Europe.

These issues, like others, ranging from what to do about Hezbollah to how best to deal with the nuclear appetite of Iran, can best be addressed by open and candid discussion befitting friends.

Mr. Prime Minister, distinguished members of the Committee on Foreign Relations, permit me to end by expressing my appreciation for the honor you have bestowed upon me by inviting me here today, my admiration for the laudable work in which you are engaged, and my hope that friendship shall always prevail in the relations between our two countries.

Presentation of the Light unto the Nations Award
to President Bill Clinton
AJC 99th Annual Meeting
Washington, D.C.
May 6, 2005

Mr. President, I think there is no one on the face of this earth who knows how to read an audience better than you do. I think it's fair to say that the nearly one thousand people here—don't tell that to the fire marshal!—who come from fifty-one Jewish communities around the world; who represent a delegation from the National Defense College of Israel; who represent universities in the United States, Europe, and elsewhere; and who hail from across the United States are grateful to you beyond words for being here today—and even more, for everything that you have done on behalf of our shared ideals.

Now I want to tell you, the audience, that, unlike Ambassador [Alfred] Moses, who did the introduction, the president did not appoint me to any position. So you will judge for yourself whether, from here on in, I'm telling the truth.

I believe it was Eleanor Roosevelt who once said that we as societies will be judged not by how we treat the most fortunate among us, but rather by how we treat the least fortunate among us. And that, consistent with the prophetic vision of which we are the heirs and trustees, has been the guiding principle of the American Jewish Committee now for ninety-nine years. It helps explain, for example, why, while Bill Clinton was president of the United States and there was a spate of arson attacks against African American churches in the South, the American Jewish Committee believed an attack on a church was an attack on the kind of society we wish to build. So we rushed in with our funds and with our own hands to rebuild churches across the South, and to adopt the Gay's Hill Baptist Church in Millen, Georgia, as our own.

It also helps explain why, while Bill Clinton was president and Slobodan Milosevic unleashed another round of ethnic cleansing in Kosovo, we went to the refugee camps in the neighboring countries and saw what was taking place on the ground.

We were particularly impressed, Mr. President, by what the German armed forces and humanitarian groups were doing. And we said as an NGO, yes, we can give funds, but we can give even more to the people of the Balkans; we can give them a message of hope. Our action can become a metaphor for hope, and what better metaphor than Jews and Germans working together in 1999 and 2000 to alleviate suffering and the consequences of ethnic hatred.

This also explains why we responded immediately, as you and President Bush so generously said, to the crisis in Asia. I especially wish to recognize Priya Tandon, our representative in India, who worked tirelessly in both India and Sri Lanka on our behalf to aid the victims of this catastrophe.

And in the same spirit, we were so pleased to partner with Israel in its humanitarian efforts, symbolized by IsraAID. We all heard a few moments ago from the representative of IsraAID. We are proud of how Israel responded. And we are proud that Israel flew the Star of David in the region, even when there were those who wished it would be hidden.

And it is why, Mr. President, just before you came, we adopted a statement on Darfur. We refuse to remain silent. Surely the history of the twentieth century has taught us this one clear lesson: We must be responsive to the least fortunate in the world at all times, irrespective of race, religion, or ethnicity.

There are many things for which to thank President Bill Clinton on this occasion. Ambassador Moses set the stage. Let me complete it, if I may, before presenting the president our award.

We wish to pay tribute to Bill Clinton for his global leadership, together with former President Bush, in the worldwide recovery and reconstruction effort following the devastating tsunami.

We wish to recognize him for his distinguished record as statesman and leader of our nation for eight years.

We wish to recognize him for his abiding friendship for the State of Israel and his relentless pursuit of peace in the Middle East.

We wish to recognize him for his remarkable and steadfast commitment to strengthening the bonds of pluralism and intergroup understanding here at home.

We wish to recognize him for giving hope to those who have been at risk of losing it.

We wish to recognize the president for his memorable speech to the American Jewish Committee at our Annual Meeting in 1996.

In sum, we wish to recognize President Bill Clinton for his lifelong commitment to the pursuit of justice and compassion, to democracy and the rule of law, to fairness and inclusion, to the prophetic ideals of a world at peace and a world in harmony—a world where, as Isaiah said, "The lion and the lamb will lie down together." Though, as Woody Allen added, "The lion and the lamb shall lie down together, but the lamb won't get much sleep."

And there's one more thing that I need to thank the president for. Please indulge me this note of personal privilege. You see, my family and I got to Chappaqua before he and his family did. And for years my wife and I were faced with the inevitable reaction—"Oh, I know that place. I used to spend summers in Chautauqua." Or else the even more devilish reaction, "Well, ah, how does it feel to live on that, ah, island called Chappaquiddick?" Or, at the very least, the simple question, "How do you spell it?"

But since President Clinton and his wife, Senator Hillary Clinton, chose to move to Chappaqua, and became, in my wife's memorable coining, fellow Chappaquainians, I get no more questions of this sort, except possibly one. And that is, "Is the best sighting in town of the president at Lange's Delicatessen or Starbucks?" I'll let him answer if he chooses to.

So, Mr. President, thank you for lightening my load by removing all doubt about Chappaqua. And thank you to you and your wife for being such committed and enthusiastic community residents.

The moral of the story is that if any institution is name-challenged, get this man involved.

He is, as everyone in this audience knows, a unique individual. Who is more deserving of our Light unto the Nations Award than Bill Clinton? It is a thrill for the American Jewish Committee to honor him today with the symbol of the Jewish holiday Hanukkah, which represents light and liberty and religious freedom.

Ladies and gentlemen, please join me in expressing our collective appreciation to President Clinton for a lifetime of service to the nation—and the world.

Presentation of the American Liberties Medallion
to Aleksander Kwasniewski
President of the Republic of Poland
New York, New York
September 15, 2005

Mr. President,

On behalf of the American Jewish Committee, and in the presence of many who have worked tirelessly in the vineyards of Polish-Jewish relations, it is my great privilege to present you with our highest award, the American Liberties Medallion.

Mr. President, the award honors champions of liberty.

You are a towering champion of liberty.

The award honors defenders of democracy.

You are a steadfast defender of democracy.

The award honors advocates for human rights.

You are a staunch advocate for human rights.

The award honors protectors of memory.

You are a courageous, a very courageous, protector of memory.

And the award honors promoters of mutual understanding.

You are a tireless promoter of mutual understanding.

For all this, we applaud you.

And Mr. President, we equally applaud you for the historic steps Poland has taken, during your presidency, to enter NATO and the European Union.

We applaud you for the unshakable bonds of friendship and cooperation Poland has maintained with the United States and with Israel.

And we applaud you for Poland's laudable commitment to the promotion of peace around the world. Mr. President, the American Jewish Committee has for decades built bonds of friendship with freedom-loving Poles. When freedom was no longer a dream, but instead had become a reality, we celebrated the emergence of a new Poland finally able to pursue its own destiny.

For too many years in Poland's noble history, larger neighbors had sought to occupy it, subjugate it, even destroy it. But, notwithstanding the enormous damage they inflicted, ultimately they did not prevail. How could they, given the indomatibility of the Polish spirit?

Winston Churchill memorably said in the House of Commons on October 1, 1939: "The soul of Poland is indestructible.... She will rise again like a rock, which may for a spell be submerged by a tidal wave, but which remains a rock."

As in so many cases, Churchill had it exactly right.

And today, democratic—and indestructible—Poland shines bright in the constellation of free nations.

Mr. President, Poland and the Jewish people have lived together for nearly a thousand years. For the Jewish people, Poland long represented the center, the epicenter, of our civilization, scholarship, creativity, culture, and vitality. As we know, it was not always easy, far from it, but then again, we must never view the arc of ten centuries through the prism of difficult times alone, either.

Our goal at the American Jewish Committee has been nothing less than to write a new chapter in relations between Poland and the Jewish people. Much of note has already been accomplished, including our unprecedented cooperation in protecting and preserving the Nazi death camp at Belzec. Mr. President, you honored us by your presence—and your powerful words—at the dedication ceremony last year.

But more remains to be done. We are eager, together with our Polish friends and partners, to look to the future.

It means broadening and deepening the dialogue between Poland and the Jewish world, especially among young people.

It means helping Jews understand the evolution of Poland into a dynamic and open society, where a proud Jewish community is rebuilding itself and looks with optimism to the days ahead. It means helping Poles understand the vibrancy and diversity of contemporary Jewish life around the world, including in Israel.

It means working together to create a world in which anti-Semitism has no place, and in which racism, xenophobia, and negative national, or other, stereotyping are fought with tenacity.

It means protecting the integrity of memory, for the future can only be built on a solid foundation of truth and accuracy. Those who would rewrite or otherwise misrepresent history, be it in books or museums, must be exposed and challenged.

We, Poland and the Jewish people, fully understand the stakes involved in ensuring that historical revisionism does not succeed.

Those who wish to portray the Holocaust as a figment of the Jewish imagination need to confront us both, standing together as one.

And those who conveniently wish to forget that Poland was the first victim nation of the Nazi German onslaught in 1939, and that those millions killed on Polish soil were overwhelmingly murdered at the hands of the Nazis, must also face us both, again standing shoulder to shoulder.

Yes, Mr. President, we have a full agenda and, I am firmly convinced, a promising tomorrow awaiting us.

In your presence, I wish to reaffirm that we shall continue to attach the highest importance to our expanding relations with Poland, and we will always be open to possible new areas of collaboration.

Mr. President, on behalf of the American Jewish Committee, I am honored to present you with the American Liberties Medallion. The award reads: "American Liberties Medallion, presented to the Honorable Aleksander Kwasniewski, President of the Republic of Poland. To an advocate of democratic ideals, whose tireless championship of human dignity includes equally within its broad vistas the past now gone and the future that lies ahead. For his exceptional contributions to the cause of liberty."

I can think of no more worthy recipient than you, President Kwasniewski.

Remarks on Receiving the
Chevalier de la Légion d'Honneur
St. Regis Hotel
New York, New York
September 18, 2005

Foreign Minister [Philippe] Douste-Blazy, Ambassador [Jean-David] Levitte, leaders and friends of the American Jewish Committee, family members, ladies and gentlemen:

As you might imagine, this is a special occasion for me. In fact, it may be even more special than you realize.

Let me explain why.

France has loomed large in my life, essentially from day one.

Neither of my parents was born in France, but both found a home there, as did so many other political refugees in the years between the First and Second World Wars.

My mother, who is here tonight, and her family fled Soviet Communism and arrived to start a new life, in Paris, in 1929. She was nearly six at the time, her brother Yuli, not quite nine.

My late father arrived in Paris in 1938, at the age of eighteen, after fleeing Vienna.

In fact, my parents met in Paris. Their only common language was French. And, who knows, had there been no ensuing war, I might well have been born in Paris and today be mangling English instead of French.

But there was a war.

Immediately after France declared war on Germany, my father enlisted. Instead of being sent to the *Légion pour les étrangers*, however, through a clerical error, he was assigned to the *Légion étrangere*, the legendary Foreign Legion. He was sent to Algeria. It wasn't easy. And when France fell, he was discharged and immediately arrested by the Vichy government, which put him in a concentration camp in Kenadsa in western Algeria. He spent three harrowing years there before escaping and making his way across the desert to Algiers. There, he joined the British Army and, later, the U.S. Office of Strategic Services, the wartime predecessor to the CIA.

My mother and her immediate family left Paris just before the Nazis entered. First, they went to Arcachon, near Bordeaux, and then, Minister Douste-Blazy, they moved to a city you know particularly well, Toulouse, where they lived for several months.

My late uncle Yuli was arrested as a stateless individual with an expired identity card. In the end, though, he was among the fortunate few. He was transferred to what was called *résidence forcé* in Luchon, where he was joined by my mother and their parents.

At long last, in two groups of seven extended family members each, they arrived in New York in 1941, via Spain and Portugal. Two years later, my mother began working for the French War Relief. While France was under occupation, the group's principal contact was with the London-based French government-in-exile. After the liberation, the group sent clothing and other essentials to those in need throughout France.

Other family members stayed behind. Several were active in the Organisation Juive de Combat, the French Jewish resistance movement. Their principal objective was smuggling Jewish children across the border into neutral Switzerland. All but one, our cousin Mila Racine, survived. Mila was arrested in October 1943 and sent to Ravensbrück, and later to Mauthausen, where she was killed weeks before the war ended.

After the war, Mila was honored posthumously by the French government with the Médaille de la Résistance.

Her brother, Emanuel, was honored by the French government in his lifetime with the Croix de Guerre avec étoile, Officier de la Légion d'Honneur, and many other decorations.

After the Second World War, our family was largely divided among the United States, France, and Israel. But French remained the lingua franca, the common denominator, of family gatherings and contacts.

I recount all this not to burden you with personal details, but rather to create a framework for the honor that Minister Douste-Blazy has so graciously presented me.

You can imagine that for my mother, my aunt Selda, who is also here and has a French story of her own, and those other family members of the wartime generation, this evening is textured with layer upon layer of meaning, memory, and emotion.

It is, then, first of all, in honor of them—those present and those very much alive in our memory—that I receive this award tonight.

In fact, it was my family's history—and the history of those around them—that led to my choice of career.

From an early age, I knew that terrible things had happened to them, to good, kind people, although it took many years to piece together the details and even longer to try to understand why.

In a way, though, can any of us ever really understand those who demonize an entire people and, in the name of that hatred, seek their extermination? Perhaps, as the Chinese philosopher Tao Te Ching said, "The more you know, the less you understand." I fear I am doomed to just such a fate.

So, yes, I was puzzled. I was also angry.

I couldn't simply compartmentalize the information I heard first-hand and over time from survivors and refugees, as well as from written accounts, films, and site visits about Communism, repression, Nazism, genocide, dehumanization, or collaboration.

Or about flight, deprivation, fear, separation, and exile.

Or about resistance, fortitude, or heroism.

In other words, I couldn't just go about my life as if all of these things were only marginally related to me, much less let them lie dormant most of the year, to be awakened only occasionally.

But I didn't quite know how to act on all of this, either, at least until the early 1970s, when I embarked on a new journey of discovery.

I came to realize, to my dismay, that the battle still wasn't over. No, it wasn't just about trying to come to terms with a difficult past, even if in so many ways the world had changed for the better, including for my family.

Millions of Jews in the Soviet Union, the country of my mother's birth, were being targeted for cultural genocide. They desperately needed a lifeline from the outside.

Israel, victorious in the 1967 war, was caught by surprise in 1973. In the first days of that war, its very existence—this state for which we had yearned and prayed since time immemorial—hung precariously in the balance. Would the United States and other countries come to its assistance, or let it fend for itself? What exactly was the responsibility of friends of Israel around the world at such a moment?

Israeli and Jewish targets were in the crosshairs of Palestinian terrorists and their ideological confrères in Europe. Synagogues, schools, planes, and Olympic athletes were all considered legitimate targets. How could I watch the selection process—yes, the selection process—of the Arab and German terrorists who hijacked an Air France plane in 1976 to Entebbe, and who sorted out the Jewish from the non-Jewish passengers, without hearing echoes of the past?

And the United Nations, an institution I had not only revered but at one point aspired to work for, turned against Israel, while disgracing itself by adopting a General Assembly resolution equating Zionism with racism.

I couldn't remain indifferent to these ominous developments, as if they somehow didn't touch me personally. My family history wouldn't allow it. And the words of Albert Camus, many of whose works I had avidly read, kept ringing in my ear: "The greatness of man lies in his decision to be stronger than the condition in which he finds himself."

I embarked on a search for a place where I could respond—both to the dangers that lurked and, yes, in pursuit of the dreams of peace and harmony and mutual respect that I refused to abandon.

I found that place. It was called the American Jewish Committee. It struck me as a unique institution in the way it approached the world and grappled with tough, complex issues.

And it is to this organization, which has given me the greatest professional gift I ever could have asked for, that I also wish to dedicate tonight's honor.

AJC's links to France long predate my association. In fact, they go back to the active presence of American Jewish Committee leaders at the 1919 Paris Peace Conference, the conference which, for better and for worse, shaped the world for the remainder of the century and beyond.

And, after the Second World War, the American Jewish Committee established an office in Paris. Its goals were to help French and, indeed, European Jews get back on their feet and, later, to seek to ensure legal protections for Jewish communities—and other minorities—in the emerging independent states of North Africa. I might add that George

Levitte, the father of the current French ambassador in Washington, was a professional staff member there for many years.

After French Jews found their footing, rebuilt their institutions, and were subsequently joined by several hundred thousand Jews from North Africa who, with or without legal protections, were uneasy about their future in the Maghreb, there was no longer a need for our presence. We closed the office.

More recently, however, we have reestablished that presence. We are grateful to our office director, Valerie Hoffenberg, for her tireless efforts on our behalf.

As profound believers in the need for transatlantic cooperation on the most pressing issues of our time—from the existential danger posed by proliferation of weapons of mass destruction, to the threat faced in every corner of the world from those who seek to murder and maim in the name of their perverted religious dogma, to the need to forge an ever expanding global coalition committed to the principles of democracy, the rule of law, and the inviolate dignity of the individual—we wanted to stay in close touch with decision-makers and opinion molders on both sides of the ocean.

Moreover, we witnessed a disturbing reemergence of anti-Semitism and distorted, at times grotesque, portrayals of Israel and Zionism in too many places in a Europe undergoing rapid socio-demographic changes. We wanted to be available to share our nearly century-long experience in combating bigotry through political, legal, educational, and other means, and strengthening the bonds that ensure robust pluralistic societies.

In a sense, we are outsiders, it is true, but we have a profound stake in France and its future. And we do, after all, live in an increasingly interdependent world.

We are mindful of Winston Churchill's admiring view of France. In 1944, the British prime minister said: "All my life I have been grateful for the contribution France has made to the glory and culture of Europe—above all for the sense of personal liberty and the rights of man that has radiated from the soul of France."

We applaud the vision of such French statesmen as Robert Schumann and Jean Monnet in forging the process of European integration—which I believe to be the most ambitious and successful peace project in modern history.

We recognize France's key involvement, not only in the European Union, where, for example, it is currently part of the three-plus-one team dealing with Iran on the nuclear issue, but at the UN, and especially on the Security Council, in the Organization for Security and Cooperation in Europe, the International Red Cross Movement, and in so many other vitally important regional and international institutions that make a profound difference in our lives.

We note with appreciation the close cooperation today between the Elysée and the White House, the Quai d'Orsay and the State Department, on matters related to both Lebanon and Syria—yet another reminder of the possibilities for collaboration between our countries on matters of common interest.

We know that France today is home to the world's third largest Jewish community. France has given the Jews, as citizens of the state, unlimited opportunity to realize their full human potential. In turn, Jews in France have contributed substantially to every sphere of the country's political, economic, scientific, intellectual, and cultural development, while fully embracing and holding dear the values of the Republic.

Nonetheless, it would be disingenuous, even on such an occasion, to pretend that there haven't been areas of concern to us regarding France—including anti-Jewish incidents on the streets of Paris and other cities in recent years, not to mention the chill that set in after 1967 in France's bilateral link with Israel.

But I think it is fair to say—indeed, it is necessary to say—that the current French government has worked energetically to address the problem of anti-Semitism wherever it surfaces, from the schools to the streets. It is a significant challenge, but the will is there, I believe, as is the recognition that the danger is both to Jews and, no less, to the very fabric of French society.

We may not yet have returned to the heyday of Franco-Israeli ties in the pre-1967 era. Even so, the recent well-received visits to Paris of Prime Minister Ariel Sharon and, before him, President Moshe Katsav, coupled with the upbeat visits to Israel by French leaders, including recently you, Minister Douste-Blazy—who have a personal record of friendship for Israel and sensitivity to its security concerns that we wish to acknowledge—are a welcome source of encouragement.

François de La Rochefoucauld was a seventeenth-century Frenchman whom my late father-in-law—a graduate, incidentally, of the Alliance Israélite school system—loved to quote. Among his many memorable maxims was this one: "There are few sensible people, we find, except those who share our opinions."

I know that you are all sensible enough to share mine when I say that we at the American Jewish Committee shall continue to attach the highest priority to engaging with France and its leaders on those many issues of mutual concern.

Ladies and gentlemen, on behalf of my two families—my own family and my American Jewish Committee family—I gratefully receive this award.

But even at the risk of stating the obvious, the journey goes on, for me, for each of us. As the American poet Robert Frost wrote:

The woods are lovely, dark and deep.
But I have promises to keep,
And miles to go before I sleep,
And miles to go before I sleep.

May we ever travel together, strive together, toward a world first envisioned by the ancient Hebrew prophets—a world at peace, a world of justice, a world of compassion, and a world in harmony.

Presentation to
Ricardo Lagos, President of Chile
Santiago, Chile
November 7, 2005

We are honored to be in the presence of the nation's president, former president, chief justice of the Supreme Court, members of the Cabinet, leaders of Parliament, ambassadors, military officials, and religious authorities.

And I wish to pay tribute to Isaac Frenkel—known to all of you, I'm sure—for organizing this wonderful event, and for all that he does on behalf of Chile and the Jewish community.

Ladies and gentlemen, we have come to Chile in a spirit of friendship and deep admiration for what your country has achieved, particularly in recent years.

You have shown the region and the world the indomitability of the human spirit—or, in the words of Pablo Neruda, *"la luz inapelable"* ("the unwavering light"). In the process, you have set an enviable standard for national development based on the robust institutions of a free society. We salute you.

We are here because of a deep-rooted belief in the importance of dialogue among the nations—and peoples—of the Western Hemisphere. We are convinced that there is ample room for growth in this arena.

We come on this trip to listen and learn, mindful of the words of the nineteenth-century British prime minister Benjamin Disraeli, "Nature has given us two ears but only one mouth."

Indeed, we attach such significance to hemispheric relationships that last year we set up the Institute of Latino and Latin American Affairs at the American Jewish Committee, directed by Dina Siegel Vann, who is here this evening. The institute sponsors research, publications, conferences, and travel missions, such as this one. Last month, we visited Venezuela and, after Chile, we shall be traveling to Argentina, Uruguay, and Peru.

As an organization, we are unabashed internationalists. We recognize the need for the United States, and for nongovernmental organizations like our own, to be engaged with the world in a spirit of mutual respect, to grasp the essential fact that we are increasingly interconnected, indeed interdependent.

While there are those in the world who wish to divide us, whether along national, regional, religious, or other lines, we seek quite the opposite—the building of strong, sturdy bridges that link us in common purpose.

Each nation has distinctive challenges, yet isn't it increasingly clear that no nation can either turn its back on the world or, conversely, go it alone, at least for long?

Whether it be the environment, trade, human development, trafficking, terrorism, avian flu, cyberspace, natural disasters, or a hundred other issues that don't necessarily respect national borders, we have a profound stake in maximizing regional and global collaboration.

Someone once said, "Talk is cheap because supply exceeds demand."

However, our goal at the American Jewish Committee has been to demonstrate that what counts in the end are deeds, and not simply words.

We are ever mindful of the admonition of Ernest Hemingway, the noted American writer, "Never confuse motion with action."

In a few months, our organization will be celebrating its one hundredth birthday. It won't come as a surprise, I hope, if I note that none of us in our delegation were present at the founding.

But we all take immense pride in the American Jewish Committee's record of achievement over the span of a century.

Our founders first met in New York, in 1906, to consider how they could help fellow Jews in czarist Russia who were the targets of repeated—and deadly—pogroms. And throughout the ensuing years, as the organization grew, it was compelled to confront one dire situation after another where Jews were in danger, whether in Nazi-occupied Europe, behind the Iron Curtain, or in much of the Arab world.

After the nightmarish years of the Second World War and the Holocaust, previously unimaginable progress was achieved in the second half of the twentieth century. Today, the vast majority of Jews live in democratic countries, such as Chile, and participate fully and proudly in the lives of these nations. This is as it should be.

Even so, we remain ever vigilant. Tragically, a foolproof vaccine against anti-Semitism has yet to be discovered.

In recent years, we have witnessed a resurgence of this age-old pathology, particularly in some countries of the Islamic world and in Western Europe. At times, it has taken the form, if you will, of classical anti-Semitism; at other times, it disguises itself as anti-Zionism, seeking to deny Jews the right of self-determination.

History has taught us that anti-Semitism can strike anywhere, at any time. As a consequence, it behooves all countries and people of good will to be on the alert. And it requires effective utilization of the tools of education to instill the values of tolerance and mutual respect in young people; political leaders prepared to speak out against bigotry; and laws that provide punishment for those who engage in racial discrimination.

We were especially pleased that, with Chile's support, the United Nations held a special session in January to mark the sixtieth anniversary of the liberation of the Nazi death camp Auschwitz.

We also noted with appreciation the visit of Foreign Minister Ignacio Walker, who is here this evening, to Israel in March to attend the opening of the new Holocaust museum in Jerusalem. As he mentioned when we met in New York in September, this was the first visit by a Chilean foreign minister to Israel. We hope it will be followed by others. We are convinced that the more contact there is, the greater will be the realization of the potential for ever expanding and mutually beneficial ties.

We were honored when Foreign Minister Walker addressed our 99th Annual Meeting in Washington last May. He made many friends for Chile that evening.

And just last week, the UN General Assembly adopted a landmark resolution, with Chile's cosponsorship, to create an International Day of Holocaust Remembrance, to condemn those who deny the Holocaust, and to promote Holocaust education as an antidote to the spread of racism or anti-Semitism.

As you can well imagine, the American Jewish Committee has had an abiding interest in the State of Israel's quest for peace. No nation, I believe, has a deeper yearning for peace than Israel or has shown a greater willingness to compromise in the interest of achieving a lasting settlement.

Difficult as it sometimes is to imagine, Israel—a country small enough to fit more than thirty-five times into Chile's landmass—remains in danger even fifty-seven years after its establishment. There are still those who seek its annihilation, as the president of Iran made so abundantly clear just two weeks ago.

This was done, as noted by the Chilean Foreign Ministry's welcome statement, in blatant violation of the United Nations Charter, which requires all member states to refrain from the threat or use of force against any member state. Incidentally, he is not the first Iranian leader to call for Israel's elimination. In fact, these same chilling words have been heard often over the span of the last twenty-five years.

What is different today, however, is that Iran has serious nuclear ambitions and a documented missile development program, assisted by North Korea. Clearly, the president's threat cannot be easily dismissed.

Nor should the frequent calls for Israel's destruction by terrorist groups like Hamas and Islamic Jihad, who receive support from both Iran and Syria, and whose spokesmen are equally blunt in refusing to recognize Israel's very legitimacy.

We hope that the Palestinian Authority will do what it must—ensure that these groups do not continue to operate both inside and outside the system. The current situation is untenable for consolidating the PA's authority and, therefore, unlikely to achieve the necessary goal of a negotiated two-state solution.

And yet Israel, as those who have visited the country readily see, is about far more than an unsolved political conflict.

Like Chile, it is a pulsating democratic nation, with a vibrant political culture, a lively press, and a diverse population that hails from many corners of the world.

Moreover, the three Israeli recipients of the Nobel Prize in the past two years alone are a reminder of the centrality of scholarship, research, and innovation to Israeli society.

Ladies and gentlemen, at the American Jewish Committee, we profoundly believe that Jewish security and well-being are dependent, yes, on relentless advocacy and education efforts, but also are inextricably linked to the political and social health of the larger societies in which Jews live.

Only truly democratic societies governed by the rule of law can ensure the rights of all, Jews included.

And in this spirit, we applaud Chile's leading role in the Community of Democracies, which unites those nations committed to protecting and strengthening democratic values, and the successful gathering of the group that you hosted here in Santiago earlier this year.

Only pluralistic societies that welcome the full and equal participation of all citizens, irrespective of their race, religion, creed, or ethnic background, can offer hope of overcoming centuries of prejudice and discrimination.

And only a world which acknowledges the indivisibility of human rights can chart a path toward peace, progress, and prosperity for all.

In a very real sense, this outlook has been informed by our heritage. As Paul Johnson, a noted Christian historian, wrote:

> To the Jews we owe the idea of equality before the law, both divine and human; of the sanctity of life and the dignity of human person; of the individual conscience and so of personal redemption; of collective conscience and so of social responsibility; of peace as an abstract ideal and love as the foundation of justice, and many other items which constitute the basic moral furniture of the human mind. Without Jews the world might have been a much emptier place.

It helps explain why the American Jewish Committee became deeply immersed in the civil rights struggle in the United States as early as 1911, and tirelessly pressed for human rights standards and monitoring long before they became part of the fabric of the international system.

It has also sparked our interest in responding to humanitarian crises, whether man-made or natural, from Latin America to South Asia, from sub-Saharan Africa to southeastern Europe.

As Jews, we believe that every human being is created in the image of God. We are, then, one extended human family, and by our actions we seek to affirm this at once simple and revolutionary concept.

We are also taught in our tradition that "the world rests on three things: justice, truth, and peace" (Rabbi Simeon ben Gamliel).

And this brings me to the privilege I have this evening.

Our Institute of Latino and Latin American Affairs has created a "Light unto the Nations" Award. The concept comes from our tradition of moral and ethical teachings.

Tonight we present this award for the very first time.

As we thought of deserving recipients, it immediately became clear that one name stood out above all others—President Ricardo Lagos, whom we first met as a candidate for the presidency in 2000.

President Lagos, you are, for us, a light unto the nations.

You are a defender of justice, truth, and peace.

During your years as president, you have earned the respect and admiration of nations around the world as a man of vision, integrity, depth, and commitment.

As Jorge Castaneda, the former foreign minister of Mexico, wrote in the journal *Foreign Affairs* (May/June 2003): "President Ricardo Lagos is rightly considered Latin America's elder statesman. When he speaks on international matters, everyone in the region listens."

You have championed human dignity and human development—the improvement of education and healthcare, a reduction in poverty and enhanced job opportunities, justice for those who were victims of injustice and protection of the sanctity of the rule of law.

In other words, President Lagos, in a world sorely in need of genuine statesmen, you have answered the call.

In our Jewish heritage, one scholar stands out perhaps above all others. His name was Maimonides. Born in Cordova, Spain, he lived in the twelfth century.

He wrote: "Every man should view himself as equally balanced: half good and half evil. Likewise, he should see the entire world as half good and half evil.... So that with a single good deed he will tip the scales for himself, and for the entire world, to the side of good."

President Lagos, you have tipped the scales to the side of good—not once but daily.

It therefore gives me great pleasure, on behalf of the American Jewish Committee—and in the presence of our mutual friends from the Jewish community of Chile—to present you with our first "Light unto the Nations" Award.

It is, as you will see, a handmade menorah, our traditional symbol, from time immemorial, of the inextinguishable light of freedom—that "unwavering light."

May you continue to go from strength to strength in your life's remarkable journey.

3. ISRAEL ADVOCACY GUIDE

Israel and the Arab-Israeli Conflict:
A Brief Guide for the Perplexed
(Revised and Updated)
August 2005

The Middle East always seems to be in the news. Hardly a day passes without a story on something going on in Israel or related to the Arab-Israeli conflict. Unfortunately, given the rapid-fire nature of much reporting these days, the discussion often lacks historical context.

This paper provides some perspectives and talking points, both historical and contemporary, but it is not intended as an exhaustive examination of the subject.

The case to be made on behalf of Israel is as strong today as ever.
When presented with the facts, people of good will should understand:

(a) Israel's fifty-seven-year-long quest for peace and security;

(b) the real dangers faced by Israel, a country no larger than New Jersey or Wales, two-thirds the size of Belgium, and one percent the size of Saudi Arabia, in a tumultuous, heavily armed neighborhood;

(c) Israel's unshakeable commitment to democracy, including free and fair elections, smooth transfers of power, civilian control over the military, freedom of speech, press, faith, and assembly, and an independent judiciary—all unique in the region;

(d) the common thread of the threats of extremism and terrorism faced by Israel, the United States, Europe, India, Australia, Russia, moderate Muslim countries, and others; and

(e) Israel's impressive, indeed pathbreaking, contributions to world civilization in such fields as science, medicine, technology, agriculture, and culture—contributions that are even more remarkable given the country's relative youth and its heavy defense burden, but that, regrettably, are often neglected in the preoccupation with reporting on conflict and violence.

No country's historical record is perfect, and Israel, like other democratic nations, has made its share of mistakes. But acknowledging fallibility is a national strength, not a weakness. And Israel's record can be compared favorably against that of any other country in the region, indeed well beyond the region, when it comes to dedication to democratic values.

Israel has a proud record and the country's friends shouldn't hesitate to shout it from the rooftops. And it began long before the establishment of the modern state in 1948.

The Jewish people's link to the land of Israel is incontrovertible and unbroken.

It spans nearly four thousand years.

Exhibit A for this connection is the Hebrew Bible. The Book of Genesis, the first of the five books of the Bible, recounts the story of Abraham, the covenantal relationship with the one God, and the move from Ur (in present-day Iraq) to Canaan, the region corresponding roughly to Israel. The Book of Numbers, the fourth book of the Bible, includes the following words: "The Lord spoke to Moses, saying send men to scout the land of Canaan, which I am giving to the Israelite people." This came toward the end of a forty-year-long journey of the Israelites in search not simply of a refuge from the Egyptians, but of the Promised Land—the land we know today as Israel.

And these are but two of many references to this land and its centrality to Jewish history and national identity.

Exhibit B is any Jewish prayer book in use over the span of centuries anywhere in the world. The references in the liturgy to Zion, the land of Israel, are endless.

The same strong link is true of the connection between the Jewish people and Jerusalem.

It dates back to the period of King David, who lived approximately three thousand years ago, and who established Jerusalem as the capital of Israel. Ever since, Jerusalem has represented not only the geographical center of the Jewish people, but also the spiritual and metaphysical heart of their faith and identity. No matter where Jews pray, they always face in the direction of Jerusalem. Indeed, the relationship between Jerusalem and the Jewish people is entirely unique in the annals of history.

Jerusalem was the site of the two Temples—the first built by King Solomon during the tenth century B.C.E. and destroyed in 586 B.C.E. during the Babylonian conquest, and the second built less than a century later, refurbished by King Herod, and destroyed in 70 C.E. by Roman forces.

As the psalmist wrote, "If I forget thee, O Jerusalem, let my right hand wither; let my tongue stick to my palate if I cease to think of thee, if I do not keep Jerusalem in memory even at my happiest hour."

One commentary on Hebrew Scripture reads: "You also find that there is a Jerusalem above, corresponding to the Jerusalem below. For sheer love of the earthly Jerusalem, God made Himself one above."

And for over three thousand years, Jews at the Passover Seder have repeated the words: "Next year in Jerusalem."

Though in forced dispersion for nearly nineteen hundred years, Jews never stopped yearning for Zion and Jerusalem.

It is written in the Book of Isaiah: "For the sake of Zion I will not be silent; For the sake of Jerusalem I will not be still...."

In addition to expressing this yearning through prayer, there were always Jews who lived in the land of Israel, and especially Jerusalem, though there were often threats to their physical safety. Indeed, since the nineteenth century, Jews have constituted a majority of the city's population. For example, according to the *Political Dictionary of the State of Israel*, Jews were 61.9 percent of Jerusalem's population in 1892.

The historical and religious link to Jerusalem is especially important because some Arabs seek to rewrite history and assert that Jews are "foreign occupiers" or "colonialists" with no actual tie to the land. Such attempts to deny Israel's legitimacy are demonstrably false and need to be exposed for the lies they are. They also entirely ignore the "inconvenient" fact that when Jerusalem was under Muslim (i.e., Ottoman and, later, Jordanian) rule, it was always a backwater. It was never a political, religious, or economic center. For example, when Jerusalem was in Jordanian hands from 1948 to 1967, virtually no Arab leader visited, and no one from the ruling House of Saud in Saudi Arabia came to pray at the Al-Aksa Mosque in eastern Jerusalem.

Zionism is the quest for national self-determination of the Jewish people.

Although the yearning for a Jewish homeland dates back thousands of years and is given expression in classic Jewish texts, it also stems from a more contemporary reality.

Theodor Herzl, considered the father of modern Zionism, was a secular Jew and Viennese journalist who became appalled at the blatant anti-Semitism fueling the infamous Dreyfus case in France, the first European country to extend full rights to the Jews, as well as in his native Austro-Hungarian Empire. He came to the conclusion that Jews could never enjoy full equality as a minority in European societies, since the sad legacy of centuries of anti-Semitism was too deeply embedded. Therefore, he called for the establishment of a Jewish state, which he set out to describe in his landmark book *Der Judenstaat* ("The Jewish State"), published in 1896.

Herzl's vision was endorsed by the British foreign secretary, Lord Balfour, who issued a statement on November 2, 1917:

His Majesty's Government view with favour the establishment in Palestine of a national home for the Jewish people, and will use their best endeavours to facilitate the achievement of this object, it being clearly understood that nothing shall be done which may prejudice the civil and religious rights of existing non-Jewish communities in Palestine, or the rights and political status enjoyed by Jews in any other country.

In 1922, the League of Nations, entrusting Britain with a mandate for Palestine, recognized "the historical connection of the Jewish people with Palestine."

The rise of Adolf Hitler and the Nazi "Final Solution," spearheaded by Germany and its allies—and facilitated by widespread complicity as well as indifference to the fate of the Jews throughout much of the world—revealed in tragic dimensions the desperate need for a Jewish state. (Apropos, Haj Amin el-Husseini, the mufti of Jerusalem, was among the most enthusiastic supporters of the Nazi genocide of the Jewish people.)

Only in such a state, the Zionist movement—and its non-Jewish supporters—believed, would Jews not have to rely on the "goodwill" of others to determine their destiny. All Jews would be welcome to live in the Jewish state as a refuge from persecution or as a fulfillment of a "yearning for Zion." Indeed, this latter point fired the imagination of many Jews who settled in what was then a generally desolate Palestine, in the late nineteenth and early twentieth century, out of idealistic convictions, and who laid the foundation for the modern State of Israel.

Speaking of the desolation, the American author and humorist Mark Twain visited the area in 1867. This is how he described it:

[A] desolate country whose soil is rich enough, but is given over wholly to weeds—a silent mournful expanse.... A desolation is here that not even imagination can grace with the pomp of life and action.... We never saw a human being on the whole route.... There was hardly a tree or a shrub anywhere. Even the olive and the cactus, those fast friends of the worthless soil, had almost deserted the country.

To fast-forward for a moment, any visitor to Israel can see the miraculous transformation of the land, as forests were lovingly planted, the soil was irrigated and tilled, and cities and towns were built.

Israel's adversaries to this day maliciously twist the meaning of Zionism—the movement for self-determination of the Jewish people—and try to present it as a demonic force. Moreover, they seek to depict the area as well-developed by the local Arabs, who were somehow shoved aside by the arriving Jews. Their larger goal is to undermine Israel's raison d'être and isolate the state from the community of nations.

This happened, for example, in 1975, when the UN General Assembly, over the strenuous objections of the democratic countries, adopted a resolution labeling Zionism as "racism." The resolution was finally repealed in 1991, but the canard resurfaced in 2001 at the World Conference Against Racism in Durban, South Africa. The Arab bloc, however, failed in its effort to have Zionism condemned in the conference documents. This time many nations understood that the conflict between Israel and the Palestinians is, and has always been, political, not racial.

Incidentally, this recurring attempt to brand Zionism as racism is a telling example of the pot calling the kettle black. The Arab nations formally define themselves by their ethnicity, i.e., Arab, thus excluding non-Arab ethnic groups, such as Berbers and Kurds. The same is true for religion. Islam is the official religion in all but one of the Arab countries (Lebanon), thus perforce marginalizing non-Islamic faiths, particularly Christian minorities.

In this vein, it's well worth remembering the comments of the late Reverend Martin Luther King, Jr., on anti-Zionism:

> And what is anti-Zionism? It is the denial to the Jewish people of a fundamental right that we justly claim for the people of Africa and all other nations of the Globe. It is discrimination against Jews, my friends, because they are Jews. In short, it is anti-Semitism.... Let my words echo in the depths of your soul: When people criticize Zionism, they mean Jews—make no mistake about it.

It is also important to stress that non-Jews have not been excluded from Israel's nation-building. To the contrary. Today one-fifth of Israel's citizens are non-Jews, including over one million Arabs, and Arabic is an official national language.

Moreover, Israel's Jewish population has always reflected enormous national, ethnic, cultural, and linguistic diversity, which became even more pronounced in the 1980s, when Israel rescued tens of thousands of black Jews from drought-stricken Ethiopia who were dreaming of resettlement in Israel. The eloquent comments at the time of Julius

Chambers, the director-general of the NAACP Legal Defense and Education Fund, bear repeating:

Were the victims of Ethiopian famine white, countless nations might have offered them refuge. But the people dying every day of starvation in Ethiopia and the Sudan are black, and in a world where racism is officially deplored by virtually every organized government, only one non-African nation has opened its doors and its arms. The quiet humanitarian action of the State of Israel, action taken entirely without regard to the color of those being rescued, stands as a condemnation of racism far more telling than mere speeches and resolutions.

The Arab-Israeli conflict was avoidable.

Shortly after its founding in 1945, the United Nations took an interest in the future of mandatory Palestine, then under British rule. A UN commission (UNSCOP, or the United Nations Special Committee on Palestine) recommended to the General Assembly a partition of the land between the Jews and the Arabs. Neither side would get all it sought, but a division would recognize that there were two populations in the land—one Jewish, the other Arab—each meriting a state.

On November 29, 1947, the UN General Assembly, by a vote of 33 in favor, 13 opposed, and 10 abstaining, adopted Resolution 181, known as the Partition Plan.

Acceptance of the Partition Plan would have meant the establishment of two states, but the surrounding Arab countries and the local Arab population vehemently rejected the proposal. They refused to recognize a Jewish claim to any part of the land and chose war to drive the Jews out. This refusal has always been at the heart of the conflict—then and now.

Some Arab countries and Iran, not to mention the Palestinian terrorist organizations, still do not recognize Israel's very right to exist, whatever its final borders, even fifty-seven years after the state's establishment.

On May 14, 1948, the modern State of Israel was founded. Winston Churchill captured its significance:

The coming into being of a Jewish state … is an event in world history to be viewed in the perspective not of a generation or a century, but in the perspective of a thousand, two thousand or even three thousand years.

Years later, President John F. Kennedy offered his perspective on the meaning of Israel's rebirth nearly 1,900 years after its last sovereign expression:

Israel was not created in order to disappear—Israel will endure and flourish. It is the child of hope and home of the brave. It can neither be broken by adversity nor demoralized by success. It carries the shield of democracy and it honors the sword of freedom.

On the subject of peace, Israel's Declaration of the Establishment of the State included these words:

We extend our hand to all neighboring states and their peoples in an offer of peace and good neighborliness, and appeal to them to establish bonds of cooperation and mutual help with the sovereign Jewish people settled in its own land for the common good of all.

Tragically, that offer, like others before it made by Jewish leaders in the months prior to the state's creation, was ignored.

On May 15, 1948, the armies of Egypt, Iraq, Jordan, Lebanon, and Syria attacked the fledgling Jewish state, seeking its destruction.
In the course of this war, launched by Arab nations, civilian populations were affected, as in all wars. Controversies continue to this day about how many local Arabs fled Israel because Arab leaders called on them to do so or threatened them if they did not, how many left out of fear of the fighting, and how many were compelled to leave by Israeli forces. Importantly, hundreds of thousands of Arabs ended up staying in Israel and became citizens of the state.

But the central point must not be overlooked—Arab countries began this war aiming to wipe out the 650,000 Jews in the new State of Israel, and in doing so, these nations defied the UN plan for the creation of both Arab and Jewish states.

There have been two refugee populations created by the Arab-Israeli conflict, not one.
While world attention has been focused on the Palestinian refugees, the plight of Jews from Arab countries, hundreds of thousands of whom became refugees as well, has been largely ignored. Indeed, many experts believe that the size of the two groups was roughly comparable. But there was one profound difference—Israel immediately absorbed the Jewish refugees, while the Palestinian refugees were placed in camps and deliberately kept there generation after generation as a matter of calculated Arab policy and with the complicity of the UN.

There is no comparable situation in the world today where a refugee population has been cynically exploited in this way.
Until now, only one Arab country—Jordan—has offered citizenship to the Palestinian refugees.

The other twenty-one Arab countries, with their vast territory and sharing a common language, religion, and ethnic roots with the Palestinians, have refused to do so. Why? Sadly, they appear to have little interest in alleviating the plight of refugees living in often squalid camps. Rather, they want to breed hatred of Israel and thus use the refugees as a key weapon in the ongoing struggle against Israel.

Parenthetically—just to give a sense of how Palestinians are treated in the Arab world—Kuwait summarily expelled over 300,000 Palestinians working in the country (but never given Kuwaiti passports) when Yasir Arafat supported Saddam Hussein's Iraq in the 1990–91 Gulf War. The Palestinians were seen as a potential fifth column. There was hardly a peep of protest from other Arab countries about what amounted to the expulsion of an entire Palestinian community. And, difficult as it is to believe, Lebanon, for decades home to several hundred thousand Palestinian refugees, legally prevented them from working in many professional sectors.

Unfortunately, the story of the Jewish refugees from Arab countries is not often told.
When the issue of Jewish refugees from Arab countries is raised, Arab spokesmen often feign ignorance or strenuously assert that Jews lived well under Muslim rule (unlike Jews in Christian Europe). Sometimes they disingenuously argue that Arabs, by definition, cannot be anti-Semitic because, like Jews, they are Semites.

It is true that there was no equivalent of the Holocaust in the Jewish experience in Muslim lands, and it also true that there were periods of cooperation and harmony, but the story does not end there. Jews never enjoyed full and equal rights with Muslims in countries under Islamic rule; there were clearly delineated rules of behavior for Jews (and Christians) as second-class citizens. Violence against Jews was not unknown in the Muslim world.

To cite but one illustration of the fate of Jews in Arab countries, Jews lived uninterruptedly in Libya since the time of the Phoenicians, that is, many centuries before the Arabs arrived from the Arabian Peninsula, bringing Islam to North Africa and settling—occupying?— lands already inhabited by indigenous Berbers, among others.

The vast majority of Libya's 40,000 Jews left between 1948 and 1951, following pogroms in 1945 and 1948. In 1951, Libya became an independent country. Despite constitutional guarantees, the Jews who remained in the country were denied the right to vote, hold public office, obtain Libyan passports, supervise their own communal affairs, or purchase new property. After a third pogrom in 1967, Libya's remaining 4,000 Jews fled, permitted to leave with only one suitcase and the equivalent of $50. In 1970, the Libyan government announced a series of laws to confiscate the assets of Libya's exiled Jews and issued bonds providing for fair compensation payable within fifteen years. But 1985 came and went, with no compensation paid.

At the same time, the government destroyed Jewish cemeteries, using the headstones to pave new roads, as part of a calculated effort to erase any vestige of the Jewish historical presence in the country.

There were an estimated 750,000 Jews in Arab countries in 1948, the year of Israel's establishment; today, there are about 6,000, the bulk of whom live in Morocco and Tunisia.

Where was the Arab sympathy for the Palestinian population from 1948 to 1967?

With armistice agreements ending Israel's War of Independence, the Gaza Strip was in the hands of Egypt. Rather than consider sovereignty for the local Arab population and the Palestinian refugees who settled there, Egyptian authorities imposed military rule. Meanwhile, the West Bank and the eastern half of Jerusalem were governed by Jordan. Again, there was no move to create an independent Palestinian state; to the contrary, Jordan annexed the territory, a step recognized by only two countries in the world, Britain and Pakistan.

It was during this period, in 1964 to be precise, that the Palestine Liberation Organization (PLO) was founded. Its aim was not the creation of a state in the lands under Egyptian and Jordanian authority, but rather the elimination of Israel and the founding of an Arab Palestinian state in the whole of Palestine.

Article 15 of the PLO Charter clearly articulated this goal:

> The liberation of Palestine, from an Arab viewpoint, is a national duty to repulse the Zionist, imperialist invasion from the great Arab homeland and to purge the Zionist presence from Palestine.

In the ensuing years, PLO-sponsored terrorism took its deadly toll, focusing on Israeli, American, European, and Jewish targets. Schoolchildren, Olympic athletes, airplane passengers, diplomats, and even a wheelchair-bound tourist on a cruise ship were among the targets of the terrorists.

How did Israel come into possession of the West Bank, Golan Heights, Gaza Strip, the Sinai Peninsula, and the eastern half of Jerusalem, including the Old City?

These days, some people reflexively refer to the "occupied territories" without ever asking how they fell into Israel's hands in 1967. Once again, there are those in the Arab world who seek to rewrite history and impute expansionist motives to Israel, but the facts are clear. Here's a quick summary of some of the major events leading up to the Six-Day War:

On May 16, 1967, Cairo Radio announced: "The existence of Israel has continued too long. The battle has come in which we shall destroy Israel." On the same day, Egypt demanded the withdrawal of UN forces that had been stationed in Gaza and Sharm el-Sheikh since 1957. Three days later, the UN, to its everlasting shame, announced it would comply with the Egyptian demand.

On May 19, Cairo Radio said: "This is our chance, Arabs, to deal Israel a mortal blow of annihilation...."

On May 23, Egypt's President Gamal Abdel Nasser declared his intention to block the Strait of Tiran to Israeli shipping, thus effectively severing Israel's vital trade links with East Africa and Asia. Israel replied that under international law this was a casus belli, an act of war.

On May 27, Nasser said that "our basic objective will be the destruction of Israel."

On May 30, Jordan's King Hussein placed Jordanian forces under Egyptian control. Egyptian, Iraqi, and Saudi troops were sent to Jordan.

On June 1, Iraq's leader added his thoughts: "We are resolved, determined, and united to achieve our clear aim of wiping Israel off the map."

On June 3, Cairo Radio hailed the impending Muslim holy war.

On June 5, Israel, surrounded by far more numerous and heavily-armed Arab forces likely to attack at any moment, launched a preemptive strike.

Within six days, Israel defeated its adversaries and, in the process, captured land on the Egyptian, Jordanian, and Syrian fronts.

Israel made strenuous—and documented—efforts, via UN channels, to persuade King Hussein to stay out of the war. Unlike Egypt and Syria, whose hostility toward Israel was unremitting, Jordan had quietly cooperated with Israel and shared concerns about the Palestinians' aggressive designs. Years later, King Hussein publicly acknowledged that his decision to enter the 1967 war, in which he lost control of the West Bank and eastern Jerusalem, was one of the biggest blunders he ever made.

Another lost peace opportunity.

Shortly after the Six-Day War, Israel indicated its desire to exchange land for peace with its Arab neighbors. While Israel was unprepared to relinquish the eastern half of Jerusalem—which contained Judaism's holiest sites and which, in blatant violation of the terms of the Israeli-Jordanian armistice agreement, had been entirely off limits to Israel for nearly nineteen years (while Jordan desecrated fifty-eight synagogues in the Jewish Quarter of the Old City and the world remained silent)—it was eager to exchange the seized territories for a comprehensive settlement. But Israel's overtures were rebuffed. An unmistakable response came from Khartoum, Sudan's capital, where Arab leaders gathered to issue a resolution on September 1, 1967, announcing the three noes: "no peace, no recognition, and no negotiation" with Israel.

In November 1967, the UN Security Council adopted Resolution 242.

This resolution, often cited in discussions about the Arab-Israeli conflict as the basis for resolving it, is not always quoted with precision. The resolution stresses "the inadmissibility of the acquisition of territory by war and the need to work for a just and lasting peace in which *every* [emphasis added] State in the area can live in security."

Further, it calls for "withdrawal of Israeli armed forces from territories occupied in the recent conflict," but deliberately omits use of the word "the" before the word "territories." The U.S. ambassador to the UN at the time, Arthur Goldberg, noted that this was intentional, so that any final settlement could allow for unspecified border adjustments that would take into account Israel's security needs. For instance, prior to the 1967 Six-Day War, Israel at its narrowest point—just north of Tel Aviv, its largest city—was only nine miles wide.

The resolution also includes a call for "termination of all claims or states of belligerency and respect for and acknowledgment of the sovereignty, territorial integrity and political independence of every State in the area and their right to live in peace within secure and recognized boundaries free from threats or acts of force."

And, not least, it "affirms further the necessity (a) For guaranteeing freedom of navigation through international waterways in the area; (b) For achieving a just settlement of the refugee problem [Author's comment: Note the absence of specificity as to which refugee problem, allowing for more than one interpretation of the intended refugee population.]; and (c) For guaranteeing the territorial inviolability and political independence of every State in the area, through measures including the establishment of demilitarized zones."

On October 22, 1973—during another Arab-launched war, which came to be known as the Yom Kippur War because it began on Judaism's holiest day—the UN Security Council adopted Resolution 338. The measure called for a cease-fire, implementation of Resolution 242 in its entirety, and the onset of talks between the parties concerned. Resolutions 242 and 338 are normally cited together in connection with any Arab-Israeli peace talks.

The settlements have been a contentious issue.

No question, but, like just about everything else associated with the Arab-Israeli conflict, there's more here than meets the eye.

After Israel's victory in the 1967 war, and once it became clear that the Arabs were not interested in negotiating peace, Israel, under a Labor-led coalition, began encouraging the construction of settlements, or new communities, in the captured lands. This practice was accelerated under Likud-led governments after 1977.

Whatever one's perspective on the settlements, it's important to understand Israel's motives in moving ahead on this front:

(a) Israel contended that the land was disputed—both Arabs and Jews laid claim to it—and since there was no sovereign authority, Israel had as much right to settle there as the Palestinians (who had never had a state of their own);

(b) there had been Jewish communities in the West Bank long before 1948, for example, in Hebron and Gush Etzion, both sites of twentieth-century massacres by Arabs in which large numbers of Jews were killed;

(c) the West Bank, according to the Hebrew Bible, represents the cradle of Jewish civilization, and some Jews, driven by faith and history, were eager to reassert that link;

(d) the Israeli government believed that certain settlements could serve a useful security purpose, given the importance of geography, and especially topography, in this rather confined area;

(e) a number of Israeli officials felt that building settlements, and thus creating facts on the ground, might hasten the day when the Palestinians, presumably realizing that time was not necessarily on their side, would talk peace.

At the same time, polls have consistently found that a majority of Israelis agree that any peace agreement with the Palestinians will necessarily entail dismantling many, though not all, of the settlements. Those settlements which are today quite substantial cities, and which are nearest to Jerusalem and other areas adjacent to the 1967 line, are likely to be retained by Israel in any peace accord. Importantly, the 1967 border was never an internationally recognized boundary, but rather only an armistice line marking the positions held at the end of Israel's War of Independence in 1949.

The United States recognized this critically important fact most recently when President George W. Bush wrote to Prime Minister Ariel Sharon, on April 14, 2004, that "it is unrealistic to expect that the outcome of the final-status negotiations will be a full and complete return to the armistice lines of 1949."

The possibilities of peace

In 1977, Menachem Begin, Israel's first Likud prime minister, took office. That did not stop Egypt's President Anwar Sadat from making his historic trip to Israel the same year and addressing the Knesset, Israel's parliament. An extraordinary peace process ensued, with all the ups and downs that come with a difficult set of negotiations. In September 1978, the Camp David Accords were adopted, containing a framework for comprehensive peace, including a proposal for limited self-government for the Palestinians. (The proposal was rejected by the Palestinians.) Six months later, a peace accord was signed, and the thirty-one-year state of war between Israel and Egypt came to an end.

It was a remarkable moment in history. Sadat, virulently anti-Israel and anti-Semitic for much of his life, and the mastermind of Egypt's surprise attack (together with Syria) on Israel that ignited the 1973

Yom Kippur War, teamed up with Begin, the head of Israel's leading right-wing party, to open a new chapter in Arab-Israel relations. It proved that with will, courage, and vision, anything was possible.

But every other Arab country, except Sudan (under far more moderate leadership then than now) and Oman, severed diplomatic ties with Cairo to protest the move. And in 1981 the Egyptian leader was assassinated by members of Egyptian Islamic Jihad, who would later become brothers-in-arms of Osama bin Laden and his Al-Qaeda network.

For its part, Israel yielded the vast expanse of the Sinai (approximately 23,000 square miles, or more than twice the size of Israel proper), which had provided a critical strategic buffer zone between itself and Egypt. Israel also gave up valuable oil fields which it had discovered in the Sinai, a big sacrifice for a country with no natural resources to speak of. It closed important air force bases that had been constructed. And, despite Begin's staunch commitment to settlements, it dismantled these enclaves in Sinai.

In doing so, Israel demonstrated its unquenchable thirst for peace, its willingness to take substantial risks and make sacrifices, and its scrupulous commitment to fulfilling the terms of its agreements. When else in modern history has a country victorious in a war for its very survival relinquished land and other tangible strategic assets in pursuit of peace?

Israel and Jordan reached an historic peace agreement in 1994.

This was a much easier negotiation than with Egypt, since Israel and Jordan already enjoyed good, if quiet, ties based on overlapping national interests vis-à-vis the Palestinians. (The Jordanians were just as fearful of Palestinian territorial ambitions as Israel.) Israel once again demonstrated its deep yearning for peace and readiness to take the steps necessary to achieve it, including border adjustments and water-sharing arrangements called for by Amman. On October 26, 1994, Israeli Prime Minister Yitzhak Rabin and King Hussein of Jordan signed a formal peace treaty at Wadi Araba on the Israeli-Jordanian border. Rabin called it "the peace of soldiers and the peace of friends."

Spurred by the examples of, first, Egypt and, later, Jordan, a number of Arab countries began exploring links with Israel. The most forthcoming was Mauritania, which became the third Arab state to establish formal diplomatic relations with Israel. Others, such as Morocco, Oman, Qatar, and Tunisia, stopped short of full recognition, but openly sought political or economic ties. And some other Arab countries, who would rather remain nameless, developed points of contact with Israel that have taken a variety of forms, but these countries have been unwilling to go further, they assert, until there is a comprehensive peace agreement reached between Israel and all its neighbors.

Another opportunity for peace was spurned by the Palestinians in 2000–01.

When Ehud Barak became prime minister in 1999, he announced an ambitious agenda. The left-of-center Israeli leader said he would attempt to reach an historic end to the conflict with the Palestinians within thirteen months, picking up where his predecessors had left off, and building on the momentum of the 1991 Madrid Conference, the first peace talks since the Camp David agreement, and the 1993 Oslo Accords, which established a Declaration of Principles between Israel and the Palestinians. As it turned out, he went beyond what anyone in Israel might have thought possible in his willingness to compromise in the interest of peace.

With the active support of the Clinton administration, Barak pushed the process as far and as fast as he could, and, in doing so, he broke new ground on such infinitely sensitive issues as Jerusalem, for the sake of an agreement. But alas, he and Clinton failed.

Arafat was not ready to engage the process and make it work.

Rather than press ahead with the talks, which would have led to the establishment of the first-ever Palestinian state, with its capital in eastern Jerusalem, he walked away, after preposterously trying to persuade President Clinton that there was no historical Jewish link to Jerusalem and dropping the bombshell demand of a so-called "right of return" for Palestinian refugees and their generations of descendants. Arafat surely knew that this was an instant deal-breaker, since no Israeli government could ever conceivably allow millions of Palestinians to settle in Israel and thus totally undermine the Jewish character of the state.

Tragically, Arafat revealed himself incapable or unwilling, or both, of pursuing peace at the negotiating table. Instead, he returned to a more familiar pattern—on occasion talking peace while consistently encouraging terrorism.

Arafat understood that the media images of heavily armed Israeli troops facing Palestinians in the streets, including children cynically sent to the front lines, would work to his advantage. Israel would be cast in the role of aggressor and oppressor, the Palestinians as downtrodden victims.

It wouldn't be long, he calculated, before the Arab world would angrily denounce Israel, the nonaligned countries would dutifully follow suit, the Europeans would urge still more concessions from Israel to placate the Palestinians, international human rights groups would accuse Israel of excessive force, and the world, plagued by a short memory, would forget that the Palestinian leader had just spurned an unprecedented chance to strike a peace deal.

Arafat wasn't entirely wrong. Much of the media, many European governments, and the majority of human rights groups played right into his hands. It was only after his death in 2004 that some, though not all, of them finally realized they had been duped by the wily, corrupt leader whom they had inexplicably chosen to trust, if not romanticize.

Moreover, Arafat presumably reckoned, Washington might eventually take a tougher line on Israel as the result of pressure from Egypt and Saudi Arabia, two Arab countries that loom large in the worldview of American policy makers, and from the European Union. And there was the long-term possibility that Israel, a first-world country, would begin to tire of the struggle and its daily toll of military and civilian casualties, the negative impact on the nation's mood and psyche—not to speak of its economy—and the potentially growing international isolation.

But here he grossly miscalculated. Israel didn't tire; instead, it stayed the course. And the United States stood by Israel, recognizing and exposing Arafat for who he was and refusing to have any further dealings with him.

What exactly is Israel expected to do to ensure the safety of its citizens? What would other states do in a similar situation?

Perhaps the recent bombings in Britain, Egypt, Indonesia, Morocco, Russia, Spain, Tunisia, Turkey, the United States, and elsewhere will help the world grasp the true nature of the terrorist threat Israel has been facing and the rationale for Israel's unflinching response.

Unflinching, yes, but also measured. The truth is that Israel, given its military strength, could have delivered a much more devastating blow to the Palestinians, but has chosen not to for a host of diplomatic, political, strategic, and humanitarian reasons.

Jenin is a perfect example. Though Palestinian spokesmen rushed to condemn the Israeli military operation in this West Bank city in 2002 as a "massacre," in reality Israel chose the most risky method of entering the city to search for terrorist hideouts precisely to avoid Palestinian civilian casualties. As a result, Israel suffered twenty-three military fatalities, while killing just over fifty armed Palestinian gunmen. Israel's alternative might have been to attack Jenin from the air, just as NATO fighter planes bombed Belgrade in the 1990s, but that would have resulted in indiscriminate killing, something Israel desperately wanted to avoid.

Interestingly, many in the West who criticized Israel for its tactics in dealing with terrorism are now adopting those very same methods, including enhanced intelligence, surveillance, penetration, and preemption.

Judging from the global full-court press against the terrorists, it doesn't look as if "restraint," "dialogue," "compromise," and "understanding" are currently part of the vocabulary vis-à-vis those who attack us, nor should they be, but these were some of the very words offered as advice to Israel by the international community for dealing with the threat not so long ago.

In the final analysis, even though Israel enjoys military superiority, Jerusalem understands that this is not a conflict that can be won exclusively on the battlefield. Simply put, neither side is going to disappear.

This conflict can be resolved only at the peace table, if and when the Palestinians finally realize they have squandered more than half a century and numerous chances to build a state—alongside Israel, not in its place.

Perhaps the most controversial aspect of Israel's policy is the defensive fence or security barrier currently being built, which opponents falsely call a "wall."

Three things in particular should be kept in mind. First, the barrier has been proven to cut dramatically the ability of Palestinian terrorists to enter into Israeli population centers and create havoc. Second, the barrier was built *only* as a result of repeated terrorist activity—an estimated 25,000 attempted attacks against Israelis by Palestinian groups and individuals in the last five years alone. And third, barriers can be moved in any direction, or even dismantled, but the lives of innocent victims of terror can never be regained.

Gaza is a test case of Palestinian intentions.

Israel's disengagement from Gaza, the brainchild of Prime Minister Sharon, not only provides a potential new start to the peace process, but also gives the Palestinians, under the leadership of Palestinian Authority president Mahmoud Abbas, an historic opportunity for self-governance. Will they begin to establish a peaceful civil society without the widespread corruption, violence, and anarchy so endemic in the past? Or will Gaza end up as an essentially lawless area, hospitable primarily to terrorists and their friends? Will the Palestinians aspire to build a model state living quietly alongside Israel, or will they use Gaza as a new platform for firing missiles and organizing terror attacks against neighboring Israel?

A key test for the leadership of President Abbas is the challenge posed by terror groups operating within Palestinian society. The new Palestinian leadership at times has condemned attacks by these groups, but it has only rarely confronted them directly, and has not sought to disarm them. Without action on this front, the chances for moving ahead successfully on the peace front diminish dramatically. Moreover, the Palestinian Authority can never establish its authority if armed groups have the luxury of operating both as political factions and separate militia groups.

In particular, Hamas and Islamic Jihad, two radical groups on the American and European Union list of designated terrorist organizations, have been operating with relative impunity in the Palestinian-controlled areas. Increasingly, so does Hezbollah. All three groups have operational and financial links with Iran and Syria.

There's one other important point. If, after the 1993 Oslo Accords, the Palestinian Authority had begun to introduce the values of tolerance and coexistence into the school curriculum, perhaps the generation of young suicide bombers we've witnessed in recent years might have acted differently. But instead they were fed a steady diet of incitement, hatred, vilification, and demonization of Jews, Judaism, Israel, and Zionism. They were led to believe that there could be no higher calling for Arabs and Muslims than so-called martyrdom through the killing of as many detested Jews—the "sons of monkeys and pigs," as some spokesmen regularly refer to the Jews—as possible.

And this teaching has been reinforced by the drumbeat of hatred pouring out of mosques during Friday sermons, the popularity of notoriously anti-Semitic books like *Mein Kampf* and the *Protocols of the Elders of Zion*, and the use of Palestinian media as a mouthpiece for incitement. When Palestinian schools, the media, and the mosques stop this outpouring of anti-Semitism and anti-Zionism, then chances for building a foundation of true peace will increase.

And no, despite Palestinian claims, there is nothing comparable emanating from the Israeli side. When lone Israeli voices resort to extremist language (or action), they are quickly condemned by Israeli society, not lionized.

Israel is a democracy and thinks and behaves like a democracy.

That's not always easy to do in light of the situation it faces. But, while Israel gets its share of criticism for allegedly heavy-handed methods, the Palestinians, despite all their shrill rhetoric, understand better than anyone that it is precisely Israel's democratic values and rule of law that they believe could be the nation's Achilles' heel.

The Palestinians know, even if they don't publicly acknowledge it, that the democratic system places brakes and limits on Israel's policy options.

They know that Israel has a multiparty political system and that these parties need to differentiate themselves from one another to have any chance of electoral success. In fact, the parties have included every viewpoint from extreme left to extreme right, from secular to religious, from Russian Jewish to Arab. Apropos, Israeli Arabs currently hold approximately ten percent of the Knesset seats (and a few of these parliamentarians have openly identified with Israel's enemies in the current conflict).

They know that public opinion in Israel counts for something and can affect policy.

They know that Israel enjoys a free and inquisitive press.

They know that Israel has an independent judiciary that occupies a respected place in the nation's life and that has not hesitated to overrule government, even military, decisions that are deemed to be inconsistent with the spirit or letter of Israeli law.

They know that Israel has a thriving civil society and numerous human rights groups that stress objectivity and impartiality.

They know that Israel protects freedom of worship for all religious communities, indeed has gone so far as to prevent Jews from praying on the Temple Mount, Judaism's holiest site, specifically to avoid tension with Muslim worshipers at the two mosques built there much later. Indeed, since the 1967 Six-Day War Israel has ceded authority for the area to the Waqf, the Muslim religious authority. Could anyone imagine the reverse happening if it were in an Arab country?

They know that Israel, based on the core principles of the Jewish tradition, attaches great importance to ethical and moral standards of behavior, even when, at times, it falls short of them.

And, as a result, they know that there are self-imposed restraints on Israeli behavior precisely because Israel is a democratic state and because, in the final analysis, its government is accountable to the will of the people.

If only the Middle East resembled the Middle West!

Wouldn't that augur well for peaceful conflict resolution and regional cooperation? When was the last time that one democratic nation launched a military attack against another democracy? Regrettably, democracy is a very rare commodity in the Middle East.

The Palestinians know how Syria's late President Hafez el-Assad dealt with Islamic fundamentalists, killing an estimated 10,000–20,000 in Hama and leveling the city as an unmistakable message to other fundamentalists in the country.

They know how Iraq's former President Saddam Hussein handled the Kurds, using poison gas to kill thousands and destroying hundreds of Kurdish villages.

They know how Saudi Arabia reacted to Yemeni support for Saddam Hussein during the 1990–91 Gulf War. Overnight, the country expelled an estimated 600,000 Yemenis.

And they know how Egypt has dealt with its own Islamic radicals— below the radar of the media, without fanfare. Thousands of these extremists have either been killed or locked up in jails without due process.

The Palestinians count on the fact that Israel will not follow any of these examples. That is Israel's strength as a democracy, but it comes with a price. The Palestinians seek to take advantage of it. But they have made one fundamental error—they have underestimated Israel's will to survive.

Israelis desperately want peace. At the same time, peace at any price is no peace.

Israelis want to stop worrying about bombs on buses and in malls. They want to put an end to burying their children, victims of terror or military engagements. In short, they want to lead normal lives, and they have demonstrated their willingness time and again to endorse far-reaching, even potentially risky, compromises in the quest for peace.

Israelis, however, have learned the painful lessons of history. Peace without secure and defensible borders can be tantamount to national suicide. And who knows better than the citizens of Israel, who include Holocaust survivors and refugees from Communist lands and from

Arab extremism, how dangerous it can be to let one's guard down too quickly, too easily?

Are Israelis simply to ignore Iran's calls for Israel's annihilation and its quest to acquire weapons of mass destruction, Syria's hospitality to terrorist groups bent on Israel's destruction, Hezbollah's arsenal of thousands of short-range missiles in southern Lebanon capable of reaching the northern half of Israel, and the blood-curdling calls for suicide attacks against Israel heard in Gaza and the West Bank?

Our world hasn't been terribly kind to the naïve, the credulous, or the self-delusional. Despite the doubters at the time, Adolf Hitler meant exactly what he said when he wrote *Mein Kampf*, Saddam Hussein meant exactly what he said when he insisted that Kuwait was a province of Iraq, and Osama bin Laden meant exactly what he said when, in 1998, he called for killing as many Americans as possible.

Israel lives in a particularly rough neighborhood. To survive, it has had to be courageous on the battlefield and at the peace table. It has passed both tests with flying colors.

Israel is about much more than conflict and conflict resolution.

While public discussion and media attention tend to focus on issues of war, violence, and terrorism in the region, there is another side to Israel which is only rarely seen, except largely by those fortunate enough to visit Israel and see it with their own eyes.

Israel is an unimaginably vibrant and dynamic country. It is both ancient and cutting-edge. It is a country of Nobel Prize winners in literature and chemistry, of Olympic medalists, of concert pianists, and rap stars. There are more scientists and engineers in Israel per capita than anywhere else in the world. Newspaper readership and book publishing are also among the highest in the world. The number of high-tech start-up companies and patents issued are astonishingly impressive for a country of just under seven million inhabitants. Medical advances, technological and communications breakthroughs, and agricultural innovations have not only benefited Israel, but also millions of people around the world.

Next time you enter a chat room, use a mobile phone or voice mail, require color imaging, depend on a Pentium processor chip, need a

CAT scan or MRI, or see a farm blooming in the desert due to drip irri-
gation, there's a good chance that Israel has lent a helping hand.

Israel. The more you know, the more you understand.

4. RADIO COMMENTARY

David Harris's biweekly radio commentaries are aired on the CBS National Radio Network and reach an estimated audience of 30–35 million listeners.

Week of January 5, 2004

The scenes from the ancient Iranian city of Bam have been shocking.

Tens of thousands killed, many more injured, and countless homes destroyed in a powerful earthquake.

This should remind us of our common humanity. After all, such acts of nature pay no heed to race, religion, or ethnicity.

In a goodwill gesture, Israel offered assistance, including its famed search-and-rescue teams.

But the Iranian government said it would accept aid from every country except one—Israel.

Think about it.

Bodies buried in the rubble. The injured desperate for medical care. The homeless exposed to the cold. And yet these compelling needs were trumped by the hatred of a regime that goes so far as to deny Israel's right to exist.

Our hearts go out to the people of Bam as they face this immense tragedy. At the same time, we pray that countries like Iran will one day be governed by enlightened leaders who put the needs of their citizens first … and who recognize our common humanity.

Week of January 26, 2004

Auschwitz. It stands as the ultimate symbol of evil.

Fifty-nine years ago this week, the infamous Nazi camp was liberated. The machinery of death boggles the mind.

At Auschwitz alone, over a million Jews were systematically murdered.

This week many European countries mark Holocaust Remembrance Day.

It's a day to recall the six million Jews, including a million and a half children, who were killed in the Nazi death camps, as well as the many other victims of Nazi terror.

It's also a day to rededicate ourselves to the struggle against anti-Semitism. Tragically, it didn't entirely disappear with the Nazi defeat.

In recent years, we've seen a new wave of anti-Semitism, particularly in the Islamic world and Europe. But no country is immune from this cancer, not even our own.

How best to fight it? People of good will must stand up and speak out. Make no mistake about it: While anti-Semites may target a specific group, their ultimate target is democracy itself.

Week of February 16, 2004

Israel.

It's in the news a lot, but the coverage rarely provides context. Instead, it tends to focus on daily events.

Yet to understand what's really going on requires more information.

Having just returned from Israel, I bring you three examples:

Geography. Israel is a tiny country. It's about the size of New Jersey and barely two-thirds the size of Belgium. That doesn't give Israel much margin for error in a region where some terrorist groups and countries openly seek Israel's destruction.

History. The Jewish people have been intimately connected to the land of Israel since time immemorial. It's not possible to understand

Israel without recognizing the link among a land, a people, and a faith.

Democracy. Israel is the only democracy in its immediate neighbor-hood. That means full voting rights for all citizens, Jews and Arabs alike, religious freedom, an independent judiciary, women's rights, and a feisty press

Israel. It's a country worth getting to know.

Week of March 1, 2004

What's that expression—"Out of sight, out of mind"?

Over 100,000 American servicemen and women stationed in Iraq and Afghanistan may be out of sight, but they should never be out of mind.

Together with soldiers from such allied countries as Britain, Australia, and Poland, they're at risk 24/7 in the cause of freedom and global security. Some have tragically lost their lives in the line of duty.

The stakes for our nation couldn't be higher.

Consider for a moment a stabilized Iraq where the country's enormous potential for peaceful development is unleashed, and where tyranny and torture never again reign.

And consider a stabilized Afghanistan where terrorists can't find safe haven and the facilities to plan their evil deeds, and where women are never again denied even basic health care and education.

Whatever our political differences, we Americans should stand united in support of our troops on the ground, and pray both for the success of their mission and their safe return home.

Week of March 15, 2004

There are some things I just don't get.

For example, while American troops are putting their lives on the line in Iraq and Afghanistan, here at home we're too often disengaged.

What can we do to help?

For one thing, we ought to be telling our elected officials that our nation must cut its dependence on Middle East oil, and that we're ready to do our part.

The situation is surreal.

We buy oil from countries that have supported terrorism, spread radical religious teachings, suppressed women's rights, and persecuted other faiths.

Meanwhile, our fuel economy standards are at a twenty-two-year low.

Isn't it high time for our elected officials to put partisanship aside and agree on a three-part initiative?

First, raise fuel economy standards for cars and trucks, and fast. Second, step up research into the new technologies that can one day replace fossil fuels. And third, call on all Americans to reduce our use of gas.

Remember: Greater energy independence means greater national security.

Week of March 29, 2004

Peace.

It's been at the heart of democratic Israel's quest since its founding, with UN support, in 1948.

Thankfully, there's peace with Egypt and Jordan. But with the Palestinians, it's another story.

They could have had a state at the time of Israel's creation. They refused. They weren't prepared to live alongside Israel.

They could have had a state as recently as three years ago. Again they refused.

Instead, they unleashed a new wave of terrorism.

Such Palestinian groups as Hamas openly declare that their goal is to destroy Israel and replace it with a radical Islamic state.

And they get Palestinian teenagers to strap bombs on themselves, luring them with a cash gift for their families and a promise that they'll meet seventy-two virgins in heaven.

When Palestinian leaders finally emerge dedicated to peaceful compromise, they'll find willing partners in Israel.

Until that day, Israel, like any nation, including our own, will do what it must to prevail against those who would destroy it.

Week of April 12, 2004

This month we mark two tragic anniversaries.

In the Nazi Holocaust, six million Jews were exterminated.

In Rwanda, 800,000 people, primarily members of the Tutsi tribe, were slaughtered in 1994.

These tragedies are graphic reminders of man's capacity for evil.

They're also object lessons in the high price of global apathy.

Nations and people of good will must never remain silent in the face of such barbaric crimes.

Take Sudan today.

An op-ed writer in the *New York Times* described the situation in this multiethnic and multireligious country: "The Sudanese government is teaming up with Arab Muslim militias in a campaign of ethnic slaughter and deportation."

To date, a million black Africans, the principal targets, have been displaced. Tens of thousands have been killed.

The voices of governments, religious organizations, students, and others need to be heard loud and clear.

Never again should massive human rights violations be met with indifference.

The time to act is now.

Week of April 26, 2004

This week Israel marks its fifty-sixth birthday.

It's an occasion worth celebrating.

As Winston Churchill, the legendary British statesman, said: "The coming into being of a Jewish state is an event in world history to be viewed in the perspective not of a generation or a century, but in the perspective of a thousand, two thousand, or even three thousand years."

President Ronald Reagan remarked that "in Israel, free men and women are every day demonstrating the power of courage and faith.... Israel is a land of stability and democracy in a region of tyranny and unrest."

And President Bill Clinton noted that "like America, Israel is a strong democracy, a symbol of freedom, and an oasis of liberty, a home to the oppressed and persecuted."

Israel. An ancient country.

Israel. A modern country.

Israel. A democratic country still yearning, after fifty-six years, for peace and security.

Happy birthday, Israel!

Week of May 10, 2004

Let's get back to basics in the Middle East.

What's the underlying problem in the region?

Accepting Israel as a fact of life.

Israel was created by the UN in 1947 and became a member of the world body two years later.

Still, there are those who seek to destroy it. Is there any other UN member state still fighting for its very right to exist?

Look at maps of Israel in the region.

Palestinian, Saudi, and Syrian textbooks show maps that omit any mention of Israel.

Instead, Israeli and Palestinian areas are combined into one country called Palestine.

Peace is a strategic necessity.

Democratic Israel has shown its willingness to compromise for the sake of peace, most recently in proposing a viable Palestinian state. The response?

Another rebuff by Yasir Arafat, who revealed once again that his goal is not a two-state, but a one-state, solution—just like the maps.

How can you make peace with those who don't even recognize your very right to exist?

Week of May 24, 2004

Albert Einstein famously defined insanity as doing the same thing over and over and expecting different results.

That's been our nation's energy policy for two decades.

As dependence on Middle East oil grows, fuel economy standards are at a twenty-two-year low and our appetite for gas guzzlers increases.

Our policy endangers America's national security big-time.

We've become dependent on nations that aren't necessarily our friends.

And our petrodollars too often fund those who preach, teach, or practice hatred toward us.

In short, this is insanity.

And even after the tumultuous events of recent years, too many lawmakers still act as if everything will be just fine.

They need to hear from constituents.

Tell them we want more fuel-efficient cars and trucks, we support serious research into alternative energy sources, and we believe in energy conservation.

And tell them the time to act is now. Our country's future depends on it.

Week of June 7, 2004

Peace in the Middle East.

It's a goal worth striving for.

But how can there be peace in this troubled region when hatred of Jews is so widespread?

When Hitler's *Mein Kampf*, the Nazi manifesto, is printed and sold in several Arab countries?

When popular TV programs and books repeat the blood libel—the medieval canard that caused so much bloodshed against the Jews?

When religious leaders demonize Jews and Judaism in their weekly sermons?

When notorious anti-Semitic forgeries are serialized on television and in best-selling books?

When conspiracy theories attribute to Jews all the evils of the world?

To make matters still worse, these lies are spread around the world via the Internet, satellite technology, and traveling spokesmen.

Peace in the Middle East is a strategic necessity, but it can't be built on the language of hatred and incitement.

People of good will must be heard. Silence has never been the answer to bigotry.

Week of June 21, 2004

Since 9/11, many people have been asking: Where are the moderate voices in the Muslim world? Why aren't they being heard?

One such moderate has recently written a book, and it's well worth reading.

Born to a Muslim family in Africa, Irshad Manji today lives in Canada, where she's a prominent journalist and TV personality.

She's also a brave woman. Her book, *The Trouble with Islam*, has received glowing reviews. But Islamic radicals haven't been quite so complimentary. In fact, she's gotten many death threats.

That's because she doesn't flinch from asking the tough questions of her fellow Muslims, such as: "Why are we squandering the talents of women, fully half of God's creation? What's with the stubborn streak of anti-Semitism in Islam? How can we be so sure that homosexuals deserve ostracism—or death?"

And that's just for starters.

Let's hope Irshad Manji's courageous book will inspire other voices of moderation to speak out.

Week of July 5, 2004

It's about time that we Americans face reality. We can't afford to live in denial much longer.

We desperately need a serious energy policy, and now.

We must reduce our dependence on Middle East oil.

Our national security is at stake.

Our insatiable appetite for oil means that we send billions of dollars overseas to countries that aren't always our friends. And since 9/11 in particular, we've learned the consequences.

We need bipartisan political leadership. Both parties should show vision and courage, and jointly sponsor a major energy independence initiative. We also need the full cooperation of car and truck manufacturers. And we need the involvement of all Americans.

We must cut our dangerous dependence on Middle Eastern oil. American know-how surely gives us the ability to do it, if only we have the resolve. It's high time to find that resolve. Our nation's future requires no less.

Week of July 19, 2004

In a world of headlines and sound bites, too many stories just don't get told.

Take Israel.

Most of the reporting focuses on Palestinian terrorist attacks and Israeli self-defense measures.

But there's far more to the Israel story.

There's Israel's thriving democracy, the only real democracy in the region.

There's Israel's protection of religious freedom for Christians, Jews, and Muslims alike, making it the only "faith haven" in the area.

There's Israel's dynamic high-tech industry. With just under seven million people, Israel ranks near the top globally in start-up companies and new patents.

There's Israel's path-breaking science and medicine. As the actor Christopher Reeve said, "Israel is among the world's leaders in scientific research ... and on the cutting edge in paralysis research."

And there's Israel's state-of-the-art agriculture, which today is helping farmers in developing countries learn how to grow crops in arid soil.

Israel. The more you know, the more you understand.

Week of August 2, 2004

Never again.

Those were the words expressed by the world after the Holocaust.

They reflected a belated awareness that too many nations had done nothing to help the Jews in the face of genocide.

But did the words "never again" have any real meaning?

Too little, I'm afraid.

In the 1970s, as many as two million people were killed by a maniacal regime in Cambodia.

The world didn't intervene.

In the 1990s, nearly a million people were slaughtered in Rwanda.

The world didn't act there, either.

And now, another crime against humanity is taking place. This time it's in Sudan.

Arab militias, with Sudanese government support, are carrying out mass murder against black Africans. Experts say this is the greatest humanitarian crisis in the world today.

How many black Africans will die or be forced from their homes by the Arab militias before the world takes decisive action?

If the words "never again" are to have any meaning today, then Sudan is the place to prove it.

Week of August 16, 2004

How many chances have there been to create a Palestinian state?

The answer: at least four.

In 1947, the UN proposed two new countries—one Jewish, the other Palestinian Arab. The Jews said yes, and Israel was born. The Arab world said no and declared war on Israel.

Over the next twenty years, the West Bank and Gaza Strip were in Arab, not Israeli, hands. A Palestinian state could have been established at any time. It wasn't. The goal remained Israel's destruction.

Fast-forward to 2000. President Clinton worked feverishly to offer the Palestinians a viable state. The offer was rejected.

And two years ago, President Bush called for a Palestinian state. But to get there, he said, the new wave of terrorism against Israel had to stop. It hasn't.

Four chances to create the first Palestinian state ever. Four chances tragically squandered.

How long will Israel and the world have to wait for the emergence of Palestinian leaders truly committed to peaceful coexistence?

Week of August 30, 2004

This year's Olympics were exceptional.

Watching superb athletes from around the world compete was exhilarating and inspiring. And we could let our imaginations soar.

How wonderful it would be if we really were one human family, if our competition were limited to the playing field, not the battlefield.

But then we were reminded that politics is never far away.

An Iranian athlete withdrew rather than compete against an Israeli in a judo match.

You see, though Israel was established by the UN and has been around since 1948, Iran still doesn't accept its right to exist. In fact, it openly calls for Israel's destruction.

Leaders of Iran, a country that supports terrorism and suppresses human rights, praised the athlete's action.

Iran should be reprimanded by the Olympic movement for violating the Games' spirit. If not, this incident will be a permanent stain on an otherwise memorable sporting event.

Week of September 13, 2004

This week, Jews celebrate Rosh Hashanah, the Jewish New Year.

It ushers in a period of introspection. We examine our own behavior in the past year and resolve to do better in the coming year.

The holiday season prompts two thoughts.

First, the essence of good behavior is to be found in the teachings of every major religion, including Buddhism, Christianity, Islam, and Judaism. It is, as the Jewish text says, "What is hateful to you, do not do to your neighbor."

We Americans know it as the Golden Rule. What a wonderful world it could be if each of us took these words to heart!

And second, the rabbis ask: Why are we told that in the beginning there were only two people, Adam and Eve? This way, they answer, absolutely no one can claim to have "better" ancestry than anyone else.

In other words, whatever our race, religion, or ethnicity, at the end of the day we're all members of the same human family.

May we always remember and act on these thoughts in the year ahead.

Week of September 27, 2004

Just as it takes two to tango, so it takes two to make peace.

But what if one side is unwilling?

That's the tragedy of the Israeli-Palestinian conflict.

Israel has sought several times to resolve the conflict through peaceful compromise.

But it's been rebuffed each time by the Palestinian leadership—the same leadership that for decades has been calling for Israel's destruction; the same leadership that prefers to keep Palestinians in refugee camps rather than give them a new lease on life; the same leadership that encourages kids to become suicide bombers and not scientists; and the same leadership that's been accused of widespread corruption by the U.S. and Europe.

Peace is a vital strategic necessity for Israelis and Palestinians alike, but it takes two to make peace.

One day soon, I pray, a Palestinian partner committed to genuine peace with Israel will emerge.

But until that day, Israel must stand strong and protect itself against those who would destroy it.

Week of October 11, 2004

Some say peace in the Middle East is impossible.

I beg to differ. This year we mark two anniversaries that remind us just how possible it is.

Twenty-five years ago Egypt and Israel made peace. Why did Egypt turn toward peace after rejecting it for decades?

Above all, because its courageous leader, Anwar Sadat, came to realize the futility of war. He found in Israel an eager partner for peace.

And ten years ago, a peace treaty was signed between Jordan and Israel. When Jordan's King Hussein was finally ready, he, too, found an eager partner in Israel.

Yes, peace is possible, but it requires leaders of vision. Tragically, that's precisely what's been missing among the Palestinians. Had they taken a cue from Egypt and Jordan, perhaps this year we'd be marking three anniversaries, not two.

Still, I'm grateful for the two anniversaries. They should remind us never, ever, to abandon hope in the possibility of peace.

Week of October 25, 2004

My fellow Americans,

It's not your vote I'm asking you for next week.

Rather, I'm simply asking you to vote.

We Americans have been given a precious gift—freedom. We should never take it for granted, yet too many do. Sadly, America has among the lowest voter turnout rates of any democratic nation.

Like many Americans, I'm from a family of refugees who came here in search of freedom.

My mother was a refugee from Communism, then from Nazism; my father from Nazism; and my wife from an Arab country where democracy was unknown and Jews had even fewer rights than others.

For those who've experienced such a brutal denial of freedom elsewhere, the chance to vote here is a sacred task. On Election Day, all Americans, whatever our backgrounds, should keep this in mind.

Yes, there will be winners and losers, but, ultimately, Election Day is the chance for us to participate in the democratic process. And that in itself is reason for celebration.

Week of November 8, 2004

Here's a quiz:

Can you name the country whose two scientists just won the Nobel Prize in Chemistry?

It's the same country that has one of the world's highest rates of patents filed and scientific papers published.

The same country that the late actor Christopher Reeve admired for its pioneering work in paralysis research.

The same country that's developed a fully computerized, radiation-free diagnostic instrument for breast cancer.

The same country that's developed the first ingestible video camera to help doctors diagnose cancer and digestive disorders.

The same country that's been developing solar technology, a renewable and clean form of energy.

And the same country that's been a leader in developing the cell phone, voice mail technology, and computer microprocessors.

The country?

Israel.

Even while battling terrorism, democratic Israel continues to celebrate life and advance the frontiers of human knowledge.

Israel. The more you know, the more you understand.

Week of November 22, 2004

Thanksgiving.

It's a wonderful holiday—a day for parades, family gatherings, football, and feasts.

And a day, we shouldn't forget, for giving thanks.

The Pilgrims originated the holiday in 1621. They drew their inspiration from the Jewish holiday of Sukkot, when Jews give thanks for the bounty we enjoy.

After 9/11, we felt that Thanksgiving was the perfect time not only for all Americans to express gratitude for that bounty, but also to emphasize the special blessing of America and the ties that bind us.

Together with several ethnic and religious partners, we created *America's Table: A Thanksgiving Reader*. It highlights our diverse roots and our shared values as Americans.

In just a few short pages, we seek to capture the unique story of America, and of nine Americans who exemplify the richness of our nation's mosaic.

Use the *Reader* at your holiday table. You'll be adding something important to your celebration.

Week of December 5, 2004

Are we on the verge of a new era in the Middle East?

It's possible, though still a long shot.

Things have changed with the death of Yasir Arafat. With him around, peace proved impossible.

Given the chance to create a Palestinian state alongside Israel, he said no. He couldn't abandon his lifelong dream of destroying Israel through terrorism.

Now the Palestinians must choose new leaders. There are lots of factions vying for power, including groups bent on still more terror.

Let's hope that moderate leaders will emerge, who recognize the need to end the violence.

Let's hope that these leaders will prepare their people for peace with Israel, and end the incitement to hatred.

And let's hope that these leaders will use donor funds to build Palestinian society, not divert them to personal bank accounts around the world.

If such leaders emerge, they'll find eager partners in Jerusalem.

Today the chances of peace may be a bit brighter, if the Palestinians choose the direction of moderation and negotiation. Let's pray they do.

Week of December 20, 2004

This is a joyous holiday season.

Christians are about to celebrate Christmas.

Jews have just finished celebrating Hanukkah.

It's a time for family, festivity, and fun.

It should also be a time for reflection.

Sometimes we Americans take our religious freedom for granted. We shouldn't, ever.

In too many countries, according to the State Department, religious freedom is restricted or nonexistent. Among these countries are Iran, Saudi Arabia, Sudan, and North Korea.

Mutual respect is at the heart of our nation's religious freedom. Americans are free to believe or not to believe, as we wish. But we're not free to impose our religious beliefs on others. Indeed, our religious diversity and tolerance are vital signs of our nation's enduring democracy.

And amidst all the celebrations, let's remember our brave troops overseas, for whom this is a particularly tough time to be away from loved ones.

May this precious season usher in a more peaceful and harmonious world.

Week of January 3, 2005

Winston Churchill said: "Democracy is the worst form of government except for all those others that have been tried."

Churchill was right.

Democracy is our best hope. Democratic nations wage peace with one another, not war. Democratic nations protect freedom; they don't crush it.

There's good news on the democracy front.

According to Freedom House, in 1984 there were 53 "free" countries; today there are 89.

In the past year alone, Afghans voted in their first free elections. And who can forget Ukrainians challenging a rigged election and prevailing?

My new year's wish is for the continuing spread of democracy.

This month, Palestinians and Iraqis will go to the voting booths. If those elections go well—a big if, of course—who knows?

Maybe the entire Arab world, which, as reported by Freedom House, doesn't include one democratic country, will catch the bug. If so, peace, freedom, and human rights could be the beneficiaries.

Week of January 17, 2005

The Palestinian elections are now behind us. Mahmoud Abbas, known as Abu Mazen, is the new leader.

Who is he really?

Is he truly committed to making peace with Israel?

Will he seek to end the terrorism against Israel?

Will he stop the teaching of hatred about Jews and Israel in Palestinian schools?

Will he use international aid to the Palestinians, which is per capita the world's highest, to actually improve the lives of the people?

Or will he turn out to be just another Yasir Arafat, his old boss, only with a suit and tie?

The same Arafat who, given every chance to make peace, instead chose violence and corruption, and thereby betrayed his people's interests.

Only time will tell, of course. But I hope and pray that Abu Mazen proves himself a credible peace partner. If so, he'll find a willing Israeli partner. And the beneficiaries are sure to be Palestinians and Israelis alike.

Week of January 31, 2005

Auschwitz.

It's a name that evokes the ultimate evil.

A Nazi death camp where over a million people, primarily Jews, were killed.

It was part of the Nazi plan to exterminate the Jews.

They came close.

Six million Jews, two-thirds of European Jewry, were murdered in Auschwitz and the other infamous killing fields.

Last week, thousands gathered at Auschwitz to mark the sixtieth anniversary of the camp's liberation.

Elsewhere in Europe and at the UN, there were also Holocaust remembrance events.

Remembrance.

It's about recalling the individual lives—and the civilization—that were cruelly destroyed.

And it's about us. People of good will must stand as one. The Holocaust reminds us why. Postwar tragedies—from Cambodia to Rwanda to Sudan—are further reminders of the need for constant vigilance.

It's been said, "Those who cannot remember the past are condemned to repeat it." We must never—never—forget.

Week of February 14, 2005

A new study by Freedom House should be required reading for all Americans.

The study reviewed 200 documents, all published by the Saudi government and disseminated right here in the United States.

The findings? The Saudi government is actively spreading hatred of Christians and Jews and urges the killing of those who convert out of Islam.

The report reinforces an earlier study by the American Jewish Committee on Saudi textbooks.

These textbooks, used in Saudi Arabia and Saudi-funded schools around the world, stress the same themes. There's especially heavy emphasis on distrust of non-Muslims. The textbooks are filled with anti-Christian and anti-Semitic references.

All this raises a few basic questions: Why do some in our country continue to call Saudi Arabia an ally? How can anyone believe the Saudi claim that they share values with us? And when will we finally develop an energy policy to cut sharply our nation's dangerous addiction to Saudi oil?

Week of February 28, 2005

There's a glimmer of hope these days in Israeli-Palestinian peace-making.

What's changed?

For years, Israeli and American officials had been saying that peace with Yasir Arafat was impossible. Arafat, they argued, was more interested in destroying Israel than making peace with it.

These officials were absolutely right, though they faced criticism from those at the UN, in Europe, and elsewhere, who made a career of defending Arafat.

Now, there's a new Palestinian leader who claims to be more interested in peace.

Still, there are many hurdles to reaching peace, among them: Palestinian terrorist groups opposed to Israel's existence haven't disappeared. Syrian support for these groups continues unabated. And Iran, hungry for nuclear weapons, calls for Israel's annihilation.

Even so, Israel is taking dramatic goodwill steps to show its desire to work with the new Palestinian leader. It's one more reminder of Israel's ongoing and unquenchable thirst for peace.

Week of March 14, 2005

The winds of change are blowing in the Middle East.

There's a democratic stirring in the air.

It's been a long time coming, and it has a very long way to go. But it's beginning.

The elections in nearby Afghanistan started things off.

Then came the Palestinian elections.

They were followed by the dramatic Iraqi elections.

Egypt is talking about opening up its presidential vote to real competition.

And now there's Lebanon. Occupied for years by Syrian troops while a largely indifferent world looked on, the Lebanese people are demanding that Syria get out.

Much more needs to be done. In this part of the world, except for Israel, free elections, women's equality, protection of religious minorities, and the rule of law haven't exactly thrived. But something is changing. That change deserves support from those committed to democracy and human rights.

A peaceful and prosperous Middle East could hang in the balance. That's a goal worth striving for.

Week of March 28, 2005

Never again.

These words became a mantra after the Holocaust, when six million Jews were killed and the world did so pitifully little to help.

No more silence, no more inaction in the face of evil, we were told. Easier said than done, it turns out.

Think of the human tragedies since the war: the massive toll of Communism; the killing fields of Cambodia; ethnic cleansing in Bosnia and Kosovo; mass murder in Sudan; genocide in Rwanda; the list goes on.

The words "never again" haven't meant all that much, have they?

Now it's Darfur. Tens of thousands of black Africans have been killed by Arab militias. Millions are homeless. And again the world dithers.

The Holocaust should have taught us two things. First, never underestimate man's capacity for inhumanity. And second, indifference to evil is not an option.

Isn't it high time for the words "never again" to have real meaning?

Week of April 4, 2005

Pope John Paul II's death is a great loss for Catholics and non-Catholics alike.

The pope will be remembered as a towering figure. He was a symbol of religious faith, interreligious dialogue, and opposition to tyranny, particularly behind the Iron Curtain.

The American Jewish Committee will cherish his memory. Pope John Paul II made a special effort to reach out to Jewish communities worldwide.

He was the first pope ever to visit a synagogue.

He was the first pope to honor the memory of Holocaust victims with a memorial concert at the Vatican.

Under his leadership, diplomatic ties between the Holy See and Israel were established.

And he was the first pope to make an official visit to Israel.

Moreover, he repeatedly condemned anti-Semitism, past and present, as a sin against God.

In this mourning period, we express our deepest sympathies to our Catholic friends and neighbors. May the pope's memory be an inspiration to building a more humane world.

Week of April 11, 2005

President John Kennedy famously said: "Ask not what your country can do for you; ask what you can do for your country."

Sometimes we take our good fortune for granted. We shouldn't.

Many Americans are putting their lives on the line for our country, particularly in Iraq and Afghanistan. We owe them a lot, and they should always be in our thoughts and prayers.

But is there something the rest of us can do? The answer is yes.

We can also help strengthen our national security. How?

By getting in touch with our elected officials and telling them that we need to cut our dependence on imported oil now. This should be an issue that unites Democrats and Republicans.

And we can also make informed decisions about our own vehicles and homes that decrease the use of imported oil.

Let's be clear. As long as we import oil from nations that are not our friends, we endanger our national security.

It's time to heed President Kennedy's words and think about what we can do for our country.

Week of April 25, 2005

This week Jews celebrate Passover.

It's a holiday associated with the exodus of the Israelites from Egypt over 3,000 years ago—a journey from slavery to freedom.

It's a reminder that, after leaving Egypt, the Israelites sought the way to the Promised Land. It took forty years of wandering in the desert, but they came to it. It's the land today called Israel, a land central to Jewish identity and consciousness.

Passover also has universal meaning. During the civil rights struggle, for example, African Americans sang a spiritual whose words include: "When Israel was in Egypt's land, let my people go; oppressed so hard they could not stand, let my people go. Go down, Moses, way down in Egypt's land; tell old Pharaoh to let my people go."

And did you know that Thomas Jefferson, John Adams, and Benjamin Franklin wanted a national seal with a scene from the Jewish exodus from Egypt?

May the triumph of liberty and religious freedom contained in the Passover story always prevail.

Week of May 9, 2005

This month marks the sixtieth anniversary of World War II's end in Europe.

Millions of Americans, together with soldiers of the Allied nations, went to war. The military cemeteries across Europe are a permanent reminder of the huge sacrifices we as a country made to help vanquish the Nazis.

Those who bravely defended our precious freedoms against history's greatest evil deserve our eternal debt of gratitude.

And we should never take those freedoms for granted.

We must also never forget the Nazi effort to eliminate the Jewish people. They almost succeeded. Of nine million European Jews before the war, six million were murdered in the Holocaust.

What's needed is eternal vigilance against all forms of racism, including anti-Semitism. Remember: The rantings of a once obscure Austrian-born anti-Semite named Adolf Hitler quickly led to his total control of Germany and, later, much of Europe.

The sixtieth anniversary of the war's end is a time for remembrance and rededication.

Week of May 23, 2005

Religion flourishes in the United States.

But in some countries, it's a different story.

Take Saudi Arabia.

The Saudis build mosques and schools around the world. But at home, according to the State Department, the Saudi government bans the practice of all non-Muslim religions. Conversion from Islam to another religion is punishable by death.

Or take Sudan.

Islam is the state religion. The activities of Christians and other faith groups are severely restricted. Conversion to Islam is permitted, but conversion from Islam is also punishable by death.

There are many more examples of religious persecution against Christians and other religious minorities. Churches have been attacked by terrorists in Iraq and Pakistan, Baha'is have been suppressed in Iran, and Christians have been quietly emigrating from the Arab world in droves.

It's time to speak out. Freedom of worship must be a universal right. People of good will should stand together and demand no less.

Week of June 6, 2005

Thirty-eight years ago this week, Israel fought a war for survival against Arab neighbors bent on its destruction.

It's a good moment to recall some basic facts.

At the time, the West Bank and Gaza were in Arab, not Israeli, hands. Had the Arab nations wanted to create a Palestinian state, they could have. They didn't.

After the 1967 war, Israel proposed peace talks. Not for the first time, the Arab world categorically said no.

Years later, first Egypt, then Jordan changed their minds. They found a willing partner in Israel, and peace treaties were signed.

But with the Palestinians, it's been tougher. Yasir Arafat led his people down a blind alley, instead of into a bright valley.

Now there's new Palestinian leadership, and Israel has again extended an outstretched hand.

Will the Palestinians confront the terror groups in their midst and seek peaceful coexistence with Israel? Or will they continue the self-destructive policies of the past? Only time and deeds will tell.

Week of June 20, 2005

The Fourth of July is just around the corner. Amidst the fireworks and family fun, it's important to reflect on the larger meaning of our nation's birthday.

Freedom is a priceless gift. We owe those who've defended it more than we can ever express.

From the beginning, America has served as a beacon of hope for the oppressed.

Just ask those who fled political and religious tyranny what America means to them.

And America is a permanent work in progress, constantly seeking to overcome its shortcomings. This, too, reflects our nation's greatness.

We know we must always do better to achieve our founders' vision that "all men are created equal, that they are endowed by their Creator with certain unalienable rights, that among these are life, liberty, and the pursuit of happiness."

On this Fourth of July, let's recall the words from the Hebrew Bible inscribed on the Liberty Bell: "Proclaim liberty throughout all the land unto all the inhabitants thereof."

Happy upcoming Fourth of July, America.

Week of July 4, 2005

Many of us are taking to the road this summer.

It's the right time to think about our nation's energy policy.

Put bluntly, we've got a problem. We're dependent on imported oil, much of it from countries that aren't exactly our friends.

As the price of gas soars, our petrodollars are flowing to places that support terrorists, repress women, and despise our religious freedom.

We need to do something about this. Our security depends on it. And our economy isn't helped by this vast outflow of funds, either.

Other countries aren't sitting still. A recent *New York Times* article spoke of Japan's efforts to become far more fuel efficient. Meanwhile, the U.S., the world's largest energy consumer, is lagging behind, the same article reported.

We need Republicans and Democrats to work together. After all, this isn't about partisan politics. It's about national security. It's about leadership.

If we have the will, we can deal with the problem. What we can't do any longer, though, is live in denial.

Week of July 18, 2005

Next month, Israel is planning another major new peace step.

It will disengage from Gaza.

The move is controversial within Israel.

Some Israelis fear that it will only invite more Palestinian terror attacks.

But Israel is pressing ahead, hoping the disengagement will move the region closer to peace.

Israel deserves credit for such a bold and courageous step.

In moving forward, Israel is giving the Palestinians an opportunity that no one else, including Egypt, which ruled Gaza for decades, has ever offered—the chance to govern themselves.

What does Gaza's future hold?

Will it become a Singapore—a compact area that, with few natural resources, has emerged as a peaceful and prosperous state?

Or will it become a Syria—a state that threatens its neighbors, supports terrorism, and disregards the needs of its citizens?

Let's hope the Palestinians make the right choice. If they do, they, and all the peoples in the region, will be the beneficiaries.

Week of August 1, 2005

I'm an optimist.

At times, it can be tough.

Radical Islamic terrorism, Iran's pursuit of nuclear weapons, and calls for Israel's destruction are worrisome—very worrisome.

But the worst thing would be to succumb to hopelessness.

I'm just back from a trip to Europe. I was again reminded why hope should trump despair.

Germany launched two major wars in the twentieth century. Now it's a democratic nation at peace with those around it.

And the Iron Curtain kept such countries as Poland, Latvia, and Hungary under Soviet Communist control. Now the Iron Curtain is a relic of history. So is the Soviet Union.

The struggle took decades, but people of vision, courage, and resolve refused to give up. They were proven right.

We need the same vision, courage, and resolve for the Middle East. Things won't change overnight, but, yes, they can change. A democratic and peaceful Middle East could one day realize its vast human potential. It's a goal worth pursuing.

Week of August 15, 2005

This is a big week in the Middle East.

Israel is disengaging from Gaza.

The Israeli government hopes the move will increase chances for peace. Opponents fear it will only encourage more Palestinian terrorism.

How will the Palestinians respond? Here are three things to watch for:

First, what will happen to terror groups like Hamas and Islamic Jihad? Will they be allowed to operate freely, or will they be reined in?

Second, what will happen to the funds promised to Gaza by the international community? Will those funds be used to build schools and hospitals? Or will they disappear into secret bank accounts and private pockets, as during Yassir Arafat's time?

And third, will schoolchildren in Gaza be taught about coexistence with Israel? Or will they continue to use textbooks that exclude Israel from maps and teach hatred of Jews and Judaism?

Yes, this is a big week in the Middle East. Israel has again shown its yearning for peace. Now the ball is in the Palestinian court.

Week of August 29, 2005

The ongoing debate in America about the proper role of religion in the public sphere has taken center stage again. In fact, it's gotten ugly.

Intemperate attacks on the judiciary, evolution, and the separation of church and state are increasing. As a result, the balance that the Framers of the Constitution sought to achieve over 200 years ago is in jeopardy.

The challenge our Founding Fathers faced was to create a form of government that respects the rights of all Americans to worship as they see fit. They succeeded brilliantly.

Surely, those efforts to remove religion from the public square completely are inappropriate.

But the American experiment in separating government from religion is the best defense against the religious strife witnessed across the globe.

It has also resulted in a vibrant, indeed unparalleled, religious landscape.

The challenge for us Americans in the twenty-first century is to learn to live together with respect for our differences.

Attempts to divide us along religious lines have no place in this debate.

Week of September 12, 2005

I'm just back from Houston.

I went to meet with people evacuated from Hurricane Katrina.

It's not easy to describe what's going on there.

The lives of countless people have been shattered. Their future is uncertain. In some cases, family members are unaccounted for and the search for loved ones goes on.

Thousands of people from all walks of life have volunteered to help. What an inspiration they are!

And many organizations and corporations have pitched in, working alongside local, state, and national government teams.

It's such tragedies that remind us that, as a nation, we have a common destiny.

Part of the funds we've collected at the American Jewish Committee is going for immediate assistance to the needy; part will go for rebuilding damaged houses of worship. That's our way of saying that Americans may be of many faiths, but, as Hurricane Katrina underscored, we are one human family.

Week of September 26, 2005

It was years in the making, but America, increasingly dependent on oil, is slowly coming to its senses.

Tragically, it required the destruction wrought by two hurricanes, as oil prices skyrocketed and supplies declined.

And it needed the wake-up call of 9/11 and the realization that our petrodollars were going to those who teach and preach hatred of us.

But judging from comments by elected officials and auto industry leaders, there's a growing awareness that it's high time to come to grips with the energy question. And in America, where there's a will, there's a way.

There's much to be done, but the first thing ought to be increasing fuel economy standards for cars and trucks. The technology is there. What's been missing is political vision and courage from Washington.

True, we have red states and blue states. But enhancing our national security by reducing our need for imported oil ought to be a red, white, and blue issue—uniting us all.

Week of October 10, 2005

It's refreshing when someone speaks the plain and simple truth.

Such was the case recently when Kim Howells, the British minister of state for the Middle East, visited the region. Here's what he said in a newspaper interview:

> The Palestinians are receiving more aid per capita than any other people on the face of the earth, and we want to see some proper response [in fighting terror]....
>
> Gaza is now in the hands of the Palestinian Authority, and there are no Israeli troops there.
>
> Sooner or later, [the Palestinians] have to take a tough decision and start disarming the armed factions within Gaza and the West Bank. If they don't, how can the rest of the world have any confidence in their ability to bring good governance to these areas?
>
> We are waiting with baited breath for a response from the Palestinian Authority.... This is not a bottomless pit that the money is coming from.... What they [the Palestinians] need is the political will to do it.

As the British would say, Minister Howells's words are spot on.

Week of October 24, 2005

When people deliberately target civilians, what should they be called?

For many in the media, the answer is simple: "militants."

But that's inadequate. It softens the brutality of going after innocent people in schools, buses, offices, or houses of worship.

They should be called by their rightful name: "terrorists."

You'd think this was a no-brainer, but it turns out that calling people "militants" is less controversial. It avoids judgments. Calling people "terrorists" entails making judgments.

Yet if we can't make judgments about people who, driven by twisted faith or politics, board a bus to blow it up, enter a sacred place to kill, or murder schoolchildren, then we're in sad shape.

The next time you hear or read a news report about a premeditated attack on civilians, pay attention to how the perpetrators are described. If it's "militants," why not contact the source and ask them to stop mincing words?

Terrorists aren't just militants; they're terrorists, pure and simple.

Week of November 7, 2005

As they say, "Birds of a feather flock together."

Look at who are best friends in the Middle East.

There's Iran, whose president recently announced that his country aims to wipe Israel off the map.

Iran's nuclear ambitions could one day give it the means.

Then there's Syria, Iran's good buddy.

While Iran denies Israel's right to exist, Syria for decades has tried to dominate Lebanon. It was stopped, but hasn't given up the goal.

Meanwhile, Syria and Iran support Palestinian terror groups like Hamas and Islamic Jihad, which make no secret of their long-term objective—Israel's destruction.

All this is a sobering reminder of Israel's challenges. Its region, after all, is not the Midwest, but the Mideast.

And Israel isn't alone. The dangers posed by Iran, Syria, and terror groups put at risk other democratic, open societies.

Will these societies stand together in confronting the dangers? To succeed, they must.

Week of November 29, 2005

Fifty years ago this week, an event occurred that changed the course of American history.

A black seamstress in Montgomery, Alabama, refused to give up her bus seat to a white man. Her name was Rosa Parks.

At the time, blacks were required to sit in the back of the bus, or even get off if seats were needed for white passengers.

Rosa Parks was arrested and fined. The black community launched a thirteen-month boycott of Montgomery buses.

In 1956, the Supreme Court finally outlawed segregation in public transportation.

Much more work—and sacrifice—were required in the years ahead to dismantle the web of segregation laws. Previously unimaginable progress has been achieved. But there's still need for vigilance against all forms of racism.

Rosa Parks died a month ago. May her quiet act of defiance remind us that each of us can improve the world by our willingness to stand up—or, in Rosa Parks's case, to sit down—against injustice.

Week of December 5, 2005

Terrorists struck again this week.

The target was a mall in Israel. Five people were killed and more than fifty wounded.

The Palestinian terror group Islamic Jihad claimed responsibility. No surprise. This group seeks Israel's total destruction and makes no secret of it. Suicide bombings are their perverse specialty.

They peddle their twisted faith to young Palestinians and send them out to kill innocent people. Oh, and the sweetener is the promise of a hallowed place in heaven for the murderers.

Let's be clear: These terrorists aren't interested in peace—far from it.

Then there's the Palestinian Authority. It's supposed to be disarming Palestinian terrorist groups. But instead it's been hemming and hawing.

In response to this latest outrage, British Foreign Minister Jack Straw said: "I call on the Palestinian Authority to bring those responsible to justice, and to exert every effort to prevent such attacks in the future."

If only his wise words were heeded.

Week of December 12, 2005

Christmas and Hanukkah are around the corner.

Amidst the holiday planning, let's remember two things.

First, we're fortunate to live in a country that protects religious freedom. We're free to believe as we wish. It's a matter of private conscience, not public coercion.

And second, not everyone is so lucky.

According to the State Department and other sources:

In North Korea, religious freedom doesn't exist.

In Cuba, the government makes life difficult for the Catholic Church.

In Iran, Sunni Muslims, Baha'is, Jews, and Christians are victims of harassment and arrest.

In Saudi Arabia, all citizens must be Muslim.

In Sudan, while Muslims can proselytize freely, any Muslim who converts to another religion faces the death penalty.

In Egypt, where Islam is the state religion, Christians encounter systematic discrimination.

The list goes on.

As we celebrate our religious freedom, we should never forget those who aren't as blessed.

Week of December 20, 2005

Perhaps the greatest Jewish contribution to the world is the belief in one God.

From that belief it follows that we're all one human family, whatever our perceived differences.

And if we're all one human family, then we should act as such.

That's why the American Jewish Committee responded immediately to Hurricane Katrina, as we did to so many other natural and man-made disasters.

And that's why, on the eve of this holiday season, an AJC volunteer group is going to New Orleans.

We'll distribute donated funds to Christian and Jewish houses of worship and to Dillard University, the historically black, faith-based school—all of which suffered extensive hurricane damage.

Shortly after, younger members of AJC will be going to help in the rebuilding efforts.

We believe in affirming what unites us as human beings.

And we believe the true spirit of this season invites us to ask how we can help those in greater need than ourselves.

Happy holidays!

Week of December 27, 2005

With 2006 just around the corner, it's time for making resolutions and expressing hopes.

Even in our tell-all society, though, who wants to hear about my exercise plans or other resolutions?

But I'll gladly share some hopes.

First, that our armed forces serving in Iraq and elsewhere will be safe and successful in their vital missions. Our thoughts should be with our troops who are in harm's way.

Second, that 2006 will be the year our nation finally gets serious about reducing our dependence on Middle East oil. That addiction undermines our national security, compromises our political independence, and hurts our economy.

And third, having just visited the New Orleans area, that we sustain the rebuilding effort along the Gulf Coast. Even four months after Hurricane Katrina, the devastation remains mind-boggling. We owe it to our fellow Americans to stay the course.

5. PRINT MEDIA

Violence Is an Attack on Both Jews and France
International Herald Tribune
January 7, 2004

In discussing violence against Jews in France, an article (Dec. 17) cites an official who links the alarming phenomenon to "Muslim youths angry over Israel's treatment of Palestinians."

In reality, the problem goes far deeper. If these youngsters are unhappy about Israel's policy, then, as residents of a democratic society, they have every right to demonstrate peacefully to voice their views. This is precisely what French Jews have done to express their revulsion against Palestinian suicide bombers who target Israelis in buses, pizzerias, and markets. French Jews, however, don't express their anger by assaulting Muslims or their institutions in France.

The hundreds of documented attacks on synagogues, Jewish schools, and even a Jewish soccer team must be seen for what they are: acts of unadulterated anti-Semitism. Motivated by hatred fueled in some mosques, pervasive anti-Semitism in the Arab media, and widespread distribution of anti-Semitic material depicting Jews in vile language and grotesque images, these youth conclude that Jews and Jewish institutions in France are legitimate targets.

Until recently, the French government underestimated the extent of the danger and, therefore, reacted too slowly and meekly. In recent months, though, President Jacques Chirac has spoken of a zero-tolerance policy, and Interior Minister Nicolas Sarkozy has adopted a get-tough approach. Anti-Semitism, after all, is both an attack on Jews and, as Chirac has stated, on France and its cherished values of liberty and tolerance.

Pesky Truths Can't Be Ignored
Financial Times
January 9, 2004

The two published letters (January 7) responding to a recent article ("Europe's moral treachery over anti-Semitism," January 5) were as revealing for what they did not say as for what they did.

Both letter writers used the occasion to engage in a frontal assault on Israel. In doing so, they conveniently ignored pesky truths that might have placed recent Israeli actions in context.

Are we to forget that three years ago Israeli Prime Minister Ehud Barak, with full U.S. backing, proposed a comprehensive two-state solution to the Palestinians, only to be turned down flat by Chairman Yasir Arafat, who once again revealed a preference for violence over diplomacy?

Are we to ignore the nearly 1,000 Israelis murdered in cold blood in the past three years by terrorist bombers who believe that deliberately targeting innocent men, women, and children will give them a hallowed place in heaven?

Are we to gloss over the fact that the principal organizations perpetrating the terror and mayhem, including Hamas and Islamic Jihad, do not recognize Jewish sovereignty over any part of Israel, instead seeking an Islamic state in all of historic Palestine?

What would any other democratic state do in Israel's place if faced with the same challenges? Obviously, negotiation and mutual compromise are the preferred paths. Israel, in its peace accords with Egypt and Jordan and its two-state proposal to the Palestinians, has amply demonstrated its good faith. The same, tragically, cannot be said for the Palestinian Authority led by Arafat, who has repeatedly failed his own people in his decades of corrupt rule.

Israel, like any other state, is subject to legitimate criticism. Indeed, as a democracy, that criticism can be read every day in the spirited Israeli press and heard in the parliament. But when that criticism comes from those who repeatedly single out Israel for vilification, regardless of the facts, and who blithely ignore massive human rights violations elsewhere in the region, despite their purported interest in the human rights of the Palestinians, something far more insidious is going on. And when the Jewish people, uniquely in the world, are attacked by some for exercising the right of self-determination, while Palestinians and others are assumed to have that right, once again underlying motives must be questioned.

Too many European governments and institutions, including the media, have watched this growing attack on Israel from the sidelines and, in some cases, have contributed to it. This, in turn, has created a far more menacing climate for many European Jews, who have witnessed increased incidents of anti-Semitism. Shockingly, Europeans, who should know better than anyone the dangers of the slippery slope of anti-Semitism, have, with a few notable exceptions, been too slow to react. While that has begun to change, it has undoubtedly left its scars.

Response: Why the Security Barrier?
Rutgers Student Journal of Israel Affairs
March 29, 2004

Many countries in the world have built security fences or walls. In some cases, it is to keep people in; in other cases, to keep them out.

Israel built a barrier along its border with Gaza. It has served its purpose. Few, if any, Palestinians living in Gaza have successfully penetrated the barrier to carry out terrorist attacks inside Israel. There has been no international outcry about this barrier because it follows the accepted boundary between Israel and the Gaza Strip.

The security barrier being built to separate Israelis and Palestinians [in the West Bank] is more complicated. For one thing, absent a negotiated settlement, there is no agreed-upon boundary between Israel and the Palestinian territory. And for another, as a practical matter, Israelis and Palestinians currently live cheek by jowl in a residential checkerboard.

Some of Israel's critics in the international community argue that they oppose the barrier only because it does not follow the 1967 border, known as the Green Line. Yet to construct the barrier along the

Green Line now would, in effect, constitute an Israeli negotiating concession—an implicit, if not explicit, acknowledgment that this represents the new border. Moreover, it would physically endanger those in communities beyond the Green Line who have lived there with the encouragement of successive Israeli governments and who would find themselves beyond the protection of the barrier. Thus, Israel's challenge is to build the barrier in such a way that it protects as many Israelis as possible, while, at the same time, disrupting daily Palestinian life as little as possible.

All along, Israel has made clear that the security barrier is a temporary measure, not a permanent political fence. Should peace talks resume and bear fruit, the barrier can easily be moved. But as long as Israelis are threatened with repeated terrorist attacks originating in the West Bank, and given that a barrier can prevent many such attacks, the security barrier serves a vital, life-saving purpose.

A Problem on the Palestinian Side
Financial Times
March 31, 2004

It all fits together rather neatly in Philip Stephens's mind ("The targeted killing of the Middle East peace process," March 26). Hardheaded Western and Arab diplomats hammering out the contours of a possible new Israeli-Palestinian deal are sabotaged by the "hardened hawk" Ariel Sharon, Israeli prime minister, whose "blinkered obduracy" has sounded the death knell of the latest efforts.

The situation is, in fact, a bit more complicated: There is a problem on the Palestinian side. With whom is Israel to negotiate? Yasir Arafat, the man who was offered a landmark two-state deal by the left-of-centre Barak government in the pre-Bush era and walked away from it, returning to his more familiar role as guerrilla-in-chief? Ahmed Qurei, prime minister, installed by Mr. Arafat and enjoying no independent authority, assuming for a moment he might wish to exercise it? Hamas or Islamic Jihad, both of which openly call for Israel's total destruction and replacement by an Islamic state? Egypt and Jordan, neither of which has been given proxy by the Palestinians to negotiate on their behalf?

Mr. Sharon, though beyond redemption in Mr. Stephens's eyes, has publicly acknowledged the need for a two-state solution and indicated that Israel would make painful compromises for the sake of lasting peace. But he recognizes, as Barak did before him, that peace cannot be achieved in a vacuum, which is precisely what exists at the moment and what led to his consideration of certain unilateral moves.

If the Palestinian Authority itself is in a state of disarray—a condition largely of its own making—and is unable or unwilling to confront terrorist groups such as Hamas, there is no foundation at present on which to build peace. But this is not to abandon hope. I trust that one day there will be a Palestinian leadership that grasps these essential points: that peace can be achieved by forswearing terror and incitement, establishing a central and accountable authority, and negotiating in good faith a durable, two-state solution.

As the UN Flogs Israel, Rights Abuses Are Ignored
Wall Street Journal
April 12, 2004

As you note in your April 5 editorial "Human Rights and Wrongs," the UN Commission on Human Rights has become a misnomer. That's a tragedy. It means that many of the world's egregious human-rights situations go largely unaddressed because of the commission's make-up, while a few countries bear the brunt of attention. Given the membership, it's no surprise that Israel tops the list.

The commission's agenda actually bifurcates the world in two—Israel and every other country. Thus, agenda item no. 8 is devoted solely and exclusively to Israel, which is presumed guilty by its separate designation, while agenda item no. 9 deals with every other country, from Sudan to Iran to North Korea.

If past practice prevails again this year, by the end of the six-week session, Israel will be the target of as many as five critical resolutions, whereas no other nation will be the subject of more than one.

Politicization of the process and numerical majorities ensure that some malefactors will get away free.

Don't count on a resolution condemning Palestinian suicide bombing, the Saudi treatment of women or suppression of non-Muslim faiths, or Syria's longstanding occupation of Lebanon. It's simply not in the cards.

Without agreement among the democratic nations to set aside petty differences and regional loyalties and put the house in order, the commission will be nothing more than a global laughingstock. The victims of genuine human rights abuse deserve better.

Neglect and the Palestinians
New York Times
April 22, 2004

If the Arab countries care so much about the Palestinian plight, they have an unusual way of demonstrating their concern (op-ed, April 21). From 1948 onward, Palestinian refugees have been granted citizenship only in Jordan, while the other Arab countries have adamantly refused to integrate them.

The United Nations Relief and Works Agency, established in 1949 to care for Palestinian refugees and their descendants, receives less than 3 percent of its yearly budget from all the Arab states combined, while the United States, the target of Arab wrath, contributes close to 40 percent.

There is a contradiction between Arab rhetoric and performance when it comes to the Palestinians.

Placing blame on the United States for the Palestinian condition may sell well in the Arab street, but it doesn't square with reality.

Holocaust Memorial Respects the Dead
New York Times
June 15, 2004

The *Times* did not cover the June 3 dedication of the new memorial and museum at Belzec, the Nazi death camp in Poland, but you published "A Trench Runs Through It," by Walter Reich (op-ed, June 12), which is critical of the memorial.

This site was neglected for nearly six decades. When I first visited several years ago, the open field was unprotected, inaccurately marked, and littered.

An unprecedented agreement between the Polish government and the American Jewish Committee—supported by the United States Holocaust Memorial Museum, overseen by rabbinical experts in Jewish burial law, and partly financed by Holocaust survivors—ended this sacrilege.

A fitting design was selected by a distinguished international panel. It fully protects the mass graves while providing visitors with an opportunity to pay their respects and learn about the tragedy that befell Europe's Jews there.

Every design has its critics. But for those 1,000 invited guests, including political dignitaries and survivors, who gathered in Belzec earlier this month, there was an overwhelming consensus that this place, at once sacred and accursed, had finally been memorialized.

Unsparing of Organized Religion
Financial Times
June 16, 2004

Ian Buruma ("Politics and blind faith do not mix," June 10) offers a thought-provoking view on the peril of excessive entanglement between religion and state. But in making his case, he invokes Voltaire, asserting that the French philosopher "would have approved of New York City which, like eighteenth-century London, has buried religious bigotry in the interests of commerce." Did Prof. Buruma mean to say "buried religion," for surely *that* would have met with Voltaire's enthusiastic approval? After all, Voltaire was a staunch opponent of organized religion. It was he who, in 1769, famously wrote: "If God did not exist, it would be necessary to invent him."

To be sure, Voltaire in principle opposed all forms of intolerance. Unfortunately, he failed to extend that condemnation of intolerance to religious and cultural differences. In particular, Judaism and Christianity aroused his ire for what he believed were their essential obscurantism, superstition, and exclusivism. Jews, in particular, endured the harshness of Voltaire's unsparing pen.

We should celebrate the prevailing attitudes of mutual respect and live-and-let-live that exist today among religious (and nonreligious) communities in enlightened cities such as New York, but seeking Voltaire's approval does not necessarily advance the argument.

Must-See Saudi TV
New York Sun
June 25, 2004

Just as insidious as communicating hatred of Christians, Jews, and the United States via Saudi television programming ("Must-See Saudi TV," June 24) is the teaching of hatred in Saudi schools.

Democracy, pluralism, and mutual respect, all bedrock American values, are absent in Saudi Arabia, where children are taught contempt for anyone who is Christian or Jewish, and the West as a whole is denigrated. The daily teaching of hatred is taking place, as it has for many years, in a nation long purported to be America's closest ally in the Muslim world, largely because of our tragic addiction to Middle East oil.

An examination of Saudi schoolbooks makes it easier, though even more disturbing, to understand why fifteen of the nineteen terrorists on 9/11 were products of the Saudi educational system, and why terrorism inside the kingdom against Americans is on the rise.

Saudi children are taught intolerance and distrust of the West and non-Muslims in a wide range of subjects, from literature to math. This is the central finding of a comprehensive study, cosponsored by the American Jewish Committee, of Saudi Arabian Ministry of Education books used in grades 1 though 10.

For example, eighth graders are told, in a geography book, that "Islam replaced the former religions that preceded it" and that "a malicious Crusader-Jewish alliance is striving to eliminate Islam from all the continents."

In a ninth-grade language exercise, Saudi youth are instructed to use the sentence, "The Jews are wickedness in its very essence," when learning the rules of the Arabic language.

Saudi schoolbooks implore Muslims not to befriend Christians or Jews. "Emulation of the infidels leads to loving them, glorifying them and raising their status in the eyes of the Muslim, and that is forbidden," states a ninth-grade jurisprudence book.

Glib Saudi spokesmen have repeatedly dismissed the indisputable fact that the demonizing of Christians, Jews, and the West is pervasive in official books used throughout the government-controlled school system.

Saudi Foreign Minister [Saud Al-] Faisal told the American Jewish Committee, as he has stated in interviews with American media, that the problematic passages are limited to about "five percent of the schoolbooks." That is a gross underestimation of the problem, and though the foreign minister asserted that steps are being taken to rewrite them, there is no evidence as yet to support his claims.

Moreover, Saudi schoolbooks are actively exported to other Arab and Muslim countries, where Saudi largess funds many schools. Indeed, several Muslim schools in the United States have been built and staffed with Saudi money, opening the door to the spread of Saudi-sponsored hate on American soil. Probing which of the Saudi books are being used here in the U.S. is vital.

To continue to ignore the hate that is integral to Saudi education can no longer be tolerated, all the more so given Saudi demography. More than half of the Saudi population is under the age of twenty. What can we expect from these youngsters after years of indoctrination? The answer should be obvious. The United States must press Saudi Arabia, which claims friendship with our country, to eliminate the hatred that permeates their schoolbooks. Until then, truly amicable ties will be impossible to achieve.

Life After
The New Republic
July 26, 2004

Ruth Franklin points out the regrettable tendency of some in the second generation to "elevate their own childhood traumas above and even beyond the sufferings of their parents." This should not, however, obscure the fact that being born into a survivor family comes with heavy psychological demands. I grew up in this milieu. As a child, it was almost impossible to escape exposure, impact, and, yes, some trauma, no matter how much my family tried to shield me from the horrors of the recent past. The same was true for my second-generation friends. The inner, inextinguishable pain of parents and other loved ones who survived the war couldn't be hidden from those born after.

The notion that evil people sought to inflict suffering on one's parents evoked very strong feelings. Some parents had nightmares and woke up the children with their terrified screams. Some children were given the names of murdered relatives. Many families were dispersed among several countries, with huge gaping holes of murdered grandparents, siblings, aunts, uncles, and cousins. There were endless debates about whether it was permissible to speak German after the war. German-made products were boycotted. The existence of God was constantly called into question. Almost every country in Europe was seen through the prism of its wartime behavior. Many were judged wanting and, therefore, untrustworthy, off-limits, and eternally condemned. Given the starvation that parents endured, meals could be complicated if children left food uneaten. The list goes on and on, all of it far from easy for a youngster of any age to grapple with.

True, we the children, are not "primary in this dark story." But we share a real consciousness—not a "false consciousness" based on vicarious experience, as Franklin suggests. This consciousness of the Holocaust is translated in many cases into action, not merely into self-reflection. The second generation is disproportionately represented among the activists and leaders in Jewish life, both here and in Israel. The knowledge, emotional freight, and responsibility carried by the children are hardly negligible, especially as aging survivors seek to ensure that their history will not be forgotten after their deaths.

Finding Peace in Sudan
International Herald Tribune
July 31, 2004

It seems unfathomable that the United Nations has yet to enact sanctions against Sudan ("EU presses UN for Sudan sanctions," July 27). After the Holocaust, the world said "never again" to genocide. These were the words of a world that had failed to confront the Nazis' Final Solution for the Jewish people. They were words not to have been forgotten.

But have the words "never again" ever carried real weight? In the 1970s, as many as two million people were killed by a maniacal regime in Cambodia. The world didn't intervene. In the 1990s, nearly a million people were slaughtered in Rwanda. The world did nothing. And now, Sudan is suffering from another crime against humanity, a crime the U.S. Congress has declared genocide.

Arab militias, with Sudanese government support, are carrying out mass murder against black Africans. Experts say this is the greatest humanitarian crisis in the world today. How many men, women, and children have to die or be forced from their homes before the world takes decisive action? If the words "never again" are to have any meaning today, then the Sudan is the place to prove it, and the UN is the place to start.

The Threat to Israel
New York Times
October 1, 2004

We take issue with the implication in "Car Bombing Kills Official of Hamas in Damascus" (news article, Sept. 27) that violence by Hamas and similar groups will thrive as long as "Israel occupies Arab lands" captured in the 1967 Six-Day War.

When Hamas and like-minded organizations refer to occupation, it is not solely to territory acquired by Israel in that war for Israel's survival. If that were so, Hamas would be welcoming Israel's planned withdrawal from the Gaza Strip and would be seeking to end terrorism so that the Road Map for peace could be carried out with the full backing of the United States.

But Hamas cannot and will not. Its agenda, pure and simple, is the destruction of Israel and the creation in its place of an extremist Islamic state. Syria remains a willing partner of international terrorism, providing a haven in Damascus for Hamas, Hezbollah, Islamic Jihad, and other radical groups.

Clearly, Israeli-Palestinian peace will remain out of reach as long as the Palestinian Authority and Arab states like Syria encourage extremism and lend support to terrorists.

In Want of a Leader
The Economist
October 28, 2004

You are right that "Palestinian leaders have every reason to show the world that [Ariel] Sharon is wrong when he keeps on saying that Israel has no responsible partner on the other side" ("Israel's unlikely dove," October 23). But will they? You scrutinize Mr. Sharon's motives, putting the onus for the stalled peace process on Israel without addressing the vacuum of Palestinian leadership plaguing the process. Am I missing something, or is there no Palestinian leader today ready to forswear terrorism and pursue a peaceful two-state settlement based on the principle of mutual compromise? Mr. Sharon's actions should not be examined alone. The real issue is whether a Palestinian leader can emerge who has the will to fight violence, marginalize the duplicitous Yasir Arafat, and guide his people to a brighter future.

The Conversion Challenge
Jerusalem Report
November 9, 2004

Your article "Why Aren't They Jewish?" (Nov. 15) was profoundly disturbing. Each time I read reports of roadblocks that some religious figures or bureaucrats place in the path of those who resolutely seek conversion to Judaism, my immediate reactions are anger and embarrassment. Instead of being welcomed, such individuals are too often treated with disdain or suspicion. Ironically, this occurs at the very same time that we bemoan our dwindling numbers and conduct endless studies on how to reverse our demographic crisis.

I have heard countless firsthand stories, particularly in Europe, of those who, for reasons of family background, intellectual or spiritual attraction, or, yes, marriage, genuinely wish to become Jewish, but are discouraged from converting. By the way, in these accounts the wealthy who marry non-Jews somehow seem to find a solution that is unavailable to others, a topic worthy of further examination.

In a post-Holocaust world where anti-Semitism has once again reared its head, and living in Israel is not without its responsibilities and dangers, are we to dismiss so cavalierly the sincerity of those who wish to join the Jewish people, lead a Jewish life in Israel (or the Diaspora), and thus share in our collective destiny?

Mountain from a Molehill
Jerusalem Post
December 29, 2004

Your article on the American Jewish Committee ("Identity crisis plagues Jewish Committee," Dec. 26) was much ado about nothing.

There is no identity crisis at the American Jewish Committee. To the contrary, we have a mission statement that has served us exceedingly well, and our institutional vital signs reveal an agency at its healthiest point in a nearly 100-year history.

The article refers to discussion about possible changes in our name or tag line. A few weeks ago the agency's senior staff gathered for a periodic one-day retreat. In discussions on internal matters, we touched on the fact that we are referred to by as many as five different names: American Jewish Committee, AJCommittee, AJC, AJComm, and Committee. This creates some "brand" confusion.

We talked about how we might address it, before moving on to more pressing issues. As I pointed out to your reporter, other institutions, like the University of Pennsylvania, have faced the same issue and solved it without changing their name. So will we.

Regarding our tag line, all institutions in the public eye seek to convey a sense of themselves in six words or less. The American Jewish Committee is no different. Every few years we ask ourselves whether our tag line does the trick. It's a regular feature of doing business—no more, no less.

We do many things—from successfully urging the U.S. government to ban Al-Manar's hate-filled broadcasts from American airwaves, to partnering with the Polish government to protect and memorialize the site of the Nazi death camp at Belzec; from building support for Jewish concerns among America's racial, religious, and ethnic groups, to sponsoring delegations of influential American and European parliamentarians and journalists to visit Israel.

It's not easy to convey this wide-ranging work in just a few words, so we're always on the lookout for a better way.

The article sought to make a mountain out of a molehill. Given the state of the world, I daresay *Jerusalem Post* readers deserve more compelling, not to mention more accurate, news stories.

Election No Surprise, but Progress Might Be
Palm Beach Post
January 13, 2005

There was no surprise in the Palestinian elections. Mahmoud Abbas handily won and succeeded the late Yasir Arafat as president of the Palestinian Authority.

In principle, this is good news. The elections went off with few hitches and an impressive voter turnout. And Mr. Abbas is believed in some circles to be a pragmatist interested in restarting the peace process with Israel.

But this is the Middle East, after all, and few things go as expected. There is a real danger in inflating expectations. And let's be frank: It is still not entirely clear who the real Abbas is.

Is he the man who, for a brief period, distanced himself from his longtime boss, Mr. Arafat, and had the courage to tell his fellow Palestinians that violence and terrorism were counterproductive to their cause?

Or is he the man who wrote his doctoral dissertation on the theme of Jewish exaggeration of the Holocaust? The man who, in recent weeks on the campaign trail, associated publicly with known terrorists and referred to Israel as the "Zionist enemy"? And the man who recently insisted that he is the standard-bearer for Mr. Arafat's legacy, while demanding the so-called "right of return," a well-known formula for Israel's destruction?

There is supporting evidence for each of the portraits. Of course, ideologues of the right will refuse to consider any possibility that he just might be talking tough now to strengthen his domestic base, but that his goal will be to strike a deal with Israel. And ideologues of the left will refuse to consider that when he uses such terms as "Zionist enemy" and "right of return," he might actually mean them.

What should we be looking for? There are several yardsticks.

First, will Mr. Abbas get serious about internal reform? The Arafat legacy was one of cronyism, corruption, and duplicity. Despite the fact that, per capita, Palestinians are the highest recipients of international aid, there was little to show for it during Mr. Arafat's tenure. While the Palestinians grew poorer, his worldwide bank accounts grew richer. Will Mr. Abbas put the interests of the Palestinian people ahead of his own?

Second, will he take on the extremist factions? Confronting Hamas, Islamic Jihad, and other terrorist groups will be vital for him to succeed. These groups pose a direct challenge to his authority. He must not coddle or ignore the extremists.

Third, will he take steps to end the pervasive incitement against Israel and Jews in Palestinian schools and the media?

And fourth, will the new Palestinian leader explain to his people that progress toward peace, based on a mutually acceptable formula, is a strategic necessity for Palestinians and Israelis alike? Will he steer the Palestinian people away from violence and confrontation and in the direction of compromise and coexistence?

None of this will be easy or risk-free for Mr. Abbas, but what's the alternative? In 1947, the United Nations proposed a two-state partition that would have given the Palestinians their own state. The Arab world turned it down. After Israel's war for survival in 1967, the Jewish state proposed a swap of the newly acquired territory, including the West Bank and Gaza Strip, for peace. The Arab world refused. And in 2000, President Bill Clinton and Prime Minister Ehud Barak worked feverishly to reach a two-state agreement with Mr. Arafat, but, once again, it was rejected.

Now there is a chance to chart a new course. Mr. Arafat is gone. Mr. Abbas has a healthy mandate to lead. A new Israeli national unity government, led by Prime Minister Ariel Sharon and including Nobel laureate Shimon Peres, has indicated its desire to cooperate. The Bush administration is prepared to help. The Egyptian and Jordanian governments are sending positive signals.

What's required is a Palestinian leader with the courage, credibility, and determination to seize the moment and move, together with willing Israeli partners, toward a new start for the region. Let's hope and pray that Mahmoud Abbas is up to the test. If so, then the region and, indeed, the world will be the beneficiaries.

A Solution Requires Accepting Mutual Responsibility
Financial Times
January 14, 2005

In reading Rashid Khalidi's article on the Israeli-Palestinian conflict ("A Palestinian map out of history's dead end," Jan. 11), I am struck, not for the first time, by the unwillingness of leading Palestinian spokesmen to engage in painful but necessary self-reflection.

Instead, it is so much easier to lay the entire blame for the Palestinian condition at Israel's door. In this way, there is a one-size-fits-all explanation for everything. How intellectually satisfying, and how off base.

To read Mr. Khalidi, one would think that Israel has no other interest in the world than to oppress another people, in this case the Palestinians, and thus to deny them their national aspirations.

He scrupulously avoids any acknowledgment that the problems faced by Palestinians today might also be self-inflicted. By wallowing in indignant self-righteousness and victimization, the Palestinians have failed to seize one opportunity after another to advance their condition, indeed to achieve statehood.

If Palestinian leaders took a page from the examples of the late Anwar Sadat and King Hussein, they would understand the deep yearning for peace, based on territorial compromise, in the Israeli majority.

Moreover, they would have grasped the seemingly obvious fact that that an outstretched hand is far likelier to create the proper climate for negotiation than a suicide bomber.

Mr. Khalidi blithely dismisses Israel's plan to withdraw from Gaza as nothing more than a ploy to hold on to the West Bank.

If the Palestinians were to cooperate with Israel to ensure a peaceful withdrawal, and to establish a governing authority that exercised responsible control, there is little doubt that support in Israel for compromise on the West Bank would rise dramatically. But, conversely, if Gaza should become a platform for terrorist acts against Israel, then what incentive would tiny Israel, two-thirds the size of Belgium to begin with, have for further territorial concessions?

Perhaps, with new Palestinian leaders at the helm, we will witness a fresh start toward two lands for two peoples. But vilifying Israel, while cavalierly ignoring the Palestinian record of terrorism, violence, and incitement that has centrally contributed to today's situation, surely is not the way to launch the process.

Mideast Messages, Clear and Subtle
New York Times
January 19, 2005

Israel's response to the deadly terrorist attack that claimed the lives of six Israelis at the border crossing with Gaza was not an "overreaction," as you assert ("A Double Blow to Mideast Peace," editorial, Jan. 15).

In fact, it is disturbing that you would even juxtapose the Palestinian murder spree with the resultant Israeli decision to hold off on talks with the new Palestinian leader, Mahmoud Abbas.

Israel is saying clearly two things. First, a resumption of peace talks is entirely possible, but only if Palestinian leaders become serious from the get-go, both in word and deed, about confronting and containing violent factions.

Second, Israel will not tolerate further Palestinian double-dealing, whereby leaders talk to the outside world of a desire for peace, while Palestinian terrorist groups continue their rocket attacks on Israeli towns from Gaza and breeze past Palestinian security forces to attack and kill Israelis.

Mahmoud Abbas has a historic opportunity to undo the damage done—above all, to Palestinians themselves—by nearly four decades of Yasir Arafat's tragic legacy of precisely this kind of two-faced policy.

In Israel, he will find a new government, now including the Labor Party, eager to pursue a negotiated peace accord.

But equivocation, mixed signals or claims of political impotence by today's Palestinian leaders in the face of continuing terrorism aren't going to persuade Israelis of a genuine commitment to peace—far from it.

Response to "How I Became a Jew"
Spectator
February 2, 2005

How are we to reconcile the contradictory statements made by Anthony Lipmann about his identity ("How I became a Jew," Jan. 22)? On the one hand, he speaks of "we Jews," yet he notes that "I was, and remain, a middle-of-the-road Anglican" and cites his worship in a church. So much for becoming a Jew.

Lipmann, however, seeks to use his claim of Jewish identity, which derives from his mother, a Holocaust survivor who had her son baptized, as a moral weapon to lambaste Israel by including Jenin in a list that also includes Darfur and Rwanda and, more generally, by accusing "Jews" of causing the "suffering" of Palestinians.

This is daft, if not downright disingenuous. While there may be disputes over whether to label Darfur a genocide, there is no doubt that tens of thousands of people have been killed by government-supported Arab militias and more than a million rendered homeless. And in Rwanda, nearly a million people were killed in what was unquestionably genocide. By contrast, Jenin was an entirely different story. Israel, determined to stop the flow of terrorist bombers coming from the city, sent troops into the booby-trapped alleyways rather than strike from the air and risk indiscriminate killing. As a result, some fifty-five Palestinians were killed, the overwhelming majority in shootouts, while twenty-three Israeli soldiers lost their lives. In other words, what in the world does Jenin have to do with Darfur or Rwanda?

And where is Lipmann's concern for the suffering of Israelis at the hands of Palestinians, who spurned the chance for a promising two-state solution offered by President Bill Clinton and Prime Minister Ehud Barak and instead unleashed a new wave of terror and violence that began in the fall of 2000?

I, too, am the child of Holocaust survivors. Unlike Lipmann, however, I learned several things. First, despite what Jews might do to support a better world—and Jews are, I am proud to note, disproportionately represented in nearly every human rights, civil rights, and humanitarian campaign—there are some who, for whatever reason, will continue to hate us. Second, take seriously those who threaten to harm the Jews, be they neo-Nazis or radical Muslims, because they just might do so. And third, cherish Israel, which, had it existed in 1940 might have offered the haven for European Jews that other nations callously did not, and understand its daunting challenge of achieving peace in a rough-and-tumble neighborhood.

Jews don't need morality lessons from those with a barely concealed political agenda cloaking themselves in dubious identity garb.

"Lake Failure"
New York Sun
March 31, 2005

The *New York Sun*'s editorial on the United Nations ("Lake Failure," March 29, 2005) criticizes the American Jewish Committee for welcoming Secretary-General Kofi Annan's statement, made in Jerusalem earlier this month, calling for closer ties between the UN and Israel and urging member states to correct the injustice of Israel's exclusion from one of the five regional blocs that determine the all-important committee assignments.

You suggest that we live in a dream world, oblivious to the daily realities of the UN, including Mr. Annan's decision to lay a wreath at the gravesite of Yasir Arafat the day before his Jerusalem speech. No other organization has devoted as much time and effort over the span of decades to pointing out the failings of the UN when it comes to Israel and the Jewish people. Indeed, only the AJC has an institute, UN Watch, founded by the late Ambassador Morris Abram, devoted exclusively to holding the UN to the standards of its own charter.

We part company with your editorial on two important issues. You've all but relegated the UN to the dustbin of history, declaring its work null and void. We recognize the reality that, like it or not, the UN is here to stay, that it has its strengths and its weaknesses, that Israel is a member state, and that we have to fight the good fight to ensure fair treatment for the Jewish state, indeed for the Jewish people. Incidentally, that's exactly the same approach taken by Israel, which also welcomed the secretary-general's visit to Jerusalem, his participation in the ceremony opening the new museum at Yad Vashem, and his forward-looking remarks on Israel and the UN. And the editorial suggests that if we make any positive comments at all—as we did in the case of Mr. Annan's speech in the Knesset—then we are ipso facto guilty of ignoring all the misdeeds done by the UN, and afflicted by naiveté or worse. That's just plain nonsense.

The Red Cross and Israel
New York Times
April 25, 2005

Re "Crosses, Crescents and Stars" (editorial, April 22):

Bravo for calling on the Red Cross and Red Crescent Movement to end its inexcusable policy of excluding Israel's Magen David Adom from full membership. Despite the movement's laudable goals of universality and impartiality, they have been violated in Israel's case. Politics has been at work in a movement that describes itself as nonpolitical. That was abundantly clear in 2000, for example, when a promising effort to admit the Israeli humanitarian group was torpedoed by some Arab and other Islamic countries.

There is a potential new opportunity to right this wrong. The American Red Cross has led the way with strong United States government support. Several European countries are also showing interest. And importantly, some moderate Arab countries understand that fixing the situation may contribute to confidence-building in the post-Yasir Arafat era.

It is high time to stop a narrow-minded minority from bullying the majority into inaction and, in doing so, trampling on the cherished ideals of a vital international institution. There are practical solutions, as your editorial suggests, for the emblem issue. The bigger question is whether there is now the collective will to see this through.

Response to "Lesson from German History"*
Foreign Affairs
May 12, 2005

Fritz Stern's "Lesson from German History" (May/June 2005) contains a statement that lends itself to possible misunderstanding. Stern describes the United States as "the country that gave haven to German-speaking refugees in the 1930s. (In 1938, at the age of 12, I came with my family to New York.)"

True enough, the United States gave haven to *some* German-speaking refugees, but certainly not to the majority of those who sought refuge. Between 1933, the year that Adolf Hitler took power in Berlin, and 1939, the year of the outbreak of the Second World War, an estimated 300,000 Germans, the vast majority Jews, applied for entry visas to the United States. Approximately 90,000 people—including, to their good fortune, the Stern family—were lucky enough to receive visas and were resettled in the U.S. The fate of the rest varied. Some were able to find sanctuary, principally in Latin American countries, China, the United Kingdom, and British-ruled Palestine. Others, however, trapped in continental Europe and unable to obtain a visa, were deported to the death camps as the Nazis overran one country after another.

American immigration policy had become far more restrictionist in the 1920s and 1930s than between 1881 and 1920. A spirit of growing isolationism had taken hold. Strict national quotas were introduced in

---

* This text is the original letter submitted. A shortened version was published.

the 1924 Immigration Act, following anti-immigration legislation adopted in 1921. Still worse for Jews in the 1930s, it was only in 1938 that the U.S. quota for German and Austrian immigrants was actually filled; in the other years of the 1930s, varying numbers of slots went unfilled, though certainly not for lack of applications.

This was, it should be recalled, a period of economic depression. Jobs were scarce, and newcomers were regarded as unwelcome competitors for any vacant positions.

Moreover, given widespread anti-Semitism, including within the State Department, the prospect of hundreds of thousands of Jews coming to America was essentially a nonstarter. Even after the tragedy of Kristallnacht in November 1938, when nearly 100 Jews were killed in pogroms, more than 250 synagogues and 7,500 Jewish-owned businesses were destroyed, and 25,000 Jews were sent to concentration camps, nearly three-fourths of Americans, according to a survey conducted by the National Opinion Research Center, opposed admitting large numbers of German Jews to the United States.

In the same vein, according to a study published by the Leo Baeck Institute, the organization that honored Professor Stern, a congressional effort in 1939 to admit 20,000 nonquota refugee children over two years, known as the Wagner-Rogers Bill, was opposed in polls by two-thirds of the American public and never even made it to a House vote.

Perhaps most emblematic of the resistance to immigration was the fate of the *St. Louis*, the ocean liner that, in May 1939, took 937 passengers, more than 900 of them Jews, westward across the Atlantic. Most desired to stay in Cuba with what they thought were valid landing permits, at least temporarily, until they could enter the United States. With the exception of twenty-eight passengers, however, none were allowed to disembark in Cuba. When the ship's captain then headed for Florida in the hope that American officials would accept the remaining passengers, the shocking answer from Washington was negative, forcing the ship to return to Europe and unload the passengers in Antwerp. Ten weeks later, World War II began.

In other words, there were fortunate German Jews in the 1930s who made it to the United States and a new start, but, tragically, there were at least twice as many who did not. It is important that both sides of this story be told.

The March of the Living and Poland
New York Jewish Week
May 16, 2005

Jonathan Mark deserves praise for raising a sensitive issue in "'March' Gets Critical Scrutiny" (Media Watch, May 13). He takes a look at the annual March of the Living, which this year brought nearly 20,000 people, primarily but not exclusively Jews, to Auschwitz-Birkenau to pay homage to the victims and to declare "Never again." Having participated in the past, I know firsthand the lasting impact this experience can have, especially on younger people, including my son.

The challenge, as Mark notes, is how to relate the march to modern-day Poland. For many participants, there has simply been no link. Poland, in their eyes, is the site of Auschwitz-Birkenau, as well as other infamous Nazi death camps, and therefore represents nothing more than a vast gravesite of millions of Jews slaughtered in the Shoah. And, in the same vein, Poland also suggests a country where anti-Semitism both before and after the war was quite widespread. Consequently, according to this view, the less contact there is with the actual country, the better.

While I can understand these sentiments, I do not share them. Yes, the death camps were in Poland, but they were German, not Polish. And yes, anti-Semitism was at times a serious, even lethal, factor in Polish life, but Poland now is a different country. We Jews shortchange ourselves if we fail to recognize the transformation.

Since its unshackling from the Soviet yoke in 1989, Poland has embraced democracy, joined NATO and the European Union, and become a staunch U.S. ally. Moreover, Poland has evolved into a key friend of Israel; the bilateral relationship is both deep and wide. The Jewish community, while a bare shadow of its prewar self, has reestablished itself with vigor. The Polish government has made strenuous efforts to reach out to world Jewry. And many non-Jewish Poles have been eager to explore their country's Jewish past, through cultural festivals, restoration projects, and academic studies.

This is not to say that all is perfect in Poland, or that anti-Semitism has been entirely eliminated (as if it were a relic of the past in other European countries!). It is to say that, in a world where friends of Israel and the Jewish people are sometimes hard to find, contemporary Poland, however improbable it may sound to some, beckons. The organizers of the March of the Living would be well served to encourage far greater contact between participants and today's Poland, particularly among young people. All sides would be well served.

For Train Riders, the Middle Seat Isn't the Center
New York Times
June 6, 2005

As a veteran Metro-North commuter, I read about the aversion to sitting in the dreaded middle seat with interest (front page, May 31).

In my twice-daily commute, I seek a measure of solitude—and the middle seat is the last place to look for it. The chance of being physically squeezed, unwillingly drawn into neighboring cell-phone conversations, entering the "smell zone" of foods eaten on board, or being subjected to music via the earplugs of excessively loud iPods is just too great to risk.

The new cars don't help. There is little legroom, making the middle seat even more claustrophobic. And maneuvering into the cramped seats facing each other takes the agility of an Olympic gymnast.

I'm not looking for "100 Years of Solitude"; 100 minutes a day will do very nicely. But it's also made more difficult by the frequent announcements that drone on, even with the convenient digital signage of the new trains. What the train conductors perhaps fail to grasp is that the more they speak, the less passengers are inclined to listen.

Gaza's Past, and Its Future
New York Times
August 18, 2005

Re "Gaza Reality Check" (editorial, Aug. 18):

While focusing on Gaza's future, historical context remains essential, especially for understanding how Israel came to govern it for thirty-eight years.

Gaza was under Egyptian rule from 1949 to 1967, as you note. In fact, it was under Egyptian military rule. Strikingly, neither the Egyptians nor the local population sought the creation of a Palestinian state when Israel was not even a factor.

The reference to "the 1967 Israeli-Arab war," when Israel captured Gaza, doesn't note how the war came about. A drumbeat of public calls from Cairo and Damascus, supported by the Palestine Liberation Organization, for Israel's total annihilation, as well as worrisome troop deployments, convinced Israeli leaders that a preemptive strike was necessary to ensure Israel's survival.

After the war, Israel sought Gaza's return to Egyptian rule as a part of a larger peace deal, but the collective Arab answer, expressed in the Khartoum Resolutions on Sept. 1, 1967, could not have been clearer: no peace, no recognition, no negotiation.

Gazans now get their first chance ever, not just in the last thirty-eight years, at true self-governance. Will they use it to build a peaceful and prosperous land alongside Israel, or as a launching pad to intensify violence and terror against Israel? Let us hope they choose wisely.

Will a State alongside Israel Satisfy the Palestinians?
Financial Times
August 20, 2005

Your editorial "Keeping an eye on the opportunity of Gaza" (Aug. 15) glosses over several critical points.

Ariel Sharon, the Israeli prime minister, deserves more credit for the courageous step of Israeli disengagement from Gaza and the northern

West Bank than you give him. Not only does it represent a sea-change in his own outlook, but also it has entailed a fierce and ongoing domestic fight. By immediately questioning his longer-term motives, you divert attention from the historic significance of what is taking place on the ground.

Moreover, to suggest that Israel now move rapidly to yielding additional territory on the West Bank and in Jerusalem may be premature. While a majority of Israelis understand that any political solution with the Palestinians entails a two-state solution, what is less clear are Palestinian intentions.

Will the Palestinians be content with a state alongside Israel, as you suggest, or is their ultimate goal a state in place of Israel, as many Israelis believe? There is a need to test intentions in Gaza, where the Palestinians, for the first time, have the chance to embrace self-government and plant the seeds of an eventual state.

It should be kept in mind that a thriving—and peaceful—Gaza is in everyone's interest, including Israel's. But will the Palestinian Authority assert control over Hamas and Islamic Jihad, or will it be the other way around? Will international donor funds be earmarked to build the Gaza economy and boost the standard of living, or will they be diverted, as in the past, to secret bank accounts and private pockets? And will Palestinian schoolchildren at last be taught coexistence with Israel, or will the demonization of Israel continue?

It is important, in other words, to focus not only on what Israel must do for the Palestinians, but also on what the Palestinians must do for themselves. Letting them off the hook by placing the onus for their condition on everyone but themselves does them—and history—a disservice.

Addicted to Oil
International Herald Tribune
August 29, 2005

Ian Bremmer's analysis of petroleum politics ("Prices transform oil into a weapon," Aug. 27–28) was sobering. As he notes, the world's leading industrial nations are increasingly at the mercy of "some of the world's most unsavory regimes" that control the global oil spigot.

While Mr. Bremmer did not offer a prescription, other than to note the absence of any short-term solutions, it is clear that the United States in particular, as the world's foremost energy consumer, needs finally to get serious about facing the energy issue. In fact, had the U.S. sustained its short-lived resolve of the 1970s to pursue conservation and research into alternative energy sources, by now we might well have begun to wean ourselves from a dangerous addiction to oil. Instead, the dependency has only grown and, with it, in the post-9/11 era an ever increasing threat to national and international security.

Europe, by virtue of its highly taxed gas, greater use of fuel-efficient vehicles, advanced experimentation in wind power and other alternative energy practices, and better urban and intercity public transportation networks, is well ahead of the U.S. in facing the challenge. Moreover, China has just announced ambitious plans to dampen a surging appetite for imported oil.

Meanwhile, the U.S. hems and haws, making a gesture here and there, but in reality still deluding itself into believing it can sustain a gas-guzzling, energy-devouring lifestyle without any real need for fundamental change. Mr. Bremmer reminds us why such an approach is no longer sustainable—not, at least, if America values its future political, economic, and military well-being.

Why Russian Jews Become Instant Patriots
Wall Street Journal
September 12, 2005

Ah, the perils of political centrism! One day, we are assailed in a *Wall Street Journal* column ("The Russians Are Coming," Sept. 9) for our alleged liberalism and apparent contempt for Republicans. The next day, those on the left criticize us for our unstinting support for Israel and the war on terrorism, as well as our decades-long sponsorship of the monthly journal *Commentary*. It's not easy in our political environment being the targets of the slings and arrows of two highly energized ideological camps.

But since "The Russians Are Coming" took a potshot at us from the right, let's deal with that.

The column's main argument is that some Russian-born Jews have challenged the views of mainstream American Jewry. As the piece acknowledges, the American Jewish Committee, which was founded in 1906 in response to the pogroms against Jews in Czarist Russia, has invested heavily—and rewardingly, I might add—in building ties with the large Russian-speaking Jewish community in the United States. But along the way, an ideological gap was supposedly revealed. Boston was cited as an example. There some outspoken Russian Jews opposed positions taken by the American Jewish Committee and began criticizing our director, Dr. Larry Lowenthal, an Israeli army veteran, for his "liberal" position on a range of issues.

It is unfortunate that the columnist, Tony Carnes, did not interview Dr. Lowenthal. He would have discovered that the American Jewish Committee, in fact, takes no position on Supreme Court nominations and has expressed no view on euthanasia. On the other hand, yes, we have clear positions on a number of church-state matters and civil rights, and Lowenthal was doing nothing more than voicing the national policy, reflecting frequent debates and votes, in a local context.

Carnes also would have learned that Lowenthal was not "approvingly" stating his own view on Jews as "the most liberal" and "least religious people in America," as the column suggests, but simply reporting the factual conclusions of Dr. Tom Smith, director of the General Social Survey of the University of Chicago's National Opinion Research Center. And he would have understood that our membership, whether in Boston or elsewhere, includes Democrats and Republicans (and independents). Would President George W. Bush have chosen our organization as the first Jewish venue to make a public address in 2001 had he regarded us as hostile to Republicans?

We are an organization open to a broad spectrum of perspectives, recognizing fully that one Jew might build two synagogues (one to attend, the other to avoid attending!) and two Jews may have three opinions. Those who would like to join and participate in our discussions are most welcome. At the same time, they should understand that simply seeking to impose a particular view on an agency of more than 150,000 constituents—and a deliberative process of decision-making—is not the rule by which we operate.

Anti-Israel Problems at UN Unimproved
Forward
September 30, 2005

Perspective and context are needed to fully assess Israel's stature in the United Nations system. A September 16 editorial shortchanges both by taking an unwarranted swipe at our television ad on the UN and Israel ("UNimproved"). The nuanced ad was aimed primarily at the unique gathering of more than 170 world leaders in New York for the UN World Summit—to remind them that out of 191 UN member states, only Israel is denied the full benefits and respect of membership.

True, there have been several encouraging developments, which you cited in your editorial, and which we also have welcomed. But the core issues affecting the treatment of Israel at the UN sadly remain.

Yes, in 2000 Israel became a temporary member of the West European and Others Group, an accomplishment that, in fact, was due largely to the efforts of Secretary of State Madeleine Albright and Ambassador Richard Holbrooke. They credited a series of our full-page newspaper ads in the *New York Times* for helping wake up the European member states to the injustice of excluding Israel from any chance of serving on the UN Security Council and other major bodies. But membership in the West European and Others Group, which is temporary and conditional, applies only to the UN in New York. Efforts to get Israel admitted to the regional group in other UN cities such as Geneva and Nairobi, Kenya, have been stymied.

Further, the UN administrative structure that has evolved with the support of most member states provides for systemic, round-the-clock promotion of the Palestinian cause. The Division for Palestinian Rights of the Secretariat, the Committee on the Exercise of the Inalienable

Rights of the Palestinians, and the Special Committee to Investigate Israeli Practices affecting the Human Rights of the Palestinian People are key UN-funded entities that divert precious resources, while reinforcing hostility toward Israel and hindering progress toward peace.

Moreover, the UN Commission on Human Rights, which convenes annually in Geneva, divides the world in two. Israel, presumed "guilty," is handled under a separate agenda item, while the other 190 member states are combined under another, single agenda item, underscoring once again the unfair treatment of Israel.

The American Jewish Committee has been actively involved in the world body from its founding sixty years ago. We support efforts to reform the UN system out of concern for its moral integrity and its future. Yet, whatever reform is eventually achieved will fall short unless UN members agree to desist from treating one member state completely different from the other 190.

Response to "What's Next for Bush?"
New York Sun
October 13, 2005

Kudos to Cal Thomas for his call for energy independence ["What's Next for Bush?" Opinion, Oct. 11, 2005].

After a promising start in the late 1970s and early 1980s, the U.S. essentially lost interest in reducing our dangerous dependence on imported oil. Once again awash in relatively cheap and plentiful oil, and having conveniently forgotten the earlier oil shocks, we assumed it was our natural right to drive ever bigger and more powerful vehicles, to freeze our homes and offices in summer and boil them in winter, oblivious to what was going on elsewhere in the world.

Even the September 11 terrorist attacks didn't immediately wake up our nation or, for that matter, a majority of our elected officials to the dangers posed by our growing addiction to oil and the massive transfer of petrodollars to countries like Saudi Arabia. Only now, with higher oil prices resulting in part from Hurricane Katrina and a growing sense of vulnerability to limited supplies, is there emerging recognition of a problem.

For the sake of our national security, it's high time to tackle this issue head on, and, as Thomas notes, no one is better positioned to lead the effort than President Bush.

Just as Prime Minister Sharon learned from changing facts on the ground and provided courageous vision and statesmanship, so is our country's leader presented with a similar opportunity.

Mr. Bush could go down in history were he to launch our nation on a full-court press to grapple with the issue of energy independence. Precisely because he is from Texas, was connected to the oil industry, has close ties to the Saudis, and is not seen as a starry-eyed tree-hugger, he has just the right credentials to stand before our country and, like Mr. Sharon, tell us what we need to hear.

With China and India growing rapidly and in need of ever more energy resources, the geostrategic competition for oil will only grow, doubtless driving prices higher in the long run and creating more tension in the international system. That will only further strengthen countries like Iran, already hell-bent on building nuclear weapons; Saudi Arabia, the chief funder of fundamentalist Islam around the world; and Venezuela, whose leader has forged close ties with Cuba and Iran.

There are no quick fixes for the challenges we face. Yes, we must seek to drive less, use public transportation where it exists, carpool, and lower the thermostat a few degrees this winter. But it will take a sustained national effort to explore existing and new technologies to move us away from our dangerous dependence. The time to start is now, and the place to begin is in Washington.

Only a Leader of Sharon's Steel Will Convince Israel
Financial Times
November 22, 2005

Henry Siegman offers a one-sided explanation for the slow pace of Arab-Israel peacemaking ("It is time to take Palestinian opinion seriously," Nov. 18). He places responsibility at Prime Minister Ariel Sharon's doorstep and, more generally, on an Israeli refusal to understand recent "dramatic changes" in Palestinian public opinion. Mr. Siegman, to judge by his prodigious writings on the Middle East, has underestimated Mr. Sharon's commitment to peace since the Israeli leader took office in 2001.

In one telling example from the Council on Foreign Relations Web site, Mr. Siegman was asked in an interview (Oct. 7, 2004) if he thought the Israeli withdrawal from Gaza would take place. He replied, "I think that Sharon may have intended the withdrawal to take place, but he has probably come around to the position that he must kill the idea and do so in a way that persuades the international community that he intended to do it, but that Palestinians made it impossible."

No such thing occurred, of course. Instead, despite opposition from within his own Likud Party, fears of violent resistance from Jewish settlers in Gaza, and even a risk of assassination, the prime minister went ahead. The Israeli Disengagement proceeded without a hitch, and Gaza is now in Palestinian hands.

Most recently, with U.S. help, a deal was struck on the Gaza border crossings, which belies Mr. Siegman's claim that Israel's policy was "threatening to turn [Gaza] into a vast prison."

Mr. Siegman has been a forceful advocate for Palestinian self-determination. He would do his cause a big favor if he grasped the essential point that the Palestinians cannot be absolved of responsibility for shaping their own destiny, instead resorting to blaming everyone else for their downtrodden condition. Citing polling data, as Mr. Siegman does, to prove a change in Palestinian attitude is, in the end, insufficient. After all, polls are like perfume—good to smell, dangerous to swallow.

When the Palestinians get serious about curbing terrorism, stop lionizing "martyrs" who seek to kill indiscriminately, and focus on building their own society rather than fantasizing about destroying Israel, they will find in Israel a serious partner for a negotiated two-state settlement.

After all, it is in Israel's vital interest to find a modus vivendi with the Palestinian people. And on the Israeli side, it will take someone with Mr. Sharon's steely determination and experience to persuade the Israeli public that the benefits of further territorial compromise are worth the security risks to a nation smaller than Wales.

On the Red Crystal Symbol
Submitted to the *New York Sun*
December 11, 2005
(unpublished)

Your assessment of the "enduring hate" of Jews, as reflected in the outrageous and bone-chilling comments of the Iranian president and the incitement that remains an all-too-prominent feature of the mosque, media, and mainstream in many Arab countries, was right on target ("The Hate That Endures," Dec. 9).

As part of this grim picture, however, you cite the outcome of the recent diplomatic conference in Geneva attended by the signatories of the 1949 Geneva Conventions, which approved an additional emblem for the Red Cross Movement. But, in doing so, you give short shrift to what was accomplished.

In a perfect world, the Star of David would be treated exactly as the Red Cross and Red Crescent. In fact, I'd go a step further. In a perfect world, there would be only one universally recognized symbol, devoid of any religious significance whatsoever, adopted by the international humanitarian movement. Perhaps that day will come, but not anytime soon. In the meantime, Israel was faced with a choice between the unattainable "perfect" and the attainable "good" of a third symbol—a Red Crystal in which Israel can insert the Star of David. Understanding that the perfect is often the enemy of the good, Israel wisely chose the latter.

In doing so, the way is now paved for Israel's Magen David Adom to become a full-fledged member of the Red Cross Movement, correcting an historical injustice that began in 1949. And the movement travels a step closer toward its own professed values of universality, impartiality, and neutrality.

This milestone development, welcomed by the Israeli government and Magen David Adom alike, did not happen in a vacuum. A number of determined individuals, prominent among them Swiss Foreign Minister Micheline Calme-Rey, U.S. Secretary of State Condoleezza Rice, International Committee of the Red Cross President Jakob Kellenberger, and International Federation of the Red Cross and Red Crescent Societies Ambassador Chris Lamb, played a decisive role. They pressed ahead, refusing to back down when the obstructionist tactics of countries like Egypt, Malaysia, Pakistan, and Syria threatened to derail the process. Moreover, the American Red Cross deserves special mention. Since 1999, it has withheld its annual contribution to the international movement to protest Israel's exclusion.

As the chairman of Magen David Adom said after the historic vote: "We are happy. It will give us more protection, meaning we will be able to take more risks to help more people. This new emblem will protect us and defend us as we carry out our work to save lives." There could be no more fitting—or uplifting—response to the hatred that endures.

Context Is All
Submitted to the *Wall Street Journal*
December 5, 2005
(unpublished)

In the Arab-Israeli debate, every word is pregnant with meaning. Your time line on key events since 1967 is no exception ("Storied Land," Dec. 2). It starts with June 1967, when, you write, "Israel conquers the Gaza Strip and the West Bank." To the uninitiated, these words convey the impression of aggressive intent on Israel's part, but the reality was rather different.

The war began because Israel had a legitimate fear of a multination Arab attack to destroy the country. Prior to the 1967 war, after all, the Gaza Strip and West Bank, as well as the Golan Heights and eastern Jerusalem, were all in Arab hands; therefore, the Arab goal could not have been to reclaim them.

On May 16, 1967, Cairo Radio announced: "The existence of Israel has continued too long. The battle has come in which we shall destroy

Israel." Eleven days later, Egyptian President Gamal Nasser declared that "our basic objective will be the destruction of Israel." Similar sentiments emanated from Damascus and Baghdad. The drumbeat of war was unmistakable.

Meanwhile, on May 16, Egypt demanded the withdrawal of UN peacekeeping forces that had been stationed in Gaza and Sharm el-Sheikh since 1957. Three days later, the UN shamefully announced it would comply with the Egyptian demand.

And on May 23, President Nasser declared his intention to block the Strait of Tiran to Israeli shipping, thus severing Israel's vital trade links with East Africa and Asia. Israel replied that under international law, this was a casus belli.

While Israel was preparing for an inevitable war on its borders with Egypt and Syria, it was sending messages to Jordanian King Hussein, via UN channels, urging him to remain on the sidelines. Instead, he placed his forces under Egyptian control. As a result, he was drawn into the conflict, during which he lost the West Bank and eastern Jerusalem. Years later, the king admitted that this was one of the biggest blunders of his reign.

Context is everything. It remains essential to bear in mind the facts that led to the 1967 Six-Day War. Israel was faced with extinction. By winning the war, it acquired territories which it later hoped could be used as bargaining chips in exchange for recognition of its right to exist in peace and security. Tragically, the process of gaining that recognition from the Arab world remains only partially complete. Would that it were otherwise!

The Plot against America
Azure
Winter 2006

In Samuel G. Freedman's essay, "Philip Roth and the Great American Nightmare" (*Azure* 20, Spring 2005), he lumps together, as he describes them, "the so-called 'defense organizations' for American Jewry," and then proceeds to accuse them of a litany of misdeeds, including, above all, "the fetishizing of anti-Semitism." In essence, he charges these organizations with an inability to accept the good news of a country that has marginalized anti-Semitism and, worse, with continuing to peddle fear and thus preying on the latent anxieties of American Jews. It is, he asserts, "a self-indulgent, self-aggrandizing exaggeration of risk."

To begin with, I am surprised that a respected observer of the American Jewish scene would make the mistake of talking about the various organizations as if they were indistinguishable from one another. In reality, they are distinguishable, just as universities, though all committed to the common goal of education, are not identical.

Needless to say, I can only speak for my own organization. The American Jewish Committee is not in the fear-mongering business. Our domestic agenda is comprised of three parts and "fetishizing" anti-Semitism does not figure in any of them.

First, the biggest danger to American Jewry today, we believe, is posed not by external threats, but rather by internal challenges. We are hemorrhaging as a people. Our numbers, both in absolute and proportional terms, are static at best, declining at worst. Ignorance and indifference about the richness and contemporary relevance of our heritage abound. And while there is also good news to report on thriving synagogues, oversubscribed day schools, and vibrant adult education programs, this cannot mask the difficulties we face in large segments of the community.

That is why the American Jewish Committee established a Jewish Communal Affairs Department more than four decades ago. The goals of the department have remained constant: to study trends in American Jewish life, enhance appreciation of the joys of being Jewish, and encourage a greater sense of connection among Jews in the United States and between them and Jews worldwide.

Second, much of our work is focused on intergroup relations. This has always been a priority for us, but all the more so with the accelerating pace of socio-demographic change in the United States. We want to be certain that the glue of American democratic pluralism holds strong for the benefit of all, that mutual respect, not mutual rancor, prevails, and that the American Jewish community has potential coalition partners on issues of consequence. That requires the constant give-and-take of interfaith and interethnic diplomacy.

And third, yes, we keep an eye on potential external threats to the security and well-being of American Jewry, and make no apology for it.

We fully recognize the coming of age of American Jewry, including the nomination of Senator Joseph Lieberman in 2000, electoral successes of (Jewish) candidates in states with few, if any, Jews, and the shattering of the glass ceiling in Fortune 500 companies and top-notch universities. Indeed, we (and our sister agencies) have devoted much of our effort over the decades to helping foster just such a climate of acceptance. Yet, we cannot simply declare anti-Semitism dead, for it is not. Being alert does not mean being alarmist; it means being attuned to currents at hand, continuing our many programs in prejudice reduction, conducting research, and always bearing in mind that things can change—for better or worse.

Just a few years ago, French Jews felt fully integrated and totally at home in France, despite occasional preoccupation with the extreme right-wing National Front Party. Now, as another article in the same issue of *Azure* reports, there is a sense of anxiety about the future, after a four-year spate of hundreds of documented attacks. Could it happen in the United States? Hopefully not. But surely that does not allow for complacency either.

6. AJC INSTITUTIONAL

Identity and Commitment:
A Personal Story
Introduction to *In the Trenches, Vol. I*
Published in Russian
Kiev, Ukraine
March 2004

In 1970, I visited Israel for the first time. I went on my own, spent time with family, and traveled the length and breadth of the country, hitchhiking or by bus. I was profoundly moved by just about everything, especially the palpable sense of excitement in building and defending a Jewish state. I admired and envied my contemporaries who proudly served in the Israel Defense Forces (IDF), at a time when the U.S. military was held in disrepute because of Vietnam and many young Americans on the left were engaging in what seemed to me, notwithstanding my own antiwar views, outlandish social, cultural and political behavior. I was drawn to the communal notion of a kibbutz, which should never be confused with a *kolkhoz,* and again admired and envied those living and working there. Soldiers, kibbutzniks, bus drivers—everyone seemed to be making this country move, survive, grow.

Israel, it seemed to me, was the place where history was playing itself out, and I quickly found myself drawn to it. America was demoralized, divided, drifting. Israel, on the other hand, after its extraordinary success in the 1967 Six-Day War—a success that galvanized American Jewry (and other Jewish communities as well, of course) and transformed our Jewish self-image and political role—was on a national roll. To my own surprise, I even began to think about aliyah. Suddenly, I wanted to be part of this bold national experiment in Jewish sovereignty, which was somehow succeeding against all the odds. I wanted to live on the edge of history. I wanted to help write that history.

If there was one moment in particular that stands out on that first visit to Israel, it was riding on a crowded city bus in Haifa, when an elderly man boarded and stood next to me. It was, I remember, a blisteringly hot day, and he was in short sleeves. I saw on his left arm a number, indicating he had been in a Nazi concentration camp. It certainly wasn't the first time I had seen such a number, but it was the first time in Israel. I began to think about the relationship between this survivor, the Holocaust, and Israel. The thought obsessed me for several days thereafter. What if there had been an Israel before the war? Might he have avoided the suffering he surely endured? How must he feel living in a Jewish state when the very idea of such a state seemed impossibly remote just twenty-five or thirty years earlier?

Thoughts of aliyah receded as I entered graduate school at the London School of Economics, which the Jewish students jokingly referred to as the London Shul of Economics. One day I picked up a book entitled *While Six Million Died* by Arthur D. Morse. It chronicled the official American indifference to the fate of European Jewry during the Holocaust. I couldn't put the book down, and I was tempted on several occasions to pound the table or let out a scream. I could barely believe what I was reading. After all, even with my own family's wartime travails, those who had sought entry to the U.S. had eventually made it, but this powerful book revealed a whole other story largely unknown to me.

I wanted to read more. I read other, more scholarly works on America's shameful wartime refugee policy. I read about the refusal of Canada and Great Britain to admit more than a handful of Jewish refugees. I read about the ill-fated Evian and Bermuda conferences on Europe's refugees. And then I went on to read books on the roots of anti-Semitism, the pogroms in Eastern Europe, the emergence of the Third Reich, the role of Righteous Gentiles during the war, and the origins of Zionism. I couldn't devour it all quickly enough.

During 1973, after returning to New York, I was teaching an English-as-a-Second-Language course for adult immigrants. In my class, it turned out, there were a couple of Soviet Jews, along with newcomers from every continent. During the break, I sought out the Soviet Jews and began speaking with them. My mother was born in Moscow, and my maternal grandparents were from Bobruisk. I had learned Russian formally beginning in high school, and I took a number of Russian studies courses in both college and graduate school. In short, I felt a natural affinity, not to mention curiosity.

Soon after the Six-Day War, some Soviet Jewish voices began clamoring for repatriation to the national Jewish homeland, Israel, or demanding religious and language rights for Jews in the USSR. These were extraordinary acts of courage, given the repressive nature of the Soviet regime. I was transfixed by the newspaper accounts I had read and Elie Wiesel's evocative book *The Jews of Silence*, and moved by the first street demonstrations on behalf of Soviet Jews I had attended in New York in the early '70s. And here in front of me, at this school on East 42nd Street, were actual Soviet Jews who had somehow made it out and were starting new lives. Sounds corny, perhaps, but I felt a calling. Before me, I saw my own family members, though they had come to the U.S. two and three decades earlier, and though Soviet-style Communism had obviously taken its toll on the Jewish identity of many.

My second transformative experience occurred during the Yom Kippur War. Like many other Jews, after the miraculous thumping of the Arabs by Israel in the Six-Day War, I had allowed myself to believe in the notion of Israeli invincibility. Thus, when Israel was caught off guard by the combined assaults of Egyptian and Syrian forces on the holiest day of the Jewish calendar, I, like other friends of Israel, became alarmed.

I rushed to my desk and, without a moment's thought, called the Israeli Consulate to volunteer for something, anything, in the IDF. I was asked a few screening questions on the phone and, being thoroughly unprepared, blurted out the wrong answer to one key query. I revealed that I was the sole surviving son in my family, which, as an only child, of course I was. Little did I know that this would disqualify me even from consideration. I had blown it and was at a loss what to do next. In the end, I had to content myself with participating in some rallies and modest fundraising efforts far from the war, while all the time cursing myself for my stupidity.

But as the saying goes, when God closes a door, somewhere a window is opened. That window opened for me less than a year later when, due to my teaching experience and interest in Russia, I had the chance to participate in a government-to-government exchange program as a teacher in the Soviet Union.

To fast-forward, nearly three months after arriving in the USSR, I was forced to leave by Soviet officials who notified me and the American Embassy that I was no longer welcome. This came after I was detained by the Soviet militia a few blocks from the synagogue on Arkhipova Street. There I had spent Shabbat with those Jews who gathered outside regularly in quiet assertion of their national dignity, to draw strength from one another, to exchange information, and to meet sympathetic foreigners like myself—always under the intrusive eye of KGB agents who sought to blend in while monitoring conversations and contacts.

I actually went to the synagogue every Shabbat. Upon later hearing this, my mother expressed dismay—mixed, I suspect, with pride—that in New York, with a synagogue on nearly every corner, I grudgingly went twice a year, but in Moscow, with the lone synagogue under constant surveillance by secret police, I had to discover religion.

This particular Shabbat there were some French Jews who, having trouble finding a common language with the Soviet Jews, asked if I could translate from French to Russian. These French Jews were unsubtle in the messages they conveyed, and in hindsight I was too caught up in the challenge of translating to give sufficient thought to what it was I was being asked to transmit. That may have been the last straw for Soviet officials, who, in any case, weren't happy to have living and working in their midst a Russian-speaking American Jew far too independent and curious for their taste. They would have been much happier had I spent my evenings and weekends enthralled by the picture-perfect ballet, circus, museums and concerts rather than at the homes of refuseniks and dissidents or at the synagogue. In fact, I suspect they would have kicked me out much sooner were it not for the fact that I was part of an official U.S.-USSR program during the era of détente.

My three months in the USSR were quite extraordinary in every respect. How many Americans at the time had such an opportunity to reside in the Soviet Union, teach full-time six days per week in a Soviet school, and completely avoid official tours and guides? And how many Americans could claim to have spent six weeks in a modest Moscow hotel occupied not by Western tourists but rather for decades by diehard Communist veterans of the Spanish Civil War and for a year by Chilean Communists who fled after Salvador Allende's overthrow in 1973? And how many Americans, armed with knowledge of the Russian language, felt sufficiently at ease to go just about anywhere on their own, day or night?

For me, as a Jew, these three months were very significant. I met some extraordinary Soviet Jews, brave beyond words. I grasped the importance for Soviet Jewish activists of Western radio broadcasts, smuggled books, especially Leon Uris's *Exodus*, and manuscripts, the pull of Israel, and possession of a Star of David or a menorah. I learned a great deal about pride and yearning and determination. I was also given an education in the state-sponsored practice of anti-Semitism and anti-Zionism. And I came face to face with the power of Communist oppression and the suffocation of any vestige of intellectual or physical freedom.

Let me mention only two personal experiences in Russia, the first in Moscow, the second in Leningrad. Simchat Torah came about a week or two after my arrival in the country, and someone in New York had suggested I visit the synagogue. I remember taking the metro to the nearest stop, walking along Khmelnitsky Street—named in memory of the seventeenth-century Ukrainian responsible for the murder of hundreds of thousands of Jews—wondering what I was doing here this evening. Surely, no one would be at the synagogue. This was, after all, the USSR and Simchat Torah must be an obscure holiday for Jews forcibly disconnected from their heritage. Imagine my surprise, then, when I came to Arkhipova Street, turned right into the block, and then stood frozen for what seemed to be several minutes as I gazed down the hill and saw literally thousands of Soviet Jews packing the street, milling about, singing and dancing. I began to cry. I couldn't stop.

Here, only a few blocks from the nerve center of the most powerful totalitarian nation on earth, Jews were gathering to send a message: We are here, we are alive, we have not forgotten, we have not bent. Fifty-five years after the Bolsheviks set out to extinguish any last vestige of Judaism and Jewish identity in the USSR through every means available to them, it was clear they had failed. No, Soviet Jews were not consigned to the dustbin of history, as Soviet leaders intended, nor would they be, judging from the turnout that evening.

I began walking down the hill and was immediately pulled into the throng. It was clear to all, by dress and demeanor, that I wasn't a Soviet Jew, which made me all the more welcome. After all, if foreigners were here, whether Jewish or non-Jewish, then Soviet Jews weren't alone in their struggle. That meant Soviet authorities, in theory at least, might have to think twice before taking measures against them. But it certainly didn't mean those authorities were paralyzed, either. Within an hour, police cars began making their way up and down the crowded street, forcing people to the sidewalks and eventually compelling them to disperse.

Two months later, I was walking along the corridor of the Leningrad school to which I was subsequently assigned, School Number 185, when a young girl passed by and slipped something into my hand. I quickly went to the nearest bathroom, found an empty stall, locked the door, and unfolded the piece of paper. The note read: "David Harris, I think you are a Jew. I feel it. If I'm right, please know that my parents are refuseniks. Would you come to our house one day after school?" I memorized the indicated address and then tore up the note and flushed it down the toilet. The next day, I saw the same girl in the hallway and simply winked as we passed one another. That night I paid the family a visit, the first of several during my five-week stay in Leningrad.

Again, I was deeply moved by the encounter. Here were parents who had lost their jobs because of a desire to establish new lives in the West and to give their children the gift of freedom as human beings and as Jews. And here were two children—14 and 10, if I remember correctly—who had grown up very quickly, far too quickly, as they had to endure the fear, tension, and fog of life in a refusenik family, which included the very real possibility that they would be vilified at school, perhaps even expelled.

By December 1974, I was out of the Soviet Union, having lost seven kilos from an already thin frame and admittedly shaken by the rough nature of my expulsion. But I was determined to act, somehow, on all that I had seen and experienced in the previous three months.

I decided to travel to Rome. I recalled those Soviet Jews in my English-language classes talking of the several months they had spent there in transit. It sounded quite enticing. Maybe there would be a job for me. It turned out there was, with HIAS—the Hebrew Immigrant Aid Society—which, together with the Joint Distribution Committee (JDC), was responsible for the care, maintenance and migration of the thousands of Soviet Jews streaming out of the USSR and seeking permanent resettlement in the West.

In March 1975 I began as a caseworker in Rome. In the ensuing period I briefed, processed, and counseled literally thousands of Soviet Jews from every corner of the country. I quickly discovered that Soviet Jews were far more heterogeneous than the rarefied types I had met in Moscow and Leningrad. There were ex-prisoners of conscience and ex-convicts; there were top-flight scientists and high school dropouts; there were those yearning for Jewish content in their lives and those fleeing from it, believing they had paid a sufficiently high price in the USSR for their bad luck in being born Jews; and there were those grateful beyond words for the support extended by HIAS and JDC and others who simply saw us as another bureaucracy, albeit one far more naive and thus manipulable than those they were used to in the USSR.

The work was not easy. Soviet Jews were, in a real sense, living betwixt and between—in a state of suspended animation—as they waited for months in Italy until their visas came through and they could depart to start a new life. In the meantime, they were entirely dependent on the Jewish agencies, unable to work, unfamiliar with the local language, and uneasy about their children's loss of education. Tensions often ran high, as the refugees could not passively accept the fact that their fate rested entirely in the hands of others, and as the caseworkers, too few in number, sought to cope with an inherently difficult situation.

I've never been able to sit still. After only a few weeks working with the refugees in Rome, it struck me that there was a gaping hole in the HIAS and JDC programs—Jewish culture and education. Virtually nothing was being done on this score, though we had, in effect, captive, and, in some cases at least, hungry, audiences. After work, then, I would head for Ostia, the seaside town where many of the refugees lived while in transit, and offer informal evening programs using whatever materials, films or expert visitors I could find.

Eventually, I decided to try something still more ambitious, again because there was a vacuum that clearly needed to be filled. I proposed the writing of a basic book on Jewish history and religion, on Zionism and Israel, and on Diaspora Jewry, targeted for the refugees and oriented to their very specific mindset and world view.

Actually, it was the second book prepared especially for Soviet Jews in both Russian and English. Recognizing that the refugees understandably had little, if any, accurate information about the U.S.—and tons of misinformation—I first wrote an introductory volume about America, *Entering a New Culture*, with the support of HIAS. To its credit, HIAS also agreed to shoulder all the publishing expenses and distribute this second book—entitled *The Jewish World*—to every refugee passing through its offices. To this day, Jews arriving in the U.S. from the now former Soviet Union receive both books, since updated several times.

I was the first to acknowledge that there were people far more qualified than I to write a book on Jews and Judaism, but no one else stepped forward. The book may have been intended for Soviet Jewish refugees, but the two years spent researching and writing it opened my eyes to the vast civilization of which we Jews were the heirs and trustees. I remember feeling cheated, in fact downright angry, that so much of this information had been unknown to me for the first thirty years of my life. Why were so many of us Jews to be counted among the world's most literate people, yet so strikingly illiterate about the riches of our own heritage? What was it about ourselves and our psychology that could explain this dissonant phenomenon? It was one thing that Soviet Jews were largely ignorant about their culture; the Soviets forcibly denied them access. But what about us Western Jews, who had the information and resources at our fingertips?

In all, my years with HIAS in Rome and Vienna were exhilarating and fulfilling. I was doing something real, something tangible in the lives of fellow Jews desperately in need of assistance, and I couldn't have been happier. And yes, I felt I was participating in the writing of an extraordinary chapter in this century's history. I had found a professional niche for myself. Instead of simply imagining what I want to believe I might have done had I been alive during the Holocaust— fighting, rescuing, sabotaging—here was my chance, on my watch, to do something for Jews in need. Here was the real-life challenge posed to my post-Holocaust generation, if only we would recognize it and rise to meet that challenge. Here was the opportunity to say yes, we Jews had learned something, however painfully, from the lessons of the Holocaust about the compelling need for Jewish self-help, skillful political organization, and abandonment, for once and for all, of our perennial fear of provoking anti-Semitism by seeking full participation in public life.

And I also found it astonishing that a little over thirty years after the war's end, Jews in Europe were once again living with a real sense of threat. Palestinian-led terrorism had prompted European governments and Jewish agencies to take extraordinary protective measures to secure potential Jewish targets, including synagogues, day schools and highly visible agencies like HIAS and the JDC. It is difficult for Americans to understand the atmosphere in Europe at the time, but the dangers were very real.

In 1973, a train carrying Soviet refugees across Czechoslovakia to Austria was hijacked by Palestinian terrorists, creating an international crisis. In 1976, the JDC offices in Rome were firebombed (only a few minutes after I left the building), together with other Western and Jewish targets. The HIAS office in Vienna received several suspicious letters, at least one of which was a bomb defused after an alert staff member notified the police. And there were any number of potentially deadly incidents thwarted by Austrian and Italian security agencies alert to possible dangers.

These Palestinian terrorists and their European sympathizers in such groups as the Italian Red Brigades and German Baader-Meinhof Gang sought to paralyze the European Jewish world, but they failed miserably. Admittedly under far more onerous conditions, synagogues, day schools and Jewish agencies continued to function without missing a beat. If anything, the determination of those working in these places was only strengthened. I certainly knew that to be the case in HIAS and the JDC, as well as at ORT and the Jewish Agency—the operations with which I was most familiar at the time.

Clearly, there was a global struggle at hand involving a multifaceted campaign to isolate and delegitimize Israel and to create a "respectable" new form of anti-Semitism known as anti-Zionism. Since this was, in effect, a war against the Jewish people worldwide, the response must also be worldwide, led by Israel itself and the largest Jewish community in the world, the American.

I made plans to visit New York in January 1979. Just before going, however, two friends and I decided to spend a weekend in Salzburg. En route, we saw a sign for Mauthausen, the site of the infamous Nazi concentration camp. We detoured. None of us had ever before visited such a camp.

The first thing that struck us was the sheer beauty of the setting. It was totally disorienting. How could such indescribable horror have taken place amidst such natural splendor? We entered the camp and within minutes, each of us absorbed in his own thoughts, we became separated from each other. I found myself in a building, and before I knew it, I was in the gas chamber, alone. Seized by panic, I rushed for the door, but it was closed. I began trembling. I looked again at the door and realized it had been open all along; it was only my imagination playing tricks on me. I ran out of the gas chamber, only to find myself face to face with the crematoria. I kept running, shaking, sobbing, until I stumbled into my friends. They hadn't yet seen the gas chamber and crematoria, but I insisted we leave as quickly as possible.

Later, as I thought about the visit, if I had had even a shred of doubt about my decision to continue in Jewish communal work, that traumatic visit to Mauthausen sealed my fate. I knew I had to do my part to protect and keep alive the memory of the six million and seek to help ensure that nothing like this ever happened again, whether to Jews or, for that matter, any other vulnerable and targeted minority.

I joined the American Jewish Committee, the "Harvard University of Jewish agencies," as some call it, in 1979. The longer I have been associated with the American Jewish Committee, the more I have come to admire it, indeed the more I am in awe of it. To be sure, I am not totally objective, but it truly is an extraordinary institution that blends the best of American ideals and Jewish values to create a powerful advocate for Jewish well-being and security and for the advancement of democratic institutions, the protection of human rights, and the strengthening of mutual understanding. This fundamental appreciation of the inextricable link between the Jewish condition and the human condition is at the heart of AJC's ethos, and central to my own.

In making my decision to work for the American Jewish Committee, I was fully cognizant of its deep involvement in Russian and Soviet Jewish affairs.

The organization was founded in 1906 with the specific aim of mobilizing American and international support for Russian Jews targeted by repeated pogroms.

One of its earliest actions, on January 27, 1907, was the adoption of a resolution, the text of which would not have read very differently from those adopted in the 1960s, 1970s, and 1980s:

> For the prevention of massacres of Jews in Russia, no means can be considered so effective as the enlightenment of the people of the western world concerning real conditions in Russia, which have hitherto been systematically concealed or distorted by the power of the Russian Government; that to this end a Press Bureau should be established to gather and disseminate correct news of affairs in Russia.

That same year, the American Jewish Committee launched its first political effort in Washington. In violation of the provisions of an 1832 treaty between Russia and the United States, American Jews were routinely denied entry visas by Russian consular officials. To make matters still worse, the U.S. State Department seemed willing to go along with this discriminatory Russian policy.

Outraged by both the Russian position and the American acquiescence, the American Jewish Committee, collaborating with key Congressional leaders and in the face of opposition from the White House and State Department, launched a struggle to force the Russian-American treaty's abrogation. It took five years, but was ultimately successful.

And it created a precedent for linking human rights issues to American diplomacy, which we were to witness again in the mid-1970s when, once more over the objections of the White House and State Department, the United States Congress adopted the Jackson-Vanik Amendment linking American trade benefits to liberalized emigration policies in Communist countries. The legislation's principal objective was to persuade the Kremlin to permit Soviet Jews to emigrate.

Other milestones in the American Jewish Committee's involvement with what then became the Soviet Union were publication, in 1951, of the first scholarly book, *The Jews in the Soviet Union*, revealing the systematic repression of Jews in the USSR; the first high-level Jewish meeting with a Soviet official, Deputy Premier Anastas Mikoyan in 1959, to voice concern about patterns of political, religious, and cultural discrimination against Soviet Jews; sponsorship in 1964, together with three other American Jewish organizations, of the first advocacy group devoted exclusively to the plight of Soviet Jews, the American Conference on Soviet Jewry, which, in 1971, became the National Conference on Soviet Jewry; quiet backing for the creation of the National Interreligious Task Force on Soviet Jewry, a largely non-Jewish effort to demonstrate broad American support for the rights of Soviet Jews; and coordination of the 1987 rally in Washington in support of Soviet Jewry, which drew more than 250,000 participants, the largest Jewish gathering in American history, and a galaxy of political officials, including then Vice President George Bush.

There is much more that can be said about the American Jewish Committee's central involvement in Soviet Jewish affairs; in fact, a separate book could be written on the subject, but suffice it to say that, given this strong connection, I felt very much at home in the organization.

One final word. For many activists, the goal of the Soviet Jewry movement was never merely to "bring Jews out of the USSR," but to help the emigrants successfully integrate into the general and Jewish communities of their newly adopted countries. In the United States, that has meant not only dealing with language, cultural differences, jobs, health care and education, but also with reconnecting Jews with their heritage and building bridges between the newcomers and the established American Jewish community.

Eight years ago, several farsighted Russian-born Jews in New York, led by Peyrets Goldmacher and Sam Kliger, approached the American Jewish Committee. They asked if we would be willing to help them develop a program to identify and educate potential future leaders of the Russian-speaking Jewish community in the New York area, which today comprises fully one-fourth of the region's Jewish population. How could we possibly have refused such a request? After all, this was the keystone, the piece at the crown of the arch that holds all the other pieces in place. Without a well-trained leadership group, what would the community's future look like?

Since that first meeting, an annual program, now in its seventh year, has been put in place to create a cadre of Russian Jewish leaders. Several hundred have gone through the program. In turn, they have created vibrant new organizations to mobilize Russian Jews in a myriad of activities, including political advocacy, and have involved themselves in the lives of established organizations like the American Jewish Committee. And now the program has expanded to Boston, another center of Russian Jewish life, with the likelihood that it will be in other American cities before long.

Moreover, we were so captivated by the success of this initiative that we hired Sam Kliger to work fulltime and to oversee these programs while developing others that would link our efforts more closely to those taking place in the former Soviet Union, Israel, Germany, and elsewhere in the Russian-speaking world. One of the immediate results has been the creation of a Russian-language Web site, which can be accessed through www.ajc.org.

In sum, these have been breathtakingly exciting times. With the Iron Curtain a relic of history, the opportunities for communication and collaboration within the vast Russian-speaking Jewish world and between that world and the larger Jewish community are limited only by our imagination and willingness to commit resources.

This book is one example of the previously unimaginable chance we have been given to talk to one another, not through *samizdat* and smuggled manuscripts but openly and fully. It addresses selected aspects of the contemporary Jewish world through the eyes of an observer and against the backdrop of the tumultuous events of the last three years that have profoundly affected Jews and non-Jews alike.

Without the vision and determination of Leonid Finberg, a distinguished scholar in Kiev and long-time friend of the American Jewish Committee, this book would not have been possible. It was he who conceived the idea of translating into Russian a number of my essays, which have been published in the United States, and compiling them into a book. It was he who oversaw the entire project from conception to conclusion. I am grateful to him—and those who assisted him—for all their efforts.

Sam Kliger was the American Jewish Committee's liaison to the project and could not have been more helpful and cooperative.

And last but by no means least, I am thankful to the American Jewish Committee, which has given me the possibility to participate in the unfolding of history in ways that I could never have dreamed possible.

I am only sorry that my maternal grandparents, Ida and Lova Chender, are not alive to see the birth of this book. I suspect they would have found in it special meaning and symbolism.

A Tribute to Harold Tanner
AJC 98th Annual Meeting
Washington, D.C.
May 6, 2004

Over its ninety-eight-year history, the American Jewish Committee has been a lucky institution.

We have been led by a series of exceptional presidents, each of whom has embodied the best of our civic culture and our Jewish tradition. Several of those past presidents are here with us, and I salute them.

This evening we have the privilege of paying tribute to our current president, Harold Tanner, whose three-year term officially ends on Sunday.

Happily, Harold's formal association with AJC will continue as he becomes the founding chair of the Transatlantic Institute, established in Brussels earlier this year.

There is a great deal that ought to be said about Harold, but those of you in the audience who know him understand that he would not want me to take up too much time in saying it. "AJC time is on time," he would gently remind me, "and we shouldn't be testing the patience or good will of our audience."

Therefore, with all my love and admiration for Harold—and it is considerable—I'm going to keep this brief, far briefer than he deserves.

Let me highlight four attributes of Harold that have particularly struck me during the three years I've worked so closely with this exceptional individual.

First, Harold has an unmatched sense of loyalty, responsibility, and duty, and the American Jewish Committee has been the fortunate beneficiary.

In his self-effacing, unassuming manner, he has devoted himself tirelessly to every aspect of this agency's work, both the external and the internal, both the glamorous and the unheralded.

He has made a point of getting to know this vast and complex agency inside out.

He has read reams of correspondence, balance sheets, projections, monographs, and memoranda.

He has attended every meeting imaginable to demonstrate interest and support.

He has made a point of seeking to visit all thirty-three chapters to underscore their importance to the organization.

He has always said yes to every opportunity to raise funds, and no one has done it better.

And he has unfailingly shown respect and consideration for the professional staff, whom he regards as cherished partners and colleagues.

Second, Harold has a remarkable commitment to the well-being of the Jewish people. He has traveled the world time and again to make the case for Israel's quest for peace and security, to express solidarity with other Jewish communities, to combat anti-Semitism, to advance human rights and human dignity, and to create new possibilities for cooperation with governments, other faith groups, and civic institutions.

From Brussels to Beijing, Moscow to Mexico City, Paris to Pretoria, Tokyo to The Hague, and Washington to Warsaw, Harold Tanner has proved himself an indefatigable diplomat who commands the respect of top decision-makers.

To each meeting, whether with German Chancellor Gerhard Schroeder, Turkish Prime Minister Recep Tayyip Erdogan, or Pope John Paul II, he brings an open mind, a talent for listening, the reliability of his word, and an uncanny ability not only to frame difficult issues but also to propose workable solutions.

Third, Harold has a deep and abiding love for America. He is a wonderful example of the unlimited opportunities this country provides its citizens. He grew up in modest circumstances in upstate New York, learned the meaning of work at an early age, attended some of the nation's finest universities, and built a career in investment banking that has earned him a stellar reputation in the field.

At the same time, Harold has always understood the need to give back, to participate in the larger life of the country, and to lend support to those educational, cultural, and other not-for-profit institutions that strengthen America's democratic fiber and humanistic soul.

And finally, Harold's personal qualities of integrity, compassion, kindness, and generosity are legendary. He is in every way a role model of how we should live our lives—as loving family members, as consummate professionals, and as dedicated volunteers.

The American Jewish Committee has gone from strength to strength under his leadership and guidance, for which we as an institution shall always be grateful.

And I have been blessed with a mentor, a partner, and a friend, for which I shall always be personally thankful.

Harold, on behalf of the American Jewish Committee, your second family, it is now my honor to present you with our National Distinguished Leadership Award.

Twenty-fifth Anniversary
of the Konrad Adenauer Foundation-AJC Exchange
March 2005

The American Jewish Committee was created in 1906 by an accomplished group of Jews of German origin with the purpose of combating anti-Semitism and other forms of bigotry and promoting human rights. For almost 100 years, this organization has grown in the vision of its founders, bringing people of all races, ethnic groups, and religions together to enhance the democratic and pluralistic fabric of our world.

The American Jewish Committee's relationship with the Federal Republic of Germany holds a special place in this history. The German annihilation of European Jewry in the Second World War stands as a singular crime—and, from a Jewish perspective, a tragedy that remains fundamentally unfathomable even today. The principle of "Never again" continues to drive our work moving forward with a decided sense of urgency.

At the same time, the American Jewish Committee embodies a central Jewish tenet—the inextinguishable belief in the possibility of a better world, and the determination to work toward its realization. This flame of hope moved the organization to help sponsor the first Jewish prayer service on German soil since the rise of Hitler to power, which was broadcast in the U.S. and Germany as a symbol of renewed life from Aachen on October 29, 1944. The same hope led AJC, just a few short years after the end of World War II, to involve itself in the U.S.-led effort for democratic political education in Germany, and finally, in 1998, to open our own office in the heart of Berlin, the first American Jewish permanent presence on the ground.

Twenty-five years ago, our belief in the possibility of building relationships and drawing from history's lessons was institutionalized in a people-to-people exchange program with the Konrad Adenauer Foundation. We celebrate that program today with deserved fanfare. The personal visits of hundreds of American Jews to Germany as guests of the foundation, and the parallel visits of their counterparts in Germany with AJC to the United States, have in their own way made history, opening the doors of compassion and understanding for hundreds of individuals and touching the lives of thousands more.

This program at its root is about breaking down barriers and facilitating genuine communication. It is about experience—the greatest teacher of all. It is an attempt to ensure that the lessons we have learned about the dangers of the slippery slope of anti-Semitism and bigotry are well understood. It is about looking to the future with a shared sense of purpose and a passion for justice.

We are grateful to the Konrad Adenauer Foundation for its partnership in this endeavor, and for the commitment and vision it has shared with us. In particular, I would like to thank Wilhelm Staudacher, who, along with a wonderful, dedicated team of colleagues, has been so instrumental in making this twenty-fifth anniversary reunion of our partnership possible. It is gratifying to have such dedicated friends.

It is fortuitous that this anniversary should occur in the very same year as another occasion worthy of celebration. The year 2005 marks the fortieth anniversary of relations between Germany and Israel, a giant leap in the history of both countries and a special relationship that deserves continued nourishing and support.

Indeed, as we observe developments in the Middle East more broadly, the previously distant dream of democracy taking hold in the region seems just a little bit closer, though still fraught with many real and potential challenges. Germany and the Jewish people know so well the power of democracy to transform and open societies, and know equally well the mortal danger of tyranny. It is, therefore, my most fervent hope that we can work together in advancing this worthy cause. In that same spirit, I yearn for the day when the people of Israel will know true peace in a region where ploughshares one day will replace swords. Germany has a key role to play in realizing these historic possibilities.

Let this anniversary year remind us, then, of the uniqueness and importance of the bonds we have worked together so diligently to develop. The German-Jewish relationship is like none other in the world. If we tend to it, it can be an ongoing source of strength and purpose, a source of continued contemplation and reflection. In this spirit, the recollections contained in this volume will provide both uplifting reading and food for thought.

The hope that we put in Germany after the cataclysmic war has not been misplaced. Our relationship should stand as a source of inspiration to others that today can be brighter than yesterday, that history can indeed move forward in a positive direction.

A Tribute to Jacob Kovadloff
AJC 99th Annual Meeting
Washington, D.C.
May 3, 2005

Few things in life give me greater personal pleasure than the chance to honor a cherished colleague.

Unfortunately, in America these days the power and meaning of words have been greatly devalued by their overuse or, for that matter, misuse. But this evening we honor an individual who truly deserves every tribute we can possibly give him.

We honor him not for a single deed, though there are many that would qualify; rather, we honor him for the life he has led and the example he has set.

We honor him every bit as much for who he is as for what he does.

We honor him precisely because he has never sought honor—indeed, given a choice, he would refuse it—but, truth be told, we didn't really give him a choice.

We honor him because, in doing so, we remind ourselves and the larger world that there are people worth modeling ourselves on—people with abiding moral courage and the physical courage that is often its necessary companion; people who possess an Ethical Positioning System, an EPS, if you will, which tells them exactly where they should be when life presents its inevitable challenges and quandaries; and people who, having been forced to stare into the abyss, still manage to see the sky.

Mark Twain wrote that "modesty died when false modesty was born." He was almost, but not quite, on target. Had he lived longer and met Jacob Kovadloff, he would have been forced to modify his statement. Jacob, you see, is one of those rare people who, as you will hear shortly, has done real things to help real people and yet considers his acts to be totally unexceptional and, therefore, undeserving of praise.

I'm personally thrilled that this evening we honor Jacob, and that we do so in the presence of his two families—his immediate family, his beloved wife, Sonia, and his children, Georgina and Eddie, of whom he is so proud, and his extended American Jewish Committee family, his professional and lay colleagues.

Argentina's most noted author of the twentieth century, Jorge Luis Borges, once wrote: "Being with you and not being with you is the only way I have to measure time." In my case, happily, I can only measure my AJC time in being with Jacob. Since I joined the staff in 1979, I have only known an AJC office in New York with Jacob Kovadloff immersed in our important initiatives on and in South America.

Now I should tell you that it's not by accident that we chose to honor Jacob at this time. It was exactly thirty-five years ago this month that Jacob Kovadloff joined the staff of the American Jewish Committee. He became the director of our South American office, which was located in his city of residence, Buenos Aires.

But before looking at those thirty-five years, let's go further back in time for a moment or two. I'm grateful to Eliseo Neuman, my colleague and Jacob's fellow Argentinean, for help in compiling the information on Jacob's life.

Jacob comes from Ukrainian and Russian immigrants who settled in Argentina around the turn of the twentieth century, as part of the agricultural colonization program sponsored by Baron Maurice de Hirsch. He was born in the province of Entre Rios, where those who came to be known as the "Gauchos Judios," the Jewish gauchos, lived.

He attended state schools and Jewish schools. He has a degree in chemistry and owned for a number of years a company that manufactured chemical products. He did graduate study in a variety of fields, including the social sciences, psychology, and Jewish literature. He served in the military.

His involvement in Jewish communal activity, including Zionism, began when he was fourteen—and has never stopped, as you know.

He learned Yiddish from his family, and anyone who has ever seen Jacob sing a Yiddish song, as I have, knows that the words don't just come from memory; they come from the deepest recesses of his soul.

Prior to joining AJC, Jacob held a variety of lay leadership positions in the Argentine Jewish community, including the presidency of Hebraica, which is equivalent to the 92nd Street Y in New York. In other words, it is both a gathering spot for the community and one of the leading cultural hubs for the city of Buenos Aires.

He was also active in so many other Jewish institutions that to list them all would use up the remainder of my time. Suffice it to say that to this day, Jacob's name—actually, in Argentina he's often referred to by his nickname, Pipo—is known and admired throughout the entire Argentine Jewish community, and that's no exaggeration.

In 1970, he was offered a job at AJC. Typically, befitting his modesty, Jacob said he wasn't sure he could meet the agency's expectations. After all, he wasn't American, among other things. But after a trip to New York to see the organization up close, Jacob said he instantly fell in love, noting, in particular, the close ties between professionals and volunteers and the open-minded, democratic culture of the agency.

His job in Buenos Aires was wide-ranging. He had responsibility not only for Argentina, which had Latin America's largest Jewish population, but also for the other countries in South America—some, like Brazil, Chile, and Uruguay, with substantial communities, and others, like Bolivia, Cuba—yes, Cuba—and Peru, with much smaller communities.

He focused on the publication of AJC's respected magazine *Comentario*, which appeared in both Spanish and Portuguese; interfaith dialogue in the wake of the historic Second Vatican Council; the promotion of better understanding of Israel; and the supervision of research and analysis on the region. As the Soviet Jewry issue picked up steam in the early 1970s, Jacob took an active leadership role. He was founder and coordinator of the first university-level course on Jewish studies in Argentina. And he edited *Comunidades*, the only Jewish year book published in Spanish and dealing with Latin American Jewry.

But there were to be other challenges as well. Argentina was headed for a bleak period in its complicated history. Political anarchy, violence, and radicalism were on the rise in the early 1970s. It wasn't safe to be an American or associated with an American institution. And being Jewish didn't necessarily make things any easier.

Things came to a head in the mid 1970s when the armed forces seized power, and arrests, disappearances, and killings became widespread.

Within the Jewish community, there was a widespread and ongoing debate over how to deal with the situation—publicly challenge the regime, with all its attendant risks, or engage in quiet diplomacy and achieve what was possible.

Jacob, as one of the community's leaders, was at the center of these discussions. But even while these issues were being thrashed out—and Jacob's view, by the way, was that there was a place for both public outcry and private negotiation—he acted.

He used every contact he had patiently cultivated over decades in all important spheres of Argentine life, including the American embassy, to save the lives of many people who were otherwise destined for a horrible fate. And while many were Jews, Jacob also acted to focus attention on the plight of other Argentines at risk, including Catholic priests.

Typically, he often worked anonymously, shunning the limelight and refusing to take credit for lifesaving deeds. When asked how many lives he saved in this period, he refuses to reply, insisting that he wasn't keeping count and, in any case, that there were others besides him who were helping.

And then came the fateful month of June 1977. It was a month that would change his life forever.

He and his family started getting phone calls from unidentified individuals telling him to leave the country at once or face serious consequences. The callers also demanded that the American Jewish Committee office be closed. And Jacob began to notice a plain-clothed policeman in front of his apartment building.

Jacob decided he had no choice but to leave. When his family returned to their apartment in Buenos Aires after accompanying him to the airport, his wife, Sonia, found a note, one of several in those weeks. This one again demanded that the AJC office be closed and also indicated that Jacob and Sonia's children were being watched.

Sonia, Georgina, and Eduardo left Argentina a few days later, after being taken to the airport by an American embassy car and being given a rough going-over by Argentine officials. A policeman, while rummaging through the suitcases, deliberately crushed Eduardo's glasses.

A week later, AJC officially closed the office in Buenos Aires. Richard Maass, then AJC's president, announced that the office would not be reopened until those who engaged in anti-American and anti-Semitic threats were pursued and punished to the full extent of the law.

Even under the best of circumstances, moving from one country to another entails many hurdles. But in the case of Jacob and his family, the circumstances were far from ideal. They were caught totally unprepared for their sudden move. They couldn't simply shake off the threats that had become their daily fare during their last weeks in the country. They left behind countless members of their family and lifelong friends. They feared for the direction of the country of their birth, a country they could never stop loving. And Jacob could no longer work on the ground in providing leadership to the Jewish community in the throes of this unprecedented political paroxysm, during which many thousands of Argentine citizens were arrested and never heard from again.

But rather than succumb to despair, Jacob and his family began to build a new life in exile here in the United States. There is an old Yiddish saying that "he who can't endure the bad, will not live to see the good." Believe me, Jacob and his family endured more than their share of the bad. Fortunately for them, and for us, they lived to see the good.

Jacob has continued his work dealing with South America from the AJC office in New York, now in consultation with Dina Siegel Vann, who staffs our Division on Latino and Latin American Affairs. He travels to the region regularly and eventually was able to return to visit Argentina, which, in 1983, reemerged as a democratic nation. He has been deeply involved in Latin American organizations here, such as the Latin American Studies Association and the Americas Society, and he helped found the Latin American Jewish Studies Association. He has been a valued adviser to U.S. governments and members of Congress dealing with Latin American issues, not to mention to journalists covering the area.

In sum, he is a treasure trove of knowledge when it comes to political, economic, cultural, and religious trends in this region so vital to our own nation's—and the Jewish community's—interests.

To this day, we benefit from Jacob's wise counsel in all aspects of our extensive work in the region to which he has devoted a lifetime. As Plato said, "Wise men talk because they have something to say; fools talk because they have to say something." When Jacob speaks, he always has something to say.

And having accompanied Jacob to Buenos Aires, most recently in July of last year, when an AJC delegation attended the tenth anniversary commemoration of the terrorist attack on the AMIA building, which killed eighty-five people, I can personally attest to the fact that Jacob continues to be a truly invaluable resource. He knows everyone, everyone knows and respects him, and, in addition, he can still tell you where to see the best tango show in town.

This evening we honor our own. In selecting Jacob Kovadloff to be this year's honoree, we're choosing to pay tribute to an individual who has devoted his entire life to defending the Jewish people, building bridges between the Jewish people and other communities, standing strong for the advancement of democratic values and human rights protections, enhancing understanding of Israel's quest for peace and security, and strengthening ties between the United States and Latin America.

For me, Jacob embodies all that is best in our Jewish tradition. We are all, in one way or another, the beneficiaries of his tireless dedication.

As an organization, the American Jewish Committee stands taller and stronger today because of this man's decades-long and unstinting efforts.

And as individuals, we all can recall moments when Jacob's infectious warmth and kindness personally touched us, whether in a meeting room, an elevator, a hallway, or on an overseas mission.

Jacob, we *shep nakhes* in being here this evening with you and your wonderful family—Sonia, Georgina, and Eddie—who have always been at the center of your life.

In your—and our—beloved Yiddish language, there is another proverb: "A man is not old until his regrets take the place of his dreams."

Jacob, please make us a promise. Don't ever stop dreaming.